Praise for

Skirting History

"A deep dive into the remarkable life of an ordinary—and extraordinary—woman. From Holocaust refugee, to wife and mother, to accomplished feminist and activist, Eva Moseley vividly recreates a troubled childhood, a complicated marriage and difficult divorce, and the mysterious death of her ex-husband. With her, we travel across the globe and through brushes with world history, on a journey of hopes dashed and fulfilled, of despair and joy, leading ultimately toward self-respect, courage, and confidence. This is an honest story of a woman seeking answers to the toughest questions we can ask of ourselves and the world around us."
—Martha Hodes, Professor of History, New York University, author of *Mourning Lincoln* and *The Sea Captain's Wife: A True Story of Love, Race, and War in the Nineteenth Century*

"Even if Eva Moseley had had only half the experiences—on several continents—she recounts here, hers would still be a remarkable life, public and private, told now with spirit and candor."
— James O'Toole, Clough Professor of History Emeritus and University Historian, Boston College

"Eva and I were philosophy majors at Mount Holyoke College. She looked to philosophy to learn how to live her life and understand the world. This search led to dissenting views, from refusing to haze another student, which was a ritual at the college, to, more seriously and much later, opposing militarism and working for Palestinian human and political rights, which is unusual for a Jew of our generation. This book tackles questions we have all asked about a range of topics, and answers them personally and clearly."
— Mary V. Coit, Professor (retired), NYU School of Professional Studies

Skirting
HISTORY

Holocaust Refugee to Dissenting Citizen

Eva S. Moseley

OLIVE
BRANCH
PRESS

An imprint of Interlink Publishing Group, Inc.
www.interlinkbooks.com

To
Jessica and Tom;
Kate, Fiona, and Sandra;
Sebastian and Bert:
whose stories, told or not,
follow on from those told here

—

First published in 2022 by

Olive Branch Press
An imprint of Interlink Publishing Group, Inc.
46 Crosby Street, Northampton, MA 01060
www.interlinkbooks.com

Part of Chapter 12, "Ten Thousand Men of Harvard" appeared in
Yards and Gates: Gender in Harvard and Radcliffe History (Palgrave Macmillan, 2004)

Library of Congress Cataloging-in-Publication Data available.
ISBN 978-1-62371-852-7

Printed and bound in the United States of America

CONTENTS

V. COMING TOGETHER

VI. TRAVELS WITH GEORGE, 1958–70

VII. COMING APART

VIII. FAMILY PORTRAITS

FOREWORD

skirt, *v.t.* **1**. To border; to run along the edge of....
3. To go or pass around or about...; as, the army skirted the marsh.
—*Webster's New Collegiate Dictionary* (1949)

"*B*urlap!" Mother spat the word out. It was 1952 and my college friend Jenny (note: this and some other names are pseudonyms) had bought yards of the stuff and asked Mother to cut out a circle skirt. You could get burlap in all sorts of luscious colors. It makes a scratchy garment, but it was trendy and cheap.

Despite her disapproval, Mother, in New York a "little Viennese dressmaker," cut out the skirt and probably stitched it up as well. It was typical that, though disapproving what some young person wanted, she would go along, sometimes skirting confrontations about matters of more moment than a skirt.

As the title of this book suggests, my parents, the whole family, or just I, lived through years of wars, revolutions, the Holocaust, other disasters, and various political movements. Katelin, my first granddaughter, after reading *The Diary of Anne Frank* in high school, said, "I'm so glad you got out." Having a grandmother who might have met the same fate as Anne Frank sharpened the reality of that story for her. My story is obviously different from Anne Frank's: I skirted the Holocaust and most lesser public disasters—but not some private ones.

At the Schlesinger Library, where I was curator of manuscripts and we collected papers of nineteenth- and twentieth-century women, we operated with the conviction that history is made by all sorts of people. I learned that some famous, important people have boring archives as they keep only the commendations and awards, while a housekeeper, nurse, or secretary might write revealing letters or keep (like Gwendolen in *The Importance of Being Earnest)* "sensational" diaries; just as newspapers report on interesting unknowns and boring celebrities. My last boss, the wonderful Mary Maples Dunn, gave me a splendid retirement event: Adrienne Rich read her poems, Arthur Schlesinger, jr. introduced me, and I spoke about my years at the library. Afterward, an old friend said, "You're somebody!" With luck, I'd found a suitable spot between the notable physicist (or pianist) I once fantasized about becoming and the stenographer, the Girl Friday, that so many 1950s "coeds" became—between "extraordinary" and "ordinary."

A caveat about memory. As I was finishing the last draft of this book, I took my daughter and son to see the Madison Boulder in Madison, New Hampshire. I had seen this huge glacial erratic before and recalled a dead-end street at most a fifth mile long, and there the rock sits, not far from some houses. In fact, the street to it is much longer, then one parks and there is an easy woodsy walk to the rock in its own "natural area." I've tried to make this book as true as possible, but some descriptions, or what I think are facts, may be erratic.

"Biography helps me understand the lives of others in new ways, so that I can understand my own life better," writes journalism professor Steve Weinberg. So here is some of the history of a woman who made her way through seventy percent of the twentieth century and some of the twenty-first, bumping up against assorted issues, trying to come to terms with more than one unhappy family and with being a secular Jew who has doubts about Israel, and carrying on—as many women do—a sporadic lifelong argument with her mother, while gradually shedding childhood timidity.[1] Much of it is a Jewish story; some of it will make some Jews angry, although that isn't my aim.

It hasn't all been gravely serious. In daily life, laughter often occurs in among difficulties, and some funny things are also serious, such as the old Jew who was asked what he thought about some important question. He thought and thought but remained silent. When pressed he said, "I know what I think, but I'm not sure I agree with it," an answer that isn't as silly as it may sound. Mother taught me that "where there are ten Jews, there are twelve political parties," and it isn't only Jews for whom the expression "to be of two minds" was invented.

Now I resemble another old Jew. In a story psychiatrist and author Robert Jay Lifton told, one solitary Jew is left alive after a pogrom. The tsar grants him a boon: for having survived, he may choose the manner of his death. This Jew has no second thoughts: "Your Majesty," he says, "I choose old age."

This choice has been handed to me, despite all the dramatic and dangerous events the world has seen during my ninety years, events I often watched—from a safe distance—as I dealt with things as trivial as a burlap skirt, or as weighty as exile, divorce, nuclear fallout, sexism/feminism, and Jewishness.

I'm immensely grateful to Michel Moushabeck and his colleagues at Interlink Publishing for taking a chance on a little-known author. I appreciate, and try to live up to, Interlink's "global, cosmopolitan perspective." Although the future looks doubtful to me now, Michel and his enterprise are surely part of the efforts that can save humanity by bringing people closer together to solve the huge, frightening dangers, most human-made, that threaten its future.

Cambridge, Massachusetts, December 2021

I.

Vienna, 1931–39

Chapter 1
A TALE OF TWO CANALS

"*B*efore the war, I lived in a virtual paradise." George Berkley, later author of *Vienna and Its Jews,* heard this from a woman with a Central-European accent in New York in the late 1940s. "[H]er face lit up and her voice took on an almost ecstatic tone.... [She] was Viennese ... Here was a mature and educated woman who still treasured glowing memories of the city that had forced her and her fellow Jews to flee for their lives. I had never heard German Jewish refugees speak with such rapture about their native cities." On first reading this, I felt that Berkley was accusing me of being irrational, for I too remember Vienna as a special, wonderful place.

I was born into this virtual paradise on Christmas Day, 1931. We Steiners lived in a lower stratum of Viennese society than Berkley's ecstatic lady, and I knew the city for only seven years, but surely Berkley's subtitle, "The Tragedy of Success," is one explanation for the lady's rapture. Vienna enchanted her at least partly because of the presence and achievements of Jews: Gustav Mahler, Sigmund Freud, Helene Deutsch, Arthur Schnitzler, Stefan Zweig, Theodor Herzl, and many others, known and unknown, religious or secular, Zionist or not. Along with the beautiful surroundings, the architecture, the music, the cafés.

My family's youthful Jewish acquaintances included future notables. Mother (born Isabella Zetlin) knew Hans Kraus, a noted rock climber and a refugee orthopedic surgeon who later treated President Kennedy's back (as well as my relatives' aches and pains), and Bruno Bettelheim, the psychiatrist who was famous, and then infamous, for his work with autistic children. The Zetlin children played with Leon Trotsky's children, if my aunt Vickie Zetlin is to be believed. Vickie and her friend, Lisl Kolberg, knew Rudolf Serkin before he became a famous pianist; Hesse,

3

the oldest Zetlin sibling, and Serkin's sister were briefly an item.

Yes, we Jews were forced out beginning in 1938, while some clear-eyed pessimists left earlier—but before that many of us lived pretty good lives there, considering the economic depression and political unrest of the 1930s. Not all Austrians were anti-Semites, and a kind of unthinking anti-Semitism was rampant in the US too.

At first I was hardly aware of being Jewish. Both parents were non-believers; we ignored Jewish holidays and sometimes had a Christmas tree (as did the Freuds as early as the 1880s), which stood on a brick stove that heated the *Salon* (living room). The candles were real, and one year my uncle Lyova Zetlin's hair caught fire. Mother imparted some Yiddish words and Jewish lore, and my aunt Anna Zetlin taught me to write Hebrew. Only after March 12, 1938, did I learn that being Jewish could be dangerous.

A trolley ride brought you to the wooded hills laced with walking paths and ski slopes of the *Wienerwald* (the Vienna Woods), or to sandy Danube beaches. Not much farther away are the Alps. Young people living in close quarters with parents, siblings, and maybe other relatives, and working all week in an office, shop, or factory, given more than one day off, would ride third-class on a night train into the mountains, sleep in the overhead luggage racks, then hike hut-to-hut, some—my father included—climbing over rocks and glaciers to snow-covered summits.

I have scattered memories of outings near Vienna and country vacations: one *Pfingsten* (Pentecost) at a lodge in perfect May weather; playing in the shallows of a lake and guiltily peeing in the water; playing with Mitzi on her family's farm in Obersdorf, Steiermark (Styria) in 1937. Photos show the Zetlin sisters in cotton dresses and hiking boots, with knapsacks and walking sticks, or groups at huts. It surely wasn't always idyllic: at those Alpine huts there must have been arguments, rivalries, blisters, sprains. A scar on my shin is a souvenir of climbing over a fence on Mitzi's farm and falling on a scythe, and late in life Vickie identified the young mountaineers in some sixty-year-old photos. "That one," she pointed, "fell to his death that day." (It was Hans Kraus's friend Marcus, whose death was an impetus for Kraus to become an orthopedic doctor.)

For my father, Leopold Steiner—Poldi in Austria, Leo here—outdoor pursuits were his vocation more than any job he ever had. He hiked, skied, climbed mountains, rode a bicycle, was a volunteer swimming instructor, paddled a *Faltboot* (collapsible boat), and sometimes went to a nudist colony. Handsome and well built, he looked gorgeous in the skimpy bathing suit that some wore then. Whether he looked more gorgeous without it is a matter of taste. For me, nudity conjures a sandy crotch and sunburned tush, discomfort, not pleasure—except swimming nude, which is delicious.

Poldi was lucky enough to have a job and so worked five-and-a-half or six days a week. But Christmas 1931 fell on a Friday and he evidently had extra days off. I appeared toward noon. Mother's water had broken that morning, so Poldi knew she was about to give birth; Paul had been born on April 6, 1929. But Poldi had plans to go skiing, so he went, for three days, maybe longer. His wife's giving birth to their—*his*—child couldn't compete with time in the mountains. Did it matter to me then? Not directly, because I had her, but *she* didn't have *him*.

I see Paul and me as being raised by Mother and her Zetlin siblings. Father was there, but in my memory very sporadically as an engaged parent, and we rarely saw his large family. Mother decided how to raise us. With Paul, she said, she obeyed the prevailing child-rearing experts, standing at the door of the room in which he was crying, almost in tears but not letting herself go in. With me she said the German equivalent of "the hell with it" and went in to pick me up.

Passersby, she told us, said she should get a subsidy so she could have more children, we were so cute and beautiful. Nevertheless, Mother left most of our care to others.

She told me that I didn't suck my thumb. Paul sucked two or three fingers. Obeying the experts, she tied those fingers up so he couldn't stuff them in his mouth. I would hold a diaper near my mouth and make sucking movements. In therapy four decades later, I had a momentary insight: the words *Daumen saugen* (suck thumb) came to me and were immediately replaced by *Gummi lutschen* (suck rubber—that is, a pacifier), as if I learned very early that thumb-sucking was frowned upon. Is it possible for an infant to pick that message up? It fits with my need to be seen as *good*, never naughty. (*Lutschen* and *saugen* both mean to suck. *Saugen* requires effort and includes intake of liquid; *lutschen* is what one does with a lollipop.)

5

Paul was born left-handed but, as was usual then, trained to conform to the majority. Whatever ill effects that had, it did not squelch an active mind. Having noticed that when you scratch a bug bite it gets bigger, he planned to start scratching his coccyx and when he had a bump, scratch that till it made another bump, and so on till he had a tail. This untested theory shows a logical young mind at work.

Logical and also sensitive, Paul must have been six or seven when he saw a deer's head hung in a grocery store and for weeks refused to eat meat. And he must have gotten over it because there is a family story about Paul and meat. He didn't like vegetable croquettes. When he refused to eat them, Anna told him they were meat. *"Dieses Fleisch mag i nett"* ("This meat I don't like") was his astute response to her fib.

Lying about food was common in our family, and perhaps more generally. Much later, nutritionist Adelle Davis told a reporter that when someone gave her son a Coca-Cola, she told him it would taste better cold. While he went out with friends, she replaced the Coke with strong, bitter coffee. Her son tasted it and never wanted another soda. I'd say that trust between parent and child weighs more heavily than the damage of an occasional soda. Ditto for the lies Paul and I were told.

Mother had quite a fixation on the alimentary canal, on eating and eliminating. So my early years were defined by the Danube Canal—an important part of Vienna's geography—and the alimentary canal.

Paul and I could each choose one food we didn't have to eat. He shunned string beans and I, *Nockerln*, a sort of dumpling. Mother's were both lumpy and slimy. This dispensation didn't excuse us from eating other disgusting things: brains is one I remember with particular distaste. Nor did it spare me from the grownups' endless worries about how little I ate. Mother and Anna seemed to worry that I would waste away, perhaps because they had been hungry during World War I. Anna's childhood diaries tell of Vickie's going to market early mornings and returning hours later empty-handed; of food rationing; of standing in line for coal; of Mama (my Zetlin grandmother) reluctantly accepting a piece of bread from a neighbor "for the little one" (Anna).

So they tried to trick me into eating something nourishing disguised by something I liked, such as a raw egg in orange juice. It takes more juice than a small child can drink to disguise a raw egg. Just as I discovered decades later, when I mixed ground-up kidneys or other organ meats by whose nutritional value Adelle Davis swore, in a meat loaf: if I used enough of the presumably repulsive meat to make any difference nutritionally, you could taste it; using too little to taste wasn't worth the effort.

Because of grownups' anxiety I had to sit over food I couldn't force down. In 1943 or even later, I still faced cooked cereal turned cold, when it devolves into a gelatinous mass and murky liquid. Hard to get down when hot and fresh—lumpy farina always made me gag—once cold and separated it caused revulsion, despair. An unanswerable question: did this happen often, even daily, or rarely? Either could make it memorable.

Worst of all was cocoa with skin on it. I've learned that stirring vigorously makes the skin dissolve, but the hot-milk smell remains. Cocoa skin was probably a daily trial, arousing disgust, almost fright.

As for the other end of the alimentary canal, Mother was chronically interested in the amount and quality of the solid waste I (or we) produced. Anxiety about elimination lasted into adulthood. She also had a firm principle about both liquid and solid waste: never hold it in. I quote this to technicians with each pelvic ultrasound or barium enema, when one has to hold it in for quite a while. They smile indulgently and go right on with their procedure.

One other health-related memory that some of my contemporaries might recall was one or more sunlamp treatments, presumably to provide vitamin D. I liked the smell of the lamp, being fussed over and lying undressed in a warm, safe place, not having to do or prove anything. It seems skin cancer wasn't yet on the agenda of worries.

Nor was food all torment. Mother made a farina pudding to take on outings; it was delicious with raspberry syrup (*Himbeersaft*). She made chocolate pudding from Dr. Oetker's mix and served it with *Schlag* (whipped cream) in stem glasses, the delicate crystal making it taste even better. I can still conjure up the taste of lemon ice sold by Italians who appeared in the summer with a little cart on a street leading uphill from our house to Türkenschanzpark, the park's name commemorating the defeat of the second Turkish siege of Vienna, in 1683. And there was chocolate with one of those crusty Viennese rolls. Anna provided it as we rode a trolley, a treat whether rare or habitual. All these favorite foods were desserts, but I liked other foods too, for instance anchovy paste.

While eating and not eating, like all children I was trying to understand the physical world and how to deal with it. In a photo, I'm at a beach wearing only shoes, socks, and a hair ribbon and looking intently at my cupped hands as a ball tossed by Vickie is on its way to me. Perhaps focusing on one's hands rather than on the ball is a common form of toddler solipsism; when playing hide-and-seek I covered my eyes, sure that, because I couldn't see anything, no one could see me. And I argued that you can't hear yourself talk; you just know what you're saying. Some older person—in the family I was always the youngest—tried to disabuse me of this belief, but, evidently like other last-borns, I often felt that others understood things that I never would.

When I learned the numbers, I saw the digits from zero to nine in color: zero and one are white; two blue; three green; four yellow; five red; six blue; seven white; eight yellow; nine brown, each with a narrow black outline. Annie Steinbach, my (Viennese) piano teacher in New York, said that seeing numbers in color is a sign of mathematical ability (which I used to have), just as some with perfect pitch see musical tones in color. During our 1936 vacation, I had an arithmetical contretemps with a boy who said proudly that he was four. "I'm four-and-a-half," I said. "But I'm *four*," he insisted, and I knew no way to convince him that four-and-a-half is more than four.

At three I had pneumonia, lying in a big bed in the room next to the *Salon*. Mother told me later that she worried as long as I was quiet and docile. Once I became cranky she knew I was better. There were no antibiotics then.

In one other memory of that room, which later was rented out, it's Sunday afternoon and about a dozen adults are sitting at a long table, with coffee and pastries, discussing politics, at times disagreeing, although—or because—most were some shade of socialist. Almost no one we knew had children, so Paul and I had to amuse ourselves. On another Sunday he and I dressed up in one outlandish outfit after another and appeared before a few grownups to amusement and applause. In one tableau Paul, wearing the parental *Lederhose*, wheeled in Father's bicycle. Other outfits are forgotten but not the warm feeling of the grownups' enjoyment.

Father had six siblings, Mother four. Of these twelve people, six married in the 1930s, another three later. Yet Paul and I have had only two cousins and one half-sister, and the few not-childless couples among my parents' friends had at most two children. Though born in late December, I was only the 1,007th baby registered in 1931 with the *Israelitische Kultusgemeinde* (the Jewish community agency). When my uncle Felix's wife Grete was born in May, there were already more than 2,000 Jewish babies for 1906. Was this drop in "fertility" due to the times: depression, unemployment, the failed 1934 revolution in Vienna, disturbing events in Germany? This is only a guess. There was no shortage of Jewish children for the Nazis to murder.

In San Francisco in the '50s, some Viennese refugees gathered—over coffee and cake around a table—at the house of Gustl and Jena Friedmann. Talk turned to a book, *Why Women Cry,*[2] and the question of mothers working. Mother gave a little speech asserting, with suspect vehemence, "Any woman with young children who goes out to work when it isn't absolutely necessary...," indicating with words I don't recall that this was one of the worst things a mother could do.

This interested me: she was protesting too much. She *had* gone out to work, employed by another dressmaker, and then, working on her own, she'd arranged childcare by others. But she always insisted, in the '30s and the '50s and as long as she lived, that it was financially necessary. In fact, ab-so-*lute*-ly necessary.

It wasn't her going out to work that was damaging; it was sending us to live elsewhere. Paul protested, but a small child couldn't ask, in a way that would force her to think and perhaps change her mind: is it *really* necessary? She soon had customers, and employees. She was a genius with cloth and clothes. She had sewed for her mother and sisters and herself as a teenager or even earlier. With pictures in a fashion magazine, lists of clients' measurements, and expensive fabrics she made wonderful garments that disguised what were considered to be deformities. Her business was successful. Yet for years Paul and I lived most of each week with Anna and her husband.

What about the financial need? Thanks to Mother's rich cousins in New York, my parents had an apartment (at Hofstattgasse 15, Tür 6) larger than the ones they'd grown up in, larger than those of nearly everyone we knew: four rooms, kitchen, bathroom, separate toilet. Three rooms have windows on the garden; the door to the garden is in the

Salon. A bedroom, kitchen, and toilet have windows on a light court. The garden, walled on two sides by adjacent buildings, had lilac bushes, a horse chestnut tree, and a sandbox. Below, off the street just down the hill, horse-drawn wagons rolled in and out of the cobbled courtyard of a factory or warehouse. We had a telephone because of Mother's business. Few Viennese had bathrooms or telephones then. Number 15 is a respectable building up the hill from Währingerstrasse, the main street of the 18th borough, with a trolley line and many shops. Farther up the hill were villas and more elegant apartments.

Mother's business prospered and Father had a job. But according to Vickie, the Zetlins had seen much better days in Russia, with a comfortable house in Kursk, a maid, a cook, a coach and a coachman. In 1905, when Isabella was four (Hesse eight, Vickie two, Lyova one, and Anna waiting to be born), there was a pogrom, Russia having lost its brief war with Japan. The Zetlin children huddled in a corner as mobs raged outside. So Vickie told me. As far as I recall, Mother never mentioned the pogrom, nor the family's comfortable life, so much more luxurious than her later circumstances.

Because of the pogrom, my grandmother, with four children and a young cousin, moved to Vienna to be out of harm's way; no one could know how much greater harm awaited them thirty-three years later. Selig Zetlin stayed, as he had a good job as a chemist with the Russian railway, though nobody has explained why the railway needed a chemist. He had taught himself German so he could teach himself chemistry—there were no Russian chemistry books. (He also published a table of prime numbers.)

He sent money to the family in Vienna, but later he lost his sight, and his job, so the family became ever poorer. Ester Zetlin and her five children lived variously in one or two rooms. The Zetlin apartment I knew had two rooms, a tiny dark kitchen, and a toilet on the landing shared with other tenants. During World War I, Hesse got work censoring Russian letters. It wasn't all grim: though they were often hungry and as enemy aliens couldn't go to school, they were part of a circle of Russian emigrés and lived a block from the Prater, a large park.

There is a special poignancy in sinking from relative luxury to relative poverty. The myth of a past golden age fastens onto a period in one's own life. I see Isabella ever after longing for the lost comfort and prestige of a house and servants and coach. The large apartment went some way toward fulfilling this wish, even if they sometimes had to rent out a room or two; her clients meant an association with wealth, even if she couldn't have wealth of her own.

I believe that her early history, besides making her try to recreate a life clear of drudgery and squalor, had already made her choose to marry a wanderer, who like her father would often be absent—a feature of her childhood she recreated to her own and her children's detriment. The reasons for Poldi's absences were different from Selig Zetlin's, but what counted, for her feelings and for us children, was that he often wasn't there. Selig stayed in Russia for political and economic reasons; my father, for his own reasons, often preferred the mountains to his family.

My father figured in the earliest memory I feel confident of, my third Christmas Eve, in 1934. We always got presents on Christmas Eve. Paul was given a model Zeppelin. I got a doll carriage, which I filled with all my other presents. (People still ask whether I felt cheated having a Christmas birthday. No. I never had to go to school or work, and I got presents on Paul's birthday in April.) In the 1970s, therapy added to this memory of a room lit by candles on the tree, a gathering of relatives, and the kind of happy warm glow that one is supposed to feel at Christmas. The addendum was that I got to sit on Father's lap, something that I believe happened rarely. I remembered it as perching on his knees, not sitting cozily *in* his lap, held, hugged by him, but nevertheless feeling happy and proud. This was probably the closest I ever got to him, in a good way, along with being carried on his shoulders coming home from an outing, too tired to walk, but I think not enjoying those rides for I was afraid of falling.

In May 1968, in a strange episode, I felt I was reliving my birth. I sensed several huge, benign female figures, and "heard" Mother say over and over: *um Gottes Willen, um Gottes Willen* (for God's sake, or God help me). My husband, children, and I were living in Oxford. Our situation—George writing his dissertation and soon to start his first teaching job—evidently pushed us into a kind of mutual psychotherapy, a risky undertaking with unreliable results, but it was unplanned, spontaneous.

11

The "therapy" soon turned out to be mine; George ducked any real introspection. In this second birth I curled up like a fetus, felt intense pressure and then cold, and perceived the giant women. Was it a memory or my mind's interpretation of past and present feelings? It felt not as if I were being born but as if, as an adult, I was experiencing how being born felt. I didn't claim, as a youthful friend did, to have seen the inside of a third (i.e., birth) canal as I was pushed out of the womb.

On Mother's next visit, I asked about my birth. No, she hadn't said anything like that. But then I told her of a memory I'd long had of our apartment in Vienna: I'm in the hall and they're screaming at each other, arguing furiously. She gasped. "We never fought out loud in Vienna, not till New York." She didn't deny that they fought soundlessly, and seemed chastened by a small child's sixth sense. So perhaps that small child knew better than the mother could admit to herself how it felt to be laboring alone to bring forth the child of the absent skier; perhaps in 1968 the accumulated impressions of the early years converged in this reconstruction of my first moments.

Woody Allen tells of two women at a Catskills hotel. One says, "The food here is really terrible." The other agrees: "Yes, and such small portions." That paradox—I'm hungry, but do I want more of this disgusting glop?—applies to my father in a not-so-funny way. He was often absent and I wanted more of him, but often I got a kind of attention I did not want. When, in my youth, I declared to Mother that he had never loved me, she said, "He loved you but he didn't know what to do with you." Which is not how I would describe what he did do, for problems with the alimentary canal were not the only hazards of those years and were at least partly caused by more disturbing goings-on. These started very early in my life, if what I recalled in therapy was true, and Dr. L., my therapist, believed it was.

The focus of the incidents I recalled was on his genitals or mine. My hope as he approached for love and tenderness often turned to dismay and disbelief as, laughing in a coarse way, he would be interested in only that one part of my body, or want me to like a scary part of his. Frightened, horrified, revolted, I told myself that what he was doing couldn't be happening, even as it was. My disbelief and revulsion produced a kind of suspended animation, waiting for whatever he was doing to be over: I couldn't protest, and at some point I decided to make sure it never happened again, taking responsibility so as to gain the illusion of control.

These incidents, however many or few there were, may account for a fear I could never explain. Paul and I had baths together in what to me seemed our gigantic tub. Mother, or whichever grownup was in charge, would wash our hair, gather the excess lather, and set it floating, like little icebergs, in the water. I was not amused by them but revolted, afraid they would touch me. Whether this happened once or routinely, I'm pretty sure I kept my fear to myself. Nor was I put off by Paul's genitals. We not only bathed together but swam and played on the beach nude, as did other children. That was easy, normal; a father's sexuality is another matter. Once I heard Mother scold him playfully, not taking his misbehavior seriously. I felt left out in the cold.

Much later, in New York, on a Saturday in the early 1940s, he came out of the bathroom naked after a shower. My room was directly across the hall. Did he laugh out of embarrassment, or lechery, or callousness? Was it deliberate to appear naked outside my room? Was he showing off his strong, well-shaped body to his pubescent daughter? I was paralyzed, perhaps recalling, though not consciously, those earlier incidents involving me involuntarily with that body.

I'm pretty sure there had been no ugly incidents in between. Although I believe Mother should have protected me early on, she found a way to do so later. Perhaps he outgrew those urges, though it seems more likely that he would take advantage of a helpless little kid but be leery of abusing an older child who could tell other adults. There is evidence that he wasn't very brave vis-à-vis other people (as opposed to rocks and glaciers). And besides, there was a general assumption, despite Freud, that what happens to a very young child leaves no residue. "You were too young to remember," Anna said when I suggested that something that happened very early in life might have bothered me later. Perhaps he too believed that his toying with me wouldn't affect me in any lasting way.

Without minimizing its ill effects—including a half-conscious, often-thwarted assumption that I will be attractive to any man who interests me; feeling ugly and repulsive; and pathetic gratitude for almost any man's admiration—I doubt the feminist assumption that all sex abuse is about power and not about sex. Poldi was twenty-eight when I was born and I think was immature all his life, so I expect he was toying with me: amusing, titillating himself, rather than trying to harm me or teach me some anti-feminist lesson.

At a 1984 forum sponsored by the Schlesinger Library, about Jeffrey Masson's book *The Assault on Truth*, in which he attacked Freud for not sticking to his belief in childhood sexual abuse as reported by his patients, there was an almost unanimous knee-jerk-feminist assumption that women patients were being disbelieved by therapists—most then male—and so were doubly abused, and deprived of the means to be cured. Disturbed by the party-line quality of the discussion, I wanted to ask what the speakers would say to a female patient who recalled repressed memories of early abuse with the help of a male therapist—something their perspective made improbable if not impossible. But, inhibited by the large audience and the personal nature of my question, I never learned how they would have replied.

The idea of memories repressed and later recovered remains controversial, and I can't swear that any of the early incidents with my father happened as I recalled them. But I recalled them in the early 1970s, *before* the later focus on sexual abuse of children, before the purported day-care scandals (which I suspected were promoted to discredit day care and send mothers home "where they belong"), and before the endless revelations about priests. *Some* of these stories may be invented or elaborated by a kind of contagion; because of resentment of a parent, teacher, or priest; a need for attention; greed; or some other motive that allows one to stretch or bend the elusive truth. But not only did I unearth these memories under the care of Dr. L. before sexual abuse of children was in the newspapers every week, he was more convinced of the truth of my memories than I was. I kept asking how one can be sure, with such early memories and with no way to corroborate them, but had to admit that the way they came floating up unbidden and unwanted—it was always painful and frightening all over again—was an indication of authenticity, the closest thing to proof I would ever get.

Not proof either but a sort of confirmation is a nightmare I had in my youth. I remembered only the moment that woke me up in a sweat: with black night all around, a light shines on a male figure, not very tall, wearing blue trousers and a sleeveless undershirt that reveals muscular arms and shoulders. He has black hair, a nasty leer, a hint of horns, and a pose that suggests a satyr. The height, the muscles, the hair, the grin all suggest Leopold Steiner, despite the horns, and even if I didn't connect the dream to him until after I unearthed those early incidents two decades later. Nothing happened in the dream: that leering presence threatening sexual predation frightened me into waking up before he *did* anything.

I don't want to be part of the culture of blame and self-pity, but I haven't found a way to think or talk or write about my father's abuse cum neglect that is both true to my memories and not self-pitying. Tolerance and sense of humor fail when I'm alone and my father enters the room. Shouldn't they? Don't we each have some region in our lives where fear or grief overcome tolerance and humor? Dr. L. (also a Jew) called my father "your own private Hitler," comparing a petty, part-time sadist (for me a sadist, even if not one clinically) to a full-time, overtime sadist with innumerably more victims—to a historical phenomenon before which just about everyone's sense of humor fails. Dr. L. often accused me of "whitewashing" when I made excuses for my parents, so I keep trying to find the balance between taking those memories of abuse too seriously and not seriously enough.

In a photo of Isabella and Poldi, not yet anyone's parents, she is reclining against his knees and seems to be sewing; she is focused on her handiwork, and he is too, or pretends to be. A homely chap with glasses sits nearby, evidently admiring her too, probably jealous of Poldi. This man adored her, she told me, and in a way she adored him. "If I thought something was black and he said it was white, I would agree: it's white." But he didn't attract her—no "chemistry"—and Poldi did. Why? That he was handsome surely helped. Gradually, as I put together what I'd always heard or remembered with what I unearthed with Dr. L's help and with things Vickie and Anna told me, a family portrait emerged that confirms the Biblical observation that the sins of the fathers are visited on the children. (Scripture sees this as Yahweh's punishment for people's sins, but I think it, and much else, shows how well the ancient Hebrews observed what's what in this world.) In being a wanderer, Poldi resembled Isabella's father. George Moseley, who became my husband, resembled my father. Each was absent for different reasons, and "wandered" in different ways; the resemblance was obscured by

Isabella Zetlin and Poldi Steiner, with a man who I believe is the one who was also in love with her. Probably 1928.

the variety of personal and historical details. It was the basic resemblance, though, that I believe made for a shock of recognition, a sense of inevitability, that may overwhelm one as one chooses a mate. It did me.

At a church supper in Vermont, a friend of my daughter asserted that souls exist before birth and choose their parents. "Given a choice, I wouldn't have picked the parents I had," I said, not convincing her any more than she convinced me. I don't believe we choose our parents. We do choose our mates, even if we don't always know why. Mother's choice of a husband was unfortunate, even disastrous, for her and for her children. (And for him? Hard to know; I suspect it was unsatisfactory but hardly disastrous.) But had she married someone else—the man in the photo perhaps—I wouldn't exist to wish she had done better.

Chapter 2
MISPLACED GRATITUDE

$\mathcal{A}$s I unearthed more of my childhood thanks to Dr. L., I became convinced that in 1938–39, a nightmarish time in Central Europe, I was happy because I (and Paul) got to go home to Hoftattgasse and stay there. The changes that made that possible were the work of Adolf Hitler and his henchmen, who would have been chagrined, as the last thing they wanted to do was to make any Jew happy. In fact, many Jews (I included) probably fared better in exile professionally and financially than they might have if there had been no Nazis. It's an ugly thing to admit but that doesn't make it less likely.

That isn't what I might have thanked Hitler for, however, nor am I forgetting the destruction of millions of lives, and the disruption of many others. So many recollections and analyses have been recorded—on paper, film, and tape, in books, artworks, plays, entire museums—about the destruction that I can add only that with each reading or hearing or viewing I try to imagine myself and my family in a freight car headed east, rather than the passenger train and ship to America that were our actual lot.

As for the disruption, a small but poignant emblem of ruined lives was an elderly refugee who visited us in Manhattan. Having been a lawyer in Austria, he carried an *Aktentasche* (briefcase), opened it with great dignity, and pulled out not legal documents but salami and other sausages, and an order pad. Too old to start over in his profession, he was doing his best to make a living and maintain his self-respect.

Back in Vienna, Mother, with her genius for dressmaking, had begun the formal steps of apprentice, journeyman, and master—the old guild stages—that would enable her to work independently. When I was born she was still going out to work for an established dressmaker.

As long as she was nursing, she sent her breast milk home midday. I understand that she wanted and needed to work, and that Anna, the underemployed trained kindergartner, and Anna's husband, Beppo, who worked evenings at the Social Democratic Party, should take care first of Paul and then of both of us during the day. So Anna said late in her life, but there may have been a nursemaid too. (Beppo is a nickname for boys and men named Josef—via the Italian Giuseppe.)

When I was three, Mother was ready to establish her own business; our large apartment enabled her to work at home. Evidently Paul and I were in the way, for on a Sunday evening in January 1935 our parents took Paul and me to Anna and Beppo's apartment (9th Borough, at Gussenbauergasse 7, Stiege [Stairway] 2, Tür 18), and left us there. Early in therapy, as I wrote on the calendar for the next January 6th, an internal voice said, "There's no such date." Hardly scientific proof, but January 6, 1935 was a Sunday; I wished there were no such date. (Now, eighty-six years later, with the insurrection at the US Capitol, January 6 has become an infamous date for many, not just for me.)

The previous winter Anna had lost half a leg in a skiing accident. She could no longer go out to work with small children, even privately as she had been doing. So just when Mother felt she needed help caring for her children, Anna became available and in need of income. Years later, emboldened by therapy, I dared to ask Anna how Paul and I reacted to the move. "We expected no trouble and there was none," she said. Spoken, as Dr. L. noted, like a *Gauleiter* (Nazi area commander), and she wasn't even German.

But she was wrong. There was trouble, even if it didn't show. She explained "no trouble": we knew her and Beppo, and their apartment. True enough, also true that she knew how to teach and amuse small children, and that Beppo was affectionate and fun. They were better parents than our parents. But they *weren't* our parents and even the trained kindergartner, who had attended lectures by noted psychologists and analysts (this is the Vienna of Freud, Adler, et al.) and who in later years was always sure of her own wisdom, evidently didn't understand what it means to a child to be sent away from home. Or perhaps she knew what it *usually* means but believed this was different, as these lucky children were going to live with *her*. (Or did she perhaps see

Isabella and Poldi's shortcomings as parents?)

To me, being sent away, even to a bright, sunny apartment with two responsible, devoted grownups, meant that those other grownups, who had given me life, whom I adored—whatever other feelings I sometimes had—didn't want me. And that *they must be right not to want me*: that I'm somehow bad or wrong, even if no one has told me how and I haven't figured it out yet.

Now I can say that this is what I felt then. At the time I said nothing. Paul spoke up, and the exchange became part of family lore, retold often to show how clever he was:

> Paul: I don't want to move to Anna's. Why do we have to?
> Mother: The ladies want their dresses.
> Paul: Let them buy ready-made dresses.

No one seemed to notice what Mother's reply said to us children—the one asking and the one listening in: that the wishes of the "ladies" count, yours don't. They must get what they want; you needn't get what you want.

I can feel myself, timid and wide-eyed, listening and observing as Paul was sometimes rebuked, scolded, ridiculed (by Father), by Lyova's admission even smacked. It seemed safest to be good, so I became—outwardly—patient, sensible, agreeable. No trouble. Much later Mother said that she used to worry because I was so *good*. But I doubt she understood why.

A related memory emerged in therapy: little Eva, not yet three, hovering around long, earnest discussions between Mother and Anna, Mother and Vickie, or among all three sisters. A phrase here, a sentence there, hinted at the idea of our living elsewhere. It was too incredible, too awful to think about, so a pang of fear was followed by obliviousness, until it came up again, or until it happened. This pattern, called denial, makes life nicer superficially, while the denied facts and feelings seethe below, causing mischief, self-destructive decisions and physical ailments among the likely results.

A trivial incident decades later made this pattern clear. I got off the bus from Medford on a lovely spring morning. As I walked toward

Cambridge Common, with trees, statues, and Harvard and Radcliffe buildings spread before me in the early sunshine and the peaceful bustle of traffic and pedestrians starting a new day, I felt: "I'm so lucky to be here." At almost the same moment another interior voice screamed in protest, and almost simultaneously I shut that voice down.

It was denial in action. Therapy had enabled me to notice the whole rapid-fire sequence, an echo of earlier denials: of Father's abuse, Mother's abandonment.

When, in my early forties, that voice declared that there is no January 6, I was unearthing from self-imposed oblivion the memory of that first Sunday evening, the first of many. All four big people seem satisfied; all is cordial. No one guesses that anything unusual or terrible is happening. Then the door shuts with finality. Paul and I are on this side; *They* are on the other side, going down the stairs together, without me. I feel lost in a huge endless bottomless cold dark void. It's no help that there are two of us in the same fix. To a three-year-old, only her own misery counts

Normal life takes over. We sleep, eat, play, learn, have baths and naps and outings. Soon I go to the kindergarten across the courtyard of this municipal housing block and, according to Anna, am a favorite of children and teachers. We hunted for Easter eggs in the kindergarten's sandbox, the

Anna and Josef (Beppo) Jarosik, Eva in Beppo's lap, Paul in background, early 1930s.
As far as I can remember, my father never held or played with me as Beppo did.

eggs' colors extra luminous in bright sunshine, and once, returning from the sandbox to the schoolroom, one child said, erroneously, that we were to run back; so we ran and then all the other children were kept after school but I was allowed to go home, relieved, but uneasy at this special treatment.

Franzi Meyer, a neighbor boy, was a playmate and I had a boyfriend, Erich, a blank in my memory who figured in another family story.

> Eva: Erich and I are getting married.
> Adult: You're too young.
> Eva: Then we'll wait till Erich starts school.
> Adult: You'll still be too young.
> Eva: But when *I* go to school, *then* we'll be old enough.

Beppo made me a dollhouse or store, a metal box painted pea green; the front folded down when the lid came off. There were tiny furnishings and tiny boxes of groceries: e.g., a triangular box of noodles resembling the grownup version. I parked my doll carriage, piled high with toys and treasures so useless as a carriage, in a corner of the bedroom. Beppo put a new paper cone in the radio's speaker and gave me the old faded one. Onto the carriage it went. I didn't know what to do with it, or with the paper bags full of horse chestnuts I gathered in my parents' garden, but I clung to these objects. The horse chestnuts were smooth and brown, the paper cone had its own sensual appeal.

But it wasn't just aesthetic. Driving to Dr. L's in the 1970s, I suddenly realized that, when I found it hard to throw something away, it was because trash wasn't just trash. Having been sent across town into exile, I identified with rejected objects. After this little epiphany, it became easier to dispose of things, knowing that they are *not* me. And soon recycling made discarding more acceptable.

The door shut the same way almost every Sunday evening. We'd go home Saturday afternoon and back to Anna's for the week on Sunday. Each summer through 1937 we went to the country for a few weeks with Anna; Mother joined us when she could. Otherwise the same schedule prevailed, and it was with Dr. L. that I realized that the second and third Sundays were the worst. On Saturday the 12th I could think: It's over;

we're home again; but on Sunday the 13ᵗʰ and 20ᵗʰ, I had to begin to see it as routine.

Lyova took us for walks afternoons. As the two youngest Zetlins, Anna and Lyova were close when little, she told me much later; they invented their own games, and older family members stepped around them and the toys they made out of discarded scraps. Did they now enjoy us as they had their homemade dolls? One afternoon Lyova made boats out of newspaper, which we sailed on the Danube Canal. A boy named Walter was with us; he slipped and fell in, grabbing my coat, so I fell in too. This incident was fodder for many a school writing assignment, as well as grounds for a lawsuit by Walter's parents.

Paul and Eva with our uncle, Lyova Zetlin (we called him Loba), on a walk in Vienna, 1930s.

Anna taught me to read and write, some arithmetic, some Hebrew. In one little notebook covered in periwinkle blue paper I wrote the first verses of Genesis in Hebrew and illustrated them. I drew a cupboard Beppo had made, with a red bowl of fruit on top, and, over and over, my ideal *Haus und Baum* (house and tree), the trees green circles dotted with red fruit, the sky a blue margin at the top of the paper. Someone pointed out that the sky comes all the way down, so I extended the blue margin down the sides of the paper like a frame, never mind the sky as I saw it. Paul became a good chess player. I learned the rules, but played the way George W. Bush fought wars, not taking into account the smart moves the enemy would make.

We played with water on the balcony or in the steamy laundry room on the top floor. Neighbors came to visit. We seemed to have what children need: our own beds, food, toys, fresh air, attentive adults, other children. But we also had evidence that our parents didn't want us. The door shut again and again. I didn't learn Hebrew and draw recognizable objects as a three-year-old. We were there not only week after week but year after year. Mother "couldn't" have us at home while she was getting established. But soon there were steady customers, and more than one employee. Why couldn't we be there too?

Anna's and Beppo's apartment was light and airy, up several flights with a view over the Danube Canal, full of fun and stimulation. Hofstattgasse 15 was older and more substantial, built not for workers but for *Bürger*—bourgeoisie. Our ground-floor apartment was (and is) relatively dark. Our parents fought, out loud or silently. Father would take off for a hike too strenuous for his wife and children. Mostly it was sober, but I longed to be there, to be truly wanted there.

Such a brew of confusing facts and confused infantile conclusions seems to have hardened into a lifelong tendency to long for what is painful or repellent, and to reject what is attractive and wholesome.

Eventually, Hitler and the Nazis brought our nuclear family together, which felt good at the time but meant that inadequate, abusive Poldi remained the model for the men in my life. So besides the irony that Hitler's annexation of Austria resulted in my happiness at going home to Hofstattgasse, there is the further irony that this happiness was doubly a delusion: not only hadn't I done anything to *make* my parents take me home, but they were no more loving than they had been, to their children or to each other.

Furthermore, Beppo made a better father and would have been a better model for a husband. Whatever happened the day of Anna's skiing accident, he remained devoted to her; he was engaged with us children in a way Poldi rarely was, if ever; and he didn't abuse me as Poldi had, nor, I believe, disparage Paul as Poldi did. So I was triply deluded in being happy, for I lost a better man to grow up with. It's really not "Thank you" to Hitler for ending my private exile but a sour "Thanks a lot."

There are some other wrinkles to this story. First, Father worked at Pick's sporting-goods store in Alserbachstrasse, a few blocks from Anna and Beppo's house. Because it was so near and Mother had no time to cook dinner, Father had his midday meal with us every weekday. In her old age Anna complained repeatedly that *he* would complain about her lentils: he wanted them cooked with vinegar; Beppo preferred them without. Anna considered her husband's wishes at least as important as those of even a paying guest (and you can add vinegar). Anna's recollections confirm my memories: my father, whose acceptance and love I longed for, was intent mainly on what went into his stomach, and only a little now and then on who was at the table with him.

I perceived his daily appearance as a test. If I could pass this test, I could go home again, but first I had to figure out what I must do to pass. Now it's easy to see this as nonsense, a result of my wish for controlling power, "infantile omnipotence." I couldn't pass the test because there wasn't one. We were at Anna's not because of any fault or crime of mine or Paul's but because of what sort of people the adults were and the decisions they made for their own reasons—with prevailing political and economic conditions a factor but not, I believe, the deciding one. But this truth was too scary, underlining my helplessness in the face of their self-absorption. Better to think that I could *do* something about it. Better the guilt of failing to do this mysterious right thing, and the hope of eventually figuring out what to do, than the despair of recognizing that I couldn't change them or the arrangements they made.

The baffling midday meals compounded my chronic problems with food. I recall once vomiting repeatedly as Anna kept trying to feed me. I remember it as a Via Dolorosa from the table to my bed. It's unlikely it actually happened that way, but Anna said, or meant (probably with memories of World War I hunger), You have to eat *some*thing before your nap. Another day I found some croquettes inedible. The last bite was in my cheek at nap time, and still there when I woke up.

There was the added twist that both Mother and Anna limped as they walked. Did this fate await me too? What must I do to avoid it? Another mystery to solve, one only to me, for Mother was born with a dislocated hip and Anna had had an accident. Neither had been "punished," nor was there any truth to an interpretation I noted in my diary in 1980: "I got the notion as a child that in our family having a man made a woman a cripple. Vickie was alone & no cripple…. The two married ones couldn't walk normally."

Were these weekly comings and goings better or worse than uninterrupted exile? Only in recent years did I realize that we could have spent daytimes at Anna's and gone home evenings, so that we clearly lived with our parents. Perhaps no one thought of that scheme, or it wasn't what the grownups wanted.

We lived at Anna's for almost four years. Was that ab–so–*lute*–ly necessary? as Mother's insistence on financial need implied. It's good that she pursued her profession but hard to believe that she couldn't have kept us at home if she wanted to. For many years I was sure that she sent us away to save her marriage (many *adult* years; as a child I didn't consider her motives), as Poldi was such a reluctant father. That she hoped, with us out of the way, he would be more devoted to her, less likely to be off swimming, looking for other women, or whatever else he did evenings.

Later I wondered about other motives. Dr. L. suggested that she was aware of Poldi's abuse and wanted to protect me from him. That makes sense, but with the irony that she sent *me* into exile, while *he* could stay with her. And yes, perhaps protect me, but mixed in, I became convinced later still, was jealousy, of my wholeness versus her disability, and as if I were a sexual rival. In a way I was; he made me one, while I just wanted to be their child, loved, cared for, taught, enjoyed. Mother had gotten into a long-term jam by marrying this man and I suppose dealt with it as best she could. There was no good way to make the marriage a close and happy one while allowing her to follow her vocation and to keep her children at home.

These family matters didn't exist in a vacuum, and eventually public events impinged drastically on private ones, as Hitler annexed his native Austria to his adopted country and, shortly after this *Anschluss* of March 12, 1938, put a young Adolf Eichmann in charge of making Vienna *Judenrein* (clean of Jews).

My parents' marriage certificate states that Poldi was *Konfessionslos* (without religion) and Isabella, Jewish. But being secular, our failure to attend synagogue or fast on Yom Kippur, made no more difference to Hitler or Eichmann than did our Christmas trees.

For my first six years, being Jewish was, or seemed, inconsequential. But one day in 1938, walking to Anna's from the Jewish school with a boy from the gentile one (these were public schools, segregated after the *Anschluss*), I feared that, as we talked about our families, he would realize that I was Jewish; by then I knew this could be dangerous. Another day, according to a story Anna loved to repeat late in life, a group of gentile boys spotted me; one of them said, "There's a Jew; let's set her on fire"; he lit a match—and I blew it out. I don't recall this incident, Anna wasn't there to see it, so it sounds like a story concocted by a frightened child trying to sound brave. I'd seen troops marching through the streets, felt fearful as we heard squadrons of planes from behind blackout shades, seen Nazi banners hung everywhere. Seeing how Austrians welcomed the Nazis, how crowds gathered in central Vienna to cheer Hitler when he came on the 13th to gloat over the city that had spurned him as a young art student, the adults must have known it was a bad time for Jews, though no one knew how bad it would become. Beppo, not Jewish, let himself be drafted into the Wehrmacht. What did I feel about my beloved uncle in that dreaded uniform? More unresolved confusion.

Along with marching soldiers and planes I heard the ominous word *Krieg*, war, and imagined an acceptable way for men to fight. I envisioned a large, grassy sports field with a high fence around it. At each end of the center line, referees sit in lifeguard chairs. The armies fight inside the fence; the referees keep score and remind the soldiers of the rules. Civilians, going by on their way to work, school, or shopping, may stop and watch for a while, then go about their business. Alas, war has never been like that; World War II was even less so. With each war, the proportion of civilian to military casualties increases.

Anna and Beppo were divorced under the Nuremberg laws, which made dissolution of mixed marriages all too easy. In 1968, belatedly emboldened to ask questions, I asked Anna about the divorce. Beppo was political, she reminded me; had he gone into exile with her, he would have felt useless, while in the army there was underground resistance. "And," she added, not very convincingly, "maybe after eight years of marriage we weren't so much in love anymore."

In her last years she told me repeatedly about the day they appeared before the magistrate (February 14, 1939), both in tears. Beppo assured her, assured himself, that sometimes it's all right for a man to cry. After she died I found the divorce decree among her papers. As a Nazi document, it is chilling in the matter-of-fact way it expounds its crazy, vicious ideology: in marrying Anna Zetlin, Josef Jarosik knew that she was Jewish but believed that to be merely a religious distinction; now Adolf Hitler had made clear to him that it is a racial distinction, that marriage between a Jew and a non-Jew is an impossibility. And that is why Josef Jarosik was now dissolving this (pseudo-) marriage. If they remained together he would of course lose his job, and they their apartment, as if this were a matter of natural law. Nothing more about what would happen to her, or to them, if they chose to stay married.

They lost their apartment anyway, along with each other, and some lucky Nazi family moved into it. Paul and I moved back to Hofstattgasse. In 1990 Paul wrote in answer to my questions:

> On Nov. 10, we were still living on Gussenbauergasse. We moved to Hofstattgasse some time later in 1938. On Nov. 10 Loba [our version of Lyova] came over as usual in the afternoon. Usually he took us out for a walk. This time I had to ask, "Aren't we going for a walk?" He said, no, it's raining. I looked out the window and said, *"Es regnet doch nicht* [But it isn't raining]." And he said, *"Es regnet Schweinehunde* [It's raining scoundrels—literally pig-dogs]." A few days later Mother told us what had happened.

What had happened was Kristallnacht. Poldi was one of thousands of Jewish men who disappeared that day. Later Mother told us that for two weeks she ran around the city with a sweater and a bar of chocolate, looking for him. The *Kultusgemeinde* assured her that no Jews had left Vienna. Eventually he sent a postcard from Dachau. Thanks to his obsession with the outdoors, he was able to withstand the rigors of concentration camp better than most. Though he never told us much (or have I forgotten?), one incident stands out. After an attempted escape, all the prisoners had to stand at attention outdoors all day and all night, without coats, hats, gloves. Several died. It was grim, but not yet the Final Solution.

I wasn't aware of the now-famous humiliations and atrocities: Nazi toughs breaking windows, looting Jewish shops, invading Jews' apartments, making Jews scrub sidewalks with toothbrushes dipped in acid. Nor do I recall yellow stars on anyone's clothes. When I asked Anna about such things years later, she said, "That must have been in another part of the city." It sounds like denial, or was my family spared all that for some unaccountable reason? Because Beppo was in the army? Nor, unlike some, were we given middle names: Israel for males, Sarah for females; we did have a large **J**, for *Jude*, stamped on our passports. In the 1980s or '90s, a bank teller gave me a jolt when he asked about my middle initial: "What does the S stand for? Sarah?" (No: Steiner.)

My illusions about *earning* permission to go home gave the events of 1938–39 a certain glamour in my eyes that they almost surely had for no other targets of Nazi persecution. Nazis, and those who welcomed them, were happy. I was happy (as far as I can recall) because we moved back home. The evidence indicates that this would not have happened, perhaps ever, if Hitler had not reunited our little nuclear family.

Paul's memories of 1938, and mine, are sparse. The apartment to which we returned was dark but familiar. There were tenants in one or two of the rooms. The nearest Jewish school was not very near, so we went irregularly. I was in first grade and went three times; Paul, in third, went four times. I loved school, even the repetitious penmanship exercises. The clearest memory, along with glimpses of a crowded class-room, is of meeting Paul at the end of the day and taking turns multi-plying by two, his classmates impressed that I knew that 2 x 8 = 16, and even more so when I said that 2 x 32 = 64. We kept it up during the long walk home, until my next turn would bring the total to a number over 100,000 and I didn't know how to say it. I was proud and happy, oblivious of the terrible things happening all around us. Mother made sure that we were sheltered from most of the horrible truth. Did I think that I had solved the mystery, found the magic thing to do so I could stay at home? I believe I felt triumphant, not just lucky, unaware of the grim irony that Hitler's annexing Austria, drafting Beppo, dissolving Anna and Beppo's marriage, and giving their apartment to Nazis should make me happy.

In the midst of this triumphant happiness, was there no anguish or regret at losing that affectionate uncle? Did I feel he had abandoned me? I can't recall *any* feelings about that and can guess only that I accepted this fact, among many others, as part of a world still largely beyond my understanding.

Meanwhile Mother must have been preparing for departure while trying to find a way for us to get out of Austria. Getting out was not the main difficulty; Hitler and Eichmann *wanted* us out, but you had to have proof that you could get in somewhere. There was talk of Australia, and Palestine, where Hesse and Ina Zetlin lived. But Mother had cousins, the well-to-do Racolins, in New York, who had helped her acquire our apartment. Her cousin Natasha ("Nalia") had married Mendel Racolin, a dentist who began buying apartment buildings and became rich. They provided the all-important affidavit, which promised that we would not become dependent on the public; the US was still in the throes of the Great Depression. (Having long heard that there were socialist revolutionaries among Mother's relations, I asked Vickie about them and learned that Nalia had been imprisoned after taking part in the 1905 uprising in Russia. Someone, perhaps her future husband, soon bailed her out and she gave up revolution. "That's it?" I asked. "That's it," said Vickie.)

Once we could prove that we could emigrate, Father was released. I recall a happy breakfast of rolls and cocoa, and Poldi with shaved head but otherwise in good shape.

We packed a large *Lift* (crate), taking some furniture: the tall mirror that Mother used for fittings and an easy chair that, with its two ottomans, became an uncomfortable bed. Mother had to leave her collection of nineteenth-century fashion plates. I had to choose one doll. Later Anna told me repeatedly that I chose an old doll that *she* had doctored, rather than the shiny new one Mother expected I'd take. Paul had to leave his electric train. He showed a neighbor who came to buy it how the train worked, and she was so touched that, teary, she declared she couldn't bear to deprive him of it. Anna was still contemptuous six decades later: he couldn't take it with him, so what use was it to weep? Better to give him some money for it. Then Paul learned that he couldn't take his bicycle. "Maybe I don't want to go to America after all," he said. But what he, or any of us, wanted didn't matter.

Friends saw us four off at the train station on the evening of February 23rd; we crossed Germany in what I recall as an uneventful trip, very different from the kind the kind planned for the unlucky ones. Officials came through to check papers, but there was, since the *Anschluss*, no border to cross. Paul recalled that, as the train left Vienna, Mother said,

"What do we do now?" and Father said, "Let's eat some sandwiches." We arrived in Hamburg next day. Paul remembered riding the subway; I remember evening window-shopping among bright lights and lively crowds. After two nights in a hotel, we boarded the ship *Hamburg*.

Before it sailed, I sat, wrapped in a blanket in a deck chair, entranced by a brass band. I loved brass bands and didn't understand what the martial music and the Hitler salute signified. Then what seemed a normal voyage, not a flight from danger; this German liner was safe from German torpedoes from German submarines. We dropped anchor briefly off the coast of England, then were on our way to New York. I recall only one day, when Mother and Paul were lying sea-sick in the cabin and Father and I saw a movie, a proud and happy moment for me. Our arrival in New York, on March 4, 1939, ended what was surely the most significant of my skirtings of history.

Nearly all the Zetlins and Steiners also managed to leave. All but one of the Steiner siblings escaped, to Shanghai, Australia, or the US, as did all the Zetlin siblings. Selig Zetlin died, mercifully, that spring (1939), the Steiner grandparents even earlier. When Vickie and I visited the *Kultusgemeinde* in 1982, we learned that Ester Zetlin had been in Vienna (but not in her apartment) until September 10, 1942, when she was sent to *Theresienstadt*, the "elite" concentration camp where thousands died of disease or starvation. She died there in October. Vickie didn't tell me what she and her siblings felt about leaving their mother. I wasn't close to my grandmother, but in 1982 I was struck by gratuitous Nazi cruelty: in most normal societies people would want to make a blind, frail old woman as comfortable as possible, not drag her off to a concentration camp. Still, the luck of the two families was incredible. Life was not easy or blissful afterward, but we escaped from a hell that claimed millions no more or less deserving than we.

A friend who also escaped from Vienna could have been speaking for my family when she said, "Why me? I wasn't anybody special." She claimed to believe she had a good angel watching over her. It's impossible to prove she did or didn't, but I don't believe she did, and to say an angel or God saved me is still a way to be special. What about the unlucky ones? Where were their angels? Why didn't God save them? No, it's chance, good or bad luck.

When Vickie and her husband returned to Vienna in 1949, a former neighbor described the years of deprivation and bombs, and asked with a sigh, "Why did you leave?" Blinded by her own suffering, which was no doubt real enough, she didn't realize how stupid and insensitive her question was. It's as hard as ever to grasp those fearful events and to find a way to feel about having skirted them, knowing what happened to millions just like us. And knowing that we suffered physically much less than Austrians who stayed, but that we might so easily have suffered infinitely more—perhaps with no help, or even sympathy, from this neighbor.

II.
New York, 1939–49

Chapter 3
10 MANHATTAN AVENUE

*F*or our first month in New York we lived in one room in a brown-stone rooming-house on West 88th Street. My first-grade teacher issued a reader and the next day demanded that I cover it. Such book covers were unknown in Vienna, but Mother found brown paper and wrapped the book as a package. Spotting it the next day, the teacher held it up. She and the class laughed. It was the petty cruelty that allows people to feel superior to an outsider, trivial compared to what we had escaped, but as the only sharp memory of those first days in America it was a not-funny parody of the incomprehensible cruelty raging across Europe.

Soon after we moved uptown, Mother, hearing murmuring through the locked bathroom door, asked, "Is someone in there with you?" For me the bathroom was peopled with obedient little children. My presumably kindlier teacher at P.S. 179 would stand on a bench in her high heels directing our games and calisthenics. Emulating her, I stood on the toilet lid, opposite the mirror, my heels propped on the backs of my oxfords to approximate the shoes that proclaimed the teacher's authority.

We had moved to an apartment in a corner building with two addresses: 10 Manhattan Avenue and 20 West 101st Street, with an interior courtyard and an elevator—the latter rare in Vienna then. Paul often reminded Mother of her trying to tell the elevator man that her husband forgot his key: "sein key" became "sei sky."

The change in language, a breeze for me and not too hard for Paul, was a major challenge for adults. Both Eva Hoffman (in *Lost in Translation*) and Gerda Lerner (*Why History Matters*) stress the difficulties of living in a new language, but Hoffman was thirteen, Lerner nineteen when leaving Europe for English-speaking countries (in Hoffman's case Canada), while I was only seven. Learning another language with little effort while retaining the first one was a gift, an opportunity.

I was baffled by some bits of English. What is a tisofthee? (As in "My country 'tis of thee...") Who is Regus Patoff? And why does he write his name in such an odd way: Reg. U.S. Pat. Off.?

Language and cultural differences gave rise to refugee jokes. The German *Herr* means mister, master, lord. So on a double-decker Fifth Avenue bus, the husband goes upstairs. When the conductor comes to collect the wife's fare, she says, "The lord above will pay."

Although the most shocking weather for us Central Europeans was the humid summer heat, winter could also be difficult. A refugee wrote his landlady: "There is a terrible train in my room and if you don't give me a new ceiling, I will have to undress." German *Zug* means train or draft; *Decke* = ceiling or blanket; *ausziehen* = undress or move out.

Some refugees changed their names to sound American, and so a mother is sitting in the lobby of her son's apartment building, unable to go upstairs. She has forgotten the apartment number and can't ask because she doesn't remember his name.

I've forgotten too. Little remains of our two years on Manhattan Avenue. Once, while washing dishes, I broke a glass and abandoned the dishes, though I'd been proud of my offer to do them. Mother was disturbed that I was so fearful and guilty about something so trivial: it was the old need to be good to avoid being sent away. Another day in that kitchen I sat at the table chattering with my chair tilted back; it slipped and luckily my head hit the window-frame, rather than the window's glass or the courtyard's pavement.

These weeks were something of a honeymoon for us four. We had escaped intact from a continent engulfed in unimaginable horrors, with much worse to come. Mendel and Nalia Racolin, who had rescued us, employed Father as elevator man and then painter in their apartment buildings. They invited us for dinner, a rather stiff affair in their formal dining room on Riverside Drive. I was bored and uncomfortable but impressed with the view, which included the Palisades across the Hudson River and, at their base, an intermittently-lit-up sign advertising Spry vegetable shortening.

Uncle Joseph, Ester Zetlin's youngest brother, had rented the brownstone room for us and took us to the country in his car. He seemed so old and eminent that I didn't know how to address him. The formal German *Sie* seemed wrong for a relative, the familiar *Du* wrong for a child to use for an old man. Relief came when I could use the all-purpose English *you*.

Vickie moved in with us. She had arrived in October 1938 and at first worked at Purepac, with which Uncle Joseph had some connection. She earned $12 packing drugs into jars six days a week. This wasn't starvation wages—milk cost five or seven cents a quart, for instance—but she did better as a bookkeeper, and then the grander space buyer, in a series of advertising agencies. Before leaving Vienna, she took classes in pastry making just in case, but that wasn't her calling.

Mother resumed *her* calling almost immediately. Some refugee ladies left Europe with at least some of their money, and refugee seamstresses needed work; soon Mother had a going concern in our apartment, not without its headaches. When she had to lie down with an actual headache, I wrote her a note wishing I could have the headache for her. Did I mean it? Love or appeasement? Both? More unanswerable questions: were her headaches "female" or due to a problematic husband? or to deadlines or difficult clients?

Dressmaking occupied much of the apartment, our rooms doubling as waiting room, fitting room, workroom; it's sobering that I alone now occupy four rooms plus kitchen and bath. Mother bought a used Persian rug at Macy's. (It's in my study). A vacuum-cleaner salesman vacuumed it, then emptied the bag, making a small cone of black dirt. Was all the dirt from our rug? Who knows—but Mother bought a vacuum cleaner, a gadget unknown in Europe, at least by the likes of us. There rugs were hung over a line outdoors and beaten with a *Pracker*, a rattan rug-beater. Another unknown gadget was a toaster; you toasted bread on one side, turned it by hand to do the other side. Father explained: "You put flour and water and eggs and yeast in and it makes bread." I believed him, for a moment anyway.

This was one of his unfortunate habits. It's wonderful when children get a joke and play along. But when they don't, I make sure to tell them it's a joke. Otherwise one is laughing at—not with—them, humiliating them. Father seemed to have a need to do this, as if bamboozling his children certified his superiority, rather than just the opposite. When we

walked along Pelham Bay on our way to Orchard Beach, he said, pointing at Long Island, "That's England." Although I knew we had sailed for
a week after seeing England, I believed him, and he didn't disabuse me. Is
that a triumph, for a man of thirty-six versus a child of eight?

For everyday outings we went to Central Park, with its playgrounds,
meadows, rock ledges, ponds. One afternoon Paul threw a stone toward
a dog and it hit me squarely on the head. That night a doctor came, put
his cool hand on my brow, and had me walk up and down to make sure
I could. Doctors made house calls then, and I was often sick. Having
had pneumonia and whooping cough in Vienna, I had measles, mumps,
tonsillitis, and numerous colds in New York, and once a mouth full of
blisters. All this illness got me Mother's attention, though she could fuss
over me only a little when she had her business and household to manage.

My sparse memories of those two years cluster around our apartment
and the family, but I vaguely remember one friend in the building, Pauline,
and a bit more clearly, a "negro" classmate who went two blocks out of
his way to walk me home, with his arm around my shoulders. Flattered,
mainly I was amazed at how uninhibited he was. Our classmates skipped
down the street chanting "Ronny has a girlfriend; Eva has a boyfriend."
Whether this happened once or daily, I can't say, nor when during the
two years it was, but an American admirer and the friendly chanting
indicated that I was accepted and at least tentatively at home, after only a
short time in New York.

In the spring of 1941 we moved a mile south to a "better" address
more accessible for Mother's clients, most of whom lived along Central
Park West or in the East 50s to 80s. However my parents felt about our
new country—I don't recall any talk about that—they were making the
best of our situation, and gradually improving it.

Chapter 4
35 WEST 82nd STREET

$\mathcal{P}$aul was twelve and I nine when we moved to 82nd Street. In April, we and two other children were treated to an afternoon at the circus. "Gayety of Circus Cheers Refugees: 4 Children See Their First Show Under the 'Big Top.'" So *The New York Times* headed its report. Paul said he liked the elephants best while I, typically, refused to pick a favorite: "It was all good—I can't remember" is what I supposedly said. At this or another circus visit, we took part in a tableau depicting our supposed exotic heritage. We were dressed in pseudo-Bedouin robes, and photographed with a camel, one of us holding a box of matzo, the other a menorah. I remember the camel's cage, with pungent animal smells, and a grainy newspaper photo. Now this feels somewhat obnoxious; then I just did as I was told.

There were no more moments of fame. For two years we lived in apartment 6C, in the rear of the building. Again our four rooms did double duty, for the family and Mother's business. In June 1943 we moved to the larger 6B. "Paul is getting the maid's room, which is terribly small, so I sort of share mine with him," I told my diary. "I don't mind, though, because it's big enough." My room, which I don't recall sharing, faced the street, as did the living room, which again served as fitting room; ladies waited in our parents' bedroom; the dining room was the workroom. Vickie moved out, giving us more space.

As in Vienna, our building sat among more elegant neighbors. My classmate Sally Lewis lived across the street in an apartment large enough to swallow ours more than twice. It had a sunken living room, very desirable in New York then. (Disabilities awareness was decades in the future.) Mrs. Lewis's dressing table was crowded with expensive perfumes; Mother had no dressing table and only one bottle of 4711 cologne.

When I was about twelve, I began to wish—sort of—that my *real* parents lived in the Beresford, which fills the block between 81st and 82nd along Central Park West. It has three entrances with doormen. I would have a huge bedroom on a high floor overlooking the park, with lots of huge stuffed animals. I named these parents Campbell, the only "American" name I could think of. They remained rather shadowy, and I had twinges of guilt about the Steiners. In my fantasies, I granted them visiting rights.

At first we had uniformed elevator operators. By 1949, the elevator was self-service, coal no longer rattled into the cellar, where there were new coin-operated washers and dryers—though Mother, because she worked, still sent the laundry out to be done professionally. The laundryman would spread a sheet on the living-room floor and heap the other items on it as he and Mother counted them.

Typically for New York, we hardly knew people in the building. In the lobby getting the mail, which came twice a day, or sunbathing on the roof, it was at most small talk. A woman who rode the elevator with her German shepherd and me referred to her husband as the dog's father. Apartment 6A housed a sedate middle-aged couple, she rather frail, he resembling Charles DeGaulle; their polite nods may have masked regret at having such uncouth neighbors. Our actual social lives were elsewhere, but it was a good place to live, near public schools, the subway, buses, the park, museums: Natural History and the New-York Historical Society around the corner, the Metropolitan Museum of Art just across the park.

Half a block west, Columbus Avenue was lined with stores. One grocery featured slabs of butter and bulk cottage cheese. The grocer cut or scooped the amount you wanted, got items off the shelves for you, and added up what you owed in pencil on a paper bag, in which you carried it all home. Another grocery included a hearty, homely German butcher with a bloody apron, a walk-in refrigerator, and a handsome son who worked there and on whom I had a crush, which worried me: I didn't think I'd want to marry a butcher. Not that he even noticed me. Friendly pharmacists on Columbus removed foreign objects from my eyes expertly and gratis, until they weren't allowed to do it any more. Despite losing this benefit, I came to realize that such regulations are needed to protect people from each other; not everyone is as ethical as those pharmacists.

Columbus and Amsterdam—the latter with at least one corner bar at each intersection—were still lined with tenements, walk-ups five or six stories high, some with railroad apartments, in which you entered each room from the next one; only one had windows on the street, and one, mostly the kitchen, a window on an air shaft; usually no bathroom, only a shared toilet on the landing. In one such apartment, a classmate's birthday party was my introduction to Post Office, Spin the Bottle, and other kissing games, the place evidence that, while we were more cramped than the Lewises, others had more modest quarters.

At a dry-goods store on Amsterdam Avenue, the clerk would take down box after box so you could buy as many handkerchiefs, socks, or undershirts as you wanted. They weren't wrapped in plastic; the boxes stayed at the store. One of Vickie's advertising agencies represented packaging companies. I remonstrated with her about the wastefulness of all these wrappings, but they were her bread and butter then.

With pride and resentment I ran many errands for Mother's business to nearby notion shops to buy supplies, to order or pick up covered buttons or pleating. Paul and I delivered finished garments, usually to large apartment buildings with doormen presiding over lobbies with polished brass and fresh flowers. Paul used the service entrance, I the front door. We usually got either a tip or a present: a scarf, a box of chocolates.

Some errands were near the library, where I read my way beyond children's books to radio plays by Norman Corwin and etiquette books for teenagers. I spent a lot of time reading. *Moby-Dick*, for instance, hardly a children's book but Vickie gave it to me for my eleventh birthday and I plodded through it, marvelling at sentences a page long.

I wrote too. In January 1943: "Went to theatre…. Saw 'Doodle Dandy of the U.S.A.' It was wonderful…. Went home. Started writing operetta, 'Romeo and Juliet.' Supper. Finished Act 2 of operetta. Brushed teeth, washed. Went to bed." Offenbach and Lehar would envy the ease with which I polished off one act before supper and the other between supper and bedtime, but I have no memory of finishing *Romeo and Juliet* off—in either sense. I composed some of a novel only in my head; it had the (terribly clever) title, "Mrs. Knit-Wit," but I just drew her knitting a long scarf. Often alone, only sometimes happily, I founded the Bathtub Exercise Club; as the only member and all the officers, I wrote its rules and planned its activities. Then and later I declared myself not a "joiner," one way to be "different," which for many youthful years was important to me, perhaps sour grapes: who wants to belong to your clique anyway?

Paul meantime might experiment with his chemistry set, once dissolving dimes in hydrochloric acid to make silver chloride. On hot summer days he would listen to away Dodgers games (*Brooklyn* Dodgers); the dreary beeping of the telegraph ticker made the heat feel more oppressive. He was briefly a Boy Scout and after two weeks at Camp Reed taught me obscene lyrics for the bugle calls. Or maybe just one, the assembly call: "There's a soldier in the grass/With a bullet in his ass/ Take it out, take it out, Boy Scout, Boy Scout." The last time I saw Paul, a month before he died of Alzheimer's, I both reminisced and sang this ditty, at which he perked up and smiled, almost laughed.

When Paul had to write a book report for high school, having inherited the Zetlin bent toward math and science, he always looked for a thin book. As a senior, faced with one last book report, he found that he had already written about all the thin books in the school library.

At first I took the wonders of Frederick Law Olmsted's Central Park for granted, as children do—it's just there: a playground a block away; a short walk to Belvedere Lake and Belvedere Castle with its weather station; Cleopatra's Needle, an obelisk made in about 1425 BCE, a gift to New York from Egypt, its hieroglyphs now nearly obliterated by air pollution; lakes, one with rowboats; a carousel, the zoo.

On Christmas Eve 1944, after we'd opened our presents, there was one more for me. Father and Paul carried in a large flat carton. I tried to look pleased as they said, "It's a new mattress." But it was a bicycle, miraculous in wartime, when almost no metal consumer goods were being produced. After learning to ride on rented bikes, having my own was bliss. In the spring Paul, a friend, and I rode on the tree-shaded Mall, well used by cyclists and roller skaters, and rode home on the one-way road that circles the park, riding the wrong way very close to the edge of the road. Soon a cop stopped us. "It's kids like you that turn into juvenile delinquents," he said. "No it isn't," I thought but kept my mouth shut. It was my first run-in with police.

The Mall featured a bandstand, where on summer evenings Edwin Franko Goldman's brass band played Sousa marches and such in free concerts. The band was excellent, the evening air was relatively cool, and sometimes a duck waddled up from the nearby lake and joined in the music. After one concert, I encountered a woman wearing the same ready-made dress as mine, only in a different color. I smiled at her. She scowled at me. People want to be fashionable: dressed like everyone else, and yet distinctive: not dressed like everyone else. Mother helped many women negotiate this conundrum, but I was in my late teens, and even earlier this wasn't the kind of "difference" I cared about.

Also in the park, on a lovely spring day, my best friend Lucy and I lay on a blanket, amusing ourselves with games or books; her mother sat on a nearby bench. A man stepped out of the bushes and opened his coat to expose himself. We were shocked and unprepared because no one talked about such things, so neither did we.

Considering how many years we lived in New York, how many people lived there, and how much I moved around the city alone, I was lucky to be confronted by very few such incidents; once, in three years of commuting to high school, an exhibitionist on a subway train, and an incident that happened on an autumn Saturday.

I took a dress to a client at 241 Central Park West. The elevator man had a few wisps of reddish hair and small, piggy eyes above puffy cheeks. As he took me up he grabbed me and kissed me hard on the mouth. I was shaken as I delivered the dress and collected my tip. Did I say anything to Mother's client? Of course not, though I dreaded the ride down and longed for protection. Luckily another man took me down. Did I tell Mother? Of course not. You just swallowed the confusion, the disgust, the fear, maybe telling a close friend in strictest confidence, as if confessing a terrible sin. (After a 50th junior high reunion, I became friendly with a classmate with an apartment in 241. It is up the same elevator and overlooks the park and he has kindly let me and offspring stay there.)

My diaries record dates with other friends than Lucy. As we moved to 6B, a forgotten Margaret and I "carried some stuff over…, and then we did something terrible. We stood at the window and yelled at people in the street. We called them the funniest names. Some of them looked up, and most of them were mad." During junior high lunch hours, we spent nickels on nuisance phone calls. "Is your refrigerator running?" was a

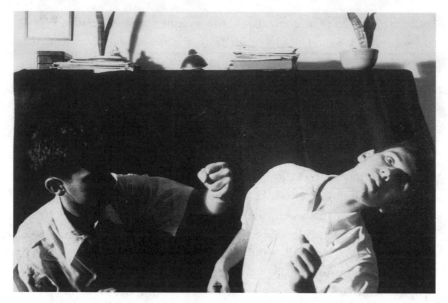

Paul knocks out Paul, in a trick photo using double exposure, taken by Paul in front of our piano covered with a dark cloth, 1940s.

perennial favorite. Or calling at random and saying "Who is this?" as if that person had called me, which I thought really clever. It's a relief that the goody-goody could be naughty and silly. I even stole a box of loose-leaf reinforcements (price 5 cents) from a five-and-ten on Broadway on a dare—daring and wicked enough to leave a long-term memory.

My classmate Audrey Manson was not pretty; her brother Roy was handsome, which seemed unfair, but she was self-assured and amusing. She and Lucy "came over and we fooled away the afternoon. Rather noisily,…but what else can you do when Audrey's around? That's right, nothing! Don't bother trying." I was once at her house on Riverside Drive and can still see the two blue barrel chairs in Roy's room and its view of Riverside Park and the Hudson.

Aside from the errands, most not dramatic, the dress-making business provided a kind of second family. In elementary school, we went home for lunch (so I walked most of West 82nd Street four times a day). I'd fill a tray with leftovers and other good things from the fridge and join the employees at their worktable, temporarily cleared of sewing implements and works-in-progress. They would comment on what I'd found; Frau

Geiringer would peel an apple and give me the one long coil to eat. Mother would most likely be busy with a customer. Often, as workdays drew to a close and she took the cutting-board off the dining table, I had to sweep the workroom. Among bits of thread and fabric were many pins, maybe a needle. Sitting on the floor, I searched the sweepings with a magnet, blowing away the fluff, returning the pins to their box. Sometimes I resented this task. It wasn't very demanding, but I wanted to keep reading or, in my teens, listening to music on the record player in the living room, with the doors shut so I could revel in this newfound joy in private. I resented being called to supper in the middle of a Beethoven symphony—after all, great music is more significant than mere food. I did see dimly that the issue was really my own pleasure versus the needs of the family.

More gratifying than picking up pins was helping Vickie at her office, even though it was Saturday, with no one else around to admire the way I worked on filing, clipping, punching, adding, etc., foreshadowing years of work in offices and libraries. It was in one of the advertising agencies she worked for and didn't have the dailiness of the pins stretching endlessly into the future to spoil it. Vickie also had Mother and me join her in working for Roosevelt's last campaign (1944). She got me to march with her union, down Eighth Avenue to Union Square, to protest the anti-union Taft–Hartley Act in 1947, and in 1948 I campaigned for Henry Wallace, the Progressive Party candidate for president, leafletting in apartment buildings and learning efficient ways to stuff envelopes. At the party's convention in Philadelphia I sang in the chorus. Pete Seeger sang with us. That was thrilling, but I was glad when it was over and we could go home. Wallace won barely 2.4 percent of votes; with our winner-take-all elections, voters who favored him, afraid "a vote for Wallace is a vote for Dewey," voted for Truman. Disillusioned by the result, I became mostly apolitical, perhaps also because of the pall thrown on dissent by the witch hunters: J. Edgar Hoover, HUAC, McCarthy.

Mother lived in Apartment 6B until she moved to San Francisco in 1960. I lived there full time until 1949, then on and off until 1957. These years saw many changes in the world, the neighborhood, the family, and me. On my way home from an exercise class on April 12, 1945, a woman stopped me on Columbus Avenue and told me that President Roosevelt had died. A blow, even for a thirteen-year-old. Who knows how different the post-war years could have been had he lived longer. Would we have had the same Cold War and persecution of left-wingers? Closer to home, Puerto Rican immigrants began to move into nearby brownstones, some right next to number 35. The West Side had been rather dull. Now people spilled out on the stoops and sidewalks, laughing, making music. Mother observed that Puerto Rican fathers were more attentive to their children than fathers we were used to. Despite the occasional fight or excessive noise, I welcomed the new liveliness.

One change in me was that I became aware of beauty, seeing aspects of the world as marvelous, not just *there*—such as the light, especially at sunset, looking toward the Hudson down 82nd Street, like many New York streets an artificial canyon, grand in its own way. Also about then I began to rage, always silently, at Mother. At seventeen, I stood in the living room after an encounter with her that infuriated me and thought, "Some day I'll have a daughter who feels about me the way I feel about Her." I'll leave it to Jessica to reveal whether I've had such a daughter.

And I came of age sexually, as interested in boys as any girl. Ben, a year ahead of me in high school, lived nearby. I walked by his corner whenever I could, hoping—in vain—to run into him. When I was eighteen, he took me to an alumni dance. I was in seventh heaven. He took me home and pushed the elevator buttons for all nine floors, so we'd have more time to kiss. Is there an eighth or ninth heaven? A final kiss at the door—and I never saw him again, a bitter lesson in how meaningless even the most romantic gesture can be.

Another change in me was physical. Mother found Paula Pogany Bennett, an admirable Hungarian lady who taught the Mensendieck system of exercise in her elegant apartment in an East Side townhouse. It involves slow, deliberate use of each muscle. The morning after a private lesson, I woke up with my left knee hugely swollen: water on the knee. A lot of viscous yellow liquid was removed and my leg was encased in a full-length cast, which probably did as much damage as the original injury. No more Mensendieck; that summer of 1949, no hiking, swimming, or any other energetic fun; and some lifelong trouble with that knee.

It was a major change in the family that affected me the most. It came to my awareness on a Saturday in June 1946, as I was about to graduate from junior high. I was at Lucy's house. Her mother, Annie Steinbach, became my piano teacher after an earlier Frau Brandt. Georg Steinbach was mild, kindly, rather buttoned up; he worked at home, I believe as an accountant, and for me was mainly the person with a movie camera; Lucy and I performed for him with devastatingly funny (we thought) "monkeyshines."

Mother called, asking me to come home. When I protested, she said: "We have something to tell you. Then you can go back to Lucy's." Both parents were there, and Paul. Mother said, "We're getting divorced and you two are staying with me. OK?" OK? Not OK, but I said nothing. I don't think Poldi said anything. It was a thunderclap, even if not totally unexpected. At least once, when he told what she considered a stupid joke, she'd said: "*Poldi, ich lass mich scheiden*" (I'm getting a divorce), and there was enough evidence of how things stood between them that I actually felt a cold hand clutch my heart.

Paul, seventeen then, told me later he'd asked questions, but I don't recall whether he got answers. Mother later told me that a marriage counselor, having seen Poldi first, then her, said: "What are you doing with a man like that?" This sounds unprofessional. Perhaps he was, or perhaps something he said sounded like what she herself was thinking.

I went back to Lucy's and said nothing, ditto during three years of high school. Life without Poldi wasn't so terrible; he wasn't much of a father. But divorce meant chaos and shame. It wasn't so rare then or even earlier, but it was usually hushed up. No one else's parents were divorced—as far as I knew. Fatherless friends had lost theirs through death. It was shame that kept my mouth shut.

Later I learned about other past divorces among Steiners and Moseleys, as new ones were added to the record. Now most parents are more forthcoming and some children suffer less from shame, although they still suffer. But children suffer as well in an intact marriage that *should* come apart, that perhaps, like my parents', was ill-starred from the start.

Chapter 5
P.S. 9 and P.S. 118

*W*hen we moved to 82ⁿᵈ Street, I was in third grade. I skipped various half grades, and my entire class polished off fifth and sixth in a year and a half, as we were in Mrs. Sanders's "Rapid Advance" class. Generally I did well and was often "teacher's pet." If other children resented me for that, they kept it to themselves. Later, but still early in life, I worried that I had no enemies, which implied not standing for anything definite.

Only in my first diary is there an inkling of a typical day at P.S. 9: "Assembly, Arithmetic, Spelling, Geography, Composition." I don't remember any specifics of this learning, nor an incident, recorded in my diary, involving Mrs. Sanders, who routinely walked down 82ⁿᵈ Street to the subway. Three days in a row, Lucy, who lived on 80ᵗʰ Street, and I accompanied her. One day she asked us to plan the class mural, the next, to make up questions for a geography test, which we also administered; the other kids were (of course!) annoyed and said the questions were too hard.

However questionable such favoritism was, Mrs. Sanders knew how to keep us interested and get us to produce. Mostly I enjoyed both regular lessons and special projects, one being the above-mentioned "mural," painted on brown paper the length of a blackboard. I had a crush on a classmate, but as we worked on the mural I associated the bad smell of the paint with him and stopped liking him, feeling ashamed because it made no sense. (This doesn't appear in a diary; the sporadic entries often omit what I would most like to know.)

Many school outings, also hazy, were to the Museum of Natural History and the attached Hayden Planetarium, or the Metropolitan Museum of Art, where we had to draw an Etruscan warrior, a larger-than-life painted figure, with arm raised to throw a spear, a huge headdress, and staring eyes. I hated that statue. Decades later, experts declared it a fake and I felt vindicated, even more so when a show in Philadelphia described the Etruscan civilization as kinder and gentler than the Roman. I like to claim that I hated him *because* he was a fake. We also learned about Greek columns. When modern versions occur—as at a corner in Cambridge, Massachusetts, where there are 19th-century wood examples of all three styles—I still reel off a short litany: sturdy Doric (flat square capital), graceful Ionic (dual scrolls), ornate (leafy) Corinthian.

Besides a full-size Brontosaurus skeleton and a gigantic whale suspended from the ceiling, the natural history museum had, and has, dioramas, with flora and fauna of various habitats—desert, veld, Arctic, and so on. Some included people (the animals were stuffed specimens, the people presumably not) and there were exhibits of things made and used by "primitive" people—baskets and such, as if part of "natural history," while the artifacts of Europeans and others like "us" were at the art museum or the historical society. It's parallel to considering Beethoven's works music and Indian ragas ethnic music, probably an untenable distinction. One could of course upend the implicit comparison that denigrated the "ethnic" cultures by declaring them *super*ior just because they are more in tune with the natural world.

The planetarium's show began with moments of complete darkness, hard to experience anywhere else. Then the stars came out and we tried to learn the constellations, which look so little like the persons, creatures, or things that the Greeks saw in them.

These outings were educational, but what determined our fate was what happened daily in the classroom. In 1943 "I got The Blue Ribbon and commendation." There is no explanation of how I earned these honors, but my grades (and probably everyone's in that elite class) were generally good, so that the teacher overlooked my frequent absences. Once, after skipping two days because of bad weather, I finally went to school, much against my will; another day I went with a heavy heart (which melodramatic expression was, I hope, self-parody). Maybe it was stylish to dislike school. In January 1944, a new reason to dislike it emerged, as we went from P.S. 9 to Joan of Arc Junior High School, P.S. 118. "I'm in 7A Rapid Advance (two-and-a-half years for seventh through ninth grades)," I told my diary. "We have an awful looking teacher, I'm not sure if I like her. I certainly miss P.S. 9."

Skimpy diary entries for 1944 feature complaints about school and record days I wangled Mother's permission to stay home. In January: "Mother didn't want me to stay home, but <u>she</u> couldn't stop me!" And in June: "Mother expected me to go to school, but I talked her out of it all-right." Despite good grades, school may have meant the ever-present possibility of failure, echoing my "failure" to make the Steiners into the ideal Campbells. Often I was bored at home and recognized this as suitable punishment: "I wriggled out of going to school…. Mostly, I had a boring time. I suppose I deserved it."

My dislike of 118 was almost surely due to "departmental," the whole class changing rooms and teachers for each subject; instead of Mrs. Sanders, half a dozen teachers, each making different demands and knowing us, and presumably caring about us, much less well. Early in the new term some of us visited Mrs. Sanders. "We complained to her about everything in 118 & then I walked home with her. I kissed her goodbye!" There was that delicious relief of unburdening myself to a sympathetic ear. Not that she could do anything but advise patience and suggest that we'd learn to enjoy 118. Which I did, though without finding any teacher there special. Soon I wrote: "Another day of school & torture! I didn't mind it too much today. I'm afraid I'm going to like 118!!" Maybe it really was trendy to hate school. And a few weeks later, "Miss Van Cook was in a good mood today & during drawing she was pretty nice." By then she and the school were no longer so strange.

While P.S. 9 was in one of those pseudo-Dutch buildings that the former Nieuw Amsterdam favored for its schools, Joan of Arc, built in 1940, was, we were told, New York's first high-rise school (eight floors), the first with elevators, and possibly the first with a public-address system. It was probably also the first, and perhaps the last, that included an entire apartment, where the girls had a course called Apartment, taught by an opinionated Mrs. Dorsey. She railed against chewing gum because it's made from the hooves of animals, then taught us to cook with gelatine, which is made from the hooves (and bones and tendons) of animals. We made chocolate pudding from scratch, learned to make beds with "hospital corners" and other techniques for "homemakers." The boys were using tools while we dusted and made applesauce.

The "awful looking teacher," Miss Van Cook, was lean, rather strict, and always well turned out; I remember a beautiful lime green linen dress. Now I wonder about her life outside school: did she live alone? Have siblings? Friends? What did she do for fun? We didn't think about this then, or I didn't, nor do I recall wondering about *Mr.* Sanders or anything else about my favorite teacher's other life.

One vivid homeroom memory dates from the first day as the teacher read the roll for the first time. The class combined children from several elementary schools. Among the clearly Jewish or otherwise familiar names, she read "Yoshio Kishi." For most of us, this was the first encounter with a Japanese name outside the pages of a newspaper or the war news on the radio. Some children laughed. I'm almost certain I wasn't one of them; I knew how it feels to be laughed at by one's classmates. Yoshio cried. I hope Miss Van Cook admonished those who laughed, whether or not I was one of them.

Did they laugh because Yoshio's name was strange or because it was Japanese? All but our last year at 118 were war years, and although my diaries rarely mention it, we were always aware of the war, and sometimes sang derisive songs: "Whistle while you work, 'cause Hitler is a jerk/ Mussolini is a meany and the Japs are saps." (Sorry if this bit of World War II Americana offends anyone.) The war, like what we studied and most of what went on at home, served as background, not something to be recorded or commented on in a diary. Only one entry concerns a contribution to the war effort: two friends and I collected nylon stockings, to provide the crosshairs in bomb sights. We also collected tin cans, aluminum foil, and bacon and other grease. How useful all this was I'm not sure, but food and gasoline were rationed and consumer goods were in short supply—none of it terribly burdensome.

Miss Van Cook taught us English. We read *Silas Marner, Julius Caesar,* and the *Odyssey* during junior high, and I suspect that most of us were too young to get much out of them. We may have read *The Tempest* before seeing the Broadway production with Vera Zorina as Ariel and Canada Lee as Caliban. The performance was magical, the play's action and colorful characters kept us pre-teens spellbound. Going backstage and getting our programs autographed added to the magic.

We also had geometry, algebra, grammar, history, Latin, gym, and so on, but I recall little of all that. One day's Latin class became memorable for me when we had a substitute teacher named Mr. Steiner. We hit it off, because of the shared name and because I enjoyed Latin. (My classmates regarded him, as we did most substitutes, as fair game.) There were also "art weaving" (needlepoint), which I disliked; learning the Dewey Decimal system from the school librarian; and another creative effort that baffled me. Dean Dixon, "the first full-time black American conductor of symphonic music" and a lively, engaging teacher, visited and deconstructed Beethoven's First Symphony for us. We then had to draw what the music evoked. One picture for four movements—and for me the music inspired feelings, not images. Neither the teacher nor I admired my picture.

Other courses are blanks—not even blurs.

For graduation, Mother made me a sleeveless white dress with a wide lace collar; I wore it for a photo shoot, with arty poses and lighting, by Rudi Pordes, who was about to marry Vickie. I was awarded the Latin and algebra medals. So I did well in those classes I've forgotten, and without inordinate effort. Much later I realized that, when real effort was required, with results uncertain, I tended to back off and do something else, again any failure evoking the early "failure" to get my parents to prove their love by taking me back from exile.

We graduated in June 1946, the same month that my parents divorced, which is probably why, when our homeroom class had a fiftieth reunion, everyone else had copious memories of the school while I remembered hardly anything. It seems the shock of the divorce threw a retrospective pall over the Joan of Arc years, leaving only sparse memories.

Chapter 6

CAMP MIDVALE 1:
SEX, HIKES, AND SOCIALISM

*C*amp Midvale belonged to the Nature Friends of America. The *Naturfreunde* began in Vienna in 1895, part of the social change caused by increased urbanization and industrialization. City-dwellers, factory workers needed a way to recreate in the outdoors, but craftsmen and blue-collar workers couldn't afford to stay at mountain hotels, so, through the Austrian and German Social Democratic parties, they organized to arrange outings, maintain trails, and build huts and lodges.

Members who emigrated to the US launched the Nature Friends of America (NFA). By the early 1920s, the group was large enough to buy a defunct farm near Midvale, New Jersey, and eventually three former farms in the Catskills.[3] At the Catskill camps we pumped water from wells and everyone pitched in, cooking meals and heating water for washing dishes on kerosene or wood stoves. The hikes in the Catskills were mostly more strenuous than those in New Jersey, but in my memory it was all beautiful, even magical, and Midvale was my childhood paradise.

When we first went there in 1942, it was thriving, even during the war. The members had built a substantial clubhouse, with a kitchen, large dining room, an enclosed porch that served as store, soda fountain, and hall for folk dancing, and upstairs a ping-pong room. The old farmhouse sported a large trail map on an outside wall; the Nature Friends maintained many of the trails. Inside were a nature museum and an infirmary. Somewhere there was an office.

European workers tended to be socialists, without the American expectation that anyone could become middle class, even rich; most assumed that workers would always be workers, and their children too.

This made for class solidarity. American Nature Friends, mostly social democrats with a few communists, put their philosophy of "brotherhood" and cooperation into practice at camp. Besides the clubhouse, the members built a sturdy brick dormitory, rolled tennis courts, laid out courts for volleyball and fistball, and cleared a hillside for skiing. The nearby woods were dotted with bungalows, most belonging to individual members, some for rent by the week; the small lots they sat on belonged to the organization. Fees were kept low, so that anyone— all races, creeds, and nationalities—could afford to stay at camp.

At first they swam at nearby Stevens Farm. One day, an interracial group went to swim and was turned away. So the members dammed a stream and built a magnificent swimming pool, two sides the natural hillside, the other two poured concrete, with low and high diving boards and a shallow kiddie pool at the natural end. The dressing rooms were in a wooden hut open to the sky, its rough boards full of knotholes, which we youngsters used to spy on members of the opposite sex.

What was paradise for me meant worries for grownups: the philosophy of inclusiveness, cooperation, and modest fees continually bumped up against economic realities, so that it was often a struggle to keep the camp going. Then, in 1947, when the NFA appeared on the US Attorney General's list of "subversive" organizations, some members opted for a non-political hiking and sports club; others felt committed

The pool at Camp Midvale, built by Nature Friends of America members after an
interracial group was barred from swimming at the usual pond. I learned to swim there.

54

to socialism. Mother, then a bungalow owner, was involved in these arguments and the eventual split in the organization. Soon I was away at college and not paying attention.

The FBI began taking down license plate numbers at the camp entrance and some in the surrounding hills, known or suspected members of the John Birch Society or the Klan, were also hostile. On October 2, 1966, the clubhouse burned to the ground. At least one member recalled that firemen stood watching it burn. This was the last straw. In 1968 the NFA signed the camp over to the American Ethical Union, which took over the debt, and in 1975 it became Weis Ecology Center, later New Weis Center for Education, Arts & Recreation. (There are three NF chapters in California and the *Naturfreunde* still thrive in Austria and Germany.)

Back in happier times, the "Kiddie Camp" was near a corner of the ballfield. Its bungalow had two bunk rooms, a porch for crafts, and a mess hall in the basement. Outside were two privies and a shed with white enameled washbasins set in holes in a wooden counter; used wash water kept the grass growing. The head counselor was a marvelous woman named Friedl Alt, who adroitly (though not singlehandedly) managed about two dozen kids in latency and early adolescence. We all did chores, and the older kids—twelve and thirteen—helped get meals from the kitchen in the clubhouse, loading pails and trays into an ancient pickup truck and riding back to unload with legs—and bare feet—dangling from the tailgate, feeling important. The driver of the truck was a veteran of the Spanish Civil War.

I learned to swim in 1943 and became a "free-pooler"—so I could swim anywhere, not just in the shallow, roped-off kiddie pool. The next summer I followed my friend Margarete up to the ten-foot diving board and jumped. Then I did it several more times, but I never learned to dive, being afraid to put my head down. One evening Friedl let us swim skinny, the girls at one end of the pool, the boys at the other, the distance between the two groups getting ever smaller.

Children came for two or four weeks so we've probably all mostly forgotten each other. I do remember, fondly but vaguely, round-faced Sheila. We were such good friends that in a time of common need we shared the single seat of the girls' privy. Evidently we shared a patch of woods for the same purpose, as we both had poison ivy simultaneously in an awkward part of the body.

Among other dangers, real or imagined, once it rained so hard that the trails were streams a foot deep; we waded happily, not worried about snakes afloat in the torrent, flooded basements, or downed power lines. On an overnight hike on or about August 12th, we did without tents and lay awake as Perseid meteors fell, but I was sure that rattlers and copperheads were waiting to pounce on my unprotected face.

We were allowed to spend Sunday afternoons with our parents, but one Sunday in 1943, "Paul, instead, went on a hike alone. It really wasn't nice of him," I wrote, enjoying my indignation. On another Sunday, I told my diary: "Sunday at supper I feel sad because my parents went home, and glad because I like the supper. Most of the other kids feel that same way."

An old woods road led to Winfield Farm, where the neglected trees still bore apples, to eat or have battles with, where we explored the empty rooms and the cellar with its wonderful cellar smell, where in a summer when yellow jackets were especially thick I put my hand on my hip and got a sting. Then on a hike a camper stumbled on a nest on the ground; some kids were untouched, but I, with more than a dozen bites, couldn't bend my knees for days. And on the last day of camp, still barefoot as usual, I stepped on a yellow jacket and had to squeeze an outsize foot into a city shoe.

We learned hiking etiquette: don't let branches snap at the person behind you, keep those before and behind you in sight. From Father I learned not to sit for a short rest; it takes more energy to get up again than you gain. Sometimes we cleared trails, and once, as some sawed or clipped and another camper repainted white circles on trees, I added a twist of the brush to insert a bright yellow disk, marking the yellow trail with a series of sunny-side-ups.

When I was eleven, ten of us older kids and two counselors went on a three-day hike, walking nine miles the first day. The next evening I wrote: "Over hill, over dale. Ouch, a blister! 30 miles today. We killed a copperhead on the way. We saw Babe Ruth. Bob [a counselor] shook hands with him. He said he was in too much of a hurry, so the boys didn't get a chance to see him. They were mad all-right!" As I recall, "we" didn't kill the snake; the boys heaved rocks at it and once it was dead threw it at us girls. In the 1940s we specialized in our sex roles: supposedly only the boys wanted to see Babe Ruth. (And I doubt we walked thirty miles.)

North of Midvale near Greenwood Lake are two hilltop lakes: Surprise Lake and Terrace Pond. Both make for especially wonderful outings, combining hiking, picnicking, and swimming. One day in 1943, two groups set out for Surprise Lake. "I'm the only one who wasn't in Group 1 who was on the three-day hike," I complained to my diary. A counselor started Group 1 off on a longer route, then took us directly to the lake. "Group 1 never got to the lake," I wrote, "but were picked up by millionaires in a Packard. They went swimming in Greenwood Lake. We went swimming in Surprise Lake. It was heavenly. They made a [phonograph] record there to prove their story. They were trying to make us jealous, but they didn't succeed." And I added, unaware of the contradiction, "I still wish I had been in Group 1."

A treasure hunt on the last evening ended at Boy Scout Lake. After supper there, we took the road back. "It was fun, marching along in the dark, singing all the songs we knew, and then listening to Friedl and Susie singing the German yodeling songs…. It was one of the nicest times I ever had in camp." I remember swinging down that road to the sound of songs I had heard, and sung, since early childhood, with Mother's alto to my soprano.

On the last day: "I hate the thought of going to the city…. When we got to the city, it really was horrible…. There is absolutely nothing nice about the city." This distaste for New York soon faded, and Midvale meant weekends all year. We took the West Side IND subway to Chambers Street, walked several blocks to the Hudson River, got a ferry to New Jersey, and a train to Wanaque-Midvale. After a slog through the town, we turned onto the road that winds across and along Wanaque Reservoir and turned up unpaved Snake Den Road to camp, four or five miles from the station. Or we might get a ride; once Mother, Vickie and I squeezed into the rumble seat of someone's Ford. In 1946, Paul was old enough to drive and we got our first car, a '37 Dodge. Then, instead of subways, ferries and trains, it was traffic jams at the George Washington Bridge.

Every summer Saturday there was a show. Pete Seeger, Woody Guthrie, Paul Robeson, or Theodore Bikel might star, or less famous but talented left-wingers. Once each summer the Kiddie Camp performed, one year a shadow play about camp life. A counselor read the roll. "Paul."

"Here." "Where?" "Cleaning the outhouse." That brought down the house. Behind the laughter, I suspect, was pride in seeing a younger generation doing humble chores in the camp's cooperative spirit.

We raised money for Russian War Relief. After the war I was baffled when the Soviet Union became the enemy. Some years had to pass before I realized that, in the eyes of most Americans, it was always the enemy (as Russia supposedly still is); the wartime anti-Axis alliance was the anomaly.

It was at Midvale that I first experienced political correctness, long before that term existed. Someone criticized John D. Rockefeller. I said that he was a human being too. "No, he isn't." Though I realized he was seen as the predatory capitalist, I was and am sure that even predatory capitalists are human. Again, when I worked at the Museum of Natural History one summer and complained about the oversize roaches infesting our apartment—two inches long, with hard shells, able to fly and swim—a museum entomologist said that migrants from tropical regions brought them in their luggage, of course not intentionally. When I relayed this information to a table-full of Nature Friends at supper one weekend, I was treated to dirty looks and veiled accusations of racism. Even then I thought that reality is not necessarily politically correct. But mostly I was in tune with prevailing Nature Friends political views. We all shared ideas about what the world would (or should) be like after the war. We didn't sing "There'll be bluebirds over/The white cliffs of Dover/…/There'll be love and laughter/And peace ever after…," but the more robust "United Nations Hymn." When the war ended in August 1945, a bonfire on the ballfield marked VJ Day, and we surely sang it then:

> As sure as there's sun in the morning
> And rivers flow down to the sea,
> A new day for mankind is dawning:
> Our children shall live proud and free.
> Chorus:
> United Nations on the march, with flags unfurled;
> Together fight for victory, a free new world."

Unaware of the horrors of Hiroshima and Nagasaki, we felt only relief and joy.

We Kiddie Campers were traversing the years between childhood and adolescence. In the early years boys were mainly yucky. "This afternoon during rest hour," I wrote in August 1943, "…Teddy was in my bed, much against my will, and Alex was in Margarete's. She seems to like him. I do. (a little.)" Almost everything I knew about sex I learned in giggling exchanges behind the Kiddie Camp outhouses, where my friend Eva Frances Steiner (also from Vienna) told me what her mother, braver than mine, had told her: that it feels good to have "it" inside one. On a hike, handsome counselor Kurt showed us bigger kids dirty postcards. Now the girls would accuse him of sexual harassment; then I just wouldn't acknowledge what I'd seen.

Although my schools were coed and I'd had crushes on boys for years, it was in Midvale at fifteen that I first felt sexual longing not directed at any particular male. That summer of 1947, the camp was teeming with veterans; they seemed heroic, larger than life. The Greeks returning from Troy couldn't have appeared more godlike than these men seemed to me, suffering not only from adolescence but probably also from my parents' divorce the year before. I padded after more than one of them, hardly knowing what I wanted or expected. Most were considerate. Lenny gently put his arm around me; tall, handsome David was friendly but distant; dark-haired Lou took some liberties that might now land him in court. As for actual sexual goings-on, of which there must have been many, a sight in a Stevens Farm pasture one Sunday afternoon baffled me until I realized that it was a bare male tush hard at work in the grass, soon followed by two voices; though still a virgin, I knew what that was about.

Earlier, from almost twelve to fourteen plus, I was in love with Paul's friend Walter, an only child whose parents had a bungalow near the dormitory. For Sunday, November 14, 1943, my diary says: "I fell in love today. Guess with whom: with Walter. I really wasn't surprised at all." On Monday: "In school today I felt very funny. I was thinking of Walter all the time. No wonder!"

Friedl had started the Nature Friends Scouts, so campers could do things together all year. Each week a postcard arrived telling us what we would do that Saturday or Sunday: a hike up one side of the Hudson or the other, perhaps with a ferry ride at the north end or a cup of hot chocolate in Ardsley, or the ferry to Staten Island and a hike there. One

February day we Scouts got off the train one stop before Wanaque, ready for a long hike to camp but not for snow a foot or more deep, looking the same on and off the trail. Ernie Jaffe came with his mother. "When are we going to *get* there?" she kept whining. Her low spirits raised ours, in unspoken solidarity against her, as the day and our feet grew colder. Eventually we got to camp and dried out, and learned (or I did) how Mrs. Jaffe, voicing the anxiety we all felt, became a scapegoat: we could laugh at her fears and so feel braver than we actually were.

Friedl also planned activities in the city. The main criterion for me was whether Walter showed up. When we played ping-pong, I was thrilled when he chose me for his team, and when I got to choose I chose him "<u>because</u> he's the best player." In February 1944, I began "to suspect that Walter likes me. He was awfully nice to me today.... Maybe it's just his nature. (I hope not.)" Is it common to want one's beloved to be a good person, but especially good only to oneself? It could be hard for the object of such hopes to get things right!

My romantic dreams got a little boost from an unexpected quarter. I was reading Pearl Buck's *The Good Earth*, and "...at Vickie's house, we were talking about the way the Chinese get married. Father said he'd choose Walter or Claudy for me & Margarete for Paul." Then I consulted the daisies:

> Monday, July 3. This morning Margarete & I...picked daisies & said He loves me, He loves me not.... The daisies this morning were 8 to 4 for me.... From the way [Walter] looked today I think he likes me.
> July 4. The daisies today said 10-2. We always do 12.

Whatever the daisies or my parents said, or I hoped, Walter's thoughts were evidently elsewhere, and in the summer of 1946 I succumbed to Georgie's shameless advances. While Walter was an incipient intellectual, Georgie was crude and extroverted, not a bit thoughtful or sensitive. But he liked me and Walter was oblivious, so immediate gratification won out. When our small crowd, too old for Kiddie Camp, hung out together, Georgie's arm was around me and I liked that, though I was only moderately fond of him.

Two years later—I was a senior in high school—Walter wrote declaring his love. When I wrote that I would have welcomed his letter a few years earlier but now it was too late, he wrote: "If there is a Devil, he must have arranged it." More letters, and poems, followed, but they couldn't move me beyond mild pity.

Walter decided to be a writer. With Paul he visited me at college and expounded his plan for—beyond the Great American Novel—the Great American Trilogy. Later, in an apartment in San Francisco next to Paul's, every available wall was lined with books. We went there with my half-sister. Toni, then about seven, having heard that Walter was a writer, asked, "Wow, did you write all these books?" In fact, he wrote—or published—only one slim book of poems. No novel, no trilogy, and he became increasingly odd. One hand hooked over his shoulder, looking down at the floor, facing the wall or into a corner, he defended bizarre opinions, his voice grating and irritable. Later still, Paul received anonymous letters calling him a balding, paunchy, middle-aged technocrat. Walter refused to admit or deny he wrote them.

In avoiding Walter's embrace, I surely skirted yet another potential disaster.[4] But memories of him can't spoil memories of Camp Midvale: the beautiful country, the hikes, sports, left-wing politics and culture, and adolescent coming-of-age.

On the ball field at Camp Midvale, 1946.
Rear: Georgie, Willie W. (future highway engineer). Front: Eva, Walter, Paul.

Chapter 7
BRONX HIGH SCHOOL OF SCIENCE

$\mathcal{J}$t may sound conceited but Bronx Science attracted kids who were bright and eager to learn, and it taught us more, not only sciences, in three or four years than did most other schools. In three years (after three of junior high), I had a year each of physics and biology, two of chemistry, three and a half of math, the required shop and mechanical drawing, three years of English, and history, civics, gym, and languages. Many teachers had Ph.D.s and the school turned out more Nobelists than most high schools, among them physicists Melvin Schwartz in our class and Steven Weinberg '50. Bronx Science is a tax-supported public school, but it is an elite school, selecting students from around the city on the basis of an entrance exam. (One classmate commuted by subway from Far Rockaway, in Queens, a round trip of about fifty miles.)

The school was only eight years old when I entered in 1946, with the second class to include girls. (One school song was changed, from "We're the boys of Science High…" to "Boys and girls of Science High….") Morris Meister, as Supervisor of Science for New York schools, saw the need for a school specializing in science and math for gifted students, lobbied for it in the face of some opposition, until he was given the dilapidated former Evander Childs High School at 184th Street and Creston Avenue; Evander had a new building. The first class entered in 1938. Meister was principal until 1958. According to his nephew Daniel, in our class, "The classes of the '40s and '50s speak of Morris Meister with reverence. Graduates from the mid '60s had never heard of [him]," and he extolled his uncle's "imagination and vision, perseverance and drive," and other qualities. I was aware of him but can't claim awareness of what we owed him. (Long after my time, Science also got a new building.)

Some or all of us sophomores were in an annex in a school on the other side of the Grand Concourse, the Bronx's grand boulevard. There was much running back and forth, as some classes were at Creston Avenue. A snafu in the schedule resulting in a missed class had one boy saying ruefully, "I didn't know the Grand Concourse is the International Date Line."

My only memory of the annex is learning basic tap dance in gym class. Not my thing. Later I learned square dancing, which *was* my thing, and got a taste of African dance à la Pearl Primus, thanks to a classmate. It was, as high school should be, one revelation after another, though not all classes were equally fascinating. European history was tedious, as Mr. Bass paced up and down, pretty much reciting what was in the textbook. I gazed longingly out the window at NYU, which then had its main campus in the west Bronx. Only later did I learn that the building I was mooning over was a veterans' hospital.

I got easy credit for an advanced course in German, took more Latin with Mr. Blume, dapper with his clipped mustache, and can still stump students of Latin with one of his homework assignments: Civili si ergo, / Fortibus es in ero. / Nobili themis trux. / Sivat sinem, causor dux.[5]

I adored math and was good at it, sometimes losing track of my math homework, lending it to a classmate, who might pass it on to others. (This would not happen now!) I was even good at solid geometry with soft-voiced Edward Lepowsky, but the true heartthrob was Dr. Julius Hlavaty, elegant and dashing, always turned out in a fabulous suit, one light green herringbone tweed, another of navy basket weave wool. Witty, urbane, brilliant, but respectful of students, he taught Math 9, that extra half year, an amalgam of probability theory, statistics, infinity theory, and other arcana. Years later, I learned that he was blacklisted as a communist. He was "the most distinguished victim" of the U.S. Senate Internal Security Subcommittee and, although "regarded by many as the most brilliant math teacher in the United States," was fired in 1953, causing the Superintendent of Schools "considerable embarrassment." He was reinstated in 1956. (A summary of his story in David Caute's *The Anti-Communist Purge under Truman and Eisenhower* made me even prouder to have been his student.)

It was odd that I did well in solid geometry because I'm not good at spatial relations, as was all too evident in mechanical drawing. Our first assignment was to draw the three views of two rectangular solids forming an L. This was easy, but the others, increasingly intricate, baffled me more and more. Somehow I passed.

Shop was another trial. We had to dream up, design, and make a scientific instrument. A balance turned out to be relatively simple and just "scientific" enough. Probably I just squeaked by. (One boy was more Groucho Marx than Albert Einstein. During World War II the shop assignment was to make something to help the war effort; as sugar was rationed, he made a coffee cup with a grainy bottom, so that the user would think s/he had already added sugar.) My classmates were making all sorts of gauges and scopes, true scientific instruments. Some did genetic studies with white mice, experimented with chemicals, or otherwise manifested real scientific imagination and ability. I got good grades, but at graduation I was a dilettante among budding experts. Not for the last time, I was skirting not disaster but opportunity, skittering away from my own possible abilities.

But I wasn't the only "Sciencite" not cut out to be a scientist. Years later, a letter came to the Schlesinger Library from Matthew Bruccoli, professor of literature and publisher of obscure American authors who deserved a comeback. When I asked if he was the person of that name in the Science class of '49, he wrote back: "Didn't any of us go into science?"

The yearbook says that I worked on *Science Survey*, the school newspaper, though I only remember taking the elective journalism course and the class visit to *The New York Times*, seeing the noisy linotype machines in action, learning how a page was prepared for the presses, and each of us coming away with a slug, the slim hunk of metal bearing a line of type, in this case our names. Foreshadowing my later work with words rather than chemicals, mice, or scopes, I chose to work on the newspaper, but according to the yearbook I was also on the Science Congress Squad and the Guidance Squad, whatever those were. I do remember singing in the chorus and finding Handel's "Hallelujah Chorus" thrilling, "Dry Bones" questionable, and the words of "O Sacred Art" corny, but not the music, a Chopin etude.

Why I took a second year of chemistry is a mystery, as I preferred physics. Analytical chemistry was a good indicator, along with shop, of how unsuited I am for laboratory sciences, but it was memorable for a non-chemical reason. We had to heat the midsection of a glass tube in the flame of a Bunsen burner and, when it was just soft enough, twirl the tube, drawing the two ends apart to form two pipettes. I messed up, making a funky shape but not a useable apparatus. So Dr. Harwell parked himself behind me, took my two hands in his, and made them turn and pull just enough. I had a crush on Dr. Harwell, so what might have been a humiliation was a thrill (for me). Needless to say, it was the last chemistry course I ever took.

Despite the WASP-y name, Dr. Harwell was probably as Jewish as most of the teachers (and perhaps 75 percent of the students). Senior year, some of us had honors English with Mr. Shaw, rumored to be né Shapiro. Whatever his name, he made us feel sophisticated. We started reading *The New Yorker* and discussed the categories highbrow, middle-brow, lowbrow, which appeared that year. We read *Hamlet* and went as a class to see the new film adaptation starring, and directed by, Laurence Olivier. Completely bowled over, I went home and memorized the "To be or not to be" soliloquy.

Some of us in Mr. Shaw's class formed the only clique I've ever belonged to, ten or twelve wise guys enchanted with our own cleverness and with being seniors, entitled to wear the cap in the school colors, yellow and green. Some of us paired off, though there were extra boys. With my partner Arthur there was no romance, but he would dutifully see me home after an evening with the gang. He was later temporarily married to another gang member, Edna. She and I were friends, then grew apart. She was an earnest student and once unintentionally put me to shame. We arranged to interview the finance columnist of the *New York Post*, Sylvia Porter, for *Science Survey*. Or Edna arranged the interview. She asked the questions, having prepared a good many. I had one, trusting that one thing would lead to another. It's risky to do an interview empty-headed, especially when the subject is such an important person with much technical knowledge. I felt like a bump on a log as Edna sailed on, getting Porter to tell all sorts of interesting things. (The *Post*

Most of our Bronx Science "Highbrow" gang, 1949. L to R, rear: Arthur Michaels, Gerald (?), Ronald Schaeffer, Ruth Loewenstein, Eva Steiner. Front: Dorothy Sachs, Arthur Kirsch, Robert Roven. Some of us were wearing our senior caps in the school colors, Green & Gold.

wasn't yet the right-wing rag it became later.)

For graduation Mother's creation was a dress of lovely pale green organdy. After the reliably moving and exciting evening ceremony, our gang had a party at my house. It was late June, all the windows were open, and in the wee hours police appeared in response to a complaint about noise, the first of (so far) two such incidents in my life. (At an archivists' meeting in Minneapolis in 1983, the New Englanders' party in my room spilled out into the hall. A tall hotel security guard took one look and left. Soon an even taller city cop appeared and told us to stay in the room and keep the noise down. The New England Archivists' newsletter reported that "The archivists offered no resistance.")

Audrey Kwit, the teacher who advised the girls, knew NYU, City College, and other schools in the city. Most graduates went to those, though many went to Cornell, which, as a land-grant university, was bound to take any student with an average above a certain grade on the statewide Regents exams. The final exam scores didn't appear until August, however. Before that, Cornell accepted the five top students in our class. Edna was salutatorian. I was the second-highest girl and sixth in the class. Did Cornell try to keep the number small because of anti-Semitism or to minimize the influx from New York City? Perhaps, from the vantage point of Ithaca, the two were the same thing.

Meantime, Lucy Steinbach had gone to private school. Her mother, by then my piano teacher, learned about Mount Holyoke from a teacher at Lucy's school who was an active alumna, recruiting likely applicants. I became one, was accepted and offered a full-tuition scholarship.

When the Regents scores appeared in *The Times* in August, Cornell admitted dozens more classmates. By then, Mother had paid Mount Holyoke a deposit, which was probably just what the powers-that-were at Cornell wanted. Whether it's a cause for regret I'll never know. One classmate hated Cornell; others didn't. Alex was disgusted when those considering him for a fraternity checked the labels in his neckties, but this could happen at any school with fraternities. At least Mount Holyoke never had sororities.

I'm pretty sure that Mother didn't tell me her doubts about Mrs. Steinbach until I'd graduated from Mount Holyoke. She suspected that Lucy's mother suggested a college in which Lucy was not interested so I wouldn't be competing with her for admission! Looking back, at first this seemed needlessly paranoid, but, recalling that I wouldn't have heard of Mount Holyoke if it weren't for Lucy's mother and Lucy's teacher, it seems quite realistic. If only Mother had told me her suspicion at the time, but perhaps it didn't occur to her until later.

At our first reunion, in 1979, I marveled at how many classmates still lived in or near New York, and how many were still married to the people they'd married in our youth. To answer Matthew Bruccoli's question, yes, many did go into scientific fields, some into physics or other sciences, about seventy into medicine, several into computer science, and some into applied math in the form of stockbroking. A 1979 pre-reunion questionnaire asked about hobbies. In the tradition of the grainy coffee cup, one chap wrote that his hobby was attending high school reunions.

Chapter 8
CAMP MIDVALE 2: BOB

A song popular in the 1940s could have been written for me: "They're Either Too Young or Too Old." One summer, eight-year-old Arnold followed me around camp, and more than one man who to me looked ancient told Mother how much he admired me. Then along came someone who seemed just right. It was the fall of 1948, my senior year at Bronx Science. Father was with us in Midvale and Sunday afternoon we went for a short hike, with Paul, one or two others, and a young man from Newark. He was twenty-two, with an air of intelligence and gentleness. By the time our little party returned to camp, Bob and I were walking hand in hand.

"Good judgment comes from experience, and experience comes from bad judgment." So read a cookie fortune that fell to me at a Chinese restaurant decades later. Back then, Bob provided the experience and I the judgment, first bad, then good.

I was in love and sure he was too. He acted as if, sort of, when he remembered about me. He was taking courses at the New School on 12th Street, and once in a while—once in a great while—he would take a detour to 82nd Street and we would kiss and pet in the dark of my room for an hour or so before he caught a train home to Newark. One frosty night we did our kissing in Central Park.

With an interest in psychology, he told me that I was more neurotic than a woman he knew who had survived the Nazi camps. Not knowing the person he was comparing me with, too inexperienced and too timid to ask how he could tell, or to scoff at the idea, I was defenseless against this vague, hurtful diagnosis. Yet I kept kissing him when he was there and longing for him when he wasn't.

On one drop-in visit I was wearing a dress with a stylish wide suede belt. Bob poked the belt with distaste: did I like wide belts? As if that were another neurotic symptom. Smitten though I was, I wondered whether the belt was simply in his way. Not that we went very far in those sessions between class and train.

During Christmas week, something he did—or failed to do—triggered my first episode of depression. I'm fairly sure that Bob promised to call and didn't. The details are lost but not the memory of days of hysterical weeping and utter hopelessness. Mother fed me a sedative (probably Baldrian) and I slept for a few hours. Waking up, I cried again, as desperately and uncontrollably as before. And so it went, crying and sleeping, for two days, perhaps more. I'm not sure how long and am only fairly sure that it ended when he finally called.

We agreed that he would come over New Year's Eve. I was still in love, apparently not resenting his casual and sporadic interest. It's harder, and more disturbing, to get inside that girl just turned seventeen, to feel what she felt, than to recall the same girl at eleven looking back at my footprints as I stomped through fresh snow on the 82nd Street sidewalk, getting a wonderful, eerie sense of myself as a person having an impact on the world. It was January 1943 and I tried to describe the feeling in my diary: "Today, when I was going home for lunch, I turned to look at my footprints in the snow. I got the funniest feeling, somehow that they were souviners of little me. I can't explain my feeling."

On New Year's Eve, Mother, Vickie, Rudi, and Anna were there. Bob asked for a typewriter and a sheet of paper so he could write out his resolutions for 1949. He had high hopes—being inordinately, ridiculously ambitious. Among them were a one-man show at the Newark Art Museum, writing the Great American Novel, a degree or two, and number 4: to find The Girl. He typed this on my family's machine, in its living room, with my relatives and me looking over his shoulder. If only I could report that this finally cured me, but no, I clung to this narcissistic, insensitive, self-centered boor even after that below-the-four-inch-belt insult. The affair and my passion did eventually fade away. Our clique of "sophisticated" high school seniors helped, providing not romance but friendship.

My infatuation was bad judgment. The experience it brought about led to a moment of good judgment. In 1965, Bob tracked me down in London, where I was living with husband and small children, and sent me a questionnaire to fill out, part of a study he was conducting, probably for a graduate degree in psychology. There was a somewhat rueful letter; after all, he wanted my cooperation.

I did not fill out the questionnaire, nor respond at all.

Good! But what if I hadn't been married? Would I have ignored it, or would I have thought, Maybe...? It's sobering to realize how many of us depend on others for validation, especially how women like me—whose fathers were absent, neglectful, and/or abusive—depend on the attentions of men, often without requiring affection or even consideration. Or, worse, thrive on abuse, because that is what we have been trained to expect as the price of attention, as part and parcel of it. Millions of men all over the world prefer the submissive woman—waiting tearfully, ready to accept punishment while hoping for something better—prefer her to the self-respecting person finding validation in her own footprints in the snow.

III.

Higher Education, 1949-55

Chapter 9
MOUNT HOLYOKE COLLEGE:
PEARSONS HALL

*P*aul drove Mother, Vickie, and me to South Hadley in the '37 Dodge, and they helped me settle into a "temp double" on the first floor of Pearsons Hall, one of four freshman dorms. (We were freshmen then; the term "first-years" was a post-women's-movement innovation.) The college paired up girls from similar backgrounds, at least Jewish girls. So I shared this single room with Roz Lyshkow, while Irma Rabbino, who was at P.S. 9 and 118 with me, shared another temp double with Edith Cohn, an almost perfect mismatch. Edith and I soon began a friendship that, with one bump along the way, has persisted ever since. Years later I realized that all my closest women friends were fatherless. Edith's father had died in Germany, before she and her mother and sister became refugees.

I hardly remember Roz, and Elsie Bartle, our housemother, whose apartment was right next to our room, is also a blur, a tall, gray, proper blur. Once, as I signed out for the evening, wearing a navy blue silk crepe dress made by Mother, with a green velvet ribbon as a belt, Mrs. Bartle said, "That's a nice color green." I wondered whether what she meant was: "I don't like your dress but I'm bound to say *some*thing nice." Or maybe she just liked that color.

The big sister/little sister cult and the class colors were among the many things strange to an exiled New Yorker. Our class was green. The juniors, collectively and individually, were our big sisters, and on occasion we sang the sister song responsively, even at meals, for Pearsons had fifteen juniors for about a hundred freshmen. "Dear old pals, jolly old pals, always together in all sorts of weather/ The yellow and the green will blend into one: '53 and '51," they sang; our response ended with "'51 and '53." I spent as little time with my (forgotten) big sister as possible,

73

not believing in assigned friends. (Admittedly when groups of students sang responsively across Lower Lake lit by Chinese lanterns, the effect was quite lovely.)

Nor do I remember the senior assigned to haze me, though our brief contact left a residue of amused annoyance. It wasn't the kind of dangerous, persistent hazing associated with fraternities; just one day of mildly humiliating stunts. In one, I had to stand on a table at the C.I. (College Inn) on one foot and sing something. I felt I should go along even though I despised the whole business, including the finale, when the senior took me out for supper and pretty much said, "It was all in good fun, right?" As a senior I refused to haze anyone.

The C.I., only steps from Pearsons, was a major attraction because I was always hungry. It served buttered and toasted hot dog buns, unknown in New York; a tearoom nearby introduced me to cinnamon toast. The college itself was a cornucopia of food unknown in Viennese or New York Jewish circles. Its cheese soufflés and lobster Newburgh were particularly unpalatable. Deacon Porter's Hat was good though, chocolate cake served with a vanilla sauce and named, as is a dorm, for an early benefactor. I gained eleven pounds, and by spring couldn't fasten some of my skirts. In 2006, I learned how typical I was via an article about the "fearsome 'Freshman 15.'"

Waiting on tables, I learned—beyond serving from the left, clearing from the right—something about group behavior. A tableful of girls from the "Main Line," the classier Philadelphia suburbs, could be insufferable, bitching about the food in a way that seemed to blame me for it. "I'm only bringing it to you," I wanted to say. "I didn't cook it." One evening I had a long talk with one of them about something we were reading in English class. She was intelligent and respectful, not at all like the hydra-headed monster she was part of at meals. Similarly, one girl at first seemed strikingly beautiful but on closer acquaintance her shallowness canceled out the glamour of her outward appearance, while another dorm mate at first seemed rather plain, but her intelligence and humanity soon gave her a glow of real beauty, more than skin deep.

We were "allowed" to sing at table at Friday supper, evidently a privilege familiar to prep school grads. The repertoire included the sister song, anthems of men's colleges, and the following:

A man without a woman is like a ship without a sail,
Is like a boat without a rudder, is like a kite without a tail.
Etc. (i.e., more things this poor guy is like)
But if there's one thing worse in the universe,
It's a woman / I said a woman /I mean a woman without a man.

It all felt silly. Now if they had sung "Peat Bog Soldiers," "Solidarity Forever," or "Union Maid," I would have joined in.

After Wednesday suppers and Sunday midday dinners, "gracious living" and skirts-and-stockings meals, there was coffee in the living room, part of the training for our presumed roles as wives of business-men, ministers, professors, or other pillars of society. (Mount Holyoke's feminist tradition blended and clashed with this view of our futures.)

Sunday dinner followed church in Abbey Chapel, an interdenom-inational but basically Protestant service. I found the occasional rabbis the most dynamic, witty, interesting, and challenging of all the invited reverends. There were brief early-morning chapels Tuesdays and Thursdays, when the speaker might be a student, faculty member, or President Roswell Gray Ham, the first male after one hundred years of women presidents. (There were two more men before Mount Holyoke again chose a woman as chief "role model.") Though often boring or irritating, all this was a useful part of my education in how the then-majority in this country lived and thought.

We had to attend half the church services each semester (one way to keep us on campus half the weekends?) and half the chapels. The college still served *in loco parentis*, taking its parental responsibilities seriously. No men in our rooms, except family members at either end of the year. Strict curfews, with earlier hours for freshmen; permission and signing out for going off campus. With all that, the hazing, big sisters, and the rest, it seemed like a girls' winter camp after three years of commuting by subway to an urban coed school.

It wasn't only meals and chapels and dorm life. We were there to learn. The English course I shared with one of the Mainliners, and with Edith, was an honors class taught by Marianne Brock, a marvelous Canadian with a raucous and frequent laugh, a sharp wit, and a kindly interest in

*With Edith Cohn outside Jack August's Seafood Restaurant in Northampton, Massachusetts,
during freshman year at Mount Holyoke, 1949-50. The man at right is my father,
Leopold Steiner. My friendship with Edith continues.*

her students. She was the ideal teacher for both literature and writing, introducing us to the arcana of bibliographies and footnotes, of ibid. and loc. cit. I enjoyed producing papers for her. The first was a critique of an Alice Meynell sonnet. Although I empathized with Meynell's experience of "having to keep at bay the insidiously pleasant thoughts about 'him'" all day (as I put it), I found her diction ("I run, I run, I am gathered to thy heart") and the tone "embarrassing" and "silly." Brock agreed with my conclusion that the poem didn't deserve serious comment.

On another paper she wrote, "You are doing excellent work this year." Praise from someone one admires is doubly welcome. But a paper called "An Amorphous Essay to meet a Free Assignment," elicited a lukewarm: "I don't think you quite pull it off." In "John Donne: He's a Better Man than I Am" (an allusion to Kipling), I detailed my confusion at the complex interrelationships of Donne's poems, ending with the "hope that I may now have Donne without fear." Brock, evidently mollified by earlier "excellent work" (and by the pun?), wrote: "You have at least given a witty account of your dilemma." Yes, Donne is difficult, but I wondered whether everyone would have been treated so charitably. Echoes of the running-back-to-kindergarten incident.

Brock steered us through other difficult poetry, most notably T.S. Eliot's "The Waste Land." I remember the first lines (with that haunting "mixing memory and desire"), which mordantly echo the start of *The Canterbury Tales*. Otherwise, I recall only that a classmate changed a famous couplet from: "In the room the women come and go/Speaking of Michelangelo," to "...Joe DiMaggio."

After a year of French with Miss Monfries including two sessions a week with a French graduate student, I could carry on a fluent, if simple, conversation with a Midvale friend who had lived in France. I have no idea why I didn't continue with French, a wrong-headed decision that has me stammering when in France, afraid to say even what I can for fear of not understanding the reply.

For phys. ed. we wore unattractive gym suits, our class's an ugly green. In deference to my not-quite-healed left knee, I was allowed to take archery, which is easy on the knees. Later I took fencing, which is not easy on the knees. I learned enough not to *do* these medieval warlike sports well but—what suited my temperament better—enough to criticize supposedly awkward or incorrect depictions of archers and fencers in drama, literature, and visual arts.

Another, one-time physical activity involved getting up very early and going by truck to pick asparagus in Hadley, "Asparagus Capital of the World." Each stalk pokes up some distance from the next; we bent over again and again, cutting stalks with a special tool, learning first-hand the "stoop labor" required to harvest that first green vegetable of the year.

In my first paper for Brock, called "Eva, Where Are You?," I listed some of the more obvious novelties: "My room in a sixth-floor apartment has given way to a temp double; I no longer eat out at Whelan's or the delicatessen, but rather at Wilbur or the C.I. The school I went to was overcrowded in one small building; now I live and study on a beautiful, spacious campus, with brick and ivy and grass everywhere."

My paper didn't mention another aspect of this new bit of the Earth that bemused me: the pedestrian buttons on traffic lights. Because

Pearsons is across College Street—Route 116—from most of the campus, we crossed the street often. In New York, traffic lights turned red and green (no yellow then) according to their own rhythm; pedestrians obeyed them when necessary, but crossed on red when safe. The idea of *controlling* a traffic light was intriguing. Sometimes we held off pushing the button to see if we could stop more cars. I also didn't mention the paucity of Jews, after the paucity of everything but Jews at my New York schools, nor another obvious change in my surroundings: that all my fellow students and more than half the faculty were women. This situation led to a temporary complication.

It happened in philosophy class. The instructor, Grace Perkinson (Perky), a recent alumna, was somewhat "mannish," as we said then, handsome rather than pretty, with a determined stride and firm voice. The course fascinated me. The questions tackled by the authors we read were serious issues for me, questions about reality, how we know anything, what is good or beautiful. I can almost hear Perky and me carrying on a lively dialogue while the rest of the class waited for the bell to ring. Soon I was as fascinated with Perky as with philosophy. I didn't know what to do with this feeling. There was certainly no chance that I would tell her, or anyone else, that I was in love with her. I would walk by her house in the hope of more talk, just the two of us, and maybe something more. But what? I couldn't visualize what I wanted to do with her, as I could with boys who attracted me. It was uncomfortable while it lasted, luckily not very long. My fascination with philosophy remained. I did not love it just because I was infatuated with Perky.

The issue of differences between the sexes already intrigued me then: what does it mean to be female or male? What are the essential differences, if any, beyond the obvious ones directly connected to reproduction? I don't recall whether I wondered why there were women's colleges. Mount Holyoke is one of the oldest, founded by Mary Lyon in 1837 as an academy that taught young women some of the same advanced fields that young men studied. It had an admirable tradition of having students do chores, which enabled women of modest means to attend. Many nineteenth-century graduates married missionaries, some thus becoming missionaries themselves. But more and more alumnae pursued their own careers, some, like Perky, returning as faculty. We all knew that

Frances Perkins, the first woman to serve in the federal cabinet, was an alumna. (When another alumna, Elaine Chao, became George W. Bush's secretary of labor and the *Alumnae Quarterly* drew parallels with Perkins, I was glad that many alumnae wrote, in effect: how dare you compare anti-labor Chao to Perkins?)

I was unaware of the long history of academic discrimination, contempt, and exclusion—unaware or, if the college tried to make us aware, indifferent. Mount Holyoke wasn't my first choice, I didn't believe in single-sex education, and I was determined to marry and have children—and don't believe that this wish meant that I was "brainwashed by society," as some second-wave feminists claimed two decades later. If I was brainwashed, it was by my own body's capacity to have children. And also—though this may be the same thing on a larger scale—by the needs of the species. Without the urge to reproduce we would have died out long ago. (Which might have been a boon to the rest of the biosphere.)

The biology department was particularly strong, with some notable female professors. I never took to biology, but at some gathering a zoologist— short and sturdy, with a mop of white hair and a suit cut like men's (though with a skirt)—told us about summers at the Marine Biological Laboratory in Woods Hole. One morning, she said, she crossed the lab's parking lot as some tourists were getting out of their car. "There goes one of them now," she overheard a tourist tell his companions as she walked by.

I admired Brock, the zoologist, Mildred Allen (who taught basic physics and had me helping out in the lab), and others like them—but didn't want to emulate them. Mount Holyoke's message about how we should spend our lives and use our talents seemed mixed, even contradictory. These seemingly independent and content bluestockings were all single, while most alumnae had triple-barreled names, successful husbands, and broods of children, and many classmates were at least as interested in who got "pinned" or engaged last weekend, where the next date was coming from, and whom to take to the prom as in what Plato had to say, or Newton or Shakespeare or even Emily Dickinson (an alumna who didn't stay to graduate), or how to earn a living if, Heaven forfend, one didn't "catch" a husband. Mount Holyoke implicitly offered a choice, I thought: career and "spinsterhood," or marriage and family and no career. Given that choice, I wanted the latter. In fact I thought that the perfect life would include work as a man's assistant, preferably my husband's, and that's how things worked out for a time—only they weren't so perfect.

To have a family eventually, one had to meet "men." Two dates that year were with Bronx Science classmates. Irving came from Harvard for a prom. He was exceedingly brainy, enough to make me a bit nervous, but we had a good time, without romance. The date with Neil at Amherst College began with my first football game, after which Neil noticed that he had lost his freshman beany. He was terrified that his sophomore would catch him without it. The consequences would evidently be dire, these assigned sophomores clearly not kindly big brothers but censorious minders. I was sorry that Neil had to take this silly business seriously.

A blind date with a prep school senior was annoying and one with someone from the University of Massachusetts, then "Mass Aggie," also went nowhere. When Paul and Walter visited, Edith Cohn joined us for a meal in Holyoke, during which, in response to something Walter said, I declared, "There's nothing wrong with the peasants of Europe." This earnest and ridiculous assertion became a "family joke" for Edith and me.

Most weekends, far as I remember, I was on campus and dateless. There were other pleasures and distractions. Reading and studying for courses, for instance, which I did despite writing a sententious bon mot about my education being interrupted by class work. And informal discussions of great issues. Perhaps it was my father and his brothers, each with his own lunch sack rather than sharing food with other hikers, that accounted for what now seems an odd philosophical outlook that I defended freshman year: I was against people doing things for each other that they can do for themselves. Why should A do for B and B for A? Why not each on his/her own? Perhaps I was reacting to Mother's entangling alliances. Now independence seems all right when necessary, but I was belittling interdependence, which we surely need. (W.H. Auden, who spent much time at Mount Holyoke, is supposed to have said: "We are here on earth to help others. What on earth the others are here for I don't know.") Behind my view was a degree of literal-mindedness that also figured in an argument about a supposed quote from Emerson: "Consistency is the hobgoblin of small minds." I insisted it must be "*in*consistency," for I couldn't accept the idea that a great thinker would disparage consistency. We were all wrong, for Emerson opposed "a foolish consistency." We could surely all agree to that, though we might not agree what makes a consistency foolish.

Sunday evenings, Professor (of philosophy) Roger Holmes and his wife Louise opened their house to any student who wished to hear classical music (or, in at least one case, flirt with Roger). Louise made delicious applesauce cake and Roger played tapes he had recorded from the radio, with what was then advanced equipment. (We didn't call them by their first names until well after graduation.)

> I have been here for one week [I wrote in that first paper for Brock].... I have been subjected to new experiences, have learned a new language, ...the geography of another small bit of the Earth's surface, and... to recognize about five-hundred faces and from fifty to one-hundred names to go with some of those faces.

The "new language" included the correct pronunciation of Holyoke, with no long 'e' sound (i.e. Whole yolk), and Amherst, with silent *h*. I can still hear choir director Ruth Douglass instructing us in a plummy and emphatic voice: "We never abbreviate the 'Mount.'" She would be horrified to know that it is now abbreviated in official college literature. Among the music Miss Douglass directed were the typical sentimental school songs:

> Oh Mount Holyoke we pay thee devotion, in the fervor of youth that is strong.
> The courage of right is thy garland, our lives, alma mater, thy song...

A student version begins: "Oh Mount Holyoke we pay thee tuition, in the fervor of youth that's gone wrong"; it's reassuring that there were other cynics to parody these flowery lyrics.

I never learned to love Mount Holyoke as many others did, but am grateful for all it taught me, some of it intentionally, some just by being so different from nearly everything I was used to.

Chapter 10

DAN

Shortly after graduation, during an evening walk on George Washington Bridge, two Bronx Science friends and I made a pact: the first to lose her virginity would tell the others. Thanks to Dan, I won that race.

A Mount Holyoke classmate got me a blind date with a boy from Hamilton College, who then invited me there for the big spring weekend, late freshman year. Friday evening we went to a party. I'd just arrived and already knew he bored me. He probably went to get drinks, because a lean, attractive fellow came over to talk; soon we were dancing and not long after that we were in bed, which both thrilled and frightened me. In 1996, when I found Dan again and we arranged to meet, it hit me: what he did was date rape, even if I wasn't his date. This suggests the ambiguities of *some* such crimes. It was and wasn't rape. I wanted what he wanted, but not so soon. It was too precipitous, he too oblivious of my wishes, I too timid and confused to make them clear even to myself.

There has been much talk about assertiveness training for girls and women so they can fend off an "other party," who may be "highly or completely self-focused," and feel "comfortable" about saying no. All very sensible, but often a woman either isn't sure what she wants, or she wants, as I did, two contradictory things: yes that, but not so fast please. And perhaps she really wants this particular chap. "If it's now or never, then the hell with him" is easier to say than to feel, and even harder to act on. Is assertiveness training enough to clarify and rectify these moments of passion and confusion?

In 1996 Dan told me that he placated my jilted date (who probably had wounded pride but not a wounded heart) by buying the tickets for the weekend's events—which we didn't go to—and throwing in a bottle of booze. Are college boys still trading in college girls?

It wasn't a one-night, or one-weekend, stand. We were in love. Though his letters are not extant, I remember rueful apologies for not being "careful"; luckily I hadn't gotten pregnant, nor did I when he came to Mount Holyoke and stayed at the C.I., where we went for a hasty, uncomfortable tryst, or more than one.

I brought Dan home with trepidation. His French Catholic father, widowed with four children, had married a woman Dan called The Bitch. Because his milieu was very different from ours, and because he meant so much to me, I was nervous about what Mother would think. I needn't have worried. They fell for each other, she presumably the good stepmother that The Bitch wasn't, and he the sort of adoring young person she couldn't resist, less problematic than her own children, with our buried resentments.

We needed summer jobs. I've forgotten what Dan found. Edith and I landed jobs at a dingy outfit in the Garment District that produced books of fabric samples, which, along with fashion magazines, were staples of our living/fitting-room. On what was not yet called Fashion Avenue (Seventh), up some rickety stairs, around a large table with eight or ten other women, we glued little swatches. No talking, but Edith and I defied this stupid rule, risking the ire of the company's Simon Legree. Years later, Edith remembered its name when I didn't.

> Du-Al Manufacturing Company. And you humming Bach while
> the nasty foreman walked around beating his leg with a yardstick.
> There were three chairs for ten people. We lasted all of three days.
> On day #4 you very wisely made me come back to pick up my
> paycheck, although I wanted to flee.

I soon got a job as a stock clerk at Roberts-Rose Textile Company, a jobber on Fourth Avenue, where for $36 a week I cruised among shelves stacked with boxes of embroidered placemats, children's clothes, handkerchiefs, and other small items, filling orders from dry-goods stores around the country. It was slightly more strenuous than pasting swatches, and almost as boring. Paul and I stayed in Mother's bungalow at Camp Midvale and Dan in one next door. We three commuted to our dreary jobs in New York, I shivering in a flimsy sweater pulled on over the sleeveless dress that would make the sweltering city almost bearable.

One day Dan told me with great relish he'd dreamt he was in bed with a woman with big breasts. I was distressed. "I didn't think you'd be jealous of a mere dream," said he. At twenty, Dan was neither sensitive nor psychologically astute. He obviously enjoyed his dream, at least in the telling. Where did that leave me, who couldn't make my breasts larger to please him? He couldn't or wouldn't tell me who the woman was. Mother had big breasts.

Other experiences involving breasts help put Dan and his "mere dream" in perspective. *Śakuntalā*, a play by Kālidāsā, one of India's greatest poets and playwrights, is an elaboration of a story in the Hindu epic *Mahābhārata*. *Śakuntalā*, of semi-divine origin, lives in an ashram when King Duṣyanta comes by and they fall in love. Her pregnancy, the result of an afternoon "one-night stand," makes her Bhārata's mother. The play details a misunderstanding and an eventual reconciliation.

We read the play in Sanskrit over the course of one semester in my second year at Harvard. One passage stayed with me. It attests to Śakuntalā's beauty via her footprints in the sand: the heels left a deeper impression than the toes. Professor Ingalls explained that this was due to the weight of her buttocks. The other requisite for female beauty, as Hindu sculpture makes plain, is large breasts. The typical twentieth-century fashion models would not turn on your lusty fifth-century Hindu. Presumably I remembered this bit of the play because I would pass muster only in the buttocks department.

As I contemplated writing about learning to accept my body as it was, I looked at *Śakuntalā* again, in English, soon finding the relevant passage. This is the Arthur Ryder translation (c.1913):

> In white sand at the door/ Fresh footprints appear,
> The toe lightly outlined,/ The heel deep and clear.

Not a clue as to what this might signify. An undated translation by T. Holme says simply "some recent footsteps." Sir William Jones (1901) has footsteps that are "raised a little before and depressed behind by the weight of her elegant limbs." This is the school of thought that considered "leg" a four-letter word.

I next turned to one Hippolyte Fauche, figuring that a Frenchman, even in 1860, wouldn't blanch at the implications of the "heel deep and clear." His footprints depress the sand "legerement ou sont les doigts, profondement a la place du talon!" And there is a footnote: "C'est-a-dire *clunium pondere*." The right part of the anatomy—no elegant limbs for M. Fauche—but he hides his blush behind the Latin.

Unlike most women in my family, I have small breasts. Does it matter? It did to Dan and some others. Some women like me were not audibly worried about it. A bunch of us freshmen, inspired by a dance and poetry evening put on by students, gathered in the room Roz and I shared. While I declaimed poetry ad-lib, Marcia did a striptease. Having put on a strapless evening gown, she began her dance by pulling—with two great flourishes—two wool gloves out of the top of her gown, a great moment for the "flat-chested."

But there was some desperation. Years before breast implants, women wore various kinds of "falsies." A young man attached his fraternity pin (to be "engaged to be engaged") too enthusiastically into what proved to be inflatable falsies (or so we heard). They could be deflated too, as could the romance.

In 1973 my new profession brought me an instructive encounter. The archivist at University of Massachusetts-Amherst proposed that I serve as the speaker at the Phi Beta Kappa initiation. At the dinner beforehand, a sociology professor sat near me. My homemade gown was more décolleté than I'd intended, but a couple of safety pins kept things decent. Decent but evidently still enticing to Professor G., judging by the direction of his glances.

He couldn't stay to hear me speak but wanted to visit the Schlesinger Library to find research materials for his students. He soon came to see the library and have lunch. As I told him about the collections, he barely listened. At lunch he picked at his food. His current (third) marriage, he said, was an "open marriage," which was trendy then. He soon called again and, upping the ante, asked me to have dinner. "I'll have dinner with you and your wife," I said. "Oh, come on," said he. I never heard from him again. It was a proud moment but an easy triumph: he didn't attract me.

Noel, whom I met in 1979, claimed to like my small breasts; his ex-wife's big ones got in the way. Dan was more typical. Even when romance is not an issue, men seem to need to look down the front of one's dress. When I caught my lawyer at it, a nice, seemingly domesticated chap, I decided it's part of the built-in equipment for propagating the species.

In my tenth decade this seems silly and sad. The men who hanker after big boobs aren't all such prize specimens, and the main thing is to accept one's own body as it is. In the showers at Harvard's pools I saw that women come in all sorts of shapes and sizes. Like most, I'm neither particularly shapely nor particularly unsightly, and surely, looking at any nude body, one cannot tell whether the person is a professor or a secretary, a dean or a janitor, nor whether s/he is content, intelligent, kind, interesting, or anything else. Maybe, if I'd seen breasts and nude bodies this way in 1950, Dan's dream wouldn't have hurt so much. In fact, I eventually decided that, given a choice between too big or too little, I'd choose the latter; one over-endowed friend agreed.

Whether or not Mother was the woman in Dan's dream, she certainly knew what was going on and allowed us privacy when she could, almost presiding over our affair. Privacy was what we needed. Once we made love eight times in barely twenty-four hours. But I was never satisfied. In those days, a woman in that fix would be considered "frigid"; now it's "female sexual dysfunction," which supposedly afflicts 43 percent of American women and is supposedly treatable with pills. Some researchers ascribe this diagnosis to pharmaceutical companies' need to sell their products.

I knew I wasn't frigid, and soon another man proved I wasn't, given patience and the right feelings. Dan was ebullient and attractive but, although in 1996 he claimed he'd been happy to find a girl he could talk with about things that mattered, what stood out was his enthusiasm for partying, which meant drinking, and it was about then that I learned that I hate being drunk. It's the loss of self-control even more than nausea and hangover, but I also observed something that I saw mentioned in print only many years later: liquor is not conducive to good sex. It may break down inhibitions or resistance but it makes muscles slack; hence the stumbling and slurred speech. The muscles needed for sex become slack too.

Around Christmas 1950 I broke up with Dan. Mother was baffled and disappointed but they remained friends for years, even after he married (and later divorced) another Eva from Vienna. Dan was one instance of what became a lifelong penchant of Mother's: befriending people in her children's generation, including my friends or Paul's—befriend seriously, trying to tie our friends more closely to her than to us. Some young people adored her, some were her acolytes *and* my friends but, looking back later, I saw that those closest to me were not close to her. A forgotten Bronx Science classmate writes that he came to pick me up for a date and Mother talked with him about Beethoven and things she did as a girl—perhaps innocently, perhaps flirting with her daughter's potential admirer. I may have been unaware of that incident but sometimes I felt her competing with me. "She was jealous of you," Edith told me later, "and tried to make me *her* friend."

Mother's friendship with Dan seemed bizarre, intrusive, a reproach to me for having thrown him over. I remained curious about it and that's why I got in touch with him in 1996. Mother had been dead for twenty-five years. He lived in Washington; I was going there on business. I wrote, asking if he would tell me what he remembered about Mother. Yes, he'd be glad to, and he offered to take me and the friends I was staying with (Marcia of the strapless gown and her husband) out on a sailboat. No. That wasn't the point of seeing him.

Over a long lunch I learned about his wives, sons, and legal career; he had worked with developers and lost a lot of money during the 1980s building bust, which aroused in me, and in Marcia when I told her about it, mainly Schadenfreude. But he had nothing to tell me about Mother. Did I not know how to ask? Did he not remember, or have something to hide? Walking to Marcia and Paul's house, pondering this frustrating encounter, I suspected that Dan had told me something by telling me nothing.

Having come on with charming enthusiasm, offering talk and the (irrelevant) sail, he then delivered just that: nothing. That was surely a major reason I told him goodbye in 1950. We were lovers but not friends, and although I fell in love I was soon frustrated, not only sexually. Over the next decades he married four times, and I didn't like him much in 1996—facts that indicate that I would have dumped him later if I hadn't already dumped him sooner.

Chapter 11
WOODBRIDGE HALL, 1950-53

*W*oodbridge Hall burned in January1969, as it was about to become a Black cultural center, and was replaced by a parking lot. It had been one of two co-op dorms and I was poor, and lucky, enough to live in it, which made my last three years at Mount Holyoke tolerable. It housed only thirty-two students and, more important, we all waited tables, cleaned bathrooms and halls, washed dishes, "sat bells" (answered the phone), and helped prepare meals.

It wasn't till senior year that I got one of the four single rooms. My sophomore-year roommate, Jeannette, had just transferred to Mount Holyoke. She had told a neighbor that she was going to study Greek. "Oh, Greek," said the neighbor, "that's Latin, isn't it?" We tried to ferment fresh cider into hard cider and once double-dated, ending up stealing plates and bowls from the kitchen and smashing them against a big tree. Wicked and satisfying!

Junior year Susan Brown and I shared a front room, where one evening non-Woodbridge Margie tried to get into bed with me. I assured her I liked her but not *that* way. My crush on Perky was a memory, and I've never been so powerfully attracted to another woman (although it could happen). Margie's family took me to see the Broadway production of *The King and I* and I visited her more than once in Miami.

Edith was in Woodbridge too, rooming with Marcia. We'd agreed not to share a room, knowing that that could spoil a friendship. Edith and Marcia remained fast friends, however, while Edith and I became estranged, even as she became entangled with Jack, one of Dan's Hamilton College friends—entangled to the point of marrying him and leaving Mount Holyoke after sophomore year. Soon I decided that our estrangement was ridiculous and got in touch in time to visit Edith and

Jack first at Lehigh University, then at the University of Vermont. He taught English at both schools.

Heather was pretty and plump, did a mean imitation of an Irish tenor, and taught me a jingle from Daily Vacation Bible School in Ashtabula, Ohio:

> Running over, running over (twirl hands around each other),
> My cup's full (cup hands) and running over (twirl hands).
> Since the Lord (point up) saved me (point at self)
> I'm as happy as can be (clap hands).
> My cup's full and running over (as before).

Hard to say which seemed more exotic to a New York Jew: that town or that summer program.

Her fiancé, Myron—they were sweethearts since high school—was at Amherst, so they were together every Saturday night. Like other couples then, they did everything but "go all the way." Myron took Amherst's course on evolution, in which each year the student with the most simian traits won a bronze ape. Most years, Myron, large, hairy, with notably long arms, would have won hands down (so to speak), but he was beaten out by a student with opposable big toes.

My junior year, the college admitted more newcomers than the freshman dorms could hold; Jenny (of the burlap skirt), a Bronx native and Bronx Science grad, was among those coming to Woodbridge. We declared ourselves sisters, ignoring our assigned siblings, and otherwise ridiculed the college's hallowed traditions. Jenny at times made fun of me; for example, while often proclaiming me her "dear old pal" (as in the sister song), she produced a series of drawings with my upper lip becoming ever thinner and finally disappearing, but her wit wasn't always acerbic: about an everyday dress she said, "I wear it every day."

There were friends, Jenny perhaps included, to whom I said or wrote things as hurtful as some of her remarks. "i hope you have gotten over your pashion," I wrote Alex (of Kiddie Camp and Bronx Science). "It is really hopeless and you know that i am much too good for you," and again: "We ought to be in LA [in August]. If you aren't there I don't care because I have someone else to take me places." Edith's Jack warned me once that if I didn't stop insulting him he would prevent me from seeing her again. The main impetus was to be clever, yet such cleverness entailed, at best, indifference to the hurt inflicted.

Many college students sent their dirty laundry home (using special shipping cases), but Jenny and I, not in that "demographic," hitchhiked to a laundromat in Holyoke. While our clothes got washed we haunted the Salvation Army store, buying what seemed marvelous garments. Those that weren't so marvelous we donated back to the store. On one trip I lost my wallet, with a $20 bill and a penny. Soon it came in the mail, with a note: "I kept your money. I obviously need it more than you do." Scholarship and co-op dorm notwithstanding, I couldn't argue with this town-versus-gown assumption. He or she left me my penny.

Sort of poor and needlessly hungry, Jenny and I gravitated to events that offered free refreshments, such as a lingerie show in the basement of South Hadley's Congregational Church. The woman in charge held up, inter alia, a capacious pair of underpants with "your low, broad bottom." I dealt with such challenges to one's composure by "hearing" a Bach organ prelude, the majesty of the music subduing my laughter.

One term Jenny and I took the same European history course. We sat together, exchanging notes and giggling a lot until the professor said, "Miss Steiner, please sit somewhere else, *anyw*here else." We sat six or eight seats apart, then slowly moved closer. When there was just one girl between us, she turned out to be the owner of a special fountain pen that Jenny had taken from the Lost and Found. Once we had mostly recovered from this embarrassment, we sat together the day the professor lectured about the the Fuggers of Augsburg, a fifteenth-century banking family. How were we supposed to keep straight faces?—even if all the other students did.

When we got our dorm assignments, I was not to be in Woodbridge senior year. I protested, first to the housemother, Mrs. Buffinton. It may have been Buffy who told me (and whose idea it was?) that I was being sent into what felt like exile because I had ruined Jenny's school spirit. Corrupting the youth, just like Socrates. As if she had any school spirit to ruin. I complained to the dean of residence and was reinstated. Pleased for having, uncharacteristically, protested and, even more uncharacteristically, overcome, I achieved a truce with Buffy. Widow Buffinton was generally kindly and sometimes in a restrained way jolly, but not brilliant.

No one could match Marianne Brock, who *was* brilliant, in making English exciting, but, unlike most students, I liked Anna Jean Mill, a somewhat dour Scot, and her English literature survey course. Spenser's *Faerie Queene* left me cold, but Milton's *Paradise Lost*, while unconvincing was interesting, even entertaining, Satan and the other fallen angels more appealing than the unfallen crew in Heaven. Knowing German pronunciation helped me in reciting a dozen lines of *The Canterbury Tales* in Middle English. But when in a paper I wrote that one thing was a function of another, a concept derived from mathematics that hadn't yet penetrated the humanities, Miss Mill questioned it and was unconvinced by my explanation; now even some literary people employ this concept.

One Friday night I landed in the infirmary with "rather severe" abdominal pains. (Stravinsky complained that, when he reported pain due to cancer, the nurses would accept at most "rather severe." He also said that with pain, it's not how much that counts, but how long.) It wasn't appendicitis but constipation. Confined to bed for twenty-two hours, I read three Shakespeare plays, found myself thinking in iambic pentameter, and wrote about my affliction in that meter, most dramatically and amusingly, I thought. Alas, that poetical work is lost, so you (and I), in imitation of Shakespeare's closing rhyming couplets: "Without the evidence to prove my claim,/ Must grant that, extant, it would merit fame."

I read Dante's *Inferno* (in translation) with Valentine Giamatti, father of Bart (late president of Yale), and grandfather of actor Paul. Rather than French, I continued with German literature, finding much of it, including Goethe's *Faust* (Part I), annoyingly sentimental. Kafka was another matter; his direct, almost journalistic prose makes horrendous events more frightening than if he had, as it were, gasped in horror. The German class put on *Der böse Geist Lumpazivagabundus* by Nestroy, once Vienna's favorite playwright. Although the only one who spoke anything like Viennese, I had only a bit part.

I took sociology as a distribution requirement and passed with a mediocre grade. I didn't think the way social scientists do and concluded, half seriously, or a bit more than half, that what sociologists discover

91

through their research is either self-evident or wrong. Philosophy continued to be congenial, though I fudged reading Kant—too dreary; found Hegel, in German or English, impenetrable; and couldn't get interested in Whitehead's invented world, which seemed not to overlap with the real world I knew. I disagreed with political scientists who considered Plato's *Republic* a blueprint for totalitarianism. According to Plato, Socrates examined justice in a city rather than an individual because it's easier to discern qualities in the larger entity: the "republic" is an analogy for the individual psyche. I don't vouch for this view now, no longer having the patience for Socrates and his merry band of talkers.

After basic physics with Mildred Allen, the lab work in Mr. Clancy's electricity course defeated me. We had to plot successive readings as a needle wavered along a numbered scale. My graph looked nothing like the elegant hysteresis curve. Twenty-some years later I mentioned this to Artie, my Midvale friend Dolly's by-then ex-husband and a brilliant theoretical physicist. He laughed about my hysteresis lump: "I always faked the lab work," he said. "Why didn't you tell me sooner?" I asked, but of course I hadn't consulted him back in 1951.

So it would be math, but integral calculus, with its endless, messy decimals, defeated me. As usual, I wasn't willing to struggle with something hard. Math had been not just congenial, but entrancing. Perhaps I should have gone on to more abstract mathematical topics, or perhaps I'd just reached my limit.

Instead I continued with philosophy. George Tovey became my adviser and a friend. I baby-sat with his son Peter and later, when George taught a course on humor at the University of New Hampshire, I told him some of my stock of jokes, which he wrote down with great interest. Soon after that he died, at only sixty-nine.

Perky soon left. Roger and Louise Holmes continued their Sunday evenings. Three and four decades later I sometimes visited them and was always received with professions of pleasure and interest (after 1975, interest especially in any prospective second husband). Roger was the son of Reverend John Haynes Holmes, a liberal minister and a co-founder of the NAACP and the ACLU. Unlike his Unitarian father, Roger was no Christian. He enjoyed undermining the faith of devout Christian students, presumably leading them through a non-believer's catechism on the problem of evil: their God could not be both benevolent and omnipotent. Can one do this kindly? Maybe not, but maybe without obvious relish.

Junior year I started Greek and soon noticed synergy (Greek for working together) among my courses: language, history, and philosophy focused entirely or partly on ancient Greece. My three years of Greek have left little residue, though I still know that phenomenon and criterion are singular and it's their *plurals* that end in –a, as they come from Greek, which isn't Latin. We read some Luke and all automatically had the angels saying: "Glory to God in the highest,/ And on earth peace, good will to men." "Look again," said Miss Wyckoff. It actually says: "peace to people of good will." The word translated as "men" is *anthropos* (human being). More significant: the Greek text implies that there is peace *only* for people of good will.

Junior year I also began lessons with the college organist. I still love to *hear* the organ but it's been like archery and fencing: I know something about it but am not good at it.

Of the men in my life during these years (about whom more later), Joe, the least likely as a mate, was most influential, getting me interested in mystical traditions, especially Hinduism, thus accounting for my undergraduate thesis, two years of graduate school, and the direction of some of my subsequent life. Surprisingly, the philosophy department let me write an honors thesis on the Hindu *Laws of Manu*. As none of the regular faculty could judge this opus, I was assigned to a visiting professor, Clarence Hamilton, a scholar of Buddhism (which isn't Hinduism but emerged from it). My focus was on the role of men and women according to the Hindu text, which carries *la différence* to an extreme, one I then approved of. The thesis helped me win the philosophy prize at commencement, another surprise.

A single room and exalted status made senior year pleasurable. Seniors were allowed to have cars after spring vacation and Mother couldn't drive hers, so she let me bring it to South Hadley. Evenings I might drive a few friends to a dive halfway to Holyoke and have a grilled-cheese sandwich and a glass of Muscatel.

One beautiful day I rode my wartime bicycle in the beautiful countryside. A dorm-mate expressed surprise that, with a "four-wheeled animal," I still rode my bike. But the car was for transportation, not pleasure, as was one classmate's bicycle: she used it to go to the college stable, where she kept her horse. She clearly belonged to a different social stratum. At commencement, as about 350 of us processed into the gym, she was one of numerous women I could swear I had never seen before, a result partly of living in Woodbridge, partly of feeling out of place, even if not as much as in 1949, and therefore socializing mainly with other misfits and relative paupers.

Looking back, ambivalence prevails: good courses, good friends, much kindness and generosity, beautiful surroundings, but, given more information, not the college I would have chosen. So I'm a grateful alumna, but not one of the fervent ones.

Chapter 12

TEN THOUSAND MEN OF HARVARD

"Ten thousand men of Harvard want vict'ry today,
For they know that o'er old Eli Fair Harvard holds sway..."
—Harvard football fight-song

*A*fter Mount Holyoke's famine there was Harvard's feast: whatever the ratio, a lot of men per woman in the Graduate School of Arts and Sciences. I wasn't thinking in feminist terms about why so few women, but about potential friends, lovers, or Mr. Right. Once one chap came to my rooming-house to see me as another left. One lived down the hall, one just across Kirkland Street.

But first I had to find that rooming-house. The housing office listed a fussy apartment near Porter Square, the landlady a widow who would watch me and any visitors. It also listed 52 Irving Street. The landlord owned 52 and the attached, mirror-image 50, lived nearby, changed our sheets every week, provided two refrigerators, and left us alone. We cooked on hotplates in our rooms, washing dishes in the bathroom sink down the hall. My trunk served as coffee table; empty Chilean Riesling bottles became candleholders. It was how graduate students should live, frugally, freely, without anyone like a housemother.

Making good use of the hotplate, I adapted Mother's recipes, such as green peppers stuffed with a mixture of ground beef, rice, egg, and onion and steamed in tomato sauce. Pinky in number 50 and I traded jokes and recipes, including desserts we invented. Hers: remove crusts of thin-sliced white bread, roll around a filling of cream cheese, dip in melted butter, sprinkle with cinnamon sugar, broil briefly, serve with canned cherries heated in their syrup. Mine: cover canned peach halves (freestone if available) with buttered bread crumbs flavored with nutmeg, broil briefly; serve hot with vanilla ice cream.

I rode my bike down Kirkland Street to Harvard Yard, and for a taste of outdoors, to beautiful Mount Auburn Cemetery. Mostly my life was at Harvard, and when on occasion I took the subway to Boston, it felt like entering another world. Day to day, aside from men and cooking, life consisted of classes and libraries.

Professor Daniel Henry Holmes Ingalls was suspicious of women students, someone told me, and in my case rightly so! But I worked hard, learning *Devanagari* (City of the Gods), the script that looks like a horizontal line with symbols hanging from it. Sanskrit is the most "phonemically perfect" language, written words reflecting changes in spoken words, and it outdoes German in constructing compound words. A short example is *ashvakovidaha*, what a knower of horses (literally, horse what knower), but many are longer and more complex. In 1953–54 the class met in the small Sanskrit library on the top floor of Widener Library, in 1954–55, in Ingalls's study, Widener 273, reading the *Bhagavad Gīta* one semester and the play *Śakuntalā* the other. Once someone knocked and Ingalls chatted briefly with a male visitor. I saw only part of a shoe but knew it was J. Robert Oppenheimer, who, while observing the first test of the atomic bomb he helped develop, quoted the *Gīta*: "I am become Death, Destroyer of Worlds." I was too shy to peer at him around the door.

Mother later questioned my choice of field. "I always thought you would stay in physics," she said, long after that could change anything. If I had become a physicist, could I have avoided joining "Oppie" in his doubts and regrets? By far the most research money was (and is) for "defense."

I took every relevant course Harvard offered: Indian history, anthropology, Buddhism. The Sanskrit library was too small and quiet, the Widener reading room—with its constant shuffle and buzz of chairs, whispers, footsteps—too big and distracting, so I frequented Harvard-Yenching Library in Boylston Hall, where I met Peter Ch'en, Mark Mancall, Roderick MacFarquhar, and other budding scholars of East Asia. Peter, seeming like a younger brother, gave me my first glimpses of Chinese culture.

As the eldest son, he was a little big shot in his family in Taiwan, but here the arrogance to which he was trained mingled uncomfortably with a wistful sense of inferiority. He told me repeatedly that he wouldn't marry a Chinese woman, but he worried that his penis was too small to satisfy a

Caucasian wife. Unable to agree or reassuringly disagree, I just listened to this endearing and repellent frankness. (That his worry had a basis in reality is clear from Jan Wong's *Red China Blues:* health agencies have condoms 106 mm. in circumference for Africa, 104 for North America and Europe; and 98 for Asia.) Peter also told me about ginseng, used to restore women's health after childbirth and considered an aphrodisiac. He relished such talk.

He invited me for supper at 367 Harvard Street, where I watched him stir-fry Chinese cabbage: some oil, soy sauce, a pinch of sugar; a few moments with a spatula and it was done. It was a revelation. I had almost surely never eaten Chinese food, certainly never seen it prepared. The term "stir-fry" was unknown; most American cooks boiled vegetables.

Peter's ancestors had migrated to Taiwan from Fujian province in an earlier century. Sandwiched between the indigenous Taiwanese, whom he looked down on, and the Kuomintang—who came with Chiang Kai-shek in 1949, when the Communists won the civil war, whom he hated—Peter harbored doubts about his future and ambivalence about being Chinese. In 1959, when I wrote him from Macao, where my (non-Harvard) husband, representing CARE (Cooperative for American Relief to Everywhere), had difficulties dealing with local authorities, Peter replied, "Once again I am reminded of disheartening way of life in Asia. Why cannot Chinese learn to live the way we do here! I am sorry that George has to go through that nasty fight.... Chinese are all alike; we cannot change them." I quoted this in a

Sitting with Peter Ch'en on Harvard's "stone turtle," a Chinese stele near Boylston Hall, which then housed Harvard-Yenching Institute, 1953-55.

letter to Professor Robert Hightower, who became a friend, adding that the Chinese are (of course!) not all alike.

Peter was at best ambivalent about the Japanese as these "ocean dwarfs" had occupied Taiwan before and during World War II. Yet his dissertation (in 1957–58 I sweated over the tortured English of the first draft) was about "The Japanese Government and the Creation of the Imperial Army, 1870–1873." In his introduction, he explains that the US had moved the Japanese military archives to Washington in 1945, where they were when he was "gathering material in Tokyo," while "shortly after my return to the United States [they were] sent back to Japan." This sort of frustration seemed to define his life. He thanks professors Edwin Reischauer and Benjamin Schwartz especially. Reischauer "permitted me to intrude upon him. He always bore with my brashiness [sic] and listened patiently to my ideas." Such effusive thanks were surely deserved; it took patience to deal with Peter, brash and humble, superior and needy.

He had some teaching jobs and several girlfriends. At last I received an invitation to a September 1973 wedding. According to my diary, I had lunch with Peter in August. "His marriage sounds difficult already and he's leaving academia in a year and opening a store in Cambridge." He was going to import things from Asia. I suggested such stores already existed but he assured me they all sold "junky stuff." Soon another announcement arrived: wedding called off. Peter did not long survive this humiliation. He died of cancer before he could move or open a store. In a 1960 letter to Robert, I had almost foreseen a bitter end: "I have the feeling that Peter's life is tragic and that there is no solution, easy or otherwise, to his dilemma." It was a short, unfulfilled life.

Some others, like Peter, didn't figure as Men. Sometimes I ate at Harkness Commons, renowned for its Bauhaus architecture—as part of the graduate student complex designed by Walter Gropius—and its terrible but cheap food. I met Ernie Schlesinger there (his daughter Eva worked for me at the Schlesinger Library three decades later); another day it was classicist Marc. I was finding *The Republic* in Greek difficult and Marc offered to tutor me at his rooms on Farrar Street. By unspoken consent there was only one Greek lesson, but we would meet up on Kirkland Street, and one day he described his digestive problems in some detail. Another day he took me to lunch at Henri IV (pronounced *a la française*), a very French restaurant on Winthrop Street. A regular, he was known as Monsieur Marc.

There were other chaps who did figure as Men, more or less. Pinky and I went to a mixer at what was then the International Student

Center and got mixed up with three charming gents from the British Commonwealth: John from England, Neville from Australia, and Ken from Canada. Neville was a straightforward, direct sort, a scientist. From our single date I recall only his good-night. My brand new, still stiff red leather jacket from Ohrbach's creaked as he embraced me. "Get rid of the jacket," said Neville with a last friendly peck, but I didn't, and my son wore it to tatters three decades later.

Ken was the one who appealed to me. We did some smooching once in his room in one of the older graduate dorms—till his roommate appeared, to Ken's embarrassment and relief. He made sure it didn't happen again, perhaps with a little regret—after all I was *there* and willing—but he didn't like being unfaithful to his fiancée, who was not there.

Pinky's first year at Harvard Law School turned out to be her last, but she stayed on in Cambridge and worked at a Boston department store (she later became an artist, designer, and art teacher, which suited her talents better), while she and her friend Phyllis, who taught first grade, and I shared an apartment at 12 Story Street (the house later swallowed by the Design Research building), under the third-floor mansard roof of Widow Pratt's house, with access to the tiny bathroom through the tiny kitchen. Mrs. Pratt had the first floor and on the second lived three male students, two at "the" law school, one later a professor there; they had rooms off an open landing and thought us girls rather uncouth as we trekked through their front hall. Decades later I twice went into the post office at the corner and asked for a book of threes, evidently what it cost to mail a letter in 1954–55.

The first year in Cambridge left sharper memories than the second. One evening I met Pinky outside the law library and heard a stentorian male voice up some stairs. I was surprised the librarians allowed a radio there, till I realized it was one law student holding forth to another.

A barrel-chested European invited me to his room on Broadway, put on a record, and got me to dance with him. It felt awkward, annoying. He was incredulous when I extricated myself and escaped, my heart pounding with (as I interpret it now) fear of someone strong enough to catch and subdue me, and anxiety at my hubris in saying no. He probably had contempt for me doubly: as a woman, and as one too stupid to value what he was offering.

Pinky and Paul, who also lived in number 50, were briefly an item, while I hankered after his younger brother Bobby, an alluring, guitar-playing freshman who rented a garret in one of the big houses on upper Irving Street. Bobby was unsure of what he wanted to do with his life—appropriate enough for a freshman—but he was quite sure that he did not want to be romantically involved with me. I consoled myself with a law student who lived in 52. The affair was meaningless and brief, but he was memorable for another reason.

He had no patience with psychotherapy. People create their own emotional problems, he declared, so they should fix them themselves. I knew there was something wrong with this argument but didn't recognize the fallacy until it was too late to confront Antonio. People *don't* create their own problems, at least to begin with; one's parents, other people, one's environment create them before one is old enough to create anything. That's the basic fallacy. Another is that only Christian Scientists believe that those who catch an infection or break a bone shouldn't get medical help. The belief that emotional problems are products of the imagination was all too common. "It's all in your head" meant you'll be fine if you just stop whining and grow up. I came to realize that, if it really is "all in your head," fixing the problem is far more difficult than treating a broken leg or an infectious disease.

My first encounter with psychotherapy, and my second with depression, took place in Cambridge. One day everything went black. I could still function, but there was a pall over everything and I felt lost and terrified. I got an appointment at the appropriate clinic at Harvard—for two weeks later. Perhaps the clinic didn't acknowledge mental health emergencies, and I was too meek to demand immediate help. Well before I saw a rather bored therapist, the black cloud had lifted. There is no way to reconstruct what brought it on, and soon I was fully back to learning Sanskrit, struggling with Plato, swapping jokes with Pinky, and meeting men.

Roger Chacon, a philosophy student from El Salvador with a world-weary air, was not a "date" but we sometimes brooded over the world's problems and our own over coffee at some cheap place. Harvard Square had its share of greasy spoons. Buddy's Sirloin Pit, a cafeteria cum grill, had a fan that wafted the seductive odor of broiling meat out over Brattle Street. Hayes-Bickford, right across Massachusetts Avenue, was a favorite hangout of the Yenching Library crowd. Later, Harvard-Yenching Institute moved to 2 Divinity Avenue, while Hayes-Bickford made way, poetically enough, for Yenching Restaurant, which lasted till 2016.

One afternoon I had a date with Stewart Thompson, an architecture student and friend of Tom Lehrer, a cabaret singer who wrote his own satirical songs, some of them political, and later taught math at the University of California-Santa Cruz. The two had been experimenting with a tape recorder to create sound effects; they crinkled cellophane in front of the microphone, Stew reported with boyish enthusiasm, and it sounded like a terrific explosion.

Pinky and I sometimes fed the squirrels in the Old Yard, defined by seven freshman dorms and Harvard's three oldest buildings. When I wore a dress made by Mother, of denim striped black, brown, and gray, a squirrel jumped up on the skirt, evidently mistaking me for a tree trunk. One evening we paused near Hollis Hall. Someone called down from an upper window and soon appeared, an excruciatingly handsome young man from Kansas City.

He was attracted, I was smitten, but he had a girlfriend at Radcliffe. Later John sent me a photo of himself and another man, presumably his father, striding down a Kansas City street, both looking at home and entitled. Perhaps it was this quality—along with his triple-barreled name (which I won't divulge, though he is dead), golden hair, good build, and gorgeous face—that captivated me, though I wasn't conscious of it then: that air, indeed fact, of belonging, which we refugees had to do without. I continued to carry a (small) torch for him; we carried on a lopsided correspondence and talked of a trip to Ireland, for which I bought a drip-dry blouse at Macy's. I had the blouse for years and a recipe for Irish soda bread that John gave me, but nothing came of the trip.

On a later visit to Cambridge, John and I walked by the river and met Professor Finley, whom John knew and whose course on *Oedipus Rex* I'd taken. Finley was walking his dog, just then running free, and as we chatted he twirled the leash and hit himself in the face with it.

I wondered whether it's typical of performers to be self-possessed in front of an audience but awkward in an individual encounter. Finley had made *Oedipus*, even strung out over a semester, truly exciting, but I forgot more Greek than I learned, for with his "performance" he did all the work.

More important for me, John told me, as kindly as he could, that he was about to marry the girlfriend. So it was goodbye. I'd arranged to meet a friend and she held me together. We saw the movie *Giant,* which was soothingly distracting until there was a wedding and the reality of John's imminent marriage came flooding back. Losing him was devastating, briefly, even though I'd never expected a life with him.

Graduate school left me unsure about my future: what to work at, where to live. And I hadn't found Mr. Right among the 10,000. I'd applied for a Fulbright fellowship to study dance in Madras, but there were no Fulbrights for India that year, more a relief than a disappointment. At least I still had an interest in Asia to focus my job search and three more or less appealing cities to choose from: New York, San Francisco, Philadelphia, less exotic and so less challenging than Madras.

IV.

Emerging Adulthood, 1955-57

Chapter 13

SAN FRANCISCO

*P*aul moved to San Francisco in January 1952 with a brand-new B.S. in mechanical engineering from City College. That summer, Mother and I—with a young Frenchman as chauffeur—drove to California, sightseeing en route, visiting my uncle Lyova (and my boyfriend Dick) in Los Angeles, and arriving in San Francisco on a typically foggy, cool summer night. The fog was invigorating after two weeks of dry heat and I fell in love with the city—unlike Mark Twain, who famously wrote that the coldest winter he ever spent was a summer in San Francisco.

We stayed at a hotel near Paul's rooming-house. Next morning Mother said, "Call your father." I didn't want to call; he was practically a stranger, and had been problematic even before he left to marry Ethel. So Mother called and arranged a visit. On this occasion and several more over the years, Ethel cooked for her husband's ex-wife and children and any friends we might bring along. Why she put up with this is a mystery.

It's less a mystery why Isabella wanted to be there if—as the Pragans, Viennese friends in New York, claimed—she loved Poldi for the rest of her life. If true it's sad. He gave her more than enough reasons to be angry while they were together. Did she really get pleasure or satisfaction from an afternoon with him and Ethel? Or was it "for the sake of the children"? If so, she needn't have bothered. These occasions were boring and painful. In the same situation two decades later, I was glad if my children saw their father but wouldn't dream of arranging the visits, let alone going along.

Back in San Francisco two summers later, I found a job at Books, Inc., staffed by knowledgeable people who stayed for years because they read and loved books and could advise customers about them. I learned about *Books in Print* and *Cumulative Book Index*, reference books used in the trade, and about one particular book, *Nightwood* by Djuna Barnes, sold there when it was daring even to mention the existence of lesbians. At night I often wandered around Pacific Heights (not far from Paul's apartment at 1985 Ellis Street), among mansions, luxuriant gardens, and the mourning of foghorns. With some serious Jews, one of whom was training to be a kibbutznik, I did Israeli folk dances, unaware that some incorporated Palestinian dance steps. I was intrigued by the kibbutzim (unaware that all or most were on land taken from Palestinians) but had doubts about a Jewish state—though I'm not sure that the contradiction inherent in a so-called democracy where some are more equal than others was clear to me then.

The next summer, having earned my M.A. and visited Margie in Florida, I was in San Francisco again. Uncertain about work, I found a job related to Asia. "I have a job," I wrote Professor Hightower in September:

> and have worked at it three whole days together. [Echoing Sir John Suckling's poem: "Out upon it! I have loved/Three whole days together."]… I feel very much like a small-size T'ao Ch'ien—the same conflicts of the distorted nature, with the desire to serve someone somehow, but the dislike of the way one has to go about it.

Hightower replied that, though all he knew about The Asia Foundation was an ex-missionary named Hoover whom he disliked, "any job in San Francisco ought to be preferable to the same thing almost anywhere else." And he would be glad to see me when I returned to Cambridge.

TAF's library occupied rooms that had housed Radio Free Asia, which resembled Radio Free Europe, but the Pacific is much wider than the Atlantic; the signal from San Francisco didn't reach its intended audiences. The studio became the reading room and the control room, the office. Jane Wilson was librarian; Tommy Tomihiro, assistant librarian; and I, clerical assistant, later library assistant. Jane conformed to the stereotype of the librarian except that she dressed well. She was single, finicky, and bossy—and knowledgeable and competent. Tommy, a Nisei or Sansei who had been interned with his family during World War II, was kind and unassuming.

I checked in periodicals, including Chinese newspapers, so I had to learn the characters for month (same as moon) and day (sun) and the numbers from 1 to 31—and typed headings on catalogue cards. Later, when Jane let me abstract periodical articles for the program officers, I learned that I could summarize articles without fully understanding them. I did understand those in *Encounter*, the monthly journal of the Congress for Cultural Freedom, and sensed something fishy. It was obviously a weapon in the Cold War. Years later it and the CCF were unmasked as CIA cultural efforts.

I hadn't yet heard of the CIA, which had only recently emerged as successor to the wartime OSS. Perhaps it was behind a mystifying development: in the spring of 1956, TAF fired all its Asian staff members except those in the Chinese News Service, and Richard Gard, a Canadian convert to Buddhism. According to a senior staff member I asked about the purge, the president had resisted pressure to do this as long as he could. "Pressure from whom?" He couldn't tell me; I guessed it was from the government. Another hint of Cold War politics was a certain book that Jane or Tommy kept in a desk drawer, listing who borrowed it. It detailed US actions in Asia, or just Korea, including those of a TAF staffer.

The purge disturbed me; I nearly quit in protest. but I wasn't sure what I would be fighting, never mind that the resignation of a library assistant would hardly be noticed in an outfit with a staff of eighty or so at headquarters, with offices in dozens of Asian countries, and with the backing of various corporate big shots and the US government. I wasn't ready to leave, so I stayed, feeling cowardly, unprincipled.

I had another Asia-related life at the American Academy of Asian Studies. Pierre Grimes was a student whom at first I took to be a teacher. In his memoir, Alan Watts, the academy's director and a student and interpreter of Asian philosophies, describes Pierre's "encounter group on the metaphysical level," which explored and broke down participants' basic assumptions about life and reality. I wasn't in this group but I too found Pierre to be "a man of compassion and humor, as well as of good sense in the practical matters of life." We became friends. Due to my diffidence vis-à-vis the great man, Watts was more useful to me through his books and radio talks than in person; he already had quite a following, at a time when Zen and Taoism were just becoming known here—as was curry: once I had the thrill of cooking shrimp curry, using a *New York Times* recipe, for Watts, the staff, and hangers-on. (In 2000, Nina Chandler Murray, a mutual acquaintance, wrote me about a visit from Alan Watts in the 1970s; he came to dinner, "proceeded to drink himself into oblivion, passing out on our sofa. He appeared on TV early the next morning without a trace of a hangover." Another side of the "great man." Watts died in 1973, at only 58.)

Pierre sometimes drove me home, or we had coffee; there are no written records, so there's no telling what we talked about, but in 1957 he became one of those mythic guides, as in a fairy tale, pointing the way out of a dilemma that trapped me.

Meantime, I found two Indian dancers who appeared at the Academy astonishing. Shy mortals, female and male, as they performed their dedicatory ritual they seemed actually to grow in stature, to become the gods or mythic beings of the dances; the closing ritual shrank them back to everyday humanity. Then Fred, whom I knew slightly from Harvard, invited me to go dancing at the William Tell, a nightclub with live music for folk dancing, one of those wonderfully odd institutions that made San Francisco irresistible. "When you've watched dancing, you have to go dancing yourself," Fred said. "Well, you don't *have* to," said I. "Yes, you do." I was delighted.

Delighted too when he invited me to go to the beach with friends. But when he picked me up in his VW Beetle a surprise awaited me. Another woman sat in front with him. I was to be in back with another man, who was blind. Without notice, Fred had drafted me as a companion for his handicapped friend. Talk about a blind date!

Hurt and angry, for a moment I thought of backing out. But I didn't, and it wasn't *just* cowardice, for, had I declined to go, besides a rebuke to Fred, who deserved it, it would have been an insult and embarrassment for his innocent friend. So I spent a miserable day with someone who interested me not at all—nor I him—while Fred and his woman had a jolly time.

During my months at TAF, I became aware of tension in my arms and shoulders and sensed that it consumed quantities of energy. A European doctor of the demigod school of medicine couldn't understand how a young person could be so tired. Tired at work, yes, but too tired to go out and have fun at night? Taking my tonsils out would fix that. For days after the operation, I put off swallowing as long as possible, it hurt so much, but I was still tired. Tonsils don't affect ingrained tension. Even years of psychotherapy didn't relieve it all. My body still tenses to ward off dangers, old and new, real and imagined.

That winter I met Norman, probably through Laura, a midwestern colleague, and her roommates, friends from back home, one of whom asserted that a woman is sexually satisfied only when she conceives. "That's a long time to wait," I thought. It was one glimpse into the sexual naiveté of many Americans, females especially. Not that I knew so much, but I knew that conception is imperceptible, while you know right away whether you're satisfied. Another glimpse came from a colleague married in about 1920, who had no idea what her husband was up to on their wedding night.

Norman was short, handsome, blond, and lost. He was gentle, not a heel, not self-centered, but not very interesting (maybe because he wasn't a self-centered heel). We flew a kite on Strawberry Hill in Golden Gate Park and left it behind in the branches of a cypress. We went sailing on a lake in Berkeley and got wet; he only *thought* he knew more about sailing than I did. We wandered around the city, two lost souls clinging together, and went to his room and got me pregnant.

Or we *probably* got me pregnant. Shortly before I met Norman I'd had a "brief encounter" with one of Laura's acquaintances. Having lived in Mexico, she socialized with a bevy of Latin men, students at UC Berkeley who hung out together, speaking Spanish and looking down on us natives. My chap was a handsome upper-class Argentinian with a wonderful multi-part name. Thanks to Google, I learned that he became a diplomat.

Partly because of the uncertain paternity, I acted as if the pregnancy was entirely my problem. Of course I didn't tell Norman that it might not be his child, and am not sure whether I asked, or he told me, what he wanted to do about it. Quite torn myself, I flew to New York to agonize about it with Mother, ambivalent toward her and toward the embryo. How I wanted that baby, but I saw no future with Norman, so finally opted for an abortion.

For years my address book listed Dr. Spencer of Ashland, Pennsylvania, a general practitioner who performed abortions for women from all over the country. Many years later, I was able to acquire letters to him for the Schlesinger Library from Michael Kaufman, a *New York Times* reporter who had gotten them from Spencer when he interviewed him. By the time Kaufman called the library, Spencer had died. The cumulative effect of the letters is heart-rending. Almost none say "pregnant" or "baby," let alone "abortion." They seek help for a "problem" or "difficulty," usually urgently. In those days, it was considered imprudent, even impermissible, to wait longer than three months.

It should have been easy, safe and cheap to go there. Perhaps Spencer was unavailable. Occasionally he would be indicted. Usually he got off, because the jurors were local people whom he had helped, with abortions or other medical needs. He was one of those old-fashioned doctors who believed that his mission was to be useful. But at times he either had to lay low or was briefly in jail.

Whatever the reason, I didn't go to Ashland. A Cuban colleague of our family doctor told him that abortions were legal in Cuba and gave him the name of the number one ob-gyn man in Havana. Mother and I flew to Miami. Margie was glad to go to Havana with us. It was steamy, but the architecture helped: stone buildings with high ceilings, arcades to shade the sidewalks. We spent a long afternoon in the famous doctor's waiting-room. Mother smoked, I fidgeted, and the haughty wealthy women—this is pre-revolution Cuba—waiting with us regarded us with contempt.

When my turn came, we learned we'd been misinformed. Abortions were not legal in Catholic Cuba. And the mighty professor did not do them. Luckily Margie had been there on the same errand with another friend and had the name of the reputed number two ob-gyn man. We got an appointment right away and he agreed to do the operation the next morning.

He was friendly and matter-of-fact. A nurse assisted him in a bright, white, sparklingly clean operating room attached to his office. He gave me sodium pentothal, everything was perfectly safe and hygienic and soon over. That afternoon we flew back to Miami, I feeling crampy and weepy.

This episode, difficult and sad at the time, doesn't loom very large on my emotional horizon. Once in a great while I think about that child, who would have been born in the fall of 1956, but the experience did not interfere with having or loving children. If the embryo felt anything, it was momentary. I'm sorrier for how I behaved toward Norman.

Back in San Francisco I took more time off from work to recover and I have an image of Norman hovering uncertainly at the edge of a small group of my friends in Tilden Park in Berkeley. What did he think? Does he remember? If he remembers me with anger, I don't blame him. A sentence in a 1972 diary evokes a faint memory of my saying, when he asked early on, that I expected "we'd last 6 weeks," the sort of "honest" nasty remark some of us wise guys would make then.

And there was Mother. She paid the doctor, air fares and hotel, adding up to real money. I meant to pay her back but she died before I had any spare cash. She was probably glad to be relied on. I would be! Long after she died, Vickie told me that Mother had had at least two abortions, one before and one after I was born. Mother never breathed a word of this, even as I was agonizing over my own wanted and unwanted embryo. If she really had been through the same trial herself—there is no way to be sure—her silence seems a betrayal, as if only I was confused and wayward enough to make such a mistake.

I don't remember seeing Norman after that afternoon in the park and only hope that he found his way in life at least as well as I have. Unlike many supposedly more interesting men, unlike the more intellectual and sophisticated Fred, he was a good soul and in our brief time together there was no meanness of which he could be accused.

After fourteen months, San Francisco's glamour had worn thin. I disliked the climate, missing the four seasons I was used to. More important, I found it nearly impossible to make friends. There was a feeling of itchiness, as if anyone might up and leave any minute, having arrived—from Des Moines or Chicago or Pittsburgh—the minute before. I'd made one friend: Barbara, another Mount Holyoke alumna, who was at TAF before I came and after I left. But I longed for a place with more history, and so I became one of those who left from one minute to the next. A woman named Jan joined TAF in 1956 and was soon ready to go back east. So in October we loaded up Mother's Oldsmobile and began a moderately eventful trip: the first day a heavy snowstorm at Donner Pass, with cars lined up trying to buy chains; next a blowout as I sped along a speed-limitless Nevada highway; then the remains of another snowstorm at a pass in Colorado, where I had to limp back down to Steamboat Springs with another flat tire. The dutiful daughter, I wrote Mother a postcard or called her every day. "What are you doing?" asked Jan. Her bemusement opened a window just a crack to a region of freedom, where I wouldn't be bound to do everything Mother wanted or expected. It took a while longer, and stronger words from Pierre Grimes, before I dared to assert my independent existence as if I meant it.

Paul stayed on after I left. After a year at Pacific Gas & Electric, he worked for many years for Cookson Company, which made rolling doors; he designed them to fit particular buildings. Although he mostly preferred chess, hiking, and folk dancing to meetings, demonstrations, and political arguments, a passage in a 1965 letter to Robert Hightower shows him in a different light. Living temporarily in a sort of halfway house, Paul,

> faced with a rent increase for employed inmates, has led the fight against the committee, on the grounds that, though they employ an extensive staff, the unemployed residents still sit around all day with nothing to do. I admire him tremendously, for the two things I am worst at when it comes to organizations or meetings is [sic] (1) taking the initiative, and (2) sticking to a minority opinion. (Cowardice is the word for it.)

Paul valued stability, and the company valued him. He was old enough to retire when Cookson moved to Arizona. Meantime he had married, at what then seemed the advanced age of thirty-nine, a lovely divorcée born Norma Knight. They met folk-dancing. She had two daughters, so Paul became a stepfather, later a step-grand- and great-grandfather. He played chess, had his chess problems printed in various publications, and turned jokes into poems. Here are some samples from his privately printed booklet, *Old Jokes for Old Folks.* (Copies available from me.)

SAN FRANCISCO

A man ran down the street so fast his legs began to hurt.
He saw a nun, ran up to her, and hid beneath her skirt.
"I'm hiding from the draft board, ma'm," he told her with a sigh.
Her voice surprised him, it was deep. She told him, "So am I."

If you want something done by him your husband must be told,
"You really shouldn't do this, dear, because you're much too old."

A man went to the doctor and he heard the doctor say
It would be very good for him to walk ten miles a day.
In a week he called the doctor. "I will need advice from you.
I'm seventy miles from home," he said. "So now what should I do?"

Chapter 14
ROBERT HIGHTOWER 1

*O*ne Harvard man became a long-time friend, and connections to his family have outlived him. Our friendship began during the years I was adrift, trying, often with his encouragement and advice, to find both suitable work in a congenial city, and a suitable mate. Psychologist Jeffrey J. Arnett calls these years between adolescence and adulthood "Emerging Adulthood," which he dates to ages 18 to 25. The concept fits my life from 23 to 26, and chapters 13-16 depict roughly these years, seen from different angles, with different players in different places.

In 1954–55, having taken all Harvard's courses on India, I took James Robert Hightower's Chinese and Japanese Literature in Translation. We read the *Tale of Genji*; the *Hung Lo Meng* ("Dream of the Red Chamber")*;* and a good deal of poetry, especially Chinese poetry. The lectures were dry but the readings eye-opening, windows on cultures I knew little about. Producing a term paper proved a major stumbling block, however. I was about to leave graduate school, destination and aspirations totally uncertain. Our household broke up, Pinky returning to Philadelphia, Phyllis off to marry David, with a posh wedding at the Plaza in New York, and I was left in our two-thirds-empty apartment with that unwritten paper. I'd picked my topic: the poet T'ao Ch'ien, but the deadline passed and I couldn't write. (In the newer transliteration system that neither Hightower nor I could get used to, it's Tao Qian. He lived 365–427.) I wrote Hightower an apologetic note, and we met in his office on the top floor of Boylston Hall.

He granted me an extension and asked about the books I had with me. Some were in German, which he knew well, having studied in Heidelberg and taught in Hamburg. We had a lengthy chat and probably began to discover a common ambivalence about Harvard—glad enough to be affiliated with it but aware of not fitting in. (Over the years I've wondered how many people feel they're not really "in" while everyone else is. The manuscript curators believed that the Society of American Archivists gave their concerns short shrift, favoring those of archivists, who in turn felt neglected. When I became a single parent, my children each complained that I loved the other one more. Finally I said: "You can't both be right, but you could both be wrong.")

But in May 1955 that was all in a hazy future. I did write the paper, using many lines of T'ao Ch'ien's poetry in German translation to reinforce my argument about his loneliness. Hightower's comments: "You write clearly but not always elegantly" and an A, which I hope wasn't due to the fact that T'ao Ch'ien was his favorite Chinese poet—which I learned only after producing the paper—and the subject of his 1970 magnum opus.

Late in our lives, Robert, as he preferred to be called, gave me a folder of our correspondence, my letters and carbon copies of his. The exchange began diffidently enough. He asked me to keep in touch, and I wanted to, though I can't say now whether more compelling feelings began that afternoon in Boylston or crept in only later. In late June I wrote to ask if he would serve as a reference in my job search; I was in New York, "investigating foundations, trying to find out what they do, besides Good."

He wrote that I was "an outstanding student," had "a degree of intellectual maturity unusual in a graduate student," was "attractive, quiet," and gave "the impression of self-assurance and competence." Professor Ingalls, who had seen more of me, also showered praise: I had done "work of the very highest excellence" in Sanskrit and "good to excellent work in related fields," and had "great scholarly abilities." More interesting are his observations of me as a person:

> Miss Steiner is rather a shy person, but by no means unattractive. She has a natural sympathy for persons as well as ideas that is very wide, perhaps too wide, for she sees so quickly how other people feel that she is hesitant to push her own claims.
>
> Miss Steiner always struck me as scrupulously honest, in fact as imposing rather Quaker-like morality upon herself. But she

does not expect as much of others…and is an easy person to get on with. Certainly the other students in my department were always fond of her, as I am myself.

I read this long after Dan Ingalls died but was as impressed by his perceptive observation about my "too wide" sympathies (an echo of my refusal to pick a favorite circus act and the worry that having no enemies signalled wishy-washiness) as I was touched by the last four words. He was more than kind to write as he did, when he knew that I wasn't going to do anything serious with what he'd taught me.

By my last semester at Harvard I knew I didn't want to be a scholar, I wanted to do something "real," something that would help people, perhaps, like Anna, teaching small children. I observed a preschool class at Shady Hill School, which had an in-service training program. Beyond its playground was Browne & Nichols School's ballfield[6], not in use when we all went outside at recess. As I wished I were in that quiet field, without the noisy, demanding children, I concluded that teaching little ones was not for me.

Nor, most likely, was social work. One summer I'd tried volunteer work in the slums of Oakland, California. Federal policy then was to help Indians (not yet Native Americans) out of poverty by getting them to settle in cities and become like everyone else. Visiting one or more Indian families, I found the poverty and hopelessness overwhelming. I wasn't sure what to do; the women I visited weren't sure what I was trying to do. This was under the auspices of the admirable American Friends Service Committee (AFSC). I was given little training, so perhaps this wasn't a fair test of my ability, but I'm better at writing checks so that those with the common touch can do the actual work.

Another "real" occupation that appealed to me in theory was farming, but I knew it demands more physical stamina than I had, so I let that go too. Only later did I learn how much modern farming involves tractors, gutter cleaners, manure spreaders, and other machines. So I worked in the library of The Asia Foundation until my love for San Francisco frayed and my dissatisfaction with TAF increased.

Uncertain as ever about my future, I called or visited every organization and agency in New York that had anything to do with Asia. One was a branch, or twig, of TAF, a small office near the UN headed by Lyman Hoover, the ex-missionary Hightower disliked. He was old-school courteous but had nothing to add to my short list of prospective employers. When I said I'd considered the Institute of Pacific Relations (IPR), Mr. Hoover said "Oh, I wouldn't do that." So I took the next bus across town and walked to 333 Sixth Avenue, a Flatiron-style building at West 4th Street that housed the IPR (as well as *The Nation*, the venerable left-wing weekly), and the director, Bill Holland, gave me a temporary job.

I also considered moving to Philadelphia. Visits to Pinky gave that city a certain allure, despite disparaging jokes. (A contest's first prize is a week in Philadelphia. Second prize is two weeks in Philadelphia.) In her apartment near Rittenhouse Square, Pinky's orgone box took up much of the front hall. It resembled an oversize phone booth lined with copper. According to Wilhelm Reich, the Austrian biophysicist who invented it, sitting in the box would improve one's "orgone energy," helping to relieve both individual and societal ills. The FDA considered it a fraud, and Reich landed, and died, in jail.

Pinky's circle of friends included a handsome poet. Sitting on her bed, which served as her couch, drinking Strega, we decided to collaborate on a translation of Rilke's *Rodin*; I would do a literal translation from German, he would redo it in "elevated" English, which I would check for accuracy. The few pages I drafted still exist but the alienation that aborted our romance also killed off our literary project. Just as well: unbeknownst to us, at least one English translation already existed, and decades later a mutual friend told me that this poet was an inveterate womanizer and not a nice person.

Still, entranced with Philadelphia's possibilities, I applied for a job at AFSC. I had done volunteer work at the Cambridge branch as well as in Oakland and admired the Friends' politics and good works, without sharing their religious beliefs. In January 1957 I wrote Hightower:

> [Last week] IPR offered me $10 more a week if I stay on the eve of a one-day trip to Philadelphia, where I was offered a fairly good job in the Information Service of the AFSC but gradually the whole Philadelphia business began to seem a bit outlandish.

All personal considerations point to N.Y. IPR is probably one of a handful of N.Y. offices where a thick skin is not required nor do they suffer from a disease which I'm afraid might be epidemic at the AFSC: enthusiasm.

Despite my professed cynicism, the no-longer-temporary job at the IPR proved quite satisfactory—although living with Mother on 82nd Street did not. The IPR was an *independent* research organization on Asia and the Pacific, focusing on both history and current events. The New York office housed the American IPR and the International Secretariat, with affiliates in various Asian and European countries. The two had formerly had separate staffs, and the office used to be in the classier East 50s, but the IPR had fallen on hard times.

Like the Nature Friends, the IPR was a victim of Cold War witch hunts, in its case (like Julius Hlavaty's) of Senator Pat McCarran's Internal Security Subcommittee. It was considered a major crime to publish works by Owen Lattimore and others who believed the Communists were likely to win the civil war in China—not that they *should* win, only that, with their ways of winning over peasants, workers, and students, and with the corruption and elitism of the Kuomintang, the Communists had a better chance of prevailing. When they actually prevailed, Lattimore et al. were accused of making the US "lose" China—as if it was ours to lose. McCarran had help from J. Edgar Hoover's FBI, which removed massive IPR archives from the Berkshires barn where they were stored and got its tax-exempt status revoked, so that it lost most of the support it had enjoyed from the Rockefeller Foundation and other grant makers, several major Wall Street firms, the author Barbara Tuchman, who had worked for the IPR as a young Barbara Wertheim, and other enlightened rich people.

This was why, by December 1956, when I first set foot in its wonderfully shabby second-floor offices, with barely adequate furniture and big windows looking out on Greenwich Village, the IPR had been reduced to a staff of about half a dozen, nearly everyone doing several different jobs. Ruth Carter, daughter of a founder, was bookkeeper, receptionist, and secretary to William L. Holland, who headed both the American and International IPR, edited both their journals and all the books that emerged from the prodigious research efforts, and organized the international conferences (variously biennial, triennial, or quadrennial). It was Ruth who first showed me into Bill's office.

It's easy to see why, with my left-wing upbringing, this place felt right to me. Not that the IPR was as left-wing as many Nature Friends, but most of its authors and supporters were open-minded and favored truly democratic governments, not the kind of regimes, many virtually fascist, that the US supported in its anti-communist zeal. Much of the work turned out to be congenial. Following Bill's superb example, I learned copyediting and proofreading symbols, and sharpened an eye for clear writing and its opposite. As I wrote Robert,

> apparently my present employers find me a good copy- and proofreader, the reason being that the articles bore me so much that I find the punctuation, by comparison, of absorbing interest. I also take pleasure in deploring, and correcting, the generally clumsy and undistinguished English of all these world-renowned scholars.

(The second sentence was truer than the first.) Soon I was in charge of getting book orders filled, assistant editor of the American IPR's monthly *Far Eastern Survey,* and book review editor of the international quarterly *Pacific Affairs.*

I worked most closely with Bill's second-in-command, Mary Healy, who had the triangular office at the prow of the building. She was one of about a dozen offspring of a Boston Irish family, and was intelligent, witty, and a very good editor. Other staff are now shadowy, except Dorothy Borg, an elegant, serene lady, with her own large office, where she worked on her own large project about the US and Asia in the 1930s. Dorothy sometimes appeared in my letters to Robert. On Nov.1, 1957, she "had given one of her opinions," about the one large table, used for lunches, by researchers, and, once a month, for the *Far Eastern Survey.*

> I was clearing it off for the Survey when she said she thought it was poor public relations to have the table all cluttered up and having someone squeezed into a corner with his research work.

> Which is perfectly true. However, part of the whole process is getting the stuff to the public—which, luckily for her, Dorothy knows next to nothing about—and this requires cluttering the table up with the Survey once a month for a day or two.... Of course both sides are right. She is lovely and exasperating.

Perhaps she was somewhat mysterious as well. On Nov. 19th, I wrote about a phone call for Dorothy, "who was out; a young man who said Please tell her her son called, to which I said Pardon me, and he said I mean, tell her her nephew called. Two minutes later she came back and wanted to know which nephew. More scandal soon."

Alas, the letters report no more "scandal"; I never did find out whether Dorothy was "a woman with a past." But in early October I wrote Robert about a day at the UN with Bill and Mary; it included a session of the General Assembly that bored me and lunch in the delegates' dining room, where I watched Krishna Menon, India's representative at the UN, "spilling his tea" and having "a rather unattractive nap." He was with, among others, "a youngish, blond Scotswoman, and it seems that they are seen together constantly. I was rather amused to hear her say, 'my husband is away just now, unfortunately....'"

Bill had worked for the IPR since 1929, Ruth had grown up with it, Mary too was a veteran, so it was something of a family. The three rented a rambling country house on a hillside in New Milford, Connecticut, a house without running water but a pump just outside the kitchen, a soapstone sink, and a kerosene stove, with large rooms full of comfortable, worn furniture, a wide porch in the trees, and a three-hole outhouse up the hill. We swam in Candlewood Lake, cooked and washed dishes communally, read and talked. Almost like Nature Friends, minus hiking and volleyball.

At the IPR, I dealt with standard office technology: typing, on a manual office machine, those blue mimeograph masters, nerve-wracking because it was hard to make corrections, and at least observing the clacking Addressograph machine, which printed mailing labels. I answered letters, dealt with the printer (a person, not a machine), and learned the whole publication process, from typescript to galley proof to page proof to published work. There was one disaster, a sentence in an article for the

Survey that I changed because I misunderstood the author's meaning. It went to press wrong, and we had to print a correction in the next issue. And one triumph, when I caught an author's mistranslation of a Buddhist term. That was one practical result of two years of graduate study.

I was at the IPR for a year and a half, and two months in the summer of 1959. My weekly paycheck grew to $70, which doesn't sound like much but which was adequate then, and generous for an employer with shrunken income.

Soon after my time there, the IPR had its day in court and was vindicated, but the loss of tax exemption had done it in. In 1960 both the American and the international IPR were dissolved. Ruth went to the Ford Foundation. Bill and *Pacific Affairs* moved to the University of British Columbia, where he initiated an Asian studies program and carried on the journal. Mary followed and started UBC's publications program. All that continued after Mary's departure and Bill's retirement.

To get back to Robert. In New York I was within reasonable reach of Cambridge. We agreed on a visit in July 1957 and he invited me to the house in Auburndale. The three Hightower children—Jamey 15, Sam 12, and Josie 8—were away, and his wife was in the hospital with newborn Tom. We talked, eventually over gin and tonic, and he asked if I could stay for supper. He cooked and we ate, and afterward we sat on a Victorian settee and he put his large hand over mine. This was not sexual harassment. It was what I wanted. Though I chose not to get all I wanted, my feelings, whatever they had been before, were much intensified when I left there that evening, which is why I also wrote about Krishna Menon and his Scottish friend: "I felt quite sympathetic toward them…. I could imagine something similar in Boylston Hall."

The next afternoon I stopped by on my way to New York, wearing a black V-neck tank top, a skirt of green and white plaid cotton, and a narrow red leather belt. Who knows why I recall that outfit so vividly and not what I wore the day before? He was glad to see me again, he said, and the correspondence, between Professor Hightower and Miss Steiner, changed character, his letters as well as mine. My letters compared him favorably with "boys" my age, whom I found wanting, and overflowed with soul searching about our situation and much longing: "[Y]our presence," I wrote from San Francisco in August, "would make pleasant things more so and unpleasant ones less so," and signed off "With all the usual sentiments in great quantities." He wrote about his rustic summer life on Bustins Island in Maine, and that he missed me "frightfully."

Besides all that, and of much longer duration, we shared political views, literary taste, opinions of people and ideas. He always voted Democratic in national races and Republican in Massachusetts races, often for good government types (called Goo-Goos). His candidates, like mine, rarely won. His political history was parallel to mine, though he had been more daring. He described his path to Chinese literature to a young friend in 1997:

> ...in my third year as a pre-med student I walked out of the university [of Colorado], determined to live outside the system and write poetry. I felt liberated, elated. It lasted a week and collapsed into despair when the father of the friend who was my accomplice accused me of corrupting his son and forbade me to see him again. I tried, not very hard, to kill myself and then went back to classes.
>
> On graduation I got as far as Paris en route to China. I had left the States with the resolution never to return; fourteen months later I was enrolled at Harvard as a graduate student in Far Eastern languages. I was still determined to go to China, and then decamp but let myself be seduced by the certain pleasures of scholarship. To assure myself I was not buying into the system, I joined the Communist Party and dutifully attended cell meetings and read Marx. The ideal appealed to me, but economics was boring, and the party members, sincere, humorless, and obsessive, were not very good company. I quietly dropped out with the outbreak of war in 1939.[7]

He made the right decision about his life's work; he was considered a giant in his field.

He seemed much readier to admire female talents and achievements, and to forgive and accept female foibles and shortcomings than those of men. I just about worshipped him, in part the way a little girl adores her father. I even wished his wife dead—before I knew her. When I did, and especially once we Moseleys lived near Boston, in 1963–64 and beginning in 1970, I felt at least as close to Bunny as to Robert. (Florence Cole Hightower was Bunny to her friends; Robert called her Pear.)

Was it a typical case of attraction between professor and student? Robert was hardly the only professor at WGU (World's Greatest University), or at every other college and university, to become entangled with students. While his letters indicate that it was mutual, we were hardly equals. Not only in that my letters were longer and more frequent than his (ostensibly because it was hard for him to find time and privacy to write): I had only vague hopes for my future while he had a wife, children, and a tenured position at WGU. As for the lopsided correspondence: "Robert, I'm very sorry I have been so awful and haven't written (i.e., that I've been as awful for two weeks as you always are)"—a moment of humor among much philosophizing and emotional outpouring. There was no sexual harassment, no quid pro quo (no A or B+ for sexual favors). I was no longer his student and I had presumably earned the A he gave me by doing good work in his course. Sometimes I was glad that, as an Elizabethan song puts it, "all our joys were in our eyes," believing that if I became his lover I could not be a friend of the family; even before I had met them, or had any idea that I might live nearby, befriending his wife and children seemed desirable. "What a smart girl she was to marry you," I wrote of the still-to-me-unknown wife. Later I learned that there were women who managed to be a friend of the family and more-than-friend of Robert.

How much Bunny knew about his outside interests is not clear. He told me that when he left for a scholarly meeting in the Virgin Islands, she joked that he mustn't bring back any virgins. It even occurred to me, and at least one family member concurs, that she might have been glad to be relieved of some of that "wifely duty." Then again, one evening in the 1970s, after one of Bunny's good dinners, I came into the study and was surprised and delighted to see that he had his arm around her.

With Robert there was, I believe, never any question of divorce. When I asked what he was like in his twenties, he wrote, "[at 25] you would have had no trouble in recognizing in me one of those unfortunate boys you keep inveighing against: selfish, cruel (the ruthless cruelty of high idealism), and with a strong instinct for self-preservation." But by the age of twenty-seven, "I had begun to grow up and had begun my interminable career as inadvertent parent." However sincere this ironic view of himself was, he had made a commitment, and, whatever else he did, he saw the family as his responsibility. Was he being dutiful? Was it just loyalty? Propriety? I think not. This is speculation, for no matter what good friends we became, there were certain things that seemed taboo—for instance, *why* the prejudice in favor of women, and did that somehow result from the death of his mother when he was barely two? That event was surely formative, but I doubt he ever delved into his own memories and feelings to trace its consequences in his later outlook, emotional state, or decisions, and I guessed that he wouldn't welcome probing questions about it—or maybe I was just afraid such questions would make him angry. But it seems certain that this family, with its successes and pleasures along with its multifarious troubles, and that house, in which he built, among other things, bookshelves for his hundreds of Chinese books (a rare collection that he eventually sold to a Canadian university), where he cut grass with a push mower, repaired everyone's bicycles, split wood for evening fires, and otherwise kept it liveable, and for many years the house on Bustins Island as well, while Bunny raised the children, cleaned the house, prepared wonderful meals, and wrote wonderful books for adolescents—all that was important enough, even *dear* enough, so that no mere amorous adventure, no matter how enticing or distracting, could ever pull him away altogether.

Chapter 15
CAMP MIDVALE 3:
UNINTENDED CONSEQUENCES

*W*hile writing here, I discovered that Midvale, with its hiking trails, was also the start of a meandering path to my adult life. I'd thought of Midvale as formative but separate—that I'd broken with that part of my life once transposed to Mount Holyoke and beyond. It *was* separate and also linked, like two mountains joined by one trail.

This trail—which explains *why* I wrote about the *Laws of Manu,* studied Sanskrit, worked for TAF and the IPR—begins with a Midvale friend, Dolly, who spent the war years in Norway with her mother before coming to live on Manhattan Avenue with her father, Harry Roth, an ebullient, charming artist. They were German originally. She was pretty, artistic, wistful, and soon attached to Artie, a brilliant sprout of a Brooklyn Jewish family who was studying physics at Princeton, knew Einstein, and was rarely unsure of what he thought, or knew, about anything.

At a party Dolly and Artie gave after Christmas 1950, we played charades and I made an impression—among others on Adam, a high school friend of Artie's—by acting out "snuff." I needed a word that "sounds like" enough and mimed sticking something up my nose and sneezing. I'd just dumped Dan, so meeting Adam, a pre-med junior at Harvard, was timely.

He introduced me to some favorite music: Prokofiev's second violin concerto, Schubert's C Major Quintet, the Archduke Trio. At a botanical garden, he showed me mimosa, which folds its delicate leaves when touched. He took me to the Old Howard burlesque theater in Scollay Square. (Both theater and square were urban-renewed out of existence, along with most of the old West End, in the 1960s.) I was fascinated and repelled, but mainly it seemed sad, for the "girls" weren't terribly talented and the show was dreary.

We visited back and forth, mostly in Cambridge, where girls were allowed in boys' rooms Saturday afternoons. When we were afraid I might be pregnant and it turned out I wasn't, I sent a telegram: "Thy rod hath comforted me, yet my cup runneth over." I was sure the college telegraph operator would catch on but she didn't; earlier she'd made me delete "damn" from a message. (Pinky, worried about pregnancy, would hopefully insert a tampon, calling it "Sending up a trial balloon.")

We each felt some impatience with the other's quirks. He couldn't understand how the sight of some houses made me happy while others depressed me; I was bemused when he was irritated that a concert didn't include any pieces he knew. But such differences in taste and temperament didn't account for the brevity of our affair. Something else was at work, in my psyche rather than his. He was affectionate and attentive and interesting, and infinitely more considerate sexually than Dan. I enjoyed our weekends at Harvard, except one unfortunate outing he planned. Equipped with a single sleeping bag, we took a trolley to the suburbs and looked for a place to camp out. It was hard to find a spot that wasn't someone's lawn, and when we did we had the worst of two seasons: it was cold *and* we were attacked by mosquitoes. We soon retreated to Cambridge, he to his Harvard House, I to a Radcliffe dorm.

We spent a day at Orchard Beach with Dolly and Artie, and a couple of days at Harry's summer house in Kingston. I felt sophisticated and happy to be in love and part of this interesting foursome. Adam and I hitchhiked back, getting a ride with a man from "Joisy City." He stopped for gas and asked for "a quart of erl," the only time I heard someone reverse the two sounds as in the stereotype of Jersey speech.

On a hot summer evening Adam and I walked on the beach and the boardwalk at Coney Island. Without knowing why, I became distressed. Standing under the El, with a train rattling overhead, I vomited and cried, at the mercy of feelings I didn't understand, feeling apologetic toward Adam and alienated from him.

Soon I broke up with him and in retrospect can only guess that it was because he was too good to me. The very qualities I craved—affection, consideration, loyalty—were also the kiss of death, the opposite of what I'd learned to expect from a man. That meant guilt at being disloyal to the first man in my life, and disappointment at not having another chance to make him, in the guise of a younger but equally self-absorbed man, love me. The rest of my life repeated this irony ad nauseam (even without actual vomiting). Either a man attracted me because he was like Father and then frustrated me with his unavailability, or (much more rarely) one attracted me and then scared me off with his un-Fatherlike emotional availability. Dr. L. compared it to Groucho Marx's "I refuse to belong to any club that will accept me as a member." I wouldn't want a man who finds me worth loving—though that is what I do want. I believe Adam was one of the very few who was *not* self-absorbed and unavailable.

That fall a letter came from another inmate of Adam's Harvard House. Joe must have seen me when Adam and I ate in the House dining hall, where the kitchen workers plopped meat, potatoes, vegetables, and dessert into the various compartments of a plastic tray. For this ungracious dining the boys had to dress like grownups; one chap, we heard, wore the required jacket and tie over an undershirt.

I never learned how Joe found me but accepted invitations to visit. No more Radcliffe dorms. He put me up at the Copley Plaza Hotel or the Statler (now Park Plaza). We ate in expensive restaurants and he got orchestra seats for *Oklahoma*. Often we sat in his suite reading Pogo comics. He never touched me.

Joe was studying Sanskrit, wrote bits of it at the end of each letter, and told me about René Guènon, Alan Watts, Ananda Coomaraswamy, and other proponents of what I came to call the One Great Religion: the conviction that all religious or mystical traditions are talking about the same Reality—more real than everyday "reality"—and aiming at the same awareness, calling it enlightenment, satori, nirvana, or whatever. There are many paths up the mountain but all lead to the summit; so says one metaphor for this hopeful view of humanity's varied quest for union (yoga) with the divine. Unfortunately, religions have rarely played a unifying role, more often fighting among themselves at the base of the mountain, or figuring as excuses for war, enslavement, colonialism, and oppression, not least of women.

I began to read Guènon and the others and was soon under their spell, which is why I wrote my honors thesis about the *Laws of Manu*. I accepted the idea that the age and authorship of sacred texts—Vedas, Bible, Koran—don't matter; the texts record eternal verities, not tied to any particular time, place, or culture. This now strikes me as nonsense. It may have served as justification for an anti-Western, inegalitarian status quo, or, more acceptably, for anti-colonialism. When Professor Ingalls said that an Indian author I admired had been part of the anti-British nation-alist movement, I was contemptuous. This had nothing to do with such mundane matters, I thought, but with the search for union with the divine principle underlying what we consider reality, which is really illusion.

Sonia, a Woodbridge friend, shared my views. She was the youngest of five children of a widowed mother. One sister lived next door, in Newton Highlands, with her family; two brothers lived at home; one was my date for a college prom. Later, when she worked in medical labs, Sonia told me about various handsome doctors who actually requited her love but, for reasons she invented for them, couldn't show it. For all I knew, these doctors barely noticed her. Surely our common fatherlessness and the resulting problematic relations with men were a major impetus for our common interest in mystical traditions that see the everyday world as illusory.

Those views figured in my third serious affair. The summer after junior year, I worked at a bank on lower Fifth Avenue. Dick, a Princeton friend of Artie's, invited me for lunch at an elegant French restaurant. I was nervous about impressing this new man, who, having grown up in a Brooklyn Heights townhouse, was used to posh surroundings. We drank one of his favorite wines: Pouilly Fuissé. I'm not sure how I got through the afternoon after that lunch, especially as I wasn't doing so well at my job.

With other summer jobs I'd pretended I wanted a permanent job. In 1951 I'd worked briefly at Electrolux on 42nd Street, in a huge open office with long rows of desks occupied by female clerks. Now and again someone brought a stack of cards to alphabetize, which took a few minutes. The other women happily discussed dates, makeup, clothes, engagement rings, weddings, but I hated the tedium, and when I tried to read, someone exclaimed, "Oh look, she's reading a book." I left after a week and got a job at Blanchard Lumber Company, in a 34th Street office that looked over Macy's to the Empire State Building. I billed and filed and learned about board feet.

At the bank in 1952, I typed letters for a bank officer, and had to retype one to a lawyer because I hadn't addressed him as "Esq." Then I had to type it again because I addressed him as Mr. So-and-so, Esq. You don't use "Mr." *and* "Esq.," a lesson I've never forgotten. My encounters with clerical work echo a definition redolent of its time: a secretary is a woman you teach to spell while she's looking for a husband.

Dick was at Cal Tech that summer. On that first trip to San Francisco we were going via Los Angeles, to visit Lyova. As a bonus, I could see Dick there. Our driver, Max Mollaret, a young Frenchman, had been training at the Waldorf-Astoria and wanted to see the US before joining his family's hotels in Aix-en-Provence. I had just flunked my first driving test: I rolled through a stop sign obscured by a double-parked truck. So Max, capable and mature, did all the driving. We took two weeks to see the Grand Canyon and other wonders. I was often grumpy and impatient. I wanted to see Dick. Max took me aside once and admonished me to be more civil, especially to Mother.

In L.A., Dick and I again ate at an elegant restaurant, driving forty or more miles each way, passing oil wells pumping away among freeways and housing developments. Late in the summer he and Paul drove back east with us. Sitting in back with Dick when Paul was driving, I sang German folk songs; whenever I paused, he asked for more. That was gratifying, and he took me for a successful driving test, along level, wide, unobstructed streets in Brooklyn.

Dick had just graduated from Princeton. Before he started medical school at Johns Hopkins, we had a weekend with his friends at a country house on Bonny Rigg Hill Road, a very Berkshires sort of name, and another at a motel in Williamstown, Massachusetts, for which I bought a dime-store wedding ring; I also wore it in Baltimore, where he looked for a place to live. We stayed at a large downtown hotel; times with Dick, as with Joe, were never shabby. The hotel's bill was made out to "Richard ___ and wf" but I broke up with him, sure that this affair conflicted with my devotion to the One Great Religion, that he would not be in sympathy with my views; when I tried to explain (over another elegant meal), he objected, rightly, that I'd never told him what these views were, so he couldn't agree or disagree. But for some reason that I can't now resurrect, I was sure it wouldn't work. Perhaps another case of Groucho Marxism: despise anyone who finds me lovable.

The trail that began with Dolly led to Adam, then to Joe, thanks to whom it led to Harvard and, after a detour with Dick, to TAF and the IPR, where I met George, who largely determined my life for the next sixteen years. I'd skirted both serious scholarship and immersion in the mystical traditions that had fascinated me. While retaining an interest in Asian literature, politics, and history, I opted for family and work in "illusory" everyday reality.

Chapter 16
1957

$\mathcal{E}$dith, dissatisfied with her marriage to Jack, learned that she could get a quick, cheap divorce in Mexico and invited me to go with her. Flights to Mexico City stopped in Miami, so we spent a few days with Margie; I'd visited her before in Coconut Grove, the Greenwich Village of Miami, and met her more or less bizarre friends. One, also in her twenties, was getting divorced and deciding what possessions to keep. When we met she was agonizing over a box of tools. Not whether she would ever need them. "Do I want to be the kind of person who has tools?" was how she put her dilemma.

On the last night of that earlier visit, Margie and I double-dated with her current boyfriend and alluring Millard Word. My dress by Leslie Morris, the custom designer at Bergdorf Goodman and a client of Mother's, was of lavender chiffon, with matching silk slip and leather belt. My pumps had a lattice pattern on the vamp, the kind Jenny derided as "shoes with a little interest in the front." We dined and danced and drank screwdrivers. (Paul's riddle: What is a Phillips screwdriver? Answer: Milk of Magnesia and orange juice.) That was one reason I felt ill on the next day's flight to L.A. Between New Orleans and Dallas-Fort Worth, in a sky full of thunderheads, we hit an air pocket and the plane dropped sharply, luggage falling off the open racks. I was so shaken that I went the rest of the way by train.

Millard also figured in our 1957 visit. He and his housemate hosted an all-day Sunday brunch, food and dancing preceded by Bloody Marys. While Millard and I danced, his housemate glowered—so said Edith. I was aware only of how attractive and sweet Millard was, even as I pined for Robert. Evidently I could entertain two infatuations at a time (perhaps echoing Poldi and Beppo), while I thought I was monogamous. There was no liaison with either one of course, only mutual warm feelings, to a degree. "If I ever get married, which I doubt," said Millard as we danced, "it will be to you." It was my most interesting proposal—insofar as it was one—outdoing Carlchen's genetically based non-proposal. Millard never did marry but if he were alive (he's not) he could now, wherever gay marriage is legal.

At dusk we all decided to cool off, and sober up, in someone's pool. Edith and I went to get our bathing suits; no one else bothered.

In a letter to Robert, I looked back at Miami from Mexico City, writing sententiously:

> The people I know there aren't quite evil, but they are bad, most of them—Margie is bad to herself, others are bad to each other.... It also made me understand about self-respect.... I sometimes wondered what the use is of saving my self-respect—I may end up with just that and nothing else. But it was clear in Miami that if you don't have the self-respect you have nothing.

The correct conclusion is something I've had to learn over and over again, but I wonder what Margie's friends would have thought about being designated bad but not evil.

Edith had to be in Mexico City for five days; when she wasn't seeing the lawyer, we were tourists. At the cathedral, the devout, praying and lighting candles, still outnumbered us sightseers. At the market outside I bought a sisal bag in multiple bright colors. The words bright and vivid came to mind often. An acquaintance of Dorothy Borg drove us to her house in Tepoztlan and took us to the local inn for lunch. The sky, the flowers, the trees were all bright and vivid. The Mexicans too. In those days a woman here would wear at most two pieces of jewelry, but there women wore as much as their necks, ears, arms, and hands could support, and in public places they stared at us shamelessly—not furtively as one would in the States—most looking amused or disapproving. We were *bollitos*, little rolls, because we were so bland, or *barbaros del Norte*.

We went to a rather dreary bullfight and to a concert. The all-female baroque chamber orchestra sat in a semicircle; both Edith and I had a theoretical crush, for the duration of the concert, on the tall, beautiful conductor. A young man someone had recommended as a guide took us to Xochimilco, the water gardens with their flower-bedecked boats; we found it kitschy but pretended to love it. "If you do ever come here, don't go to Xochimilco," I advised Robert, but was otherwise positive about Mexico.

> There is certainly much more dignity and pride here…, irrespective of economic status. In fact, there are many admirable things. Time flows differently—people move and speak more surely—in five days we saw no baby-carriages, no homosexuals, only one drunkard. But we both realize that we are Americans and have to make our way with television, neuroses, boredom, desperation.

With an effort I can forgive my twenty-five-year-old self for presuming to understand a culture I had known superficially (with almost no Spanish) for only five days, for describing it so awkwardly, and for supposing that television, neuroses, boredom, and desperation were unknown in Mexico. But it's impossible to understand what's wrong with seeing baby carriages or homosexuals, and how I knew we hadn't seen any of the latter. How surprised I would have been if someone could have told me that in 2009 Mexico City would legalize marriage for such non-existent homosexuals.

Edith got her divorce, a major turning point, and flew home. A major turning point awaited me in San Francisco, when I saw Pierre and complained about my life, despite the satisfactory job. In New York, I'd run into an actor I knew from Midvale. When I told him I was back from California and living with Mother, he said, with obvious Schadenfreude, "And you'll be there for the next twenty years." Even if he was being vengeful because I had (mostly) spurned his advances, I feared he might be right. I felt stuck.

I *was* stuck. I couldn't define myself vis-à-vis Mother. Whatever I did or thought of doing, she purported to accept, even approve. Did I suspect then or only later that often she pretended to approve so as not to alienate me? That's not a good way to keep a child's affection. Coming home and finding understanding was comforting, and there was admiration for her wisdom, yet often it was too much of a good thing, like a smothering blanket.

Often I raged against her silently for hours. With hindsight, this rage wasn't just a response to annoying mannerisms, overbearing opinions, or her making plans for other people; surely it was a delayed, unconscious response to the abandoning mother of my early years, who contrasted so sharply with the domineering, clinging person I faced as a young adult. She was more present when we no longer needed a mother, presumably because she, divorced and living alone, needed us, and perhaps it was half-conscious, inept (because unexplained), belated atonement for sending us off to Anna's.

My rage increased when I was most dependent on her. Having my leg in a cast after that bout of water on the knee was maddening; so was Mother. I'd reach for a towel and she would jump up to get it for me. As someone who suffered with a lifelong disability didn't she know that one wants to do as much as possible oneself, to depend on the able-bodied as little as possible?

There was surely extra tension because I was hobbling too, even if temporarily. As if that childish fear had come true: anything short of angelic and I'd end up like Mother and Anna. The anger was again particularly strong as I recovered from the tonsillectomy. Mother hovered, solicitous, ever ready to help even when I could help myself, as she had *not* been when we were little and needed such care from her.

Despite this fury, I never showed my anger or said anything critical. If I had, it could have helped me define what was Eva and what was Isabella. But, like her, I was afraid to arouse anger, maybe afraid of what my rage might lead me to do or say. Better to appear meek and mild and have her accept whatever I did. Need an abortion? She comes along to Havana and pays for it. When I had Dr. Elias fit me for a diaphragm and add it to her bill, I sensed that she (rightly!) thought I should pay for it, but she paid without a word.

"I always thought you would find a roommate and share an apartment," she said after I returned in October 1956. When my Bronx Science friend Ruth found the apartment she occupied lifelong and her roommate wasn't ready to move in, I had a chance to try it. I packed a suitcase. As I bent down to pick it up, I realized it wasn't what I wanted to do. It was what Mother wanted me to do. I stayed at home, comfortable and miserable. But not for twenty years.

I told Pierre that Mother's inevitable but not always genuine acceptance of everything I did felt as if I were being sucked into a morass, limbs struggling with warm, gooey stuff that wouldn't let me go. Pierre urged me to be myself rather than the dutiful daughter. "Stomp on her, kick her in the belly." It sounded cruel, but he was right. Somehow I had to separate myself from her, cruelly if she wouldn't let go.

He didn't mean it literally, of course. How was I to get free? Unintentionally, Mother herself offered an answer. There was *one thing* she couldn't understand: young people living alone. By the time I was back in New York I knew that that would get me out of her apartment and prove to her, and to me, that I could do something she didn't approve of. And it was what I *wanted* to do.

I was lucky to find an apartment for $56 a month when I was earning $70 a week. Number 415 is one in a row of small brick nineteenth-century buildings on the north side of West 56th Street. My place was up one (walk-up) flight, just one small room with two windows, a full-size refrigerator, stove, and sink crammed along one side of the short passage to the normal-size, windowless bathroom, a closet across from the kitchenette. The 57th Street building opposite reflected a pearly light; there were even a few trees. I bought a narrow couch as a bed, a table with folding leaves, shelves to hang on the wall to save floor space. It was too far west to be fashionable, but my phone number began with the fashionable PLaza. I moved in September and after a week wrote Robert:

> There are of course a thousand things to buy or do or clean or call
> the landlord about.... It wouldn't hurt if I was a more demanding
> tenant but that generally is more effort than it's worth. Last week
> I had one lonely day but I have had the identical feeling when
> living with my mother or with other girls.

It wasn't only with Mother that I was meek and mild! With the arrogance of youth, I analyzed "my mother's surprisingly exaggerated reaction," which "seems to show that she is wrapped up in me in an unhealthy way, and it makes me doubly glad that I decided to move out and break all this up a bit."

Furniture arrived, from the Salvation Army and elsewhere. "Wednesday the first batch of Peter's thesis came, and the last pair of curtains went up. I also have chairs now, there is a screen to conceal the kitchen. So I can think less about the apartment and more about the Japanese army." Soon people came for a meal, including Mother. It was glorious to do what suited me—not because it was bad for her but because it was good for me. I was actually a separate person, not an extension of her, nor a doll for her to dress or dancer to live out her dream.

A letter to Robert that fall was about Joe:

> I received a letter from a young man I had just seen in Cambridge: He is in love with me. This is someone I've known for about six years, and I spent my junior year at Holyoke pining for him—he was at least 50% of the reason I took up Sanskrit. Two years ago, he asked me to lend him $30 to get his wife, who had heart disease, out of the hospital. I lent him the money, not ever expecting to get it back—he is rather out of touch about such things. Later, he was divorced and this summer, just two years after this transaction, he told me that his daughter, whom he sees as little as possible, was just two years old. So you can see he is not a good risk. But because I feel vaguely fond of him I foolishly thought maybe I should consider it. When I had my tonsils out, as I got better, I would think about a series of men—the first, when I was feeling most like death, being this one.

I remembered the so-called loan but had forgotten the declaration of love till I saw this letter half a century later. As with Walter, first I'm in love, then he is. It's hard to say which of them would have been more dangerous. The association with dying is realistic, but Joe wasn't out of touch about practical matters; he knew how to find a "soft touch." I got the money from Mother, who was appropriately reluctant but provided it nevertheless.

In 1976 I somehow learned that Joe lived nearby. Out of curiosity, and the old hope that the frog had turned into a prince, or could be made to by me, I wrote him a note, realizing that, in the unlikely event he responded, I probably wouldn't want to have anything to do with him. But he called and I told my diary, "He thought it wd. be fun to get together. I hope so!" We agreed on a Sunday afternoon. Partly sure he wouldn't show up, partly hopeful, I also thought he might bore me. On the "big day,"

> Joe admired the house & we sat in the kitchen & talked for an hour & a half. He has 2 daughters, Sarah 21 & at U.Mass. Boston (loves it, he says) & Kate. He goes to Guatemala on contract to AID now & again, is rather negative about things. I never found out whether he's still married but didn't really care. My mentioning my divorce evoked very little response. About 5 he said he wouldn't take any more of my time, & I wasn't sorry to see him go. So that was that: It was rather boring!!

The alert reader will have noted, as I did then or later, that Sarah was 1955's "heart disease" and 1957's two-year-old daughter. Both Joe and the One Great Religion were safely in my past.

The job at the IPR continued to be interesting and the people mostly congenial, I saw friends and family often, and spent many evenings editing Peter's dissertation. After Christmas I had a party—a good party although it cost me a friend. Charles, whom I'd met in San Francisco, was of no romantic interest but amusing, attentive, and a source of unusual presents, among them a little plastic horse that walked downhill, and a fat dictionary I gave away as too big for my unsettled life.

Charles appeared unpredictably. He had once called at 2 AM, from a ship on the DEW (Distant Early Warning) Line, stations and ships near the Arctic Circle meant to warn of a Soviet attack.

> Charles: Hello, Eva. It's Charles Smith. I'm on a ship on the
> DEW Line. Over.
> Eva: Oh, what a surprise.
> Pause. Charles: You have to say over when you're done talking.
> Over.
> Eva: OK. Over.

I really wanted to say, "Do you know what time it is, for Christ's sake? Over."

He made himself memorable again, appearing early for the party before I was dressed. There was nowhere for him to wait, so I asked him to come back in an hour. He returned much later. When he saw that my sixteen guests and I were playing charades, he left in disgust. I never saw him again.

Early in 1958 my life changed again, so that I gave up my little apartment after barely six months, admitting to myself that I wouldn't have been happy living there alone for long. But as a first step beyond Mother's too-warm embrace, it was just what Guru Pierre prescribed.

V.

Coming Together

Chapter 17

1958

Soon after Bill Holland, Mary Healy, and Ruth Carter left for Lahore for the IPR's last international conference, a letter came from a man with experience in Asia who needed a job. I replied that there were no openings but I'd make sure Mr. Holland saw his letter. Soon he appeared and talked about a job and a soon-to-be-published article. I didn't tell him I had the only job that might suit him. Then I resumed working, editing Peter's dissertation, and living on 56th Street.

Ten days later, George Van Horn Moseley III came back. "There's something I forgot to ask: Will you have dinner with me?" I made him wait a week. On Monday, February 3rd, we dined and danced. He was a good ballroom dancer; I was stiff and awkward, as I hadn't been with others. He didn't mind, or didn't notice. When we left the restaurant and walked to the subway, it was snowing peacefully. He kissed my cheek.

I agreed to see a Chinese opera that Saturday. Then he called Friday: Could I have dinner that night? He had something to tell me. No, I had to edit. He persisted and I gave in.

We sat at a table for two, very close to two other tables for two, as he told me, in an almost accusatory tone (as the song has it, "You made me love you; I didn't wanna do it"), that he had fallen in love with me and wanted to marry me. I was flattered but annoyed at feeling rushed.

He didn't demand an immediate answer; he wasn't *totally* unreasonable. On Saturday, going shopping with Phyllis, I complained, "Some guy comes down from Vermont and decides he wants to marry me. What does that have to do with me?" Years later I met a woman who had married a man who threatened to kill himself if she didn't marry him. George's insistence was less extreme, but ten years later he told me that if I hadn't agreed pretty quickly, he would have been gone. True or not, it hurt—as intended.

The Chinese opera was exotic and tedious. I found the high-pitched singing, the stiff striding about on thick-soled shoes—the higher the wearer's status, the thicker the soles—ludicrous and annoying. My views were so negative that I said nothing. George was anything but ebullient. "That's that," I thought.

He took me home and I must have invited him in, for we sat up talking till the wee hours, as the heat went off. I have *no idea* what we talked about, who said what, but am 99 percent certain that I did most of the talking. Soon I was sure I wanted to marry him. It was a 180-degree turn, from being unable to imagine anyone I could want to marry (except Robert?) to feeling already married to this stranger.

How could this be? Surely subconsciously I recognized my father in another guise. Yet I "counted the ways" he was *not* like my father, aware that I was likely to be attracted to an equally poor choice as husband and father of any children. George, having made his precipitous proposal, probably felt he needn't do more, and he was right. It was barely two weeks since we'd met, our third date. But I was *so sure*. He wanted to go to bed right then, but I asked him to go and come back another time, as if just *one* abstention would be proof of love and maturity. He left early Sunday morning and called that evening to ask if we could have lunch Monday. "Yes, and can you come over now?" I was evidently almost as impatient as he was.

George was an Army brat, the second son of Van and Kay: George Van Horn Moseley, Jr., a retired colonel, and Katharine (Payne), socialite and artist. His older brother Henry was a career officer, the third generation at least to graduate from West Point; his sister Kathy was ten years younger. George chose the University of Colorado, purposely putting many miles between himself and his family then living at "The Farm" in Vermont, and graduated with a degree in Chinese history and an ROTC commission. He did a stint at Ranger School and a tour in Vietnam, where he worked for Colonel (later General) Edward Lansdale. He and Lansdale were frustrated by US policy, which ignored the "democratic center," considering only the extremes: Ngo Dinh Diem's faction as friends (or puppets), Ho Chi Minh's as enemies. After the time he owed the Army, he worked for Lansdale—whom he admired, even adulated—as a civilian, traveling in Vietnam and Laos, writing reports for Washington that he was sure nobody read.

For much of 1957 he lived at The Farm and worked on a novel about his junior year in Japan during the Korean War, when Van rejoined the Army and Kay and Kathy lived in Tokyo. George went to university there and fell in love with Japan and with two women. One was Betty, daughter of a Chinese dealer in Chinese antiques, and the mistress of Gene, an American with a family and an import business in New York, who was often in Tokyo buying antiques.

When winter came, the other Moseleys left and George had little time to write, having to chop firewood and, he said, hunt small animals for his supper. So he came to New York, rented a room, and did some job hunting while writing the novel and getting a book of youthful poems published by a vanity press: *A Student's Quest*, by Tom Austen. The pseudonym honored his favorite grandfather, "Uncle Tom" Payne (Kay Moseley's father, head of the Reed Candy Company), and grandmother, Alice Austen Moseley (Gadgie). George hoped to make money with the book but, instead of sending an announcement to everyone he knew, he sent everyone a copy of the book. So sales numbered zero.

He came that night and we did have lunch Monday. His hand over mine, he said, "We're going to be very happy." Was there a hint of "And that's an order"? Was he reassuring himself as much as me, hoping more than predicting?

We had some common interests and inclinations: interest in Asia, fairly similar political views, love of the outdoors, though enjoying it in different ways, often the same reactions to particular people. But as the years went by I often felt we clung together, two lost children in a hostile world (as I'd felt with Norman), which seemed unhealthy. Partners can look obsessively at each other, or side by side out at the world. We achieved the latter only now and then.

He was born on September 6, 1931, Labor Day weekend; his parents were having a party. When George appeared, did Kay feel—even think or say—"I already have a boy. I wanted a girl"? The party, and that she wanted a girl, were part of Moseley family lore; the rest is speculation.

George's only fixed home was The Farm, where he rarely lived.

He and Henry were probably raised largely by servants (in China in 1935–36, an amah), while his parents led an active social life with other officers and their wives: Kay, beautiful and vivacious, watching Van play polo, or with Van watching others play polo, followed by parties with plenty of liquor. One story had little George getting his head stuck between two bedposts as his parents were about to go out. An amusing incident, or a child's clumsy attempt to keep his parents at home?

Another telling moment: as Kay's mother, Grace Goldsborough Payne, known as Mama, and I leafed through an album, she fixed on a photo of Henry and George as small boys sitting on a stoop with a couple of dogs. "Oh," she exclaimed, "they were such cute dogs." Not a word about her only grandsons.

Even after decades of Moseley time, I can't claim to understand this family. But bits of George's early history fed my conviction that he was a black sheep. He may even have used that term himself. In that family I *wanted* him to be a black sheep. I also believe that what I learned about George's early years—and probably much I didn't learn—helps explain the cracks in our marriage, at first barely visible fissures that eventually widened into a gulf. Partly, while pursuing adult pleasures and responsibilities, we *were* two lost children clinging together. But back then I ignored any signs of trouble, expecting to continue to be happy.

Because I felt so thoroughly married to him already, when I packed to move to our new apartment, sure I was finished with that old life, I threw away my Bronx Science yearbook and a shoebox of letters from friends—interesting, amusing letters from interesting people, some of them dear friends. It was an irrevocable mistake that I learned to regret. When I became a manuscript curator, in charge of many collections of letters and other private records, I told those with papers: "You can always throw them out, but once you've thrown them out you can never get them back."

We went to visit friends of his on Long Island, and dined and danced at the Savoy Plaza, where I introduced us to the bandleader, father of a Woodbridge dorm-mate, whom *The New Yorker* dubbed "the scintillating Irving Conn." We spent a weekend in Northfield, Vermont, so I could meet his parents. Van was commandant of students at Norwich University. His mother, Gadgie, lived there too. I soon saw why she was

George's favorite grandmother. She made me feel welcome while Kay and Van were lukewarm, perhaps because they weren't getting along.

The next time we saw Kay, Van had thrown her out, so that weekend was the only time I saw them together. I was cold and nervous, with them and when skiing with George, who was good at it and enjoyed it; I wasn't and didn't. The visit made me realize, as I tried to explain to him, that he came from a social stratum with some control over its own fate and over that of the "lower" classes and the country as a whole—unlike us Steiners and Zetlins.

I believe Kay wasn't sure how to feel about me. Mount Holyoke and especially Radcliffe (she'd wanted George to go to Harvard), which had given me some contact with members and enclaves of the ruling classes, probably made a slightly bigger plus than the minus of Jewishness. Besides, George had considered marrying a Chinese woman (the other flame in Tokyo?). Jewish was preferable to that!

I wanted George and *my* friends to meet too and suggested dinner with Ruth and Edith. He wasn't going to eat out with three women. This was a clue to how rigidly tradition-bound he could be, but I didn't protest, although down deep I thought his objection stupid. Early on, when we disagreed about what a wife should or shouldn't do, I often agreed that he knew better. But why? He was only three months older and, although he'd "been around," so had I.

The IPR staff had a party for us and as a wedding present gave us a pendant on a gold chain—really a present for me. George was right to take offense. It was probably Mary Healy's doing: when Mitzi, a previous incumbent of my job, left to marry Bernie, Mary asked, "Do you have to get married? Can't you just be friends?"

Mother was in California visiting Paul; we agreed to marry when she returned in late February. It's hard to understand what the hurry was, but it seemed urgent, to George especially. Hoping for something better than City Hall, we met with Algernon Black, director of Ethical Culture. "What are you going to teach your children about religion?" Black asked. "Nothing," George replied. "It's children of people like you who become Catholics," Black warned. This struck us as another kind of intolerance.

Instead we got an appointment with a judge at the Old County Court Building for Friday morning, February 28th. Gene, to whom I took an immediate dislike, Ruth, and Mother made up the entire wedding party. Mother had returned Wednesday night; Thursday we bought turquoise wool fabric and she made me a suit, which, unlike the typical wedding dress, I could wear on other occasions. Friday was rainy. When we got to the judge's chambers, he was at a funeral and wouldn't return till afternoon. So we had lunch first and some of us had drinks and were a bit fuzzy for the wedding. The judge had us married in a few minutes, mispronouncing Moseley. City Hall couldn't have been more perfunctory. But I was duly and truly happy.

Sunday I wrote Robert:

> Most of my friends are amazed at the speed with which it all happened, but what amazes me is its perfection. We seem to have everything either of us ever hoped for in a marriage, and then some—though neither of us really felt confident that anything like it was possible. For the first time I feel completely a woman—I'm neither his little girl nor his mother, but entirely his wife. Also I think for the first time I have had a clear perception of the divine and free both in another person and in myself. I know that we are now both our age, and ready to live an adult life. I always wanted an "older man" in the sense that I wanted him to have been through a little of the purifying fire and to have come out all right. But then, only last year, I suddenly realized that what was even better was to grow with someone. I got both. When we met, we were both just about ready to begin a new life, having both just about reached the end of the tether with the old.

After describing how we met and our few dates, I continued this now embarrassing effusion:

> There were at least two things that I had come to think would probably be inevitable and I had better get used to them. One was that I would have to be the more active and confident. But clearly he saw the whole thing first, and it was he who made sure that I

saw it. The other thing was that I expected at least an occasional twinge that, as you once put it, I was "throwing myself away." But there has been nothing of the kind, not since I made up my mind. In general I feel that we deserve each other perfectly, and occasionally, when, as he does again and again, he surprises me with his wisdom and strength, I feel a kind of awe and admiration for him and am terribly proud to be his wife.

Without doubting my sincerity, I wonder what he said or did to surprise me in such a wonderful way and how I knew that he too saw our marriage as perfection; and, again, I doubt he "made sure that I saw it," but believe I talked myself into it. I do acknowledge that he *was* wonderful in many ways, and there was a good deal to this marriage, despite those fissures.

He was intelligent and articulate, and disciplined in a way I'm not: wanting to learn Chinese, he got a book and worked at it, without instructors or courses. He could be fun too, yet a certain awkwardness often remained between us. Driving home from a square dance years later, I was inspired to sing folk songs but, sure he wouldn't listen, sang under my breath. Was I right to assume he wouldn't appreciate them as Dick had back in 1952? Then again, George had no interest in watching or hearing about team sports. That was a relief, though hardly of primary importance. More significant was that, as I continued to work at the IPR, when over supper I told him of doings at the office, he often didn't listen. This hurt and, deep down, made me angry. After all, it wasn't any old office but one where he had supposedly hoped to work.

Choosing an apartment was also problematic. Instead of one George liked in a 96th Street brownstone I preferred one in a bland modern building, 312 West 23rd Street. It was the first of several times I chose, in effect, Anna's new, antiseptic place over my parents' older building, the one with character. Much later I speculated in my diary: "Thinking about apartments: 96th St. vs. 23rd St., my choices were always the sunnier, boxier places & I can see now that I was afraid of what would go on in the others. I felt resentful at Anna's but perhaps safer?" (This was true only when we chose places to live together, not when I did so on my own.) From 312 I could walk to work. It wasn't a good neighborhood for trees and grass, but we didn't live there very long.

We had a jolly party to celebrate a month after the dreary wedding. Nearly everyone we knew in New York came. Uncle Rudi demonstrated skiing moves and otherwise amused our friends. Kay came alone from Vermont. We prepared refreshments ourselves, he the drink, I the food. I bought a wheel of blue cheese, four inches high, six in diameter. Our guests consumed barely an eighth, so wherever we went for the next two months I took a wedge along and left it behind. Four decades passed before I looked at blue cheese again. George drank too much and I had to drag him to the bedroom, which he firmly denied ever after.

I hadn't met his siblings yet but one evening Margaret Goldsborough— Kay's maternal aunt, a "maiden lady" who lived in Baltimore on inherited money, traveled and visited—treated us to dinner at the Tudor City Hotel. Large and jolly and friendly, she explained why she frequented Vermont, that "the Jews had come and ruined New Hampshire," where she used to go. "Aunt Margaret, Eva is Jewish," George said quietly. Oh well of course she didn't mean me, and she may have claimed having Jewish friends.

In the fall of 1960, General George Van Horn Moseley came to New York and George met him for lunch. We had a baby girl, so I couldn't join them, a missed last chance as he died that November. (In response to our birth announcement, the General, father of three sons, had sent a *blue* baby blanket.) When George told him I'm Jewish, the general did actually say, "Some of my best friends are Jews."

His ex-wife Gadgie regarded both Jewish and Polish Catholic grand-daughters-in-law as welcome additions to the family. Having admired the fine young Army officer she first met in the Philippines, Gadgie divorced him in the 1920s—although then and later wives were *said* to initiate divorces to protect their reputations, even when divorce was entirely the husbands' wish. The General remarried; Gadgie did not.

General Moseley figured so prominently in Joseph W. Bendersky's book, *The "Jewish Threat": Anti-Semitic Politics of the US Army*, that the review in the *New York Review of Books* led off with a summary of a Moseley speech, in which he insisted that, to protect good American stock, Jewish refugees should be admitted only if they agree to be sterilized before leaving for the US. He didn't hate individual Jews but abhorred "the Jew" because

148

Jews are not loyal citizens. That was how an anti-Semite could have Jewish friends. (He thought "the Negro" a loyal American but not a good soldier; that "he" runs when the fighting gets too rough.)

He was a hero among some on the loony right. Max Wallace, in *The American Axis,* described a plot "to seize the White House and place [him] … in the Oval Office as a military dictator" (a plot the General may not have known about). The day he retired from the Army, he declared that "The Roosevelt administration …was manipulated by the 'alien element in our midst,' [and in 1939, that] 'The war now proposed is for the purpose of establishing Jewish hegemony throughout the world.'"

The General was hardly the only prominent person who welcomed Hitler's program to destroy what they considered undue, dangerous Jewish power. According to Albert Lee's *Henry Ford and the Jews*, Ford, famously anti-Semitic, "refused to build aircraft engines for England while building five-ton military trucks for [Hitler's] Germany."

George's defense was gratifying (although in my presence he had to say something), and would have been reassuring had I thought reassurance necessary, but I was convinced he rejected his family's reactionary views and that my being Jewish was neither here nor there. Years later he admitted that, at the job interview at CARE, he said we had both come to New York to get married, so the interviewer wouldn't think I was a New Yorker—as if most New Yorkers were Jewish. It's unlikely that the interviewer would share this convoluted reasoning. (Much later, when I surmised that an elderly gentile New Yorker believed that most New Yorkers were Jews, I headed off any anti-Semitic remarks by saying innocently: "When my family and I arrived from Vienna in 1939 ….") At about the time George admitted this, I told him some of the horrors I was reading about in a history of the Jews; he said he'd like to see such a history by a non-Jew. So my Jewishness *was* a problem for him. But that wasn't apparent (to me) in 1958.

CARE hired George. He called me at work: we were going to Macao. *Where?* I found it on a map of China, and with mixed feelings packed up things to take and things to leave, for my first trip abroad, save the brief ones to Cuba and Mexico, since immigrating in 1939. Knowing George barely four months, I was about to accompany him to the proverbial ends of the Earth.

Chapter 18

VERMONT

"*W*hen are we going to get to Vermont?" asked a small voice from the back seat as we drove from Plainfield, Vermont, to Grafton, Vermont. To Jessica and Tommy, then eight and seven, Vermont had always meant The Farm, the brick house in the hills between Grafton and Chester, and its many acres. In 1933, Van and Kay visited Mrs. Moseley, as Kay Moseley called Gadgie, at her house in Townshend. They went for a drive, saw the old brick house for sale, with its ramshackle outbuildings in its secluded valley, and bought it. To George, this was *home*, in his childhood of Army bases and for the rest of his life.

I first saw Vermont in 1948, when we drove across it from the White Mountains to the Adirondacks. It was nearly ten years before I set foot there again, with my soon-to-be husband, and then it became one of the points of my compass, even if not magnetic north as it—The Farm especially—was for George. "Birches are white only in Vermont," he told me more than once. Forget it, you who love Maine or Canada or Russia; you only *think* birches are white there.

The Farm sits west of Old Stage Road[8]. An old photo shows open fields, stone walls, and an inn in the notch between two hills west of The Farm; now it's mostly woods. Behind the house, across a field—or mowing, as some Vermonters called it—and a small brook, were the remains of a sugarhouse, where the Moseleys made maple syrup, using a horse-drawn sleigh to collect the sap in wooden buckets hung on trees along Sugarhouse Road, a rough track lined with maples. Kay called The Farm Highclere. George more aptly called it Hedgehog Hollow.

Old Stage Road is still a narrow dirt road off Route 121, which in 1958 was also unpaved. One of the few neighbors was Fred Thomas, a lean, leathery bachelor who left Vermont only once, to go "across the water" in World War I. His place was like a park; he mowed with a scythe even around trees. He drove an ancient Ford, used a wood stove for cooking and heat, and in winter kept a toilet seat by the stove to take to the outhouse. This wasn't indulgence: when George and I went to the closed-up Farm on a wintry night and I took a pan out of the cupboard, my fingers stuck to the icy metal; given a little time, it will pull the epidermis off. Fred was often at The Farm, chugging up the driveway in his Model T, advising about chores and building projects, and often staying for dinner, sometimes bringing an animal he'd shot.

This was my first encounter with hunting and private guns; far as I knew, Nature Friends didn't hunt. Kay too was a good shot. One day in the early 1960s she spotted a porcupine up in the elm next to the house. She got out the shotgun and let fly. The beast fell to earth, scattering barbed quills all over the lawn, where Tommy was crawling and Jessica running barefoot. When they were older, George taught them to shoot.

Between The Farm and Fred's place is Potato Hill, its determinedly rustic house built by Ted Steele and Eric Hawke, who lived in Darien, Connecticut, and commuted to New York, where Eric worked for Standard Oil and Ted taught at Columbia. (After Ted, who was divorced and had a daughter, died, Eric, to my surprise, married a woman.) This "odd couple" entertained at Potato Hill every summer Saturday night. The menu never varied, roast beef and Yorkshire pudding at its center. Nor the drill: drinks (outdoors if the bugs weren't too bad), dinner, then songs around the piano followed by hymns around an organ, echoing Friday singing at the table at Mount Holyoke.

One evening Ted and Eric, in their hale and hearty voices, told us guests that they had totted up what Potato Hill cost each year, entertaining included. They surely didn't mean to be rude, but I thought it odd to lump the whiskey and roast beef they invited us to consume with their taxes, repairs, and utility bills. Or odd to tell us about it.

(We had another taste of WASP frugality on a bright, cold January day when we and our two toddlers visited a couple George knew. After coffee on arrival, nothing—for the grownups anyway—during hours of talking, walking, and playing in the snow. At sunset our hostess finally retrieved supper from the fridge: four large tomatoes stuffed with tuna salad.)

151

Kay entertained often, once serving a raccoon or woodchuck cooked up by Katherine Wright, another local friend. It was tough and stringy. More often we had a steak, with much to-do about grilling it over apple-wood in the fireplace in the old cellar kitchen.

The tug between generosity and frugality afflicted the Moseleys too. I understand Kay's ambivalence—wanting company, and peace and quiet; liking to feed people, yet relishing solo meals; wanting to provide delicious meals, yet worrying about the cost. But once this ambivalence had rather odd consequences. George started a fire before Kay returned from garden club and we took the chicken meant for supper out of the fridge. It had been dead too long, so George buried it. When Kay came home and heard what he'd done, she was so suspicious that she dug it up.

Good cook that she was, Kay rarely got an entire meal on the table at once. Usually the potatoes lagged behind, as Kay—it being drink time—put away a double bourbon or two. As we sat down amid noisy talk and raucous laughter, she gave conflicting orders: eat before it gets cold; wait for the potatoes. At Thanksgiving at her Washington house in 1969, she had us eating turkey as she continued to produce other dishes. She made a point of the heirloom table linen. Her friend Richard, tackling a drumstick, wiped his fingers on his napkin. "Well," she snapped, "if you're going to get it greasy...," as she snatched it away and gave him a paper napkin.

Kay had met Richard in Mexico. She spent winters there or on Spain's Costa del Sol, painting and socializing. Richard was the black sheep of the family for which Hastings Law School was named.[9] A debonair, amusing but rather sad Anglophile, he loved horses, bet at the track, drew and painted horses and burros endlessly. His mural of a Mexican town with burro dominated the downstairs bathroom at The Farm. There is a persistent echo of his exasperated "Oh, Katharine!" They seemed to thrive on mutual irritation.

Richard and I discovered a common interest in Zen, long before most Americans had heard of it. Or I *thought* it was a common interest, till he explained that he used Zen to get the numbers on the horses. He probably never won, Zen or no Zen.

On that Thanksgiving trip to Washington, George and the kids and I visited Mount Vernon. There was an omission then that has since been corrected. The outbuildings: smokehouse, washhouse, and so on, did not include slave quarters. The next time we were at The Farm, over dinner George referred to the absence of slave cabins as a rewriting of history. "Well, of course they had slaves." Kay vehemently missed his point. "You don't think George and Martha did their own work." And she went on in this vein until George said, quietly, accurately but tactlessly, "Mother, you're drunk."

She went after him and there was a scuffle. Henry kept them apart so there were no black eyes, but the invisible bruises took a while to heal. As we four left to drive back to Gadgie's house, where we were staying, Kay followed us. "Goodbye, Jessica," she called out, "I'll probably never see you again."

After another good dinner, Henry lit into Shakespeare, how much he hated this or that play. Then, with barely a pause, a similar tirade against Gilbert and Sullivan. Aside from all being Brits, what did the three have in common? I suspect it was that Van, who taught English at West Point and later elsewhere, admired both the Bard and G&S and had been enthusiastic about both, which could be enough reason for his first-born son to detest both.

Van, out of the picture since he ordered Kay out of the commandant's house in Northfield, was fair game. I never learned what the problems between them were, nor what had kept them together, but they clearly had one thing in common. In 1958 they owned The Farm and *two* houses in Houghtonville, a small cluster of houses where Old Stage Road leaves Route 121. One was once a general store. The other has an attached barn, where George showed me the top of a wood stove, which had, with repeated freezing and thawing, sunk inch by inch into the dirt floor. Neither Kay nor Van could resist an auction or a bargain. Both were plentiful then, as other farms, like The Farm, went under.

From those auctions they brought home many wonderful heirlooms for their offspring—until then other people's heirlooms—and more *things* than they had room for, which meant buying more houses to put things into. The barn at The Farm was jammed full of wagons, sleighs, tack, farm tools. Wooden wheels hung everywhere. Luckily, after Kay got The Farm in the divorce settlement she found someone to buy all that before the sagging old barn caved in. From George I learned that you have to

At The Farm, July 4, 1963. *(Surname Moseley unless stated otherwise.) Back row,*
L to R: Isabella Steiner, Margaret Goldsborough (Kay's aunt), Kay, Richard Hastings, Henry,
Kathy, Grace G. Payne (Kay's mother), George; middle row: Helen (Henry's first wife), Eva,
Fred Thomas; front row: Noel, Jessica, Holly, Henry Jr., Kathy with Tommy. (Kathy, Henry Jr.,
Holly and Noel were children of Henry and Helen.)

keep the roof in good repair, or water gets in and rots the beams and posts. But Kay was away winters and had much else to attend to.

Her yards and yards of flower beds, for instance. She was a talented and determined gardener. Someone gave her a very small azalea in a flowerpot. She set it out some yards from the kitchen and reminded us endlessly that azaleas like acid, so the unpromising little shrub was fed coffee grounds and tea leaves, always with her admonition about acid soil. Last I saw it, that shrub measured seven or eight feet in each dimension and was a blaze of orange when it bloomed. Kay knew what she was doing, in the garden and also in improvements to the house, which she accomplished without changing its nineteenth-century-farmhouse character. I used to worry in what respects, in marrying me, George had married his mother. As a kid I kept mentally rearranging my room; in Midvale I took old pots and dishes to an island in a brook where I planned to build a hideaway; and I still enjoy planning renovations, though not as endlessly as Kay did.

Kay was impatient, outspoken, irreverent. She sometimes took my children visiting; as they left one friend's house she admonished them—before giving them a chance to speak: "Say 'Thank you,' damn it." After Van divorced her, and again after Richard died, she lived alone at The Farm for weeks or months on end. The family had lived there year round after World War II and she had friends all over southern Vermont. So she had visitors and was often out socializing or shopping, but many days and nights she was there alone. She worked for pay only one year, after her separation from Van, in a Washington lamp and shade shop, but gave that up in favor of gardening, sewing, and remodeling The Farm. She painted landscapes and portraits, fixed things, and was the center of a family of her three children, seven grandchildren, a few step-grandchildren, and eventually nearly a dozen great-grandchildren. Long after Kay died a cousin told Jessica that Kay had wanted to be an architect but her parents wouldn't hear of it. If that's true, it could explain much about the sort of person she became, and it makes me feel less critical, and more sympathetic.

The first time I saw The Farm was late that spring of 1958. We had been married two months when Van threw Kay out and she retreated to Houghtonville. We drove up to see her in Mother's Oldsmobile, my first encounter with Vermont mud. On parts of Route 121 the mud was a foot or more deep. As we approached each mire, George floored the accelerator and the car bounced wildly between high snowbanks. There were no seatbelts then and it was frightening, but the car neither sank in the mud nor lodged in a snowbank.

We walked through snow a foot deep on unplowed Old Stage Road so I could see George's beloved Farm. Mostly he commiserated with Kay. I felt remote from her and her trauma, which must have reminded me of my parents' divorce and my emotional paralysis. Kay had been sending us things that vexed me. I thought a rug not the thing to send to a daughter-in-law whose taste one doesn't know yet, but what irritated me most was an overcoat for George, as if telling me that she still needed to take care of him. Not that it was a special overcoat, except in being a bargain—and I gloated inwardly when he looked like a waif as, too big, it hung forlornly off his shoulders. The rug was a bargain too, and looked it.

If I barely saw The Farm on this first visit, I saw more than enough of it later. It has its charms, but there was almost nowhere to walk except the road, places to swim were miles away, Kay was always gardening, visiting, or running errands, George fixing or building, till drink time, and that—as I pointed out to him—was often with people we didn't care about or even disliked. There was no electricity then, which meant reading and sewing by kerosene lamp.

No electricity also meant that one summer I had to wash one hundred diapers a week by hand. A feminist scholar researching the history of housework claimed that modern household appliances haven't saved labor because, as machines improved, standards of cleanliness went up so women had to work just as hard as before. Having washed those hundreds of diapers in a soapstone washtub with no tool but a scrub board (and the sun to bleach out stains), I see the washing machine as a true labor-saving device, despite expectations for ringless collars and clean overalls.

The Moseleys could have had electricity brought in free under the New Deal's Rural Electrification Administration, but Van wouldn't have it. The once and future English professor was writing a novel. We found heaps of soggy typewritten pages in the ruins of the sugarhouse; a rusty Royal "office machine" still sat forlornly on the equally rusty evaporator twenty years after Van died. He wouldn't have electricity because, when the crew came to The Farm to shoot scenes for a movie based on his Civil War novel, electric poles would spoil the setting.

Not that I ever heard this reasoning from him; it was a Moseley family anecdote. (Gadgie told us another family story: when Van and his younger brother Francis were boys, she once found Van's to-do list. Number 1: Kill Francis.) Van wrote elaborate letters but perhaps wasn't good at fiction. At any rate, there never was a finished novel, and often no wood for the furnace till Van, or George or Henry, went out and chopped some. (Last year's wood burns much better than new wood.) Cars broke down. Horses were gone by 1958, but Mama and Aunt Margaret were scandalized—still buzzing about it years later—at the way Van kicked and swore at the horses.

He was a martinet with the boys too. After they mowed the lawn, they had to crawl around the edges and clip every last blade by hand. George liked Kent School—one of his several secondary schools—because sheep were the lawnmowers there. (And because he could substitute farm work for team sports.) He'd learned a lot about country living—and I from him and from Kay. He built a car out of the remains of a Dodge and a Buick and called it a Buidge. I lobbied for Dodgick, liking its Russian sound, but no one paid attention. He spent the summer of 1959 building a shed almost single-handed, with beams and boards from the late barn. It held our furniture when we lived abroad, and was long there, sturdy and weathered and nestled in the landscape. Later he spent many days reopening the old woods road to the notch where the inn had been.

George was proud that he could fix or build a car or a house, that, while doing academic work, he knew carpentry and other manual trades. Other academics, especially in Britain, looked askance when they learned of these déclassé skills—but I admired them even if such work sometimes took him away from the family. He was usually happier working solo on his woodsy track up the hill than hiking or playing with the rest of us.

He did take us along to Vermont though, unlike my father, who often went to the mountains without us. When we lived in the Bronx, on many a Friday, I had dinner ready and the kids ready to go to The Farm when George came home from work. We'd leave late evening and George would tear up the Taconic Parkway. Once a state trooper stopped us for speeding. As he started to write a ticket Tommy, a few months old and asleep on his tummy in his car bed wedged in behind the driver's seat, woke up, raised his head, and smiled at the cop, who relented and just admonished George not to endanger his family. Tommy always woke up smiling.

We'd put the kids to bed at The Farm after midnight. George and Kay would have a drink and catch up on news and gossip; I'd try to stay awake and not feel left out. It was only when we lived in Plainfield, our own corner of Vermont, that I began to develop real affection for that beautiful state, of which the beautiful but problematic Farm is after all only a very small part.

VI.
Travels With George, 1958-70

Chapter 19
MACAO, 1958–59

As George fished out his wallet at a store on 23rd Street, he laid his book, *Teach Yourself Chinese*, on the counter. "Is that possible?" asked the cashier. It was for George, being disciplined and as a child having learned "gutter Chinese" in the streets and servants' quarters of Tienjin. After our skimpy wedding I'd gone back to work and George had resumed job hunting, writing his novel, and studying Chinese. We'd have our honeymoon later, he said. When he landed the job with CARE, he assured me that everybody in Southeast Asia honeymooned in Macao. For him it meant getting as close as possible to China, as the US didn't allow its citizens to visit the People's Republic (PRC) itself.

In San Francisco in late May, George met Paul, and Leo and his family, and we had lunch with a former colleague at TAF, a Pakistani who, when lunch was over, offered to pay only for his and mine. George rightly took offense, but soon I learned that he was quite inconsistent in what he considered offensive or rude.

We had two weeks in the Philippines so that George could learn from CARE operations there. The chief of mission, Allan Kline, a rather smooth New Yorker, had a glamorous wife, Paula, who, while the men talked shop, introduced me to Manila, including a huge, colorful market and my first mango. Mangos were in season and could easily pass for ambrosia. Otherwise Filipino food was not memorable.

One evening we all went out to dine and dance. George and Paula danced the cha-cha-cha, which I hadn't gotten the hang of. The place was noisy and I was tired and when I asked to go back to the hotel at an early hour George accused me of being jealous. I was; I wanted to dance like that with my new husband, and hoped for patience and understanding while thousands of miles from home among strangers. He took me back to the hotel and accused me of being rude to our hosts. I spent much of that night awake and in agony while he slept; I felt ill and tried to make myself throw up.

The next day the Klines were coming to use the pool at our hotel and had promised to call in advance. I looked down and saw them there. They hadn't called. I pointed this out to George, but it didn't matter. As I got to see repeatedly over the years, to him a man in authority could do no wrong. Allan Kline was such a man.

After a week in Manila, we visited Iloilo and Cebu with friendly Paul Arnaboldi. A takeoff, smooth despite a driving monsoon rain, in a DC-3 prop plane left from World War II proved that the Filipino pilots knew their stuff. A ride in a double-outrigger boat also went well, and I liked the two provincial cities much more than smoggy, frenetic Manila.

We were booked on a ship from Cebu to Manila, leaving after lunch. As we ate in the hotel dining room, George and Paul discussed

Presentation of an American Bookshelf to Far Eastern University, Manila, P.I., June 1958.
L to R: George and Eva Moseley; university president; Paula Kline; Allan Kline, chief of
CARE mission for the Philippines; assistant to university president; Bob Manley, assistant
chief of CARE mission. (The names of the two Filipinos were not recorded with the others.)

CARE business. I had packing to do and wanted to rest, so I soon excused myself and went up to our room. George came up a while later, livid. As his wife, I was supposed to sit there until he and his colleague were ready to leave. This was even more of a challenge to my intelligence and self-respect than the Kline incident, but had I dismissed this demand as authoritarian nonsense (the concept of "sexism" was still in the future), he might well have sent me home, or wanted to. I doubt the marriage could have survived any show of independence on my part; like many other women then I valued marriage more than independence, or even self-respect.

Independence and self-respect were barely part of my mental landscape. Uncomfortable as it is to contemplate now, I had not only non-feminist but anti-feminist convictions. Months earlier I had written Robert about Phyllis, who had one toddler and was pregnant:

> One can see in [David] the ill effects of our modern prosperity: the young family living separately, with no aunt, grandmother, cousin or maid to help, thus the husband becoming involved as assistant housewife. This means that he spends a lot of his time doing chores, because he hates to see her becoming a drudge. She also limits his money and time for card-playing, etc., which I find intolerable but she finds necessary.

These retrograde views stare back at me in black type on IPR stationery. Of course it's good to have others nearby to help with children and chores, but why only women? Why "assistant housewife" when it was his house too? I was still in tune with the *Laws of Manu*, in which the man is king in his household, his wishes the commands all others must obey. (A king was duty-bound to care for and protect his subjects, but equality was not part of the picture.) I did resent George's demand that I sit there till he was ready to leave, but his view of his prerogatives conformed to Manu's dictates; my resentment didn't. My inner feminist had to keep hiding.

George was the only halfway familiar person or thing in my surroundings. So I swallowed any rebellious thoughts and we found our ship. It pitched and rolled as it plowed through large monsoon waves. Our cabin overlooked the forward deck, which was crowded with dozens of squealing pigs. What with their smell, the motion of the ship, and the recent rebuke, I was miserable; George as usual was happy on shipboard. A crew member urged me to eat some soup and that helped. George's lack of sympathy didn't.

His reports on our travels to headquarters in New York, with his observations about some of Allan Kline's programs in the Philippines, show that he needed to learn and to make a good impression, and I had to contribute to that good impression in accordance with his criteria, not mine. My state of mind was not a priority for him as he got ready to run the Macao mission. Perhaps it was unrealistic to expect him to wonder, or ask, how hard or pleasant or interesting these new experiences were for me. I'm not sure he ever did. And it was probably impossible for him, like most American men captive to the call to "manliness," to admit to any anxiety or weakness, to ask me for understanding and support, thus allowing me to feel useful, equal.

Macao, a tiny Portuguese "overseas territory" (as Portugal called its colonies), across the Pearl River Delta from Hong Kong, was and is known mainly for its gambling establishments. No newlyweds ever crossed my path but Macao was colorful and virtually unknown in the US. With houses small and crowded and the weather tropical for most of the year, life we keep behind closed doors spilled into the streets: chopping vegetables, small children taking care of tiny ones, people arguing, making furniture or baskets. You could see into small temples, watch shipwrights build junks and sampans, and smell exotic or familiar odors: of cooking by street vendors, joss sticks (the Chinese incense), raw meat and seafood in the markets, lumber for furniture or boats.

Macao consisted of a small (4.5 square miles) urban peninsula and two rural islands, Taipa and Coloane. We saw a "leprosarium" on Coloane, and on Taipa, a firecracker factory, where the work was done outdoors, in sections separated by high walls, to localize any explosion. (Macao is no longer a colony but part of China, and there are bridges, causeways and an airport where in 1958 there was water.) This was the time of the Great Leap Forward, when the PRC instituted eighteen-hour workdays in a bootstrap operation to strengthen China's economy. Many escaped to Macao or Hong Kong, some swimming across the Inner Harbor at night.

But some people, finding that schools in this corner of the so-called free world charged fees, went back to China so their children could get an education. We both felt some sympathy for China—George from having lived there as a child, I with my left-wing upbringing—and I at least wanted the PRC to succeed. His work was for the refugees; I had no particular assignment except to keep house for him and, for my own sanity, try to find something useful to do.

Soon after we arrived in Hong Kong, George's boss—George Taylor, chief of mission in Hong Kong—accompanied us to Macao to introduce George to government officials. We stayed at the Posada (Portuguese for inn), until we could furnish the house that CARE had reserved for us. The Posada's manager, Angelo, knew everyone and was proud of his culinary efforts. Here we first ate the delicious crusty Portuguese rolls, the fish called grouper, and multi-course Portuguese meals.

That fall George Taylor was transferred to Korea, and CARE moved us to Hong Kong so George could run the mission until a new chief arrived. By Christmas back in Macao, having to find another house, we shared the Posada with Orson Welles and others making a movie called *Ferry to Hong Kong*. Up in our room after supper when the crew came in, we could hear Welles's jovial booming voice. I wanted to meet him but George wouldn't go down. Obedient wife, I didn't either. A minor regret.

The trouble with this so-called honeymoon was that George was usually off with his assistant Augusto visiting refugee groups, government officials, or schools, where he initiated a milk-feeding program. Augusto (work name of José Jacinto) was a typical Macanese, a mixture of Chinese and Portuguese, and he was honest and kind; both George and I had many reasons to appreciate him in the short time we knew him.

The milk-feeding program landed CARE, and both Georges, in the thick of Cold War politics. The governor of Macao, "His Excellency Commandante Pedro Coreia de Barros," insisted that all schools must be included, even those run by Chinese Communists. George Taylor wrote to headquarters in New York for advice; New York wrote, in effect: if we can work in Yugoslavia, we can work with Macao's communist schools. George soon reported that "Happily, all of the really Communist schools have refused to participate," and that of twenty-seven nominally Communist ones, "only twelve were aggressively Communistic and anti-American." I didn't see this memo till my foray into the CARE archives in 2002. In 1958 the Cold War tone would have disturbed me. Perhaps George wanted to sound like one of the boys. Or perhaps he was more one-of-the-boys than I thought or hoped.

Some beneficiaries of the CARE milk-feeding program, Macao, 1958.

For a "small, cramped, dirty Nationalist school," the water was boiled at the headmaster's house and his wife mixed the milk. At a school in the Tin Hao Pagoda, the children came for seconds and thirds. Chinese families had sold powdered milk included in CARE food parcels and wouldn't buy milk. As many Chinese cannot digest dairy products, this program may have been one of the good intentions that pave the road to hell.

George also distributed books, school kits, fishermen's kits, tools and machines for self-help projects, and an appropriate food parcel: rice, tea, and some combination of dried beans, dried fish, soybeans, salted cabbage. The E in CARE originally stood for Europe and the original parcel contained cheese. Chinese and Vietnamese unfamiliar with dairy products complained: "This soap doesn't lather."

Now and then George took me along to a food distribution or presentation of sewing machines, but mostly I was on my own. I took Cantonese lessons, went to market, made curtains, shopped a bit for Chinese antiques—and felt useless. I couldn't find a niche. Welfare agencies were official (Assistencia Publica), Catholic, Protestant, or political: Communist or Kuomintang (Nationalist). There was no organization of secular Jews! I missed woman friends, and having work of my own.

In Eisenhower's America, thrift was virtually unpatriotic and recycling unheard of, but in Macao some women had sidewalk businesses mending nylon stockings. Used jars and tins, old tools, everything was mended if necessary and reused. In our second house in Macao, we had two burglaries. On a damp winter day, the housekeeper hung the wash in the garage. The door was locked but the transom wasn't. All the laundry disappeared. (When we hired this housekeeper, I made a weekly schedule of different things to clean each day, but she did them all every day. She had her own house and family to take care of too.) Then I left a small pot soaking in the sink; at night someone reached through the grille and took the pot. How could one not sympathize when there was so much true poverty? We lived with ambivalence.

Not everyone did. The Portuguese administrators were mildly sympathetic but generally not passionate about relieving poverty; in a letter to Overseas Operations in New York, George mentioned the "dissatisfaction" with his "zeal" of Alberto DaSilva, a neighbor and government official. Theirs was the good life. I liked their multiple-course meals: soup, fish, meat, salad, and so on—small servings of various foods rather than the big portions of meat and potatoes that Americans tended to prefer. There were cooks to prepare such complicated dinners, and servants to wait on table. I felt rude when I entertained, repeatedly leaving the table to clear one course and serve the next. Again ambivalence, for the elegant ways that we could afford were both appealing and obnoxious, our democratic ways virtuous but déclassé.

Sra. DaSilva next door had booties, covers of white embroidered cotton, for her stem glasses, and servants to wash and iron them. At the house of other DaSilvas, as we sat in a circle before lunch, the hosts' daughter, a child of about seven, was brought in and in her frilly white dress went from guest to guest, kissing each one on the mouth. I found this "charming" performance appalling, though the girl seemed to enjoy it. The booties and the kisses seemed to me emblems of a tired, outdated colonialism, as was Macao itself with its comic-opera air. African soldiers from the "overseas territories" of Angola and Mozambique wore rumpled khaki uniforms and maroon fezzes. Government officials often wore cool white, clearly having servants to keep the clothes clean and pressed. Jesuit priests wore long white robes. While many Chinese wore black pajamas, older men appeared in long gray scholars' gowns and wispy beards, and young women in colorful *cheung saam* (long dress), the sexy, close-fitting dresses with high collars, frog closures, and slit skirts.

Shopkeepers were Chinese, Portuguese, or Indian. In many shops one was expected to haggle, which I never learned to do well. It's supposed to be an art, a bit of theater. A college friend told me that, when the family returned to the States after twenty years in China, her mother went into Altman's, once one of New York's finest department stores, and tried to bargain with a sales clerk.

Except for November and December, Macao was humid, and mostly hot. In January and February it could be as cool as the 40s; our kerosene heater attracted more visitors than usual, while most people made do with padded garments and hot tea. During the summer, there was a minor typhoon (from *t'ai fung*, big wind), with windswept rain and a tree banging rhythmically against our house. Worst was early spring—cloudy, damp and warm. For weeks I cleaned mildew off leather bags, belts, and shoes every day. There were huge slugs and almost equally huge cockroaches, the kind Margie—referring to their Florida cousins—called palmetto bugs. One night one fell on me as we turned on the ceiling fan.

Our acquaintances were varied and exotic. The DaSilvas next door had an aristocratic air, perhaps from their years in the colonial service in Africa and Asia; an Austrian engineer had a Chinese wife who spoke only Cantonese and seemed more servant than equal; a witty and irreverent Portuguese Jesuit priest turned out to be our most amusing acquaintance; and a frequent visitor was Gyorgy Teliatieff, a Russian from Shanghai, anglicized to George Tully. I compared it to a diet of caviar and pheasants' tongues, without any good plain bread.

George Tully related an (apocryphal) explanation for the Cyrillic alphabet, with letters that resemble Greek or Roman ones but stand for different sounds. The tsar sent Saint Cyril to Byzantium and Cyril came back with each letter on a separate piece of parchment. As he mounted the steps to the throne, he tripped; the letters went flying and got all mixed up. Gyorgy was amusing and rather sad. Trim and not old, with one lame leg, surviving on disability pay, he had an air of aimlessness, riding his bicycle—riding was better than walking, he said—to visit friends, evidently having nothing useful to do, unlike Linson Dzau, who had established Linson College. An earnest Christian, he was proud when his students went on to university, many to the US, Canada, or Australia, and to careers in academe or business. It flattered us to be befriended by this scholarly Chinese gentleman.

Roque Choi—like Augusto of mixed Chinese and Portuguese ancestry—directed the radio station. Each weekday he read in a different language: Mondays Portuguese, Tuesdays English, and so on. I'd bought a Portuguese-English dictionary, but soon decided to try to learn what ninety percent of the people spoke: Cantonese. My teacher, Rose Tong, herself a student, came afternoons dressed in her school uniform. I never learned much and found, as with other languages, that having a little knowledge can be risky. Knowing numbers from checking in Chinese newspapers at TAF, I looked at the sign on a pushcart and asked the owner: "Are these apples four for a dollar?"

"*Sik k'ong* (can speak)!" he exclaimed, this being the chauvinistic expression for speaking Chinese. And out poured a stream of happy chatter, of which I understood not a word. I bought the apples and wished I really could speak. Another encounter was even less successful. At a market-stall I asked how much for a catty (the Chinese measure, roughly two pounds) of shrimp. The seller replied and I asked for half the amount, needing only half a catty. He shook his head: "*M t'ak*" (Can't do). I went away baffled and only later realized that he thought I was offering him half price. The shrimp, when I managed to buy some, were so fresh that they hopped around on the wrapping-paper. Chinese dishes mostly call for raw shrimp, so I had to break the heads off their live bodies.

A similar challenge was a brace of Tianjin pheasants. A delicacy there too—but there we could easily afford them—they arrived in full regalia, the hen in sober brown, the cock in multiple hues. Macao's fancy grocer readily took them back and sent them again in the nude.

When I expressed disapproval at seeing a lot of cooked rice in someone's trash, Gyorgy reminded me that almost no one had a refrigerator. The Chinese shopped every day, or nearly, going home with numerous bundles, big ones of vegetables, very small ones of meat or fish, each parcel tied with something like raffia and dangling from shoppers' fingers.

For our first house, 86 Avenida Republica, on Barra Point, the tip of the peninsula, we hired an amah, who cleaned, did the laundry, and cooked lunch. Watching her I learned about egg drop soup, fried rice, *baak choi* (white vegetable), stir frying, and various sauces and spices. She left in the afternoon and I cooked supper. She took a fancy to a shiny stainless steel ladle shaped like a bird's head we'd brought from the States. What was it called in English? Because the L sound, as in ladle, is hard for Chinese to pronounce, I said "Spoon." "*See poon, see poon*," she repeated again and again, laughing. Rose explained that this is the Cantonese term for chamber pot—more precisely, piss pot. But the amah also said "*Ho leng*" more than once: "Very beautiful." By the time it occurred to me that I should have given it to her, according to the (supposed?) Chinese custom, she was gone.

She was gone because of another baffling incident. George invited a welfare agency worker to tea. The amah made tea but, when she saw who the guest was, refused to bring it upstairs to the living room. We kept insisting and she kept refusing, so we let her go, feeling—as we so often did—uncomfortably colonialist. Augusto explained: the guest's agency was associated with the Kuomintang, while the amah's daughter was an active communist.

It wasn't just the Chinese who saw everything in political terms. George Taylor seemed to consider every pat on the head of a Chinese child another small blow at communism. He embodied the American attitude that George had decried in an article, "U.S. Aid to Indo-China," published in *The New Leader* the week we married:

> It is a standing joke in South Vietnam that anyone who calls himself an anti-Communist is automatically eligible for an American handout. By interesting ourselves in national welfare rather than anti-Communism as such, we will avoid being blackmailed by opportunistic ruling cliques which keep the endless largess flowing from Washington by periodically threatening to fling themselves into the arms of Peking.

This applied wherever American aid was distributed. Another *New Leader* article, "Problems of Southeast Asia," which he wrote in Macao, still applies; just substitute terrorism for communism. It was especially striking in 2005–06—when one of George W. Bush's advisers attempted to mitigate anti-American feelings by telling other countries how good we are—to read these still apt words from 1959: "American propaganda should be drastically reduced so as to permit concrete achievement to speak for itself." This of course assumes there is "concrete achievement." The mostly destructive "achievements" in Vietnam, Iraq, Afghanistan, Yemen, and elsewhere don't make for favorable propaganda.

Before they moved away we saw the Taylors on frequent trips to Hong Kong. Like most Americans there, they lived in a fashion to which they were not accustomed back home. (As we flew first class and stayed in the best hotels, I kept thinking of American schoolchildren dropping coins in little cans to help the starving people overseas.) The Taylors' good intentions, like those of other aid workers, mingled and clashed with the US pursuit of the Cold War, as it allied itself with dictators and other scoundrels as long as they avowed anti-communism, and so undermined the effects of CARE, AID, and other foreign aid agencies.

I found Ellen Taylor a good person but not stimulating company; perhaps I was too inexperienced to elicit what was interesting about her. While trying to keep their son Georgie amused, Ellen took me to the beach, entertained me at their posh apartment in Repulse Bay, and gave me a Chinese cookbook I still use. George Taylor admired George Moseley, as I learned reading his letters in the CARE records years later. He thanked "Fred Devine for assigning a man of George's caliber to Macau. I'm certain he is going to prove a valuable addition to CARE's Overseas Staff." Glowing words also came from New York about George's "excellent research paper on Macau." These admirers didn't know it, nor did we yet, but the stint with CARE was part of a detour on the way to an academic career; research and writing came more naturally to George than dealing with prickly government officials and corrupt welfare workers.

We lived in Hong Kong for only six weeks. We furnished an apartment, in a new high-rise building still smelling of damp concrete, part-way up Victoria Peak. On the roofs of buildings below ours, our Chinese neighbors grew gardens and raised chickens. An outing to a fishing village involved a ride in a junk, and once we visited a more elegant apartment that belonged to an American consular official, with a grand piano belonging to Betty (later known by her Chinese name, Li-chiao), who figured prominently in George's novel and his past, as one of his Tokyo loves. She *was* beautiful—though in a brassy way, I thought, and noted, but didn't say to George: "She has scrawny arms." Her presence was threatening.

Another attractive young Chinese woman worked for CARE and was neither brassy nor threatening, even though she had (supposedly) been George's almost-betrothed. She and other staff sometimes took us to lunch. As each superb dish appeared, those sitting near George and me served us the choicest morsels with their own chopsticks, before feeding themselves. One weekend we ate at that restaurant. George spoke a little Cantonese, knew Mandarin but not menu Chinese. We got tasteless, leftover glop, not the perfectly cooked dishes of those CARE feasts—one way of putting *sai-yan* (Western people) in their place. Xenophobia and racism aren't Western inventions. Chinese had several insulting terms for us, among them "big noses" and "foreign devils."

During our short time in Hong Kong I had my third, and so far last, encounter with depression. As I recovered from the flu, the world went black. I lay or sat in bed crying, unable to do the simplest household tasks. Reading made it worse. George tried to be sympathetic but was baffled and exasperated. Finally I saw a psychiatrist, who assured me it was an after-effect of the flu, I was not sliding into psychosis and would soon be over it. He was right.

We were back in Macao before a cool, damp Christmas, back to the two-to-three-hour ferry rides, which made me hungry. Usually I ordered fried rice, a huge heap served on a plate, and when I complained about not being given chopsticks, George said, rightly, "Chopsticks were not designed for eating from a plate." Ferry menus also featured "different kinds of assorted cake." A cigarette packet promised: "Guaranteed make no thirst and help thinking." Augusto baffled us with a report about a refugee: "They change his head." One of us figured out that it meant what Americans called brainwashing. Another way to change a head gave us a glimpse into Chinese syntax, when Augusto said: "I go to the barber and cut my hair." But the malapropisms weren't all on one side: it was George Taylor whom I first heard calling Americans living abroad expatriots.

After we were settled in our second Macao house, I found a way to help alleviate some of the overwhelming poverty. Among the car horns, pedicab bells, and cries of vendors in Macao's streets there was music; the musicians were blind and they were good. Augusto helped me round them up. They gathered in our living room, drank tea, spat on the floor, and performed so I could choose the pieces likeliest to appeal to Western

Two blind musicians playing in Macao's streets. At left is a two-stringed yee-wu,
at right a hsiao played by Lai Tak, who once said Good Morning to me;
his son had learned some English at his Chinese school.

ears. Then Augusto and I marched them to Radio Vila Verde, down Avenida Ouvidor Arriaga from our house. Roque Choi provided a studio and sound engineer. The musicians performed, I paid them something, and they went back to playing on the street.

Augusto found Chung Meng-kee, who translated the lyrics and provided some history. I wrote Moses Asch at Folkways Records and elicited tentative interest. When we returned to New York that summer, I brought him the tapes, the translations, and photos of the musicians at our house, at the studio, and on the street. Yes, he would publish excerpts, for a lump sum of $100 or royalties. I chose royalties and sent the money to Augusto, who was to keep some for himself and distribute most to the blinds, as he called them. When Asch sent copies of the record, it was disappointing, Augusto wrote:

> The design the cover and the material are all very good. I know that for the Europeans it doesn't matter, but all the Chinese knows these songs and they are very sorry for they aren't complete. Mr. Alvares wanted to put it in the Radio but as they aren't complete he can't play it. I played them in the HAP FAT KEE Cafe to all the blind peoples. And there were many other costumers that said they were feeling sorry for they aren't complete. Some of

them wanted to by the records, too [T]he Johnson & Universal
Records Co… wanted to order some but they didn't do it cause
they weren't complete. [T]hey wished that you instead of putting
12 musics in each record, you could put 6 or 7 but complete.
Tham they could sell them. [Letter dated 15-9-60. Spelling etc.
in the original, as in other letters quoted.]

Asch had geared the excerpts to Western patience, or impatience, frustrating those who wanted to hear the whole story. There was another
disappointment as well, as Augusto wrote in April 1961.

I wish to let you know that I received a cheque of US$37.85
which was given to the blind. [The exchange rate was about
HK$6 to US$1.] On the contrary, the blind supposed you sent
over US$1000 to me. I was very patient to explain to the blind
this misunderstanding. On your part, you would know whatever
I did by night, appeared by day.

The royalties were meager, although in total much more than $100. They
continued to trickle in, and Augusto to distribute them, keeping small
amounts. In 1960 he wrote that "my salary is just enough for eating,"
and "I don't have enough cloth to pass this winter." We sent clothes and
sometimes money.

In June 1969 he distributed

Macao money $264.69. Twenty three blind people is not a player,
I gived five dollars each. I only see six of that player, I givd Ten
dollars each, and one of the player told me, still have one, but he
is suicede to death, few days ago. I gived his family Fifty dollars….
I took thirty nine dollars and sixty nine cents.

Before the record appeared, Asch, entrepreneurial but disorganized,
kept losing papers, took months to return the photos, and violated the
contract, which stipulated that I would be credited as the source, but
my name is not on the jacket, and the booklet accompanying the record
names Augusto, Mr. Chung, the sound engineer, and, most prominently:

"Chinese Music/ Excerpts from Cantonese Music Drama/ by Henry Cowell." This distorted history. How did the musicians come to record at Radio Vila Verde? How did Folkways acquire the tapes? The text gives no clue.

I wasn't a feminist yet, but I was angry. I imagined Moses Asch asking this well-known composer to write a few words because some woman who didn't know beans about Chinese music had brought him these tapes. It's speculation that he left me out because I'm female, but all those named were men.

Phyllis's husband, a lawyer, advised that it wasn't worth suing: not enough money involved. So there was just a mild protest from me ("I was rather surprised at the star billing accorded to Mr. Cowell"), and an offhand promise from him that in any second printing he would add my name. There was no second printing. Moses Asch died and the Folkways archive is at the Smithsonian. The blinds got some money and perhaps a few non-Chinese got some pleasure from record #8880, *Chinese Opera: Songs and Music.* I got to feel useful, but not the credit that any other fieldworker would get.

In Hong Kong again in 1966–67, we visited Macao briefly. An article in the *South China Morning Post* for March 27, headed "Unexpected Windfall For Blind Musicians," plays fast and loose with the facts and ascribes imaginary feelings to me in language I would never use:

> [I]t was a mission she felt bound to fulfill—to turn over to the blind the results of their efforts. Royalties from the sale of the records…had obtained a tidy sum of money… enough to provide some of the blind folks with something for "yam-cha" ["drink tea"; cf. French pour-boire, German Trinkgeld].

According to the article, Augusto "toured the city" with me "to look up her old blind friends." We met "only two of the old crowd," a zither- and a banjo-player. "They no longer play their instruments which are now deposited in a glass cabinet in the Centre for the Rehabilitation of the Blind, where they learned how to make their hands work for them without the use of their sight." As if their hands hadn't worked for them as musicians. The article ends with more clichés: "…this visit of theirs has provided Mrs. Moseley with a thrill and the satisfied feeling of a job well done."

The royalty checks had dwindled even further; we had no largesse to distribute, so our visit meant more to us than to Augusto or the musicians. The idea that they were part of an "old crowd" of friends is fanciful nonsense, and their trading music for perhaps steadier indoor work seems a mixed blessing, perhaps less arduous and uncertain, but also less creative. And the visit made me sad, not self-satisfied.

Back in 1959, we had to decide what to do next. George was fed up with the job. Only people who belonged to an association could get food parcels; those too poor to pay dues were out of luck. Parcels lasted only a few days, but a family couldn't get another till the next month—and then might have to take its turn among other families. Asked for playground equipment, George visited the site and found old slides and swings that hadn't been maintained. Sewing machines that he provided for training refugee women were sold right after we left. Often middlemen siphoned off much, or all, of the aid meant for refugees.

After being accepted for graduate study at the University of Hong Kong, he decided to go to Yale. This suited me, for I was, at last, pregnant (one reason for all that fried rice) and would rather have the baby in a more familiar place, nearer to family and friends. At some point that spring I spontaneously gave up coffee and alcohol and started drinking milk. No morning sickness, just an unruly appetite.

As a Chinese packer expertly managed the dishes, vases, and other fragile items among our few acquisitions, I was happy to be going home, and George, as always, was happy to be moving and starting yet another new life.

Chapter 20
NEW HAVEN: JESSICA, 1959-60

*N*ew Haven was on the edges of my consciousness ever since I met Jenny, but I didn't spend time there till the mid '50s, when Edith was in graduate school at Yale and Marcia lived there with her first husband. Over one New Year's, Marcia and Jerry had a party, fed us *boeuf en daube*, played Elvis records, and had sleeping bodies disposed around the house. Early in the morning Herb—friend of Dan's once briefly attached to Edith—and I went for a slow walk, he on crutches, thanks to a serious car accident.

Jenny's brother studied math at Yale and lived at Pooh Haven, as did Tom Paley, mathematician and one of the New Lost City Ramblers, who visited Jenny at Mount Holyoke with a sandwich or two in his banjo. He consumed everyone's leftovers, so was dubbed Garbage Paley. He sang a plaintive Appalachian ballad, "Knoxville Girl." During one evening walk, the singer "knocked that poor girl down."

> She fell upon her bended knee, for mercy she did cry:
> "Oh Willy my dear, don't kill me here, I'm unprepared to die."
> She never spoke another word....

As she "had a dark and roving eye," she "never could be [his] bride." So this self-pitying chap made sure no one else got her.

I hung out some with Jenny and Tom, but I barely knew New Haven when George was admitted for graduate work in East Asian studies at Harvard and Yale, and chose Yale. Back in New York for the summer, we lived with Mother on 82nd Street and I worked part-time at the IPR. Riding the bus I got a foretaste of my baby's personality: whenever the bus stopped, she started kicking, quieting down as soon as the bus moved.

I got another insight into my husband's personality when, after a very few scenes of *The Magic Flute,* George whispered angrily, "This is silly. Let's go." Of course it's silly—entertaining silliness set to lovely music. But I couldn't find a way to make him stay, again constrained to be the compliant wife.

I loved being pregnant, except for that unruly appetite. A British obstetrician in Hong Kong permitted gaining a pound a week—a total of nearly forty, clearly too much; Bianca Steinhardt, the gynecologist Mother and her sisters were devoted to, set the total at eighteen. I'd already gained more than that, so I tried to fill up on carrots and celery.

After running around New Haven one day from one unfamiliar address to another, my belly heavy and ankles swollen, we rented the top floor of 140 Cottage Street, off Whitney Avenue. The house was for sale, the second floor kept empty for new owners, a friendly couple on the first floor. We found two overstuffed chairs and other ugly but serviceable furniture in the house; Goodwill provided the rest.

Our baby was going to be born at Grace-New Haven, Yale's teaching hospital, then the mecca of natural childbirth in this country; my doctor was Richard Hausknecht, the head ob-gyn resident, like me a New York Jewish wise guy. I kept house, sewed and knitted for the baby, cooked, shopped, and got to know the neighborhood, with a few social or intellectual events. Yale and New Haven toilets were all either upstairs or downstairs from the events. Like pregnant women generally, I had to pee often and climbing stairs was a pain. But it was all worth it. I had longed for this baby for years.

The official due date came and went. At my last checkup all was well. On November 30th I painted a crib from Goodwill. On the 1st I went to the butcher and came home feeling unusually tired. Labor began in the middle of the night. A taxi whisked us to the hospital, where my water soon broke. It looked dirty, which made me wonder, and sure enough it was a "breech presentation." George was with me in the labor room, but soon the baby's heartbeat became dangerously slow. They rushed me into a delivery room, put me under, and hauled her out with forceps. (Now they might do a C-section. I'm grateful that was a last resort then.) When I woke up briefly George told me we had a beautiful tiny girl (six and a quarter pounds) with dark hair, her head round as it hadn't served as a wedge. He was teary but I wasn't conscious long enough to learn why: the doctor wasn't sure Jessica would survive. Thinking George was just excited and happy, I gave in to the anesthetic; by the time it wore off, she was out of the woods.

The hospital, where we spent the normal four or five days, featured rooming-in as well as natural childbirth, so Jessica and her parents began to get acquainted right away. Well enough acquainted that, when a night nurse brought me a baby to feed, even in my sleepy state I sensed something wrong. The identification bracelet confirmed that it was not Jessica. It gave me a jolt and made me wonder why the idea of nursing—and possibly going home with—another baby is so repellent. But a particular baby had been in my body, sustained by it. The chemistry between mother and infant is not only emotional, but genetic and physical.

I shared a room with three other mothers. At almost twenty-eight, I was the only first-time mother. The others were all younger; some already had more than one child. Their views on family planning interested me. Catholics and full-time mothers, they all wanted birth control, but their husbands wouldn't have it. Connecticut and Massachusetts were the last states to lift bans on birth control.

At my six-week checkup, Dr. Hausknecht produced the set of graduated rubber rings used to fit women for diaphragms. "I'd rather be caught with an atomic bomb," he said, and, admiring his handiwork, "No one would guess you'd been pregnant." His expert cutting and stitching disguised the effects not only of a breech birth but even those of a normal delivery. He had told me that he looked forward to his stint in gynecology. Obstetrics was boring. Perhaps a breech birth provided an interesting challenge. Did he appreciate that? Did he get a kick out of our banter, as I did?

The first weeks at home were hard. Jessica cried a lot. I was worn out. Nursing helped me heal, but I didn't realize till I had Tommy how hard this birth had been for me, if not as dangerous and perhaps frightening as it was for Jessica. My fatigue probably interfered with milk production and I sometimes felt we were in a downward spiral: the more she cried, the more nervous and exhausted I was, the less milk I had for her, so she would cry more. When I called Dr. Hausknecht for advice, he said not to "make a fetish" of nursing. It wasn't yet known here, I think—or not by the medical profession—that nursing has benefits for the physical and psychological health of baby and mother. In 1960 many thought that artificial was good, while natural meant primitive.

Much later, at the Schlesinger Library, I noticed Dr. Hausknecht's name among the founders of the National Abortion Rights Action League. So I forgave him his youthful brashness and insensitivity. I had a crush on him back then too. Is it normal for a woman to fall in love with her obstetrician? A man (usually a man then) of knowledge and authority who briefly has her life in his hands, and that of her infant. I did anyway, until his "fetish" remark. When Tommy was born, there was further doubt, not about Hausknecht's competence but about his bedside manner. He made clear how hard this birth was for Jessica, and for him, but not how much harder than a normal birth it was for me. Had I known that, I might have expected less of myself.

Mother was there when I came home from the hospital. She told a three-year-old neighbor boy that a new baby girl had just come home. He was delighted. "Can she come out and play?" Much as I loved this baby, and having a baby, it often felt as if we would never get out to play. Foolishly, I weighed her before and after each feeding and recorded how much she drank. I did *not* do this with Tommy!

Mother was and wasn't a help. She could burp Jessica, change diapers, mind her so I could get some rest. But when Jessica was fed, changed, and put down but instead of sleeping cried, Mother fussed over her: she's hot, she's cold, she has indigestion, or some other imagined affliction. With Tommy I discovered that, when his crying reached a crescendo and it seemed I'd *have* to pick him up, if I didn't he'd be asleep moments later. Babies work hard: arms, legs, fingers and toes are moving most of the time, and sucking, especially from the breast, is strenuous. Maybe Jessica was crying because she was worn out. Picking her up wore her out even more. George sometimes walked her up and down. One evening when she fussed anyway, he said, "This baby is going to flunk me out of graduate school," a reproach aimed at me rather than helpless Jessica.

Her other grandmother presented an interesting contrast to Mother. She sat on the couch, Jessica resting peacefully against her left shoulder as Kay nonchalantly smoked a cigarette and turned the pages of *The New*

York Times. She wasn't solicitous or worried, and evidently the effect on Jessica was soothing. (Both grandmothers smoked.)

Van came with Gadgie, who seemed too frail for winter travel. He hustled her up the two steep flights and soon down again, giving her only a little time to meet her namesake: Alice Jessica. Gadgie's actual name was Alice. I wanted a Jessica, and we preferred Alice Jessica to Jessica Alice. We'd explained all this to Gadgie and she was more than satisfied: Alices she'd known were called Allie, a name she disliked. Gadgie died soon after this visit; we were glad that she had a chance to meet her namesake.

Mother made me a wool coat with a hood and I took Jessica out every day the weather permitted, in our second-hand baby carriage. Usually she slept as long as we kept moving. As spring came and she slept through the night, life became easier. In March I wrote Robert an enthusiastic report:

> She really is a delight, more so all the time. She's been making funny faces all her life and about six weeks ago started adding funny noises. But this is all old hat to you. I'm a bit upset these days since I'm having trouble nursing her and think bottles are pretty awful. But between feedings she's wonderful.

From our kitchen window, this delightful baby on my arm, I watched the young man who rented the garage polish his small sports car. It struck me that such cars are both womb and penis: curled up in the constricted space in something like a fetal position, the driver zooms around aggressively in his phalloform cocoon. This observation impressed Dr. L. (who owned a sports car) when I recalled it decades later. Still later, I wondered whether the act of polishing this phallus–womb smacks of masturbation.

I observed something interesting about motherhood at that window too. Jessica was lying on her Bathinette and I was at the window, my back to her, one foot on the sill, cutting my toenails. Without knowing what alerted me, I put the scissors down on the sill and turned in time to catch her about a foot from the floor. She hadn't previously turned over on her own, so this move was unexpected. The apparent rapport between infant and mother was amazing and reassuring: I had sensed her movement but not heard anything.

Marcia and Jerry moved away, but others from my past turned up. Dick Gard, the only non-Asian TAF fired in 1956, appeared at Yale. I asked about his wife. "She's fine. She has two children now." "*She* has?" I thought, filing his remark away as an unwitting revelation of one man's attitude toward his family. Edith, working on her doctorate in English, had met Peter Milton, soon to be her lifelong second husband. They came for dinner. George had met Edith only once and neither of us knew Peter, yet the four of us became silly and hilarious, unusual for George, who could be funny but was rarely silly.

We bought an old Packard, a big car I couldn't drive, not having learned standard shift yet. This made outings possible and we discovered how exclusive the Connecticut shore was, nearly every inch either private or reserved for local residents. One exception was a beach we visited with Leo, Lorna, and little Lisa Teller. Leo, also once a Viennese refugee, knew George's Burmese friend Shwe from Woodstock School in India. That's how we got to know the Tellers. Leo had migrated to Australia and married Lorna there. He was studying forestry at Yale. We lost touch with them, but I found them in 1986 in Beijing, where Leo was working for UNESCO. Lorna irritated me by criticizing the way I'd raised my children. Back in 1960, Leo impressed us by having been present at Lisa's birth and even taken photos, and me, because he was such a nice person.

Hod Briggs was another would-be sinologist. He and Mary Ann became our lifelong friends. Soon Hod switched from sinology to court reporting, eventually with his own business in L.A.

Lee and Marian Ash also came for dinner. Lee, devoted to books and libraries, compiled useful guides and directories. I'd consulted him about library work when we were both in New York. I made cream-cheese pie for dessert:

> Crumb 16 graham crackers (or buy crumbs). Mix with ¼ cup melted butter, press into pie plate and bake 10 minutes at 350. Or use a ready-made crust.
>
> Mix 8 oz. cream cheese (at room temperature), 2 large eggs, ½ cup superfine sugar, and 1 tbsp. vanilla. Pour into crust, bake 20 minutes at 350. COOL.
>
> Mix 1 pint sourcream or yogurt, 2 tblsp. superfine sugar, and

1 tsp. vanilla. Spread over filling. Bake 5 minutes at 350. Cool and refrigerate.

Best made the day before.

As I brought the pie out, Lee exclaimed: "Sara Lee, I love you!" I quietly set him straight. Sara Lee's was good. This is better.

Then we had dinner at their house. A tour included an upright freezer, then a novelty. One packet of leftovers was marked "Horrible lamb stew." Presumably they kept it for their cats. I'd just made lamb stew, also horrible.

George earned an M.A. and wanted to work toward a Ph.D., combining East Asian languages and geography, with a thesis on national minorities in China, but such an interdisciplinary degree was too radical for Yale. So he got a job in New York and we left New Haven, I with some regret.

> I have one of the country's best maternity clinics at my disposal, and am finding New Haven to my liking to a surprising degree [I'd written Robert in October]. It's probably a ridiculous little city, but it's relaxed and friendly and somehow very comfortable and pleasant. I find none of the snobbishness or phoniness which exasperated me in Cambridge, and I also have the feeling, though no real evidence for it, that there is less of a schism between the university and the town than one finds almost anywhere else.

The sophisticated take on New Haven was that it's a good place to be because it's near New York, but—even if some of what I wrote Robert was itself snobbish, and some of it nonsense—we, or I anyway, actually liked it for itself.

Chapter 21
THE BRONX: TOMMY, 1960–63

*"Trust me, if you've ever tried being a stay-at-home mom, going to
medical school is like a vacation. I learned something I like all day long.
Nobody was pulling on my skirt, or yelling."*
—From a speech by Dr. Virginia Latham, mother of five sons, quoted
in her obituary, *The Boston Globe*, April 28, 2017.

*A*s we hunted for an apartment in New York, I wrote Robert hopefully: "George is going to work for the Council on Foreign Relations
[CFR]….I rather dread the miles of brick and pavement. [But] we can
afford a fairly fantastic rent and so can probably live in a fairly desirable
area."

"Probably"—or not. My old West Side neighborhood was our pref-
erence, but the only large-enough apartment we could afford was the
basement of a brownstone near Riverside Drive. The location and the
tiny garden were fine; George liked it, but it was dark and I didn't relish
spending long days there with Jessica while George was at work. Again I
preferred Anna and Beppo's apartment to my parents'.

We settled on the sunny top floor of a boxy, boring, almost-new
brick two-family house in the Bronx, at Yates and Allerton avenues.
"George just isn't making enough for us to live what we consider a
civilized life in Manhattan," I wrote Robert. "Our landlord and lady
are very nice and most helpful; I have the use of their washing machine
and yard, such as it is." The Baraneks were Slovak. Mrs. Baranek was
grandmotherly and friendly until Jessica—whom she translated to
Yessichka—began playing with pots and cans and, worse, as she started
to walk and pushed the metal-legged chairs I'd bought for 56ᵗʰ Street
around the kitchen.

We chose the northeast Bronx because a nearby subway line has a stop one block from the Council at 68th Street and Park Avenue, and because it is the corner of New York nearest to Vermont and The Farm. (Lyova calculated that the distance from our house to Anna's in Coney Island is the same as that between Jerusalem and Tel Aviv.) George called the Bronx "one big bourgeois slum." We never developed any loyalty to it, even though we lived together there longer than anywhere else.

Mother and her sisters often remarked how happy Jessica and I were that summer. Pretty, curious and sociable, no longer a fussy infant, she happily hitched herself around the floor on her bottom. Meantime I was slowing down, though at first I didn't know why. I was lugging not only my growing daughter and the groceries up two flights of stairs, but also a growing belly. Dr. Hausknecht admired his work so much that, guided by those dangerous rubber rings, he gave me a diaphragm *smaller* than the one I'd used earlier. So I was pregnant again.

George was director of meetings at the Council. At twenty-nine, he had three women helping him arrange private sessions for members with notable speakers, among them Hastings Banda, Willy Brandt, Dwight Eisenhower, Pierre Mendès-France, Nehru, Tito. The sessions were nominally off the record, so George recruited "rapporteurs," who sat in back listening, not permitted to write anything down until afterward. Some were young lawyers, one became a friend.

The director of the Council, George Franklin, and his wife Helena invited us and others for lunch once. I got a babysitter and wore my wedding suit. During drinks before lunch I bit into a cherry tomato. It squirted on my suit and the carpet. Helena summoned a maid, who came running with a towel. I felt like an inexperienced silly goose, not for the first or last time.

The Franklins also invited us to their summer house in Oyster Bay. There were servants to prepare and serve lunch, mind the children, and dry our suits in the dryer after every swim. After lunch George and I—the children were too small—were taken out in the Franklins' sailboat, and I learned that, unless I can help sail the boat, sailing soon becomes boring. But the day was wonderful; the Franklins, despite their posh life, were unassuming and down to earth.

On a few other occasions I joined George downtown. At a CFR Christmas party I met two Polish gents and, as I told them, first understood why Warsaw is called the Paris of Eastern Europe. They were totally unlike the insulting stereotype of the boorish, dim-witted Pole. There was also a dinner at the apartment of the South Korean ambassador to the UN. Early on the talk turned to things and people Chinese and never left that topic, which seemed to confirm what I'd heard: that many Koreans were in awe of China and its culture.

Mothers at the playground were my usual company. I found the neighborhood somewhat dreary. Immediate neighbors were largely Italian-American and led to what I called a postjudice: a prejudice that, based on *some* contact, not just hearsay, promiscuously applies to unknown members of the group judgments drawn from contact with a few. In *The Devil's Dictionary*, Ambrose Bierce defines a prejudice as "a vagrant opinion without visible means of support."

My impatience with some neighbors made me realize that I'm a democrat in my head more than in my heart. In a letter to Robert, I was embarrassingly snooty about the Bronx, finding "the neighborhood as dull and Philistine as it can be… most of the people are just unbelievably primitive, but at least it is friendly and relaxed—not at all New Yorkish." But more on my mind than the neighbors were Jessica and then Tommy, and later peace work, along with daily chores, the vagaries of marriage, and trips to The Farm.

Just before Tommy was born, Jessica had a fever of 105° F for three days. After my repeated anxious phone calls, the pediatrician conceded that I might bring her in—into a waiting room crowded with little kids and their mothers. It didn't seem to matter that it might be harmful to drag a child with a fever, or an injury, out of bed and out of the house. The doctor found a somewhat red throat and Jessica soon got well, but we began to wonder about the care she was getting, so when we heard of a refugee doctor who made house calls, even on Sunday, we dropped the pediatrician for this relic.

Vickie and Rudi still lived in the Bronx, and their physician, Dr. Ballen, became my obstetrician. He was dismissive of natural childbirth. The point was to get the baby out safely and the doctor could do that best, preferably without interference from the mother. He didn't *say* this but he might have had I tried to insist. After missing Jessica's birth because of the danger she was in, I agreed that what happens afterward between parents and child, beginning with the intimacy of rooming-in, is more important. Still, it would have been good to have both: conscious childbirth *and* rooming-in. Bronx hospitals didn't offer natural childbirth and only ours had rooming-in—all of four beds.

When we showed up at Lebanon Hospital the night of March 9, 1961, the nurse checking me into the labor unit said, "Kiss your husband goodbye." In New Haven, the individual labor rooms resembled hotel rooms, with subdued lighting, window drapes, a comfortable bed, an upholstered chair for the husband. (It was virtually always a husband then.) At Lebanon, after I changed into a hospital gown, was shaved and treated to an enema, the nurse left me alone, flat on a cold, hard gurney in a brightly lit room. Now and then a nurse came and checked on me. "Can you stay with me?" I pleaded. I wanted a hand—not my own!—to squeeze when the pains came. Surprised, she claimed that most women want to be left alone. No one did stay with me—staffing there was not geared to this frill—and all I remember of the birth is the little head feeling like a grapefruit filled with lead as it made its way out.

This baby emerged very early on the 10th, head first and, by the book, in four hours, just half Jessica's time. Again I woke up for a moment to hear George say, "We have a boy." "Oh good," I thought, "then we don't have to have any more children," and went back to sleep. A sexist thought perhaps, but we had a girl, we wanted a boy, and I'd fulfilled a childhood prediction: I too would have one of each but the girl first because I wished I'd been first. Like Jessica, Tommy weighed six and a quarter pounds. His head, unlike hers, was briefly wedge-shaped. His hair, like hers, was straight, silky, dark brown, but with a blond streak at one temple. In those days some young bloods would bleach a clump of hair for the same effect. We named him Thomas after Kay's father, Thomas Payne. Evan, Tommy's middle name, combines my name with Van's.

Mother came to take care of Jessica and stayed to help with both. Petite at fifteen months, Jessica looked huge after four days with newborn Tommy. No long novels while nursing this time, as I talked and played with her, with the baby at my breast part of the scenery, at most sharing the spotlight with her. Though I had been the displacing second child, I wanted to minimize the pain I assumed she felt at being elbowed away from center stage by this new creature.

Soon I was taking both kids out for air, but one day Mother minded a sleeping Tommy while we went out, Jessica in the carriage's toddler seat facing me, chanting "Nonnie, nonnie." Mother understood that, missing Tommy, she chanted his name as best she could.

Luckily, it was much easier to recover from Tommy's birth than from Jessica's difficult one, as there was now more lifting and carrying and many more diapers to wash. (There were no disposable diapers then and I probably wouldn't have used them if there had been.) Having the children so close together had its benefits. Soon Jessica could barely remember not having a little brother, and once Tommy could raise his head, he amused us with deliciously funny faces and noises. He seemed to know he was being funny. This probably helped Jessica love the little intruder, balancing any jealousy.

But did jealousy cause her tantrums, which began when Tommy was very small? Who knows what other slights and frustrations she suffered? For me the tantrums were a difficult test, provoking much guilt (at not being the perfect mother), anxiety (about what I'd done to cause her misery), and impatience (due to excessive demand on my limited energy and humor). Unlike many parents, I didn't send her to her room to scream it out alone. That felt like blaming her. Some parents seem to believe that toddlers produce these rages deliberately, but she seemed in the throes of something painful that she couldn't control, and my task was to ride it out with her.

Later, when Tommy was a toddler too, they marched around the living room chanting "Ann Horgan, Ann Horgan." I'm not sure who deciphered that as George's middle name, Van Horn. Then, as both crawled through a concrete pipe at a local playground, she fell on him and broke his new tooth. That evening Jessica, not yet toilet-trained, used the potty successfully. George was surely right that this act of self-control was a way to work off the guilt at what she had done, and also appeasement: Don't be angry; look what a good girl I am.

I was grateful to have two whole, healthy children. From a neigh-borhood mother, one of whose three children was what was then called "retarded," I learned how such a child absorbs all (or more than all) the parents' attention and energy, depriving its siblings. Tommy did have bowed legs. For a few weeks they were in tiny casts, which clicked quietly as he moved in his sleep, a sad little sound but he was unperturbed, and evidently the casts fixed the problem.

One afternoon—Tommy napping and I busy in another room—Jessica suddenly cried out, obviously in pain, due to a staple in the heel of her hand. She'd climbed up on the desk (the door-across-two-old-desk-ends George had concocted for 23rd Street) and found this intriguing gadget. I pulled the staple out and fixed her boo-boo. She was happy with her Band-Aid, so I went back to my chores. When I checked on her moments later, she had climbed back up on the desk and was reaching for the stapler.

Some of George's rapporteurs came for dinner, some with wives, and some made me feel defensive for, with all my education, staying home with the children. One mother worked full time and had had her three-year old's IQ tested. It was, of course, in the 98th percentile, or 99th. I thought it crazy to test such little tykes. It made more sense to be there to encourage their learning. If I had it to do again, I might go out to work *very* part-time, but the northeast Bronx wouldn't have provided likely opportunities. Sometimes a daytime babysitter took the children out so I could be home alone. I don't recall how I spent that time, only that it was more restorative than leaving them home with a sitter and going out to work, shop, or amuse myself.

The choice to be a full-time mother was largely my reaction to having first a very part-time and then almost-no-time mother. On one of her visits, I told Mother that I found it hard to do for the kids what hadn't been done for me. She nodded, evidently accepting this as a statement of fact and not a criticism. She had always protected herself with the certainty that it was ab-so-*lute*-ly necessary for her to work and impossible to establish and maintain her business with us children at home. My choice was based—beyond my love for the children and the wish not to do what she had done—on the fact that it was so interesting to watch them try to understand the world, and learn their own powers to make things happen in it. Like all children, they said and did many things that were amusing or unexpected. There are virtually no written records, only a few memories.

Few because my once prodigious memory for details began to fail then: with small children things happen so fast, one has to respond quickly so often, that there is no time to register and store new memories properly.

As Jessica systematically removed diapers from a bureau drawer, I took photos before shutting the drawer and turning the bureau around. Ditto for her dabbling in the toilet, before I shut the lid and the bathroom door. Not much later she often borrowed my shoes—calling them heel-highs—and other gear, so as to clomp around in imitation of adult women. (Some thirty-five years later, her daughter Fiona explained to her little sister: "I'm going to town now and do my paperwork.")

Sometimes there was an astonishing insight. We came home from the playground during a heating-oil delivery. I pointed out how the oil went from the truck through the hose into the nozzle by the front door. "Yes," Jessica said, "it goes right into the belly button," an amazing observation, for the nozzle and hose are a good analogy for the navel and umbilical cord. How did she know? *Did* she know, or was it just a lucky guess? She said it as if she knew.

Tommy surprised us in a different way. He was a year old when we had a party for Mother's friends, eight or ten people in their fifties or sixties. Before dinner we brought the kids, bathed and ready for bed, out to say goodnight. George led Jessica by the hand around the circle of guests and I followed carrying Tommy, who, on his own initiative, kissed every one of them, to their delight—but unlike the girl in Macao, not on the mouth. When we finished the circle he was ready to go around again.

He figured in another incident, one that says more about Kay, and maybe George, than about Tommy. Having his diaper changed, he lay with feet and bare bottom toward the door of the kids' room, kicking and gurgling, enjoying his momentary freedom from diaper and plastic pants, as Kay walked in. "Oh Tommy!" she said in a disapproving tone. Tommy wasn't doing anything to disapprove of. I wondered whether she had shown distaste for Henry and George's nakedness too.

When Jessica was two-and-a-half and Tommy fifteen months old, we took them to Orchard Beach on a bright spring day, took their shoes off and led them to the water. Letting go of George's hand, Tommy waded in a short way, the gentle waves lapping his ankles. He looked up at us with an ecstatic smile, enchanted by that cool, ever moving water.

When he graduated beyond baby food, the only meats he liked were hamburger and bacon. Aware of my family's lies about food, at supper I would make him taste whatever meat the rest of us were having before he could have his hamburger. If this was torment, it was brief. Eventually he ate just about anything, and as an adult he became a creative cook.

Tommy would crawl down the hall pushing a pot lid, making vehicular noises. Jessica never did that, nor was she as visibly fascinated by large, noisy trucks. Does that prove anything about innate differences between boys and girls? Probably not. As Carlchen would say, you can't make statistics from two toddlers. And Mother pointed out that I drove the children in the car—a Pontiac the kids called "Ponyack"—more than George did. Did Tommy, despite this, know that he and George had the same anatomy and I didn't? Or, because we adults knew it, did we somehow transmit sex-based prejudices to the children? I tried not to, but can't swear that we—and others—would not give Jessica dolls and Tommy toy cars.

Motherhood was absorbing but not easy. I was often in despair at my impatience and wished for psychotherapy, to make me a better mother. But there was no money for that. George, the source of all our money, saw no point in it—or perhaps too much point: what might emerge about him? So I muddled on, having the children I'd wanted but not being the mother I'd hoped to be. I wrote Robert in September 1962 about visiting Cambridge and having people admire my children. "They really are the kind of kids that nearly everyone stops to admire [sounding like Mother with her would-be subsidies], and sometimes I would like to give them to the first person who does so." This wasn't serious of course. I couldn't imagine letting anyone else have them, but raising children is hard. Later, when the women's liberationists proclaimed their right to "do their own thing," I wondered whether some weren't just trying to avoid one of the hardest jobs in the world. (The idea, eventually promoted by Betty Friedan and others, that both parents should be involved in raising the children *and* have other work lives has almost become conventional wisdom.)

Having company connected me, if briefly and tenuously, to parts of the adult world, and sometimes it amused the children too. Both were enchanted by Howard Boorman, who was at Columbia working on a biographical dictionary of modern China. Howard bent down to Tommy. "I have a little boy too," Howard said. "He used to be like you and then he grew, and grew, and grew," his hand marking each stage of growth as he straightened up, the kids watching with big round eyes. Howard was as charming and lovable as his then wife, whom we met later, was cold and haughty.

Robert wrote repeatedly about a possible visit that never happened, but we did entertain the man who had taught him and George Chinese. Earl Swisher of the University of Colorado, a mild-mannered gentleman with right-wing political views, came for lunch while in New York for a conference. When I told him that we had hoped to invite Bill Holland as well, he only smiled, though he wouldn't have relished breaking bread with someone he probably considered a communist or fellow traveller. Admiring his composure, I thought that that was just how a scholarly Chinese gentleman would respond. George was fond of Swisher but not in sympathy with his pro-Kuomintang views.

In fact, with his awe for men in positions of authority, George would often come home enthusiastic about a new acquaintance, only to be disappointed soon after. (Perhaps I was one such enthusiasm!) I write this with some sympathy, even if it sometimes irked me, for a 1979 diary entry expresses similar enthusiasm for two "marvelous" archival acquaintances, one a volunteer at the Schlesinger Library, the other well known in the profession. Soon, while I still admired their intelligence and accomplishments, my enthusiasm was tempered by evidence of their more than ample self-regard; at first I'd uncritically accepted their views of themselves, rather than wait for adequate evidence for my own judgment. That may be what George often did too.

Despite long days at work, George often gave the children their bath. Sometimes he mopped the kitchen floor. A dozen years later, when talk of the sexist division of domestic labor became pervasive, I assured women who complained about their husbands that even a man who does domestic chores can be perfectly sexist in his outlook. George was helping me with *my* work when he mopped or minded the kids, and in his view the family revolved around him. But at the time I didn't mind. I shared the dominant view summed up by *Vive la différence*.

He wasn't writing much, so my editorial chores were minimal or non-existent. His novel, *Beyond Yotsuya*, was long finished. Vickie had put him in touch with Alan Green at her advertising agency for publishing advice. In writing Green, George referred to it as "my first novel," but at one of our dinner parties he held forth, in all seriousness, on the death of the novel, claiming no more novels would or could be written. As the loyal wife, I said nothing, though I thought this tirade utter rubbish. Only later did I connect his eulogy for the genre with the failure of his novel to see the light of day. His scholarly writing was intelligent and articulate but the novel didn't merit publication, though I never said as much to him.

Lacking editorial work, I still wanted to do something non-routine. Eventually I joined Women Strike for Peace to work for a ban on nuclear testing, helping persuade President Kennedy to sign the partial test-ban treaty in 1963. WSP later focused its activism on a cause George knew much about, Vietnam. During our Bronx years, the US was getting more entangled there, with increasing numbers of "military advisers." George's job left little time for political activism, but once he was on a local radio station, explaining the situation in Vietnam as he had learned it first-hand, eloquently opposing the Kennedy administration's drift toward military involvement. If only the powers-that-were had listened. Few such voices got any air time then.

The George of that radio talk was the man I believed I was marrying four years earlier. Often, though, he was withdrawn, absorbed in unexpressed private thoughts. Although most details of our life then are forgotten, limited hindsight shows George as at least moody, perhaps tending toward depression. I wonder whether some such scourge, some head full of demons, tormented George then, and more and more later.

One sign of unease was that, after barely two years at the council, he was ready to quit. I put my foot down. Too soon; doesn't look good to change jobs so often. He agreed to stay another year and began to look for fellowships so he could pursue what became his major research interest: national minorities in China, the non-Han peoples who live around the periphery, and the policy of the People's Republic toward them. By the fall of 1962 I was ready to move too. There was a slim chance he might join a project on China at the council, and we looked for a house in Westchester, where houses were expensive and sidewalks rare. "[W]e might buy a house [I wrote Robert]…, if we can find one that won't land us in the poorhouse. George is tired of the subway, I'm tired of my landlady, who hasn't spoken to us since April, and of not having a yard to turn my wild animals loose in." The Baraneks' yard was a narrow, unfenced strip of grass.

The council project didn't materialize but George got a Rockefeller Foundation grant. Friends invited us to spend a weekend at a vaguely left-wing resort in the Catskills. It was gray and chilly, with more verbal than physical activity. When George explained his plan to study national minorities in China, a woman exclaimed: "I didn't know there were Jews in China."

There have been Jews in China. The refugee colony in Shanghai during World War II that included two Steiner uncles was one instance; much earlier there were Han Chinese in Kaifeng who practiced Judaism. George's work had nothing to do with either one, but this woman's myopic remark reminded me of a story about the earlier bunch. Rabbi Rabinowitz is traveling in China. He wears a long black coat, fur hat, and prayer shawl, has a beard and sidelocks. He is in Kaifeng on *Shabbes* and goes to temple. After the service a Chinese Jew comes up to him and says, "I see you know our prayers and ritual." "Yes," says Rabinowitz, "I'm Jewish." "Oh," says the Chinese Jew, "you don't look Jewish."

George chose to use his fellowship at Harvard. I looked forward to returning to a familiar place with some familiar people, not as a student but in a role both more lowly (a mommy) and more exalted (scholar's wife). And we found an apartment with a back yard on a street with sidewalks.

Chapter 22

THE BRONX: WOMEN STRIKE FOR PEACE

"One should...be able to see that things are hopeless and yet be
determined to make them otherwise."
—F. Scott Fitzgerald, "The Crack-Up"

*T*hrough the 1950s and into the '60s, I avoided political activism—
until we lived in the Bronx. With no editorial work to do for George, I
still wanted to do *some*thing beyond meals, naps, outings. What fell in my
lap was work, with Women Strike for Peace (WSP), for a ban on nuclear
testing, my most significant political effort during the years with George.

We subscribed to the *Bulletin of the Atomic Scientists* and *I.F. Stone's
Weekly* and were in tune with their views, quite different from main-
stream Cold War dogma. Some friends worshipped President Kennedy;
we didn't. The Bay of Pigs fiasco made us skeptical, and during the
Cuban Missile Crisis we were more afraid of what the US might do than
of Cuba. Why wouldn't Cuba arm itself? The US had already invaded
it, via its Cuban surrogates, and has never accepted the Castro (and successor) government, nor acknowledged that the Batista regime Castro
overthrew was anything but democratic and good only for a slim stratum
of the wealthy, and for American sugar companies. And we had missiles
in Turkey; why was that all right but not Soviet missiles in Cuba?

Through George's work at the Council on Foreign Relations (CFR)
we met Cuban émigrés, one of whom, reminiscent of the haughty women
in the Havana doctor's waiting room, told me with great pathos that in
Havana she had had separate closets for dresses, skirts, and so on, while
in New York she had only one closet and had to iron each garment once
when hanging it up and again to wear it. Considering that most of her
countrymen and -women had had neither closets nor much to put in them

before the revolution, and many had earned a pittance cutting cane under a blazing sun for those sugar companies, it was hard to weep with her.

Earlier, when World War II gave way to the Cold War, once the Soviets also had the Bomb, every siren suggested nuclear Armageddon; New York would be a prime target. The (nonsensical) hiding-under-the-desk drills came later. We learned first to live with nuclear weapons and then to ignore them—foolishly, as they're still a menace.

Testing itself was a menace. According to Amy Swerdlow, a WSP activist who became a historian, by the end of 1958 the US had held 125 above-ground tests, the Soviet Union 44, and Britain 21.[10] Radioactive fallout from these tests included Strontium 90, an isotope common in milk and so a hazard for children especially. But we "had to" keep testing, "improving" our weapons, in our arms race with the Soviets.

Women Strike for Peace, and George and I, saw the matter differently. The US and the USSR each had more than enough warheads to destroy the other several times over. The weapons were (and are) unusable unless one is ready to end human—and not only human—life on Earth. Fallout shelters and other "civil defense" measures were mainly ways to make the arms race acceptable. Just stock your shelter with canned goods and water and toilet paper, and guns and ammo to keep the undeserving out, and we can ride out the blasts, the fires, and centuries of deadly radioactivity. This, more or less, was the government's message, but the experience of Hiroshima and Nagasaki—with tiny bombs compared to the monster H-bombs—made such preparations seem a bad joke.

Somehow I found the local WSP group, or it found me. Miriam Chesman, an "old leftie," made the meetings and demonstrations, the discussions of policy and strategy, tolerable. She also enlightened me about matters only indirectly related to WSP, one an explanation of why it's considered rude to ask how much rent someone pays. According to Miriam, it's a conspiracy to keep tenants from comparing notes so that landlords can charge different rents for equivalent apartments. From Miriam I also first learned about the competition between Jews and African-Americans about whose people had suffered more.[11]

I wasn't the only reluctant activist. Swerdlow cites a study of WSP members, in which "Only 66% had taken part in a demonstration [and] of those only 19% said they had enjoyed it." But this issue *was* urgent, and WSP was an admirable bunch of assertive women. The president, Dagmar Wilson, testified fearlessly before unfriendly congressional committees, and there were frequent marches and demonstrations, with signs, balloons, and strollers. I marched reluctantly once or twice, in Manhattan near the UN, but, though I could see how effective a parade of mothers and small children was, I didn't take the children, not wanting to use them as props. My activism was hard on them anyway: while I attended meetings and demonstrations, made phone calls, and wrote leaflets to make the world safer for my children, much of this activity deprived and frustrated them. As I hung up the phone after one WSP call, two little faces lit up. They fell again as I picked up the phone for yet another call. Swerdlow writes that some WSP couples joked that the organization was "not a Communist conspiracy, as the extreme Right suggested, but a plot by AT&T to increase its revenue." I contributed less to AT&T's profits than more active members, but the memory of my little ones' disappointment remains vivid.

In the early 1960s, most middle-class women devoted themselves primarily to housework, child rearing, and shopping, with perhaps some volunteer work, most not as voracious of their time as was WSP. Christopher Wilson, Dagmar's husband, supported the peace strike in November 1961 with which she launched WSP. He "even coined the principal slogan of the day, 'End the Arms Race—Not the Human Race.' But as the movement continued, he grew impatient with the way it upset family life."

Another woman, "asked about her husband's and children's reactions to her nonstop WSP activities, responded, 'They couldn't wait until it was all over.'" She realized only later that "her children resented the lack of attention and her preoccupation with people and events outside the home," though by their teens they understood what she was about and "became very supportive." Her husband admired "her courage and perseverance" but resented "'the fact that dinner was not ready.'" Had I been as dedicated, George would have been another resentful husband, but I must always have had dinner ready. I'm pretty sure that George never felt that WSP interfered with his comfort.

The world is no less dangerous now but somewhat less poisonous thanks to the partial test-ban treaty Kennedy and Khrushchev signed in

1963. It banned above-ground tests and limited the size of underground tests. The John F. Kennedy Library celebrated the 25th anniversary in 1988. As reported in *The Boston Globe*, speakers included Kennedy administration officials, Senator Edward Kennedy, and two Soviet ambassadors. All the speakers were men, and if the article was accurate, they recalled discussions and conflicts among members of Congress, the executive branch, and the Soviet Union, with no mention of any popular movement. Disgusted, I wrote the *Globe*:

> ...In 1961–63, thousands of women in dozens of US cities, organized by Women Strike for Peace, lobbied and demonstrated for a test ban.... Although no one at the conference seemed to remember anything but the high-level discussions, the concerns and decisions of the powerful few, isn't it possible that the peace movement helped bring about the test ban treaty?... Too bad very few journalists see fit even to speculate on the connection.

Not only was the all-male, all-government conference an all-too-familiar distortion of history, but—at the library built to honor his administration and his memory—it distorted and dishonored President Kennedy's words and actions. Although no one can say whether he would have pursued the treaty without WSP clamor, Swerdlow shows that he generally agreed with WSP demands, despite the very different message coming from the "military-industrial complex." In January 1962, with a WSP picket outside the White House, for instance:

> Kennedy stated that he had seen the women, believed them to be sincere, and had received their message.... [He]...also stated that the greatest disappointment of his first year in office was his failure to get an agreement on a nuclear test ban treaty. (p. 85)

After the treaty was signed but ratification by the Senate was still in doubt, Kennedy,

> estimating the importance of mothers' pressure in getting the... treaty...ratified, agreed to an interview with the editors of seven

leading women's magazines, in which he exhorted women…to…
[discuss]… arms control and disarmament questions in…women's
organizations of all kinds…. He explained that there was a great
deal of pressure against peace efforts and that without women's
groups helping to balance the pressure he…"would be very
isolated." (p. 95–96)

Kennedy realized that the few thousands of us who marched and leaflet-
ted and testified represented many millions of voters. And surely some
in government understood the dangers of nuclear testing. Swerdlow
points out that, while the WSP women were "pragmatic and canny" in
their choice of "the [politically] most vulnerable targets in the Cold War
arsenal," including testing in the atmosphere and air-raid shelters, they
were naive in not speculating on

> the president's motives…. Nobody asked whether Kennedy was
> downplaying the nuclear force in order to upgrade tactical weap-
> onry for small wars in Latin America or Southeast Asia. In fact,
> there was little theoretical discussion in WSP publications about
> the causes of the Cold War or of war in general.

Surely the Kennedy Library event wrote WSP out of the story largely
because we were women. But there were signs in the movement that
women not only don't all conform to the then prevailing "feminine"
model—as seen in the forthright expression of opinions and WSP's effective organizing—but that many don't conform to the soon-to-emerge
"sisterhood" model. We learned that one of the New York leaders was
leaving WSP for other work. During the discussion of how to thank her
for her prodigious contributions, one woman dissented: "Why should we
thank her? She only did it for herself."

That bitchy remark broaches a question that rarely has a simple answer:
Why do some people throw themselves into political work? Principles
may mix with personal motives: to be followed and admired, escape from
mundane domestic chores, test one's independence or abilities, impress
or oppose a husband or parent. As Swerdlow put it, "WSP women, free
for the most part from paid employment and from childcare, angered

by the nuclear recklessness of the superpowers, and frustrated by what they perceived as the timidity of the traditional peace movement, made a conscious choice to step forward to save their children and the planet. On a less conscious level they perceived an opportunity to do something important, useful, and rewarding."

Like many others, I learned about organizing but was a reluctant, rather timid, and very part-time member. I ventured to speak in public only once, at a community center, and was not effective in reaching my audience or answering questions. I was doubly glad when the treaty was signed, because of our success and because I could stop protesting and making those phone calls. But whatever our personal reasons for activism, surely we were all serious about making the world less radioactive. I hope that the distraction caused by my small part was not too much to ask of my two toddlers as the price of that boon.

The peace movement persisted, but nuclear disarmament seemed to me pie in the sky, though I was glad that others, to mix metaphors, kept tilting at that windmill. In 1982 I joined the nuclear freeze movement with considerable enthusiasm; it was a finite, achievable goal. Some reductions in missiles and warheads have been achieved. As for WSP's anti-Vietnam War work, we missed most of that movement by living abroad and then being preoccupied with private concerns.

Chapter 23
BELMONT, 1963–64

*T*he move to Massachusetts in June 1963 was difficult for three reasons, first: finding and agreeing on a place to live. I wanted to live in Cambridge but not in the dark, cramped, oddly arranged apartment that George liked. We agreed on the lighter, roomier first floor of a two-family house on Park Road in Belmont. Also difficult were moving from five rooms to four, and that Mother was with us. She was a help, but she also helped polarize our family: she and Jessica vs. George and Tommy, I in the middle.

Fitting into less space was a challenge. The children got the good-sized bedroom. The dining table filled much of the kitchen and George cobbled together a kitchen dresser with spice shelf and painted it blue, a favorite item that moved with us for many years. The dining room served as living room, and the living room was our bedroom. I figured out how to arrange the bedroom furniture after George declared it impossible, just as I sometimes managed to squeeze all we needed into the trunk of the car after he said it couldn't fit. This always annoyed him.

The rubber ring, which kept the wooden handle from clanking on the side of the metal pail for Tommy's diapers, had split. Mother picked it up. "Tommy, what's this?" "A washer." It certainly resembled a washer. "He knows a washer," Mother complained to me, "but he's still in diapers." At twenty-seven months, he wasn't toilet trained. Three years was soon enough, for me and for Dr. Spock, who advised that, before that age, it's the mother who is trained, to put the toddler on the potty in time.

In his forty-first year, I asked Tom how he remembered Grandma. "Critical," he said. "Kind of mean." "Disapproving?" I asked. "Yes."

Tommy got the short end of the stick not only from Grandma, who preferred little girls. Stearns Village Nursery School had a place for Jessica. Parents helped with maintenance and as teacher's assistants, the latter mainly mothers. The teacher, Fern Clark, required mothers to stay until their children were content, overcoming separation anxiety gradually, a fine practice, but I had to leave Tommy, too young for nursery school, in tears with a neighbor who minded a handful of tots, so that I could keep Jessica from feeling abandoned. The next year Tommy was in a nursery school that didn't permit parents to stay.

It broke my heart. But Stearns Village was wonderful. It had started in Medford, as part of Tufts, then moved to Cambridge. We carpooled with the only other Belmont family. Tommy Fredrickson, in Jessica's class, called me "Jessica's mother." His father George wrote books on race relations, including *White Supremacy* (1981) and in 2021 his younger sister, Caroline, was appointed to President Biden's commission on the Supreme Court.

Miss Clark was forthright, humorous, imaginative, and devoted to the children, never impatient or exasperated. Wise too. I was helping out when a child complained to her about something Jessica either would not let her (or him) do or was making her do. "Why don't you tell Jessica?" Miss Clark encouraged the child in Jessica's hearing. "She's a good listener." If Jessica *became* a good listener (as later with her own children), very likely Fern Clark started her on that useful path. She already had a degree of self-confidence that I couldn't match till my forties or fifties. "Mr. Clark," she would call. (She says that she probably just heard "Mr." rather than "Miss.") I was in awe of the ease with which she called out clear across the room, expecting to be heard. I would go up to Miss Clark and not speak until she noticed me.

At a parents' work evening, I became aware that, as we cleaned, painted, and repaired furniture and toys, I tried to make sure that someone, or several someones, were aware of what I'd accomplished. Distressed by this need for recognition, I've lived with it by trying to give others their due, hoping to get mine in return.

We three were often in the "Ponyack," sometimes going to the S.S. Pierce store in Cushing Square, where I bought orange marmalade and coffee by the case. (S.S. Pierce, a local gourmet grocery chain, disappeared years ago.) As I drove up Belmont Street, a car pulled out in front of me, dangerously close. "You S.O.B.," I yelled, though only the kids could hear me. An echo came from the back seat: "You S.S. Pierce!"

The children made connections with the neighbors, playing with the older girl upstairs or with Kevin next door. I can still hear him shouting, "The Germans are coming! The Germans are coming!" as he ran down the driveway with a toy gun. His grandmother, admiring him, told me how *devious* girls are, as opposed to boys. That was her word.

Devious? Some families—hers included—seemed to *make* girls something like devious: with fluffy clothes suggestive of a future sexuality, remarks about being "daddy's girl," and squelching signs of physical or mental robustness. Jessica had none of this, I like to think. With her sturdy self-assurance, she looked forward to acquiring adult power. "When I grow up and you're the child," she said to me one day, though I don't recall what she promised or threatened to do with this power.

With a neighbor couple, members of Mensa, we went to an interracial dinner that I had reluctantly gotten involved in. It seemed contrived. Better for people to work together, I thought, for civil rights or some other cause, or to play together, than to spend so much time and effort on a single social event. There was much goodwill, but I also thought that, if I were Black, I would feel patronized. Perhaps more came of the effort after we left Belmont.

Maybe I had doubts about the dinner because, drafted by a fair-housing committee, I had visited a Black woman who, with husband and child, had just moved to nearly-all-white Belmont. We were mismatched as far as tastes and interests went, and she seemed baffled by my awkward attempts at friendship—like the Indian women a decade earlier in Oakland.

Civil rights was a major issue then. In April, comedian Dick Gregory and the Freedom Singers filled Harvard's Sanders Theatre, raising money for the Student Nonviolent Coordinating Committee (SNCC, pronounced "snick"). Later I wondered whether we helped send Chaney, Goodman, and Schwerner to their deaths at the hands of white supremacists, having helped send them to Mississippi. True heroes, they went into that hell of bigotry and hatred with their eyes open. It took something as drastic as their murders to push the federal government toward taking civil rights seriously.

I raised $300 for SNCC—real money then, enough to earn thanks in the Gregory event's program—from fellow residents of Belmont, including Ann Kissinger. George knew Henry K. from the Council, so, when the Kissinger and Moseley children shared the swings at Waverley Oaks playground the previous fall, the daddies introduced their wives. Ann let me visit her and gave me a contribution, small, she said, as she had just returned from getting a divorce. George and I went to hear Dick Gregory. Mercury in fish was a new issue. He had bought his mother-in-law a nice present, he told us: a case of canned tuna. I remember only that anecdote and being vaguely annoyed by it. *The Feminine Mystique* was also new, but it would be years before the movement it helped launch made such mother-in-law jokes unfunny.

Also that spring I contributed to a fundraising art sale for civil rights. In 1956 I'd gone gallery-crawling along Madison Avenue with Vickie and for $85 (more than a week's salary) bought a wonderful line drawing of the head of a young woman by an unknown Italian artist. George didn't care for this picture, and I disliked a sentimental painting of a mother and infant he'd bought in Tehran on his way home from Vietnam. So he hung his picture at The Farm; I (regrettably) gave my drawing to the art sale, where it fetched $40.

Not a regret but a mistake showed up another cultural divergence between the Moseleys and me. Kay sent a Virginia ham, which I ruined. My cookbook said to boil it to get the salt out. The ham fell apart. Kay was contemptuous. I was duly but not excessively sorry, feeling as I had when she was outraged that I *washed* a cast-iron frying pan. "There are worse crimes," I muttered to myself. In turn I was annoyed at Mother for not treating the copper bottoms of my Revere Ware pans with due respect, but eventually I agreed that life is too short for copper cleaner.

It was a year for learning, about others and myself, which can be unpleasant. We had bought an old piano, an ornate upright, and when the time came to sell it I made an oral agreement with one chap, then wanted to sell it to another who offered more for it. The first one was censorious: an oral agreement is as binding as a written one, he told me sternly. I thought he could be less stuffy about it.

Then, one summer afternoon days before we were to move again, the kids playing outside, all the doors open, and I getting ready for dinner guests, a salesman from the nearby Electrolux store appeared. He ignored the fact that I was busy. Moving to England with its different voltage? We could get a transformer. My reasons why I was not going to buy made no impression as he demonstrated the vacuum cleaner's considerable virtues. When he started to write up a sale, I finally said no clearly enough for him to believe me. It wouldn't take me so long to stop him now. Later I saw what irked me most: a stranger barges into my house uninvited and gets me to explain to him why I won't buy what he's selling. I didn't owe him an explanation. If I didn't want to buy his machine, I didn't. Why was my business, not his.

I also learned, or taught myself, how to deal with illicit desires, as in Jimmy Carter's "lusting in one's heart." It was the first but not the last time during our marriage that I was attracted to another man. They were all less assertively "manly" than George. Fortunately, none of them was attracted to me. The object of my desire this time was a young man connected to a civil rights group. We had a joint task to do and he was quite business-like about it, with no further interest in me. So I daydreamt about him for two weeks, or three, not letting anything show, and then it was all over. No one knew I'd been anything but George's wife. The private fantasy, better than trying to squelch unwelcome desires, is an acknowledgement that you can't help what you feel: the desire arises unbidden, is in fact a nuisance. But you *can* help what you do about it. Daydreaming while saying and doing nothing turned out to be the perfect way to humor my desires while remaining the loyal wife. Admittedly it would have been harder were my feelings requited.

Some questions about the man I was loyal to arose that year, beyond those that arose earlier. After that admirable radio talk about Vietnam the year before, George had a letter published in *The New York Times* endorsing escalating US military involvement. This was probably the first time I wondered how different his political outlook really was from the Moseleys'. Were his dissenting views only remnants of adolescent rebellion, not considered political convictions? Mark Mancall, who was advising him on his research, asked George: "Do you really mean it?"

I'd known Mark in graduate school and George told me that, when they'd met and George mentioned me, Mark exclaimed, "*You* married Eva Steiner?!" Mark hadn't indicated to me that he considered this, or

me, special. He was rumored to be adept at learning languages, supposedly becoming fluent in Russian in two weeks in the USSR. While there
he had an appendicitis attack and in Belmont regaled us with the story.
Scarce anesthetics were reserved for heart and brain operations. For a
mere appendectomy, he was weighted down with iron bars. You go into
shock when cut open, he told us. Yet another way we live sheltered lives,
anaesthetized for dental fillings, let alone abdominal incisions.

It was odd to be back near Harvard, in a kind of limbo, neither the
purgatory of graduate school nor the empyrean where dwelt the faculty. I
recall only one significant social occasion involving Asian studies scholars,
a reception to launch a book. A large crowd sipped their drinks at the
MIT Faculty Club as John Fairbank spoke, with jokes in English, French,
German, Chinese, and Japanese. At each witticism different parts of the
room broke out in laughter.

Robert was not there; his field was literature, not history. We did see
something of the Hightowers that year. Bunny and I took my two and
her Tom, then about six, to children's theaters, and we four adults went
to adult plays, about which Robert and I usually shared an opinion, and
Bunny and George a different opinion.

Although we hadn't worshipped Kennedy as some of our friends
did, his death in November was a blow. One was inevitably moved by
that young widow and those two tiny, now fatherless, children. Had JFK
lived, would US actions in Vietnam and elsewhere have been different?

Whatever made George write the *Times* letter may have been behind a
dream I had: I was in the hall near our front door. It was night. Suddenly I
noticed, only a few feet away, a man lying across the threshold face down,
his legs stretching onto the front porch; he was dead, trapping me. I woke
up, my heart racing. Although I couldn't see his face, or even his whole
body, in the spooky gray twilight of the dream, I knew it was George. The
house was our house but also my body, and my psyche, both of which he
inhabited and somehow bottled up, thwarted, with his dead weight.

Surely this was a sign of trouble, as was what I learned at the dentist:
that I grind my teeth. And it was surely connected to the man George
stood in for, though I wasn't made to see the resemblance till years later:
my father, who came to visit us with his third wife over the Fourth of July

in 1964. One morning I lay in bed pretending to sleep, George annoyed because he had to entertain Leo and Elsie, who were not scintillating company.

In photos Leo took, the children look rather stiff, unfamiliar, as if he had imposed his personality on them. But there is one touching memory. In Marblehead on the Fourth, Leo was holding Tommy when the fireworks began. Our three-year-old, frightened, buried his face in Leo's shoulder, trusting as usual, even with someone he hardly knew.

Distressed by the dream, and wanting to understand us and our marriage better, I wrote Erich Fromm for advice. We'd heard him lecture in New York, and I was reading his book about fairy tales. I asked why he wrote that Little Red Riding Hood got her hood representing menstruation from her grandmother rather than her mother, and whether he knew a local psychiatrist I might usefully see for an hour. He wrote that he had no time to answer about Little Red Riding Hood, adding that "it is a matter of luck whether one gets anywhere" from "speaking with a person for one hour," but giving me the name, address, and phone number of a female doctor: "I would not know of anybody with whom it would be more worth while spending an hour."

I didn't follow up, mainly because I had no money. Soon it became impossible, for, having gotten a taste of getting paid, if not handsomely, for full-time research and writing, George secured another fellowship, one that would take us to London, the second of six consecutive annual moves. Moving enabled me to put off deciding what to do with my time and talents; there was no chance to settle into anything serious, so I postponed even thinking about what I would do if and when we stayed put for more than twelve months.

For the children, the moves were, I hope, only marginally disruptive. For George, moving not only made sense in terms of his interests and career, but also fed a deep-seated need, as he looked to new places for fulfillment and perhaps tried to run away from himself. Many of our happiest times together were when we shipped our stuff and moved ourselves and the children to another city or, better still, another continent.

Chapter 24
LONDON, 1964–65

*J*n February 1939 England was a dark streak on the horizon as the *Hamburg* stopped to take on passengers. In September 1964, as the *Maasdam* docked in Southampton after a crossing from Boston, England became our temporary home. We had two weeks at the Waverley Hotel in Bloomsbury, near the University of London, where George was to spend the year at SOAS (pronounced "so as"), the School of Oriental and African Studies. The hotel introduced us to fried eggs swimming in mutton fat, and to those perverse toast racks, little radiators cooling the toast. Two elderly British ladies remarked how well-behaved Jessica and Tommy were, unexpected praise for two little Americans in sedate England. We let them be active and noisy when it didn't matter, so they could be well-behaved when necessary.

One place they worked off steam was a playground in nearby Coram's Fields, strikingly peaceful compared to the often frenetic playgrounds back home. My theory was that British parents shared values and expectations (boys don't cry, for example) that, whether or not best for children, made for certainty and so tranquillity. Americans had a mish-mash of cultures and conflicting values, so parents were uncertain, contradictory.

Maybe something similar was true of social class. Americans thought of the US as classless: a pretense of social equality here versus fairly sharp distinctions in Britain. Speech, dress, some habits and customs varied by class; while somewhat rigid and confining, this arrangement let people know where they stood and what was expected of them. Here, going to an Ivy League or Seven Sisters college, as I did, might seem your entree to a "higher" social class, yet that class might not accept you.

Our little Americans made house hunting hard. London landlords didn't welcome children and there were no laws to force them to—possibly no fair housing laws at all. One day I was on the phone with an agent about a promising rental. Hearing my American accent, he asked, apologetically, "Are you colored at all?" Instead of suggesting we were pink, I said "No" and immediately regretted it. But pink, brown, or "white," no children wanted.

We looked further and further out, learning that "just around the corner" might mean a twenty-minute walk. Finally we found 10 Green Road in Whetstone, just around two corners from the Totteridge and Whetstone station, the penultimate stop on the Northern Line to High Barnet. Totteridge is up the hill; Whetstone is along the High Road, with shops and modest houses. Number 10 is an attached house: four small rooms, kitchen and bath, a walled garden with apple tree, and a carport. The helpful owners lived elsewhere.

We sometimes walked in a nearby strip of woods; once I was wearing stockings and learned that the poison of stinging nettles clings to nylons, prolonging the pain. A solo winter walk produced another sort of pain. The pollarded street trees looked like evil clubs; the "terraces" of identical houses rose in dark gray layers toward a gray sky. I came home close to tears, it was all so dreary. How odd that a friend came from Paris because *Paris* was dreary at Christmas. "Drearier than London?" He assured us it was. Hard to believe. Along with the grayness, on Christmas and Boxing Day (the 26th) everything was shut and hardly anyone left home.

An "infant school" for Jessica was really just around the corner. We found a nursery school for Tommy. Having left him crying while I helped Jessica get acclimated at Stearns Village, I now left him crying in this very brown church hall. But we felt he should have the company of his English contemporaries—and he didn't cry for long.

Everyday life was different in many small ways. An under-the-counter fridge meant shopping for food almost daily at multiple shops: greengrocer, baker, butcher or fishmonger, Sainsbury's for butter, cheese, smoked meats. The raw materials were surprisingly good considering what the English did with them. Beautiful vegetables, and then you could smell cabbage boiling all afternoon, the antithesis of Peter Ch'en's stir-fry. Pork was especially good, and in the country later we saw why: free-range pigs rooting in the dirt.

A common sight in English high streets would have delighted my roommates at New Haven Hospital but not their husbands: chemists' shops (drugstores) displaying condoms, diaphragms, spermicides. In the States one still asked for the stuff *sotto voce*, even where it was legal. The British were relatively open about sex; we saw couples smooching in public, then still considered scandalous in the States. Perhaps such behavior was new in the 1960s, as was, in an article about au pairs in the *Sunday Observer*, "the use, in discussing husbands' attitudes, of the term 'easy lay,' which I don't think one would find in the Sunday NY Times Magazine." (Unless otherwise noted, all longer quotations are from my letters to Robert Hightower.)

Rented houses came equipped with linens, china, pots and pans, but our new gas "cooker" was ineffectual. Each burner had a single straight row of flames. A pan on the largest burner would be bubbling down the middle while the food on each side remained cold. I complained but people at the gas company couldn't understand what the difficulty was, evidence of an endearing and maddening impracticality. The toast rack is another example, and how about auto mechanics dressed in long *white* coats? Standard dress then.

Impractical English heating is, I think, well known, but, thanks to the open coal fire in our sitting room, I learned about wing chairs. An open fire, needing air, creates a draft; you might feel the air whizzing past your ear—unless you're in a wing chair.

In 1964, London no longer had its classic fogs; soft coal, which caused the fogs' famous opacity, had been outlawed, but coal fires were still common. George tended ours and also faced the discomforts of the old Public Records Office. He had to get there early to snag a seat with heat *and* light. The Brits did already have electric radiators on wheels, which are effective and economical, and eventually we resorted to electric underblankets, which you turn on before bedtime and off when you get into bed, and oh what a difference.

We had the usual "geyser," for instant hot water, a sensible system, less wasteful than tanks that keep gallons of water hot day and night. One day our geyser quit. The repairman soon found the problem: the diaphragm;

he showed me the large worn rubber disk. He was not embarrassed. Though it looked just like an oversize contraceptive diaphragm, the Brits called that a cap.

And not only were they more matter-of-fact about sex, I got the impression that they were waiting to grow old and be shut of all that stuff. Older folks in the shops appeared content, even serene, calling each other Love and Duck/y; evenings at the laundromat they helped each other fold sheets. They had probably met at the laundromat for years, perhaps grown up together. For an English neighbor to say "Good morning" could take years, and to be invited to an English house was rare, although our sinological connections helped. One occasion was a dinner at the house of "Richard Harris of the *London Times*. Howard Boorman wrote George for us to invite ourselves at the Harris's so we did. The food was good; we have had good food in two English homes now." It was probably there that we first had trifle, which calls for cake (stale cake works well), sherry to soak it in, custard, and such embellishments as jam, fruit, nuts.

Our neighbors in the house attached to #10 were a middle-aged couple. He washed shop windows in nearby North Finchley. On Guy Fawkes Day ("Remember, remember/The fifth of November") *we* invited *them* for sparklers. I was in their house only once, to use their phone when ours, a pay phone in our tiny front hall, was out of order. A repairman soon fixed it. Needing to make sure it took incoming calls, he checked his watch; he'd have to wait twenty minutes before ringing the exchange. "They're having their afternoon tea." "All at the same time?" "Oh yes."

Used to American hustle and claims of efficiency, we had to get used to this more sedate pace. We'd been in Whetstone two months and had an account at the local Barclay's Bank, when I asked about a statement. "We try to get one out every six months," the manager told me. I explained that the checks for George's fellowship were paid directly into our account in dollars; we needed to know what we had in pounds. Could he tell me the current exchange rate? Whereupon he fished that morning's *Times* out of the dustbin and gave me the figure from the financial page; I thought he'd have inside information. This leisurely modus operandi had a good aspect: if funds were insufficient to clear a check, the bank would wait to see if the needed funds were coming, rather than bouncing the check immediately.

There wasn't always a good aspect, however. George read in the *Times* that the P&O Lines, though British, had to buy six new ships from Japan before they could afford to buy one in England. The Brits took too long, easy to believe once I'd watched construction workers crossing the high road after a tea break. I'd never seen anyone able-bodied move so slowly.

When I mentioned this surprising problem to Viennese friends of my parents, Fanny Lovington (in Vienna Löwy) ascribed it to immigrants from the British West Indies. I was skeptical, believing that working-class Brits were aping their "betters." Surely the upper classes, whose speech and manners were meant to be exemplary, were also models of indolence, even if more decorative indolence than that of factory or construction workers.

And it wasn't anything new, as was much of the West Indies influx. Our portion of Greater London took its unusual name from an actual whetstone set in the pavement outside a pub in the High Road. In earlier times, farmers would come to the village to sharpen their scythes and sickles, we were told, and indeed the stone is worn in the middle, presumably by all those blades. Everywhere else a farmer would have a sharpening stone in his pocket. He would work on the blade and keep mowing. No stroll to and from the pub, no "natter" with his "mates."

That was another set of things to get used to. The quip I'd heard attributed to Mark Twain, that the British and the Americans are two peoples separated by a common language, may actually be a bon mot of George Bernard Shaw or Oscar Wilde. Perhaps all three said it. Some words were simply different: the verb for vacuuming was "to hoover"; an acquaintance scoffed that blowing your nose should be "to kleenex." A toilet was a loo—which *may* come from the French "gardez l'eau," called out before emptying a slop pail into the street—and to "spend a penny" meant paying the fee to open the door of a public loo. An apartment was a flat, an apartment building, a block of flats; a baby carriage was a pram, short for perambulator; a stroller, a push-chair; and a car had a boot and a bonnet, not a trunk and a hood. Jessica learned to say "tidying up" and "May I have a go?," at first with an American accent.

Some expressions had different meanings. "She went back to sleep after the butler knocked her up," did not refer to hanky-panky; the butler had woken her up. Some words indicated British sedateness vs. American dynamism. We run for office; they stand for it. Our stores carry goods; theirs keep them. Or sometimes not. A friend couldn't find an item she had come to like on the usual shelf. When she asked the grocer about it, he said: "Oh, that was so popular we couldn't keep up with the demand so we stopped keeping it."

There has been much mutual influence since the 1960s. Brits now say "I guess," a source of amusement when I said it in 1965, and "step up to the plate," which makes me wonder whether they know about "home plate." Americans flaunt such Britishisms as "spot-on," "that said," and "at the end of the day," and also truncate a British saying to "The proof is in the pudding." Does this mean anything? The actual saying is "The proof of the pudding is in the eating."

There was a different sense of time too. Writer Earle Hitchner noted that "Americans think 100 years is a long time" while "the English think 100 miles is a long way." A fifteen-year-old building that in America would be torn down was considered new there. When New College, Oxford, was built in 1379 it was newer than eight other colleges. After World War II the master of New College learned that the roof beams in the "hall," where the scholars eat, needed replacing. Where was he to find such massive oak beams? Not to worry: the college's forester assured him that he and his predecessors had been growing oaks in the college's forest for just that purpose for 600 years.

And there was the currency: twelve pence to the shilling, twenty shillings to the pound, twenty-one shillings to the guinea. At first I sympathized with the Yank who, faced with a price tag in sterling, asked, "How much is that in money?" But having gotten used to it I was sad, years later, to see it displaced by the more rational, more boring metric currency.

Two other things took us by surprise. One was British driving. Usually polite face to face, in their cars, anonymous behind the "windscreen," many Brits drove like maniacs, resembling those other island dwellers, the Japanese, with their rigid social rules and their all-bets-off behavior both in crowds and on the road.

An American long resident in England introduced us to the other unexpected trait when he spoke appreciatively of British bawdiness. What in the world was he talking about? But there was the au pair article mentioned above, and we went to the Pantomime, an annual theatrical review full of slapstick and racy humor. It's probably a matter of social class. The "Panto" had a working-class air. Somewhere I read that the upper class had looser morals as its members could do what they pleased; the working class ditto because it wasn't going anywhere; while the middle class, intent on getting ahead, behaved with caution. The empire was a factor too: bearing the "white man's burden" can make one watch one's behavior and one's language. There was no more empire in 1964, but some of its habits persisted.

Perhaps it was its very sedateness that left Britain open to the cultural revolution led by the Beatles, the Rolling Stones, and King's Road fashions, with their super-short skirts and unisex clothes. The motherly owner of the local toy shop sighed as a long-haired chap walked by. "The only way you can tell the boys from the girls," she complained, "is that the boys have frills on their jeans."

Tommy loved the Matchbox toys she sold, little well-made and inexpensive vehicles; he often slept with a bed full of them, like the Hindu bed of nails. When I walked him home from nursery school, I tried to get him past the toy shop window without stopping. One day he begged and begged. I was doubtful. "You'll want me to buy you something, and you'll cry if I don't." He promised he wouldn't, I let him look, and, as we walked on, he said, "See, I didn't cry." It reminded me of an incident the year before when I'd let Jessica put a fragile object in her pocket and, afraid she'd take it out and lose or break it, was reluctant to let her take it into another room. "I'll try not to take it out," she said. It thrilled me to hear the children wrestling with their own impulses, see them dimly aware that they weren't entirely in charge of their own actions, and their triumph when a budding character overcame some unruly appetite.

With both children in some sort of school, I longed for another baby. Whenever I passed a pram or pushchair, a few tears flowed. But George wouldn't have it, and even I realized that it soon wouldn't be a baby any more.

> Being a woman, I sort of kind of sometimes want a baby [I wrote
> Robert]; it's the female way of wanting to stop the clock—or the

calendar—a stupid way, since before you know it the youngest is weaned, going to school and telling you off. So there you are, old again.

A Roma ("Gypsy" then) woman sold me some "clothes pegs" and told my fortune: You don't want a large family but will have another son. (Edith explained that, as a clairvoyant, the woman "saw" all my pregnancies; I'd already had three. Perhaps there's something to that idea.) And I remembered what Robert wrote me when Jessica was three months old: "If he is admitted, my son James will be starting at Harvard next fall. My son Thomas is two years older than Alice Jessica. Let that be a lesson to you."

So I shopped almost daily, cooked on that maddening stove, taught myself to make pie crust, and watched the children change, not totally aware of how they were changing.

> Last week we were on a bus going from Oxford Circus to Islington, when J. began to interrogate me. God was ok & I got on with baby Jesus but now they've heard that he died & came back to life. How could he do that? Does Jesus live in a house? (No, Jesus is a baby, cries T. from across the aisle. [Presumably referring to dying, not to living in a house.]) Does that building reach to Heaven? Where is heaven? I told her it was any place where people are happy. Tommy started to sing about "little old Jesus." I suggested it might be little Lord Jesus, so for a while he tried little old Lord Jesus. Jessica was using "When We Were Very Young" as a hymn-book. Last night she said her prayers: Jack and Jill went up the hill and finished up by chanting Pray him, pray him.

Despite Christianity in school, the British seemed quite irreligious. Many belonged to the Church of England or to one of the "low" churches, but this seemed more tradition and social cohesion than piety. As an adult, you could pretty much forget about Jesus except in a pro forma way on Sunday, or just at Christmas and Easter—or so it seemed.

School went on through most of July, ending with an outdoor fair punctuated by rain showers. Summer weather—rain, a bit of sun, clouds, more rain—was like being at sea, with the occasional squall. Evening weather reports might include "eight minutes of sunshine." Not that the sun came out for eight minutes, but scattered moments added up to eight minutes.

Perhaps it was the damp, cool climate that caused Tommy's frequent ear infections. Dr. Covington, kind, amusing and handsome, made house calls. He examined Tommy and chatted to us parents, curious about these Americans. He inspired a verse I wrote to the tune of *Oh Susanna*:

> I come from 10 Green Road with a boo-boo on my knee.
> I'm going to North Finchley now Dr. Covington for to see.
> Oh Dr. Covington, oh don't you cry for me,
> Just put on some mercurochrome and a Band-Aid on my knee.

(Whatever we poison our children and ourselves with now, we try not to do it with mercury, in tuna, mercurochrome, or anything else. But this was many years ago.)

Tommy eventually outgrew the ear infections. On his fourth birthday George took him to the Imperial War Museum, which Tommy called the "Men's Mezoom." Later he stood in front of the fireplace and asked, "When am I going to be four?" "You're four already," I told him. "I am?" His hand moved wonderingly over his chest and tummy and his face lit up. While he had a "softer" side, he played the usual boys' games, some of which imitate what the Men's Mezoom commemorates. Dr. Who and the Daleks were popular, and Tommy threatened family and friends, arms straight out in front like the Daleks' weapon, and in a droning robot voice declared: "I am a Dalek. I will extroy you."

In January George was "a tutor at a conference of British army officers on Far Eastern doings, in Oxford." In March, "he was offered and accepted a studentship at St. Antony's College, Oxford." Because we would be on a British fellowship, we both found menial work so as to save up some money, he as a gardener, I charring (cleaning house). Being relatively poor was instructive. When all our income went for such ephemeral necessities as rent and food, I developed an urge to buy things that would last. It helped me understand Vickie's six-foot shelf of pocketbooks after years of Zetlin poverty.

My employers, conservative, conventional, and kindly, shared a double house with her mother, who would occasionally come through the door connecting the two lounges (living rooms) and find me hoovering. "I see you're working like a black boy," she said one day, presumably the unthinking racism left over from empire days. One Sunday they invited us to tea. The table was spread with many carbohydrates and a jar of meat paste; no vitamins were present. The English were said to consume more sugar per capita than any other nationality.

Rod and Emily MacFarquhar invited us and others for a meal that was memorable in a different way. I'd known Rod in graduate school, a handsome, charming Brit, self-assured without being obnoxious. He founded Britain's *China Quarterly*. Emily, née Cohen, was American, a journalist with an interest in China. We sat on a daybed in their tiny flat eating soup with slippery rice noodles and a dessert of fruit-filled dumplings. Wow, I thought, George would never let me get away with such a supper, least of all for company. But he didn't complain when another hostess provided such interesting but slender fare.

Emily told us about her interview with Madame Chiang Kai-shek— "audience" would be more accurate for it took great effort to secure an appointment and Emily had to approach Sung Mei-ling (Madame's own name) as if she were royalty. Nor did Emily get much information out of her. "Why did you want to interview Madame Chiang Kai-shek?" George asked—a question I appreciated but Emily understandably did not.

Like the MacFarquhars, and us, Hal and Sandra Kahn were a half-Jewish couple but with the genders reversed: Hal was about as Jewish as I am. I served roast pork when they came for dinner and he not only relished the meat but asked for the fat. Hal's field was also Chinese history. According to an August letter, "I have done some editing and typing for [Hal], on his thesis, and am working on a translation of an article in German for [Sandra]." The article, from a 1942 issue of a German journal (i.e., during World War II), reported on visits of professors and traveling exhibitions from Japan, "which seems a bit spooky." And I'd edited, typed, and indexed the two books George had begun at Harvard: *A Sino-Soviet Cultural Frontier: The Ili Kazakh Autonomous Chou* (this *chou* [prefecture] is in Xinjiang), and *The Party and the National Question in China*, mainly a translation of the PRC's minorities policy. Both were published in 1966.

Despite the sharp memory of George's disturbing 1964 letter to *The New York Times*, I couldn't recall what he thought about Vietnam in 1965 until, decades later, I read a note from him in Ed Lansdale's papers at the Hoover Institution: "It's beginning to look like the ingredients for a third world war are present in poor little Vietnam. I am outraged by the whole drift of things (in the foreign field) under Johnson." It must have been a relief to have him back in the anti-war camp.

My only political effort that year was to hear Reverends Martin Luther King, Jr., and Ralph Abernathy speak, and to join in singing "We Shall Overcome." I grabbed the hand of the nearest (startled) Brit and swayed left and right as was usual in the civil rights movement.

It was good to live abroad for a time, but it meant skirting the major '60s US political upheavals: civil rights and anti-Vietnam War.

Chapter 25
VIENNA REDUX, 1965

A plaque in a church in Innsbruck that Hilde Steiner (my uncle Ignaz's widow) and I visited in 1985 explained that it had been rebuilt because in 1944 or '45 it was hit by a bomb. It did not say what nationality the bomb was and I speculated that the adults did not want Tyrolean children asking, "Why did the Americans bomb Innsbruck?"

American bombers struck Vienna too. In 1949 or '50, when reconstruction had barely begun and everything was extremely cheap if you had dollars, Vickie and Rudi were the first in our family to return. Their attempts to start a business came to naught and I, absorbed by college and other youthful pursuits, showed little interest in their experiences in Vienna. But when Mother suggested she and we four Moseleys go there in June 1965, George was willing and I was curious, with none of the reservations that for many years kept Anna from returning—even though Beppo asked her to come back.

Mother had a new VW station wagon delivered in London, so we could drive to Vienna and back before she shipped it home to sell as a used car. After a (luckily unmemorable) crossing on the Channel ferry, our route across northern France took us through small towns and past many enclosed farmsteads. When we looked for lodging among farms that offered it, Mother worried about privies that required squatting, and she would inspect the sheets for signs of bedbugs past, a likely indicator of bedbugs present. Aside from these features of rural life, the trip was our introduction (only George had been in France before) to cuisine. Not that we ate where it was haute, but everything in the simplest restaurant in the most undistinguished town was, while inexpensive, perfectly prepared.

In Reims we took a quick look at the cathedral; in Basel we swam at a very busy public pool. We avoided Germany on the trip east; Switzerland was more scenic and twenty years after the war Germany still seemed repellent. It would be another twenty years before I learned that many Austrians were "better Nazis" than many Germans. We drove back through Germany, as quickly as possible.

Austria was beautiful. We were never out of sight of at least one snow-capped peak. We may even have seen the highest, Gross Glockner, and a near rival, Dachstein, names with echoes from early childhood, though the highest mountain I "climbed" back then, in 1937 at five and a half, was the Kampl, outside the village of Obersdorf. I doubt I got anywhere near the summit. I never had the urge to climb anything really high or really dangerous, and in 1982, when Vickie and I were in Kärnten, I discovered that I liked looking *up* at high mountains. The local snowy peak, Reisskofel, loomed over my daily solo hikes, helping me see mountains as metaphors for large or important humans, who look down on you, making you feel threatened, or protected, or both. Some climbers who try to "conquer" them are killed, as if punishment for daring to challenge their greatness.

In among mountains, we saw a sight that was amazing for 1965, or for any year: an elderly couple plowing, the man guiding the plow, the woman hitched to it, the bridle around her forehead. Was this a remnant of a once-common practice or a rare, even unique, kind of exploitation, due to necessity, or cruelty? As we zipped past at many kilometers an hour, it just left a puzzling memory.

A happier memory is of an inn south of Salzburg, where an impressive stove cooked the meals and heated the house and the water. George decided he would import such stoves.

One other moment stood out en route to Vienna. As we ate our lunch on the roadside, a native on a motor scooter called out "*Mahlzeit*," short for "*Gute Mahlzeit*" ("Good mealtime," *Bon appetit*), but pronounced "*Moytseit*." I'd forgotten this familiar expression; it was as if he'd said, "Welcome home."

Mother, ever adept at arrangements, had asked Julius Donner if we could stay with him and his wife for our week in Vienna. My parents had hidden him after he took part in the failed 1934 revolution. I remembered Julius, a cabinetmaker who had lost part of a finger to his craft, as affectionate and delightful, Minnie as reserved but kind. In 1938 we had supper with them and I watched entranced as Minnie bathed Martin, their first-born, gently cleaning his ears and nostrils with cotton swabs. It was warm there and quiet, serene, so different from what I was used to that it left a lifelong memory.

We found the Donners' apartment on the fourth or fifth floor of a building on the Franz-Josefs-Kai, on the edge of the Inner City overlooking the Danube Canal. Further embarrassment, in addition to benefiting from Mother's sponging: the main connection had been with Julius but he and Minnie were living apart; she was there, he wasn't. To my regret, we saw him only for minutes on our last day. Minnie was more than hospitable; we five filled most of her apartment, but she behaved as if she had invited us.

Mother embarrassed me again when she and I visited Hofstattgasse 15 and she rang the bell of our apartment. She told the occupants, a couple probably in their forties: "We used to live here and my daughter would like to see it," not bothering with "May we come in?" Our successors were stunned into silent acquiescence, perhaps not only by the peremptory nature of this unexpected visit. Paul told me that a young Nazi pair were foisted on us (or rented a room from my parents) in 1938. If they were eighteen or twenty then, they would be in their forties in 1965.

In 1997, about to take sixteen-year-old Katelin to Vienna, I wrote to the occupants of both the apartments I'd lived in. Those in Anna and Beppo's didn't reply but there was a gracious letter from Hofstattgasse. Paul Raimund Lorenz, a professor of linguistics at the university born after the war, could only guess at what we had been through; he and his wife would be glad to have us come see the apartment. Which we did. In 1965, I just walked down the hall and glanced quickly into a couple of rooms. This time we saw all the rooms and the garden, took photos, had tea and much pleasant talk. We learned that Viennese tend to stay put once they have their apartments, and that before the Lorenzes an aged widow had lived there: the wife of 1965 and the Nazi bride of 1938? Attempts at archival research haven't provided the answer, but in any case we Steiners had to leave, somebody the Nazis approved of got our apartment, which survived the war intact, and now this nice couple had it. The bathroom and kitchen had been modernized, the sandbox and the brick *Kamin* were gone, but the layout of the rooms remained the same. No more silently fighting parents, no more young, handsome, coarse father prancing about naked. Austria eventually paid compensation for the lost apartment, as well as pensions for refugees. Some of mine paid for Katelin to study Arabic and Islamic philosophy, some went to Israeli activists for Palestinian rights, including IDF "refuseniks" who wouldn't serve in the occupation—a small way for a Jew who had escaped the terrible fate visited on most of Europe's Jews to support other Jews who refused to use the Holocaust to justify Zionist oppression of another people.

Vienna was beautiful and interesting. Anti-Semitism one heard about; I didn't experience it, but found many Viennese—more industrious than the British—rude and impatient. Riding an English tram or bus you got up when it stopped and descended in a civilized fashion. In Vienna, if you weren't ready to jump off as the trolley slowed down, the driver or passengers grumbled and scolded. And as I turned a corner in the Inner City with the children in tow, the large carton I was carrying grazed the leg of a man going by. "*Schaun'S wo Sie gehn*" ("Look where you're going"), he snapped, ignoring my apology. The contrast with the Brits was striking.

Despite the carton, we didn't shop much but I had to buy Jessica new sandals when hers came apart. The saleswoman asked what size. I didn't know; continental sizes are different from British and American sizes. Her look said: What kind of mother doesn't know her child's shoe size? I was delighted, as her look also meant: What kind of *Viennese* mother are you? I sounded like a native.

A native who speaks High German with an Austrian accent, not one who knows the Viennese dialect (*Wienerisch*). Father and Paul spoke *Wienerisch*, Mother and I didn't. Poldi and his siblings were natives, although their parents were not. The immigrant Zetlins likely felt different from, perhaps superior to, the Viennese masses, which may be why Isabella shunned the dialect. It certainly accounted for something surprising she said as we left Vienna.

But first we took the children to the zoo at Schönbrunn and to the Prater, where we rode the *Riesenrad*, the "giant" Ferris wheel made famous by *The Third Man*. One evening George and I went to an outdoor dance in a park along the Ring. Instead of my vision of waltzing with my husband near the "Blue" Danube, it was the usual Twist and free-form movement of the '60s to what seemed to me un-Viennese rock. Besides an evening with Ignaz and Hilde Steiner, there was a more significant afternoon with Beppo. We met him and his sister, Mitzi Medved, at the sprawling restaurant on Kahlenberg, the second hill from the Danube west of the city. Beppo and Mitzi spoke no English, George and the children, no German, so Mother and I had to translate. George wished we had left him and the children out of it but I wanted this favorite uncle to meet my new family, even if they couldn't readily converse.

Afterward I did something stupid. Beppo wrote me in London; in the prevailing style his letter was somewhat formal and he used standard abbreviations. The one I remember, used more than once, was *lb.* for *lieb* (dear)—e.g., *deine lb. Kinder*. I was so put off by this that I didn't answer, out of the same youthful arrogance that had me sneering at George's relatives who signed off "Affcc." How affectionate can they be if they can't even write out the word? Ms. Superior huffed. There's something to that in theory, but people are imperfect and lives finite. From my childhood I remember Beppo's affection as in no way abbreviated, and my love for him was complicated only by the fact that he was not my father and his apartment not my "real" home. I'm immensely sorry that, world history having torn us apart, I rejected his invitation to stay in touch. I might have learned a lot from Beppo in future letters; might have given him some pleasure rather than the pain of rejection via silence; might have visited Vienna again sooner so as to see him again. By my next visit, in 1982, a bad heart had killed him. A major item for the list of regrets.

Beppo carrying Eva, early 1930s.

As we left Vienna, Mother said, "Of course, I never felt at home here." For me this was a bombshell. There was no previous hint (to me) about such alienation. Had she kept it to herself? Or did she just realize it then, returning briefly to the city that was her home between the ages of four and 37? Too stunned (too timid?), too absorbed in Moseley concerns to ask how or why, I simply tucked this pregnant statement away, but years later it helped me see another parallel between her life and mine. I've speculated that we each married a wanderer because each had a father who wandered. But her bombshell makes me suspect that, in marrying Poldi, an assimilated Austrian Jew, Isabella attempted to become part of an "in" group, as did I by marrying George, with his reputed Mayflower and Huguenot ancestors and his more than triple-barrelled name. If I'm right, then another unconscious motive for marrying Leopold Steiner was that he was a native, quite at home in Vienna because he had known no other home—even if his mother was Czech and his father Hungarian. Thirty years later I let a native American, grandson of a general and a successful businessman, reputedly descended from John Alden, sweep me off my feet. Were Mother and I each hoping to become more at home, more accepted, through our indigenous husbands? Perhaps, but it was all unconscious.

Although marriage to George Van Horn Moseley III gave me new connections to American and foreign people and places, and although I wouldn't say that I never felt at home in the US, there is a kind of at-home-ness that eludes me—one I do and don't want. The kind the children later encountered in Plainfield, Vermont, and Medford, Massachusetts, where some schoolmates had never left their states and hardly their towns. Like Palestinian scholar-activist Edward Said, I find love of a country hard to understand. Interest, political participation, gratitude, yes, and attachment to particular places within it, but not the unconditional love behind "My country right or wrong." Isn't that egotism: I love it because it's mine? And tribalism: even when wrong, it's still the best.

Like Mother, I've never felt the love called patriotism—in the name of which many people shun, or otherwise harm, those whom they see as not belonging.

Chapter 26
OXFORD, 1965–66

*K*ay Moseley visited us in Whetstone, and on a rainy day in May we all went to Oxford in a rented car to get a look at our next habitat. As we ate our picnic lunch in the car, a Roma woman tried to sell Kay some lace. Kay didn't respond but, as I wrote Robert Hightower, had her fortune told anyway: she would live to 100. Not quite 60 then, she did live to 96 and a half.

Robert had lived in Oxford a year, with Bunny, Josie, and Tom. I'd written him about George's "studentship" at St. Antony's College. "It means three years for a doctorate and one of the years apparently in Hong Kong and of course they pay only his way. [I]t isn't at all clear we won't have starved to death before he leaves for Hong Kong; the stipend comes to £600, plus £3 a week housing allowance." Questions about life in Oxford elicited a mixed review:

> [M]y memories of Oxford are uniformly grim. But I can give you lots of advice. Josi's school is just behind St. Antony's. It is not a church school, but they give them a lot of indoctrination all the same. It is a good part of Oxford to live in, near some quaint shops (North Parade) where you can buy withered carrots and vegetable marrow [zucchini] all year round. There is a fish shop (avoid the fish) and another for meat (cheating butcher). All very cheery, servile, and in some vague way insulting. Get bicycles and ride them due west; you are out of town in five minutes. Three years? Are you crazy?

I enjoyed his jaundiced views without sharing them. We lived around the corner from North Parade, at 5 Winchester Road. I did avoid the expensive butcher and fishmonger; sometimes patronized the stationery/ sweets shop cum post office called Leisure and Pleasure (in England they rhyme); found the produce at the greengrocer's good, and became friendly with Rebecca Smith—a person of sardonic wit and unconventional opinions—who staffed but didn't own the shop.

We did get bicycles (I had to learn to manage hand brakes) and often went west, by wheel or on foot, across the Oxford Canal via Walton Well Road or Aristotle Lane, to Port Meadow, an enormous common on which people pasture horses and cattle. The Isis, which below Oxford becomes the Thames, runs along its western edge. When we took our supper to Port Meadow for a swim and a picnic on a long summer evening, we would meet Oxford denizens in Wellingtons and gardening clothes, carrying hoes and baskets of produce harvested from their allotments along the canal. Swans lived on the canal, in the spring with their cygnets. To me it was idyllic.

Mostly we were content without car, shower, telephone, or television. I rode my second-hand bicycle around town too: to buy staples at the Coop—dingy but with good prices—and fresh food at Sainsbury's in "the High" (High Street). Like everyone else, I parked the bike up against the "kerb"—no need to lock it—one pedal on the curb holding it upright.

An early walk on May 1, 1966, a bright, perfect Sunday, provided surprises: droves of students on Oxford's other river, the Cherwell— punting, drinking, falling in on purpose—and troops of Morris Men dancing down Cornmarket, the main shopping street, boots stomping, bells jingling, ribbons fluttering. Maybe the Brits aren't so lazy after all, I thought, but it was May Day, not a normal Sunday. (A punt is a long flat-bottomed boat propelled by one person with a long pole. George took us out in one and—classically—got hung up on his pole when it stuck in the river bottom and the boat glided away.)

Our flat consisted of a kitchen and living room on the ground floor, slightly below grade, and bedrooms and bath on what was the parlor floor. The living room was George's study. We did our living in the kitchen, which ran the width of the house, with windows on the walled back garden. The brighter end featured a coal heater, an improvement over Whetstone's open coal fire, as well as the dining table and my desk and sewing machine, a venerable treadle machine that I still use. Off the kitchen end the former coal cellar was mainly a source of slugs. The cat, acquired as a kitten in Whetstone, would stare at these creatures and paw them gingerly. In the spring she had four kittens. We fixed a bed for her in a closet and she brought them forth silently all by herself. As a mother, I felt a kind of kinship with her and also awe, thinking of all the help and fuss, the buildings, special staff and furniture, machinery, and drugs we modern human mothers, many of us, use to perform this eons-old mammalian task.

A neighbor stopped me one day and invited me to attend the nearby church, St. Philip's and St. James's, also the name of the school (known as Phil and Jim) Robert referred to, which is nominally but not physically attached to the church. I told her I'm Jewish so she wouldn't keep asking. Tommy started "infant school" there and Jessica moved on to the next form. According to a letter to Robert, "Tommy cried the first day & for a while he used to run home at outdoor play time but that soon stopped." When we moved in, the school was directly across Winchester Road from number 5 in what appeared to be a nineteenth-century outbuilding, part of St. Antony's, a former convent.

During 1965–66 Phil and Jim moved to bigger and less dingy quarters in Leckford Road. Here I had a run-in with the headmistress, Mrs. Peacocke, about her wanting a small outdoor pool at the school. As it would close along with the school late in July, it made more sense to have the city build a larger pool—preferably indoors in view of the climate—that would be open to everyone all year. I wasn't very forceful and didn't think of persuading other parents to join me, so Mrs. Peacocke got her pool. Whether or not it's still there, by the 1980s the city had built a good-size public indoor pool off Banbury Road, for which I can't take credit but which I've used.

As in London, nearly all our social life was with other foreigners—of whom there were plenty at St. Antony's, specializing as it did in international studies. We were friendly with the Chakrabartis, especially their son Suma, a mild-mannered boy a year older than Jessica (later Sir Suma Chakrabarti). He joined us for sparklers on Guy Fawkes Day. We'd made a Guy using old children's clothes and the question arose whether we should burn him, as was traditional. Jessica was all for it, but both boys, perhaps identifying with this effigy, were vehemently opposed. No statistical conclusion but an anecdotal refutation of the usual sex stereotypes.

The Chakrabartis were tangentially involved with our Easter week vacation. We celebrated Easter together, each family contributing some colored eggs, which for this Hindu family were a novelty. Some Chakrabarti eggs came along as we set out Monday morning for Higher Cheriton Farm on Exmoor in Devonshire. We stopped for lunch along a quiet country road and George tapped an egg on the side of our rented car. That's when we learned that I'd evidently taught Gayatri only half the theory of Easter eggs: she had colored but not hard-boiled them.

Exmoor is a sparsely settled rolling plain with many deep, wooded clefts. The coast is lined with steep cliffs, its most famous town, Clovelly, so steep that cars stay at the top of the cliff and one visits the town on foot. We did this on the first day, as it started to snow. Propelled by a stiff wind off the Atlantic, the snow came horizontally, blew into the attic above our room, melted, and dripped down. It was more serious for the sheep and just-born lambs. George joined the farm crew as they poked long sticks into enormous drifts to find the sheep trapped in them. Always ready for outdoor work, George was happy, and there were other children as company for ours. I don't know how I amused myself but, reminiscent of childhood summers on Austrian farms, the week had an aura of romance about it. Besides, without any help from me, Susan Ash fed us well three times a day.

And there was always more to learn. On a walk on the moor George and I found a ewe that, weighed down by her wool, had fallen over and couldn't get up. Two lambs were bleating nearby. George grabbed two handfuls of wool and pulled the ewe to her feet. Lambs will nurse only from their own mothers, so these two might have starved had we not come by. Mrs. Ash wrote me later that her "husband and Fred spent a day cutting off the lambs tails, 475 altogether, we went around to see all the lambs last night, they seem none the worse for it, and they look lovely."

The weather remained chilly and cloudy until our last day, when the sun came out—and Jessica came down with chicken pox. Lyova invented a rule that he didn't obey: Never make plans with people with small children.

There was no danger of our starving, but to make sure we didn't I found a short-term job at the Institute of Commonwealth Studies, where I was meant to sort the pamphlets and periodicals that overloaded the library's shelves and tables. There I met wonderful Anita Jackson, a South African Jew, sister of the writer Dorothea Krook and married to an agricultural economist who later worked in Botswana. Anita and I shared walks and long talks; she got me to read Patrick White, the Australian novelist who later won the literature Nobel; and she made gentle fun of me for calling myself Mrs. George Moseley (even if I did so only socially, never at work). Feminism was barely in the air then, let alone in the news, but clear-eyed Anita had a mind of her own.

I soon found a longer-term job in the cataloguing section of the Bodleian Law Library. The "Bod" is one of the oldest extant libraries; its original building is a beautiful creation of the fifteenth and seventeenth centuries. The earliest books were shelved in the order in which they were accessioned, and in 1966 the catalogues in the "Old Bod" were still large, unwieldy volumes with cards and slips pasted in. The plan was to go straight from these tomes to an automated catalogue. The law library is in a modernist building near the University Parks, by bicycle five minutes from Winchester Road. It had a card catalogue, as all modern libraries did then, over which Martin Smith presided with meticulous care. Mostly I typed cards, or headings on printed cards, as I'd learned to do at TAF, but soon got a more interesting assignment: translating German book titles for the subject cataloguer. The only title I remember is *Überhang und Überfall* (literally, "overhang and overfall"). I thought of it later in Medford, where a tall weeping willow next door dropped branches in my yard and its roots kept most things from growing there; the book, far as I could judge, gave me the right to lop its branches off at the property line.

One female colleague and I became friends of sorts, although on the weekends she was usually off on what seemed a mad but not terribly satisfying social whirl, after which she regaled me with tales of friends and lovers (or hoped-to-be lovers, she doing most of the hoping). She gave me pause when she quoted an aphorism: that single women are always trying to get what married women are always trying to avoid.

A Pole, Kazimierz Michalski, worked with foreign law books and I have an impression of him exhibiting symptoms of the proverbial "great

Slav soul." We once had a long chat about my background and my name, and he remarked with some satisfaction that, if my parents had been Orthodox Jews, they would have said Kaddish (the prayer for the dead) for me when I married a Gentile. (Though if they had been Orthodox I probably wouldn't have married a Gentile.) Martin wrote me later that Michalski was "a bit of an anti-semite" and "complained that Polish Jews did not consider themselves to be Polish," echoing General Moseley's complaint about American Jews.

George as always slept little and worked hard, down there in his sanctum filled with books, papers, and typewriter. He had contracted to write a brief history of twentieth-century China and so was juggling several tasks and obligations. I no longer know whether he had to do anything for St. Antony's beyond research for his dissertation on non-Han peoples living along China's southern border, mainly in Yunnan and Kwangsi. The term "professor" applied to his nominal adviser, Geoffrey Hudson, perfectly, as he professed to teach Chinese history but, as far as we could tell, didn't actually teach, or do, anything. So George worked on his own, which was the way he liked it.

Unlike Robert, I would have been glad to spend three years in Oxford, but the dissertation required research in Hong Kong and field work among the peoples George was to write about. We found a home for the cat and her four kittens—they would all stay together with a family that already had many cats. As far as I remember, it wasn't wrenching to leave as we knew we'd soon be back, resuming a life of genteel student poverty among the Brits for one more year.

Chapter 27
HONG KONG, 1966–67

*G*eorge did not go to Hong Kong alone. First we had a summer in the US, with time at The Farm and for me a weekend with Ruth Loewenstein in New York, where it was 106° each day, and in the evening the heat radiated from the pavement. George went to Washington to do research at the Library of Congress, mainly in Chinese and other newspapers, staying near Dupont Circle, "where the action is," one of the centers of his universe. This was our first lengthy separation. As always during our unsettled existence, I threw all letters out after I'd answered them—his included. Too bad; I'd like to read them now. He spent time with Shwe and one or two other friends. What else, personal or political, took up his time? And did he (could he?) tell me about it?

I soon took the children, then six and five, to San Francisco, where we moved in with Mother, in her half of her two-family house north of Golden Gate Park.

> We are supposed to be in Hong Kong already [I wrote Robert on September 1st], but George found stacks of material at the Library of Congress + so postponed everything. He'll be here tomorrow....The last hurdle is for all 4 Moseleys to spend 8 days in a 4-room apartment with Mrs. Steiner.

I showed the children off to our San Francisco friends, and to Paul and his new friend Norma; they married two years later. Tommy too fell in love with her, calling her Norman, and one day he climbed a tree in a nearby park, hung from a low branch by his knees, and asked, "Where are we now?" There would be more places to confuse him: Tokyo, and then Hong Kong.

Lyova came from Montrose in his red convertible, drove us up Highway 1 to Point Reyes, and stopped at a waterside restaurant. Tommy was fascinated by something in the water. I walked on slowly, calling to him to come, but before he did, Lyova grabbed and smacked him for not obeying. It was time to eat!

Probably it reminded Lyova of the Danube Canal incident, but with me there, he wasn't responsible for Tommy. Used to living alone, he had little patience with other people's whims and he was already angry at me because Jessica and Tommy—evidently sensing my nervousness around him—hadn't taken to him as other children did, which shows in the photos he took of them that morning. Lyova was sure I'd turned them against him. In a way I had, but unintentionally.

Once George arrived, he too met Norma, we had dinner with Poldi and Elsie, and I made George see *The Russians Are Coming The Russians Are Coming*, a new movie that I'd seen and loved. He was unenthusiastic, which disturbed me as the movie wasn't just funny and well acted but also daring in those Cold War days, treating the Russian characters as sympathetic.

Thanks to his junior year in Tokyo, George read and spoke Japanese, and was probably the only scholar I ever met who liked China and Japan equally. I found Tokyo overwhelming. *The New Yorker* once reported on its "kamikaze" taxi drivers: during a "Taxi No Accident" week there were more accidents involving taxis than ever. There seemed to be daily protests, battalions of angry young people, wearing white headbands and wielding banners, noisily taking over already crowded streets.

George had scholars to see. Knowing only a few words of Japanese and unable to read street or shop signs, I found being on my own with the kids trying, even frightening: as we walked through a small park we were followed—if that's the right term—by a man who actually walked a short distance in front of us but kept turning, leering at me, laughing what seemed a dangerous laugh, resembling the satyr-like man in my youthful nightmare. He never came close; perhaps he only seemed dangerous because of that daunting city.

After a nerve-wracking day, we put the kids to bed. When Jessica popped up again, I, at the end of my not-very-long rope, raised my right arm to threaten her, and threw my shoulder out. Evidently I was trying to make two contrary motions at once. Decades later—after I dislocated the shoulder three more times and had it repaired surgically in 1975—I wondered whether behind my pulling back was the message from brain to arm that it wasn't Jessica I wanted to hit. She was acting up but it was George who had left us adrift in that unfamiliar city. Had I agreed to a day alone with the children? Had George given me a choice? I have no idea, but, given the choice, I would probably have been the compliant—and resentful—wife.

The shoulder hurt almost as much as childbirth. George got the hotel to send a babysitter and took me to the nearest hospital, where he could answer the questions of the doctor on emergency duty, a urologist. It was a struggle to put the shoulder back and a great relief when it was in place. The doctor, wanting to ask *me* a question, went to get a German-Japanese medical dictionary; I thought this rather sinister—in view of the World War II Axis—until I remembered that Berlin and Vienna used to be meccas of medical research, treatment, and training. His question: Does it hurt?

We started our new life in Hong Kong with my arm in a sling. This time we aimed to live in Kowloon, near the Universities Service Center, where, as I wrote Robert, George shared "an air-conditioned office & a typewriter with one Englishman—he can get lunch, xeroxing, stationery, tea, &c. for little or nothing—also a research assistant, who also provides language practice." The USC was founded in 1963 to foster research on contemporary East Asia, especially China, because "in 1949 neither an existing body of knowledge nor a corps of trained personnel was available for systematic research on Mainland China." (Compare US ignorance of Vietnam, Afghanistan, and Iraq. Someone quipped that Americans learn geography when the US goes to war.)

The center found us a furnished flat, rented from Chinese owners, on the twelfth floor of 210 Argyle Street (the center being at 155), with two bedrooms, a living/dining room, and a balcony lined with pots of jasmine. The kitchen was too small for all the appliances we take for granted so the fridge—which the Chinese didn't take for granted—was in the front hall. On the two television channels, Chinese and English, you could watch *Ngo Wai Woo-See*, or *I Love Lucy*.

A roof garden came with the flat. There the kids met neighbors and played in a plastic pool on hot days; and there we celebrated Christmas Chinese style, with firecrackers. Anthony Dicks, scholar of Chinese law, was with us. Tony was another of those "soft" men whom I found attractive in a way that George wasn't. On that front there was a change too. In Macao I'd noticed that I didn't regard Chinese men as sexual beings and worried that this was a form of racism. This time I found a young shopkeeper quite appealing. Not to the point of mooning over him, but there was pleasure in winning a smile, and transacting business in his meager English and my meager Cantonese.

I rode crowded buses and was never jostled or harassed, never felt threatened. At Chinese New Year, the children and I were invited to celebrate with our amah (who cleaned our flat and did laundry twice a week) and her family in one of the numerous housing blocks the government built to get at least some of the thousands of refugees out of the shanties that illegally covered various steep hillsides. The monsoon rains often washed whole slopes bare of shacks, carrying along possessions and any residents who had the bad luck to be at home. So the housing blocks—graceless concrete monsters with long open corridors, laundry hung everywhere on bamboo poles, much noise and commotion and no privacy, with only one room per family—were better than shacks of corrugated iron, tarps, or other odds and ends clinging precariously to hillsides. No quiet or privacy there either. As I keep reminding myself, dwellings that seem shabby and depressing to me may look good to their inhabitants compared to what they've escaped.

Jessica and Tommy with Yip Wai-yee in our flat in Kowloon, Hong Kong, which Wai-yee's mother cleaned twice a week, 1966 or '67. As with Lina Dunayevskaya in Khabarovsk later, the children played together without a common language.

New Year's is an important time, so it was noisy. Concrete floors and walls amplified the din of firecrackers, usually a string of them going off machine-gun style, and reduced the danger of fire. As far as we could see, we three were the only Big Noses there, eliciting the usual surprise, curiosity, and friendly laughter.

Our children knew the amah's daughter, Yip Wai-yee, as her mother sometimes brought her along to our house. The three kids played together with no common language. We taught Jessica and Tommy to say *tso-san* (good—literally "early"—morning) in Cantonese and to count to ten—though they transformed 9 and 10, *kow sap*, into "cow plop." Vickie Mayne, the center's secretary, was a favorite of theirs; they also befriended a pretty Chinese art student in our building. Vickie took the kids on the harbor ferry to the queen's birthday celebration—held because it was a British colony, without the queen (and probably not her actual birthday). We decided not to send them to a Chinese school as some foreigners did, because by the time they made friends and learned "to speak," our short time there would be nearly over. So they went to Kowloon Junior School, continuing their British education.

Only three of us celebrated New Year because George was doing field work. The Chuang, Miao, Yi, and other minorities live both in China's Yunnan and Kwangsi provinces and in countries of Southeast Asia. So he spent six weeks in northern Thailand, an opium-producing region, interviewing non-Han people and smoking opium ("only once, to see what it's like"), perhaps a way to win his subjects' trust.

Kay came in time to see him and stayed for part of those six weeks, ostensibly to help me with the children. She was helpful in her usual breezy way, but preferred shopping in duty-free Hong Kong. Living there was cheap enough so that even on George's fellowship I could have dresses of fine fabrics made to order. They were beautifully cut and stitched, and fit perfectly as long as I didn't gain more than an ounce or two.

English-speaking Chinese asked, "Do you live Hong Kong side or Kowloon side?" Victoria is on Hong Kong Island, one of several islands that, with Kowloon peninsula, make up what until 1997 was the Crown Colony. Kowloon means nine dragons and refers to the arc of hills that form the edge of Kowloon City and that made landing a plane there so exciting. (Kowloon's Kai Tak has been replaced by a larger airport on one of the islands.) George once took a weekday off and we hiked a short, steep path to Kowloon Pass. At the top we encountered an elderly Chinese woman with two large crates of bottled drinks and snacks suspended from a bamboo shoulder pole. She had come the more gradual way from a village in the rural New Territories, but she was probably twice our age and I couldn't have shouldered her load, let alone carried it any distance.

She wasn't unusual. At a school under construction opposite our balcony, women were among the workers who melted tar on the sidewalk, sent it, hot and glossy black, up to the roof in small vessels raised by pullies, and spread it on the roof. Did they prefer this work to less arduous occupations? Were they paid more than for cleaning or sewing or ironing? Were they paid as much as the men? Watching them, while much of the year I barely managed domestic tasks in that sweltering climate, made me feel both privileged and feeble, as many white folks among what Kipling called the "lesser breeds" generally are.

My work was less arduous. According to an October letter to Robert, MIT Press had published *The Party and the National Question in China*, I finished the index for George's monograph on the Kazakhs, and was supposed to sort out, cut and paste 12 pounds of xeroxed material from the Library of Congress. I also did a little journalism. Mother was making dresses for the wife of the publisher of the *San Francisco Chronicle* and had pulled the right strings to get me a challenging writing assignment. I had to produce interesting, accurate, sometimes amusing observations without pretending to be an expert on Hong Kong or matters Chinese; I didn't, for instance, investigate the work or lives of the women construction workers. Contrasts of modern versus traditional and Chinese versus European were readily available themes.

It was Deputy Director M.H. Su of the USC who pointed out a meeting of East and West that I hadn't noticed. He and others came for dinner. For dessert I made Ginger Cream Mold, unpoetically named by Craig Claiborne of *The New York Times*, a delicious concoction featuring preserved ginger and whipped cream. Mr. Su observed that ginger is a staple of Chinese cooking; cream is never used. It was a scholarly observation, maybe indirectly a rebuke to a thoughtless cook. He had no ill effects from digesting a dairy product—as far as I know.

Though the population was overwhelmingly Chinese, there was

plenty of cream to whip. Even more than Macao, Hong Kong was an easy place for Westerners. You could live on Chinese ingredients or buy groceries at a Dairy Farm store and eat cream cheese and chutney on white bread (crusts removed) at an English-style restaurant in central Victoria. There were dragon boat races and there was polo. The cultures also merged, as in my dessert: it was a Chinese dentist who pulled a wisdom tooth (which kept breaking) using Western methods. During the hour-long ordeal I could watch both junks and freighters in the harbor.

An impacted wisdom tooth could happen anywhere, but another health hazard is now rare in the States. In 1960, when we lived in the Bronx and Jessica was eight months old, I went to the toilet and felt something odd. It was a worm over a foot long. I had the presence of mind to put it in a jar and take it to the city's parasite clinic. It was a roundworm and was probably invisible when I ingested it. It appeared thirteen months after we left Macao, where I used to make salads. In Hong Kong I used a chemical to clean raw vegetables and cooked things more thoroughly. An English public health nurse whom I met at a party told me I'd been lucky: most people vomit roundworms up. Back in Oxford, I had us all tested for parasites; we'd skirted that hazard.

As in Macao, events in the People's Republic sometimes impinged on our relatively easy and placid lives. Looking back on our two separate years on the coast of China, I saw that we had been in Macao during the Great Leap Forward and in Hong Kong at the start of the Cultural Revolution. In the spring of 1967, youths marched in solidarity with the Red Guards across the border. A movie, *The East Is Red*, showing Mao Tse-tung with ecstatic crowds of adoring youth in Tien-An Moon Square, was a mixture of exciting and tedious. The communist department stores stocked the "little red book" of Mao's sayings; the demonstrators flourished their copies as they marched. There was some labor unrest, but we benefited from it: when the workers at the municipal water plant walked off the job, instead of shutting the water off as the rationing schedule required, they left it on.

The Cultural Revolution heated up after we left, in both China and Hong Kong, and we skirted another major event that June. Months earlier, George had suggested finishing our trip around the world by way of Siberia; he had scholars to visit along the way. The Six-Day War in the Middle East happened as we were traveling and might have made the usual route problematic. Another stroke of luck, due to no prescience on our part.

Chapter 28
BAIKAL AND BAIKAL, JUNE 1967

*A*s we boarded our Soviet ship, the *Baikal*, in Kowloon, Chinese dock workers moved nimbly and noisily about, shouting, spitting, staring, pointing, laughing. A Russian sailor, towering over them, stood like a statue guarding the approach to the ship, arms by his side, immobile, unsmiling, his furtive sideways glances confirming a stereotype. Many Russians had that same aura of heaviness, as if amply but not well fed, suspicious, and perpetually dissatisfied. Such impressions led me to conclude that what was wrong with the Soviet Union was not that it was communist but that it was Russian. Centuries of inequality and oppression predated the Revolution—indeed made something like it necessary—but life was still very hard. Housing was cheap but for most meager; shortages of food and goods meant long lines at state stores. Daily life seemed to press down on the working masses, while the elite were relatively slender and well-dressed, but not very numerous.

Among the few passengers on the *Baikal* were another American family and one Chinese man. The way he hung about suggested another stereotype: that Chinese are so enmeshed in their families and clans that one alone is lonely and lost[12]. Our kids played with the other American kids—on hot days in the saltwater shower on deck, which served in lieu of a pool. Meals often included red caviar, salty and tasty. In the evening there was Russian music, and the social director liked to chat with us, showing off his English, much better than my limited Russian: after two stabs at beginning Russian, I could speak a little and read signs and menus.

On Sunday afternoon in Yokohama—or Yokogama, as the h-less Russians call it—we took a fast train to Kamakura to see the Daibutsu, the Big Buddha. He is indeed very big and there were big crowds to see him. Returning to Yokohama, the last stop, I was the last to get off. The new passengers rushed on and knocked me to the floor, my second unpleasant encounter in Japan. In two years among the Chinese I'd never been hurt or molested.

The weather on the last leg was gray and unsettled, but we soon reached Nakhodka—near better-known Vladivostok, a military port so off limits. We disembarked on a chilly day in mid June and got on a cozy overnight train to Khabarovsk. We had three of the four extra-long bunks (things tended to be big in the USSR) in our compartment. Tommy and I shared one. The fourth was occupied by Victor Dunayevskii, an engineer originally from Baku, then living in Khabarovsk. We put the kids to bed and we three adults repaired to the dining car, ate, drank vodka, and talked about life and politics. Victor's English was considerably better than my Russian. He said he went to work where his government needed him. Kamchatka, the large peninsula in northeastern Siberia, was a future possibility. His wife taught English; daughter Lina was about Jessica's age. As we talked about the rivalry between our countries, Victor asked: what if he and George were to face each other on the battlefield? Soon he sang a song about peace.

The next evening we met Victor and Lina in the town square; his wife was busy with exams. As with Wai-yee, our kids and Lina couldn't converse but were soon laughing and running around together. It was a lovely interlude, the kind of encounter that makes the annoyances of travel worthwhile.

I must have written some time later, as Victor wrote from Kamchatka in February 1970. He had been working there but would soon be done and they hoped to move back to "the central regions of our country." He reported on Lina's progress in school, and that they now had a fourteen-month-old son Igor. He hoped we could stay in touch and that our children would know each other. "This is so noble!" It would have been, but it's possible that, because of all that was happening, I never answered him.

From Khabarovsk we flew to Irkutsk. I had purposely not bought film before leaving Hong Kong, thinking it would be more interesting to buy it in the USSR. "Interesting" *da* (yes), "buy" *nyet*. I went to the relevant state store, crowded with shoppers, or would-be shoppers, and (in Russian) asked for film at a showcase full of cameras. They had no film.

Where could I get some? The saleswoman didn't know. Our guide from Intourist, the official Soviet tourist agency, said that often professional photographers couldn't get film—another cliché, about the distribution of goods. Artie, erstwhile communist, once explained about Soviet goods. State planners decreed how many bathtubs and stoppers would be made. Rubber stoppers wear out faster than bathtubs, so even hotels were left with tubs that couldn't be filled. So Artie told me gleefully.

We had a few days in Irkutsk because George had someone to see about minorities policy; the Chinese policy was partly based on the Soviet one, and Kazakhs, Tadjiks, Mongols, and other minorities lived in both countries. He and the kids didn't join me in visiting a certain church. At least two people in Hong Kong had told us about happening to visit as a service was in progress. When I entered, a tall priest in a long robe faced about a dozen women, most not young. Without pews or benches, they stood except when one of the women, usually an old one, knelt and kow-towed (Chinese for "knock head"). The priest chanted in a beautiful bass and the women responded with harmonies so heavenly that, while this a capella music couldn't make me a believer, it was hard to tear myself away. I guessed that there was *always* a "service" in progress, a continuous litany familiar to those taking part.[13]

Our guide took us all to Lake Baikal, a very deep lake with its own microclimate: it was noticeably chillier by the water. Baikal was also said to be very clean and pure, but later stories about pollution suggest there was already some in 1967.

One day, as we left our Irkutsk hotel, the kids were arguing. Soon it was a scuffle. It wasn't serious but an excitable passerby tried to break it up, lecturing the children in Russian. "*Nichivo,*" I said, "*nichivo,*" a useful word meaning "never mind" or "it's nothing." Ever inclined to jump at generalizations, I concluded that the destruction of World War II, which devastated much of European Russia and killed something like twenty million Soviet citizens, made ordinary Russians leery of any violence. Perhaps the stranger was just a busybody, but his manner suggested that he was truly distressed to see children fighting.

We flew from Irkutsk to Moscow and learned first-hand what is obvious from any globe: that the nearer to either pole one is, the narrower the time zones are. A retired American psychology professor and his wife were on the same flight, which also included a couple with a swaddled baby. I had long wondered whether the brooding ill humor now and then exploding into violence, another cliché based on Russian reality, might be partly a result of swaddling, which used to be common. This baby was in a rigid package; it could move its eyes and mouth and maybe its head but nothing else. This could provide a sense of security but must also be frustrating. I asked the psychologist what he thought of swaddling. He had nothing to say, leaving me to my speculations.

This was probably a family from the hinterland, perhaps going to Moscow for a once-in-a-lifetime visit to the Kremlin and Lenin's tomb. Another passenger was a man from Tashkent or some other romantic-sounding city in Central Asia, taking a basket of plums picked much too early to a weekly market. By plane! This may have been a form of subsidy for farmers in a non-Russian soviet republic, like the Irkutsk church a way to defuse discontent. I bought two barely edible plums.

The Hotel Metropol is around the corner from Red Square and the Kremlin. Built in 1898 and once frequented by statesmen and other notables, it was still elegant but rooms had been split in half; ours was long and narrow. I don't remember whether the tub had a stopper, but old women with a downtrodden air cleaned the acres of Oriental carpet in the wide corridors using whiskbrooms and buckets of water. Our young guide took us to Moscow University, and introduced us to *kvass*, a fermented drink sold from little tanker carts. St. Basil's Cathedral with its colorful onion-shaped domes was closed for renovations and we passed up the chance to see Lenin. Because between Irkutsk and Moscow every hour of flight time equalled an hour's time difference, I woke up each day at about 4 A.M. On an early walk I saw that the line for Lenin's tomb already stretched around the corner of the Kremlin. Foreigners could go to the head of the line, which struck us as obnoxious, while waiting in line was a waste of our short time in Moscow.

Because of George's impatience with sightseeing, we passed up the palaces and treasures of the Kremlin, missing much of what is beautiful in Moscow. Beautiful architecture was not among the good things the Revolution brought. Handsome structures dated from the bad old tsarist days. We did go to Gorky Park of Culture and Rest, with its well-tended lawns, flowers, venerable trees, and various rides and amusements. For each entertainment one had to queue up to buy tickets and again for admission to the thing itself. No wonder so many Russians had that air of resentment and fatigue. (Not that this air is unknown in the West.)

The kids and I also experienced the famous Moscow subway. It did *not* live up to its earlier reputation, as in an anecdote from my childhood. Russian-American Igor is back in Moscow visiting relatives. Cousin Sasha takes him to a subway station, a palace of marble pillars, frescoes, soft lights, and fountains. They admire it all. Then Igor says, "It's very beautiful, but where are the trains?" Sasha shoots back: "Do I ask you about the lynchings in the South?" There *were* trains and one took us to a large public swimming pool.

Another day we went to GUM, an acronym for *Gosudardvenie Universalnii Magazin* (government department store). It was *Universalnii* in another sense, as the entire population of Moscow seemed to have converged on it that day. Inching along between artless displays of clothes, groceries, housewares, I found film—pricier than in Hong Kong.

I'm glad to have seen something of the land of Mother's birth. I don't recall talking with her about it. Perhaps, having been there as an adult, I knew more than she did; she'd left when only four. Nor do I remember her ever speaking Russian, but I must have heard it at my grandparents' house, for Russian always sounds both familiar and beautiful.

Prague was our last stop before England. It was the year *before* the Prague Spring and the ensuing Soviet crackdown. Though Czechoslovakia was communist, Slavic, and somewhat dispirited, in some undefinable way we felt we were back in Europe. Fresh fruit was hard to get here too but the hotel staff used vacuum cleaners. After a brief visit to the city where Kafka wrote, in the country from which my father's mother had migrated to Vienna, it was a short hop to London, completing our piecemeal circumnavigation of the Earth.

Chapter 29

OXFORD, 1967–68

$\mathcal{W}$e lived at 5 Winchester Road again but on the upper two floors, with bedrooms below, living room and kitchen above. (Soon it sounded odd when someone said "I'm going up to bed." We went *down* to bed.) It was good to be back at the same address, and that fall we were delighted to learn that Aaron, one of George's CFR rapporteurs, was coming to St. Antony's.

If only I had kept a diary that year. The decades between the two childhood diaries and late 1971—when I resumed writing—are, archivally, nearly a blank, with barely a written record. A datebook for 1968 did survive. It notes but doesn't describe parties, visitors, medical appointments, events, and the hours I worked at the small Latin America library at St. Antony's— raising more questions than memories, for some names are now unfamiliar and events forgotten. That year we returned to the States and I began to solve a mystery dating from my thirtieth birthday, when the thought "In only six years I'll be thirty-six" inspired dread. What did that mean? I found out only gradually.

Tommy returned to Phil and Jim, Jessica went on to Bishop Kirk Junior School. George finished his short history of twentieth-century China. Aside from typing, editing and possibly constructing the index, I wrote a section about writers, in print under four pages, for which I read history, criticism, and fiction, some of it propaganda, some heartfelt but clumsy, some true works of literature, notably the masterpieces of Lu Hsun—such a great writer that the communists claimed him, just as they claimed classics from China's literary past as "progressive" for their times. In February I wrote Robert:

How I have been looking forward to writing this letter! ... because

I had made up my mind that I wouldn't write it (or any others for that matter, except an occasional one to keep my mother quiet) until the book was done. Last Friday we took it to the publisher and the sense of relief has barely diminished since then.

For Friday, February 2nd, the datebook says: "London—A.M." (With a drink with Aaron at 5:30 and a play at 7:45.) I admitted to some let-down when discarding my notes and reading lists, but the dominant feeling was relief. The book appeared that year as *From Empire to People's Republic*, and in 1970 in the US as *China Since 1911*.

George still had to write the dissertation. He hoped to finish by June so he wouldn't have to return for his "viva," as the live thesis defense is called. And he had to find a job.

Several things may catch up with George, one being age [almost 37], the other being the lack of a discipline (he'd like to teach political science, but has never taken a course in it, therefore isn't able to sling around the proper lingo) [so I wrote glibly, as if vocabulary was all there was to it], and the third being the lack of a patron. Being a student of Geoffrey Hudson is about as useful for getting a job as being a student of Jessica's teddy-bear. Do you know him? A sweet old man who never answers a letter and hasn't written a book about China since 1931.

(An aside about the teddy bear. We bought a good-sized one for Jessica and I made it a pinafore out of remnants from her school uniform. Christmas morning, Tommy saw the bear and his face lit up; then it fell when he learned that it was for Jessica. I treasured such signs of tenderness, not only because they defied sex stereotypes. It was reminiscent of his and Suma's solicitude for the Guy.)

The datebook mentions a party Geoffrey Hudson gave in February and his wedding in July. I recall neither event, only a visit to his house, all four of us, to meet his Japanese bride, who was decades younger and spoke no English; Hudson knew no Japanese. She brewed what may have been the ceremonial tea. I found it unpalatable and remembered Kay's telling us how she suffered through a tea ceremony in Tokyo, hiding the equally unpalatable pastries in her handbag. Our afternoon was awkward, but at least George could serve as interpreter between wife and husband.

George had two books in print (plus his pseudonymous poems) and one forthcoming, but he didn't finish the dissertation until 1970. Possible jobs were all over the place, according to a March letter to Robert: "Have you ever heard of Goddard College? It looks as though that is where we are going." Other schools I listed as possibilities included

> UC Santa Barbara [where funding was uncertain, thanks to Governor Reagan]; Central Wash. State College; Moorhead State C. in Minnesota.; Louisiana Polytechn. Inst., with a high salary and a free hand in setting up an Asian Studies program, but uncertain funding; School of Advanced Internat. Studies in Wash., D.C.; Victoria Univ. in Wellington, N.Z.; Windsor Univ., Ontario. This is not exhaustive but they are the main ones.

Only Goddard and Louisiana Polytech had actually offered George a job. Goddard was small and somewhat bizarre, but the one student I'd known, a co-worker in the Henry Wallace campaign, seemed admirable. It meant living in George's favorite state, although Goddard is nowhere near The Farm.

> Last week the president of Goddard [Royce ("Tim") Pitkin, also the founder] was in London. To my surprise, he is a Vermonter, straightforward type, realizes his "experimental" college is anathema to the D.A., the local press & many neighbors but is prepared for an endless, intermittent battle. George would advise the kids as well as teach them something about Asia—what would be up to him & his students.

Alex, my Midvale and Bronx Science friend, warned us that at a small college in a small village there would be too few people from among whom to find friends. He wasn't wrong, but George was sold—even though Tim was going to retire in 1969. Goddard became the first of three schools where George pioneered East Asian history and Chinese language.

We had a fairly steady stream of visitors. Suma came for a weekend in March, the family having moved to London, and his parents came for the big dance in June. Earlier that day the Hollenbergs came with Fred and Martha Gruenberg, who were visiting from New York—all Viennese refugees. Martha, as usual fussing over me affectionately, worried that I was too thin.

Ruth and Jerry Opper, San Francisco friends, came as they dragged two teenage daughters around Europe. Sinological friends included Sandra and Hal Kahn, and Howard Boorman twice, in May with Margaret, whom I disliked, as did nearly everyone, and in July with Scott, the little boy who had grown and grown. Obviously brilliant, Scott, living in Harvard's Quincy House with several hundred other students, assured me that none was worth knowing. He couldn't have been more different from his relentlessly charming, gregarious, irresistible father.

Ruth Lovington came from London for Sunday dinner, and George said he found her sexy. Later he said that about New York Ruth; she'd lain on the floor and he said he'd wanted to lie with his head on her belly. Neither was an innocent "I like your friend." Both Ruths were small and black-haired, more "Jewish-looking" than I was. In view of George's ambivalence about my Jewishness, this is intriguing. But when he actually looked elsewhere, she was not Jewish.

Vickie and Anna came in May, and one day we went to Salisbury, where we had an unappetizing lunch in a deceptively charming tearoom, and to Stonehenge. I'm grateful to have visited it before it was fenced off. It's harder to feel the magic seeing it through a fence. We bought the children ice cream at a stand right by the monument. As Tommy hopped about, the scoop fell out of his cone and sat there like a microlith among all those megaliths.

On their last day the aunts taught us Russian advice for travelers: pack, get ready to leave, then sit down before facing the exertion and excitement of travel—good advice I rarely follow. (Anna also related a rule from a Russian knights' etiquette book: when standing talking in a circle, spit outside the circle, not into it.)

Along with the forgotten St. Antony's names, we clearly socialized a good deal with Tej, an attractive and engaging upper-class Thai, and with the Brandts: Conrad, a German sinologist, and Beate, a Swiss dentist. In

1971 I asked Conrad to serve as reference for my job hunt. He and Beate were dividing their time between Basel and Paris:

> Apart from brief returns designed to wind up our affairs, we have not been back to Oxford since July 1968, because I knew already then that Chinese studies in general were going to be abolished in the University, just like Indian studies 2 years earlier. Now that David Hawkes has resigned the Professorship, only Dawson remains—and Dawson, I am told, is the one who brilliantly removed the rest of us.

Conrad had "actually done pretty well helping people to get jobs—or at least better than I have done placing myself." He believed Dawson was "born a villain," accused Hudson of "consummate hypocrisy;" and others at St. Antony's of misleading him, perhaps innocently, about his future there, while two St. Antony's professors, Carr and Zeldin, behaved well toward him. Was this "age discrimination," Conrad being all of fifty? Was Conrad paranoid? Difficult to work with? not a good teacher or scholar? For us, the Brandts were congenial company. Childless, they enjoyed our children. A later Christmas greeting from Conrad is addressed "to George, Eva, Tommy and General Moseley," not meaning George's grandfather. He looked forward to "Jessica becoming the first woman to head the Joint Chiefs of Staff" as she had "once made Winchester Road safe for an aging academic <u>without resorting to violence or even threatening to do so</u>." Probably some neighbor kids approached Conrad and Jessica told them to leave him alone.

Jessica especially made friends with the Crawleys, who had our former flat in number 5. William was studying India and played the cello. Bonny was his new Indian wife. Most memorable was a note William found one evening: Wife on strike, needs to be taken out for dinner. As with Emily MacFarquhar's soup and dumplings, I was in awe of such wifely chutzpah.

By April George had a job. He almost had a doctorate. He felt good, expansive. He grew a beard, and on May 23rd went to Paris to experience the student uprising, returning two days later with a paving stone that

Picnic in the back garden of
5 Winchester Road, Oxford, spring 1968.
L to R: Grace Bear, Jessica, George, Tommy.

had hit him on the shoulder, pleased to have been part of "the action." I wasn't so thrilled but was interested to see that cobblestones reach a foot or more into the ground.

A major cause of such demonstrations was the Vietnam War. My only Vietnam-related memory is of graffiti on the outside wall of the women's loo at the Oxford Railway Station: "YANKS GET OUT OF VIETNAM–COME TO BRITAIN." Clearly not a political statement.

That George felt good was probably only half true. Very likely he was anxious about his future and the dissertation. Something about our situation led him to begin the mysterious process partly described earlier, in which we supposedly probed our own and each other's psyches—but increasingly just mine. In May, shortly after a visit from his sister Kathy (noted in the datebook but totally forgotten) and in among my aunts' visit, there are notations in a tiny script: labor, E. birth, G. labor (1), G. birth (2), and later, in June, J.&T.'s "birth."

I did undergo something that felt like labor, though neither as long nor as painful as the real thing; attaching names made sense to me then, if not later. George hovered about and sometimes was helpful. One episode ended with a headache and he brought me aspirin and milk to swallow it with. But more and more he used this opening of my emotional Pandora's Box to criticize my sexual and other shortcomings as he saw them. Mine, not his.

In June my half-sister Toni and her mother stayed with us. I never cared for Ethel, not as a "homewrecker" (Poldi/Leo was the homewrecker) but because she seemed stupid, insensitive. She criticized me for not wearing makeup, supposedly not caring to please my husband. If George longed for me to wear makeup, he didn't say so. It felt as though Ethel sensed and echoed his critical mood, joining him in finding fault with me. More double standard: if he was dissatisfied, it was my fault; if I was dissatisfied, that was my problem.

Also in June George came home with a Mr. Jackson, whom he'd met on the street and invited to lunch (which of course it was my duty to provide). As I prepared a meal, George remembered that he had a lunch date with Conrad. Of all the things he might have done—taken us both along, given Mr. Jackson a few shillings to buy lunch—he simply left, leaving me on the fourth floor with this stranger, no one else around, no phone. It turned out all right—although reputedly homeless, Jackson was a gentleman: jacket and tie, well spoken—and George may have apologized for leaving me with Jackson. Was it just inconsiderate or also hostile? Did he do it *because* it was dangerous?

For the next day the datebook says: "fight." All I recall is feebly punching his white-shirted chest. He was unscathed physically; I acquired a black eye, which our acquaintances pretended not to notice; only Rebecca Smith, the greengrocer lady, remarked on it; I appreciated that.

Such storm clouds had started gathering the autumn before, or even sooner.

We saw a good deal of Aaron. Drinks in his rooms at St. Antony's, dinner at our house, and so on. One day we all went out somewhere, the kids and I following behind the two men. George was short but carried himself like a soldier, very erect. Aaron was even shorter, with thick black hair, Jewish looking in the traditional Diaspora way—seemingly an indoors, studious person (although in a later letter he mentions gardening and riding horseback).

Watching me cook, he admired the way I didn't measure precisely but added ingredients according to feel. His praise thrilled me, for I was smitten, and my usual practice of fantasizing until my feelings evaporated didn't work. My feelings didn't evaporate. Eventually I told them both; I don't recall how or when, whether together or separately. I made clear to George that I loved him as before and didn't want to change anything, but perhaps it was this that was eating at him when he started criticizing me that spring. And even when I got over it, was it a permanent factor in how George felt about me? If so, he failed to understand, or acknowledge, that I found the situation painful and was dealing with it as best I could, and that it was the old double standard: all right for him to look elsewhere (he seemed to know where Betty/Li-chiao was), but not for me. Not that I wanted to. "If the fool would persist in his folly, he would become wise," Blake wrote in "The Marriage of Heaven and Hell." I was trying to do that, rather than dissemble, or suppress feelings.

I quoted Blake to Aaron but he disagreed and thought we shouldn't meet for a time. He was practicing *"Zivilcourage,"* which I think to him meant the proverbial British stiff upper lip: one does the right and proper thing, suppressing feelings as necessary. He'd told me that his mother was ill and unavailable when he and his twin brother were infants, and about research showing that an infant does best when it forms, especially between the ages of six and eighteen months, an attachment to a particular adult. He hadn't had that and I had the impression that he did without close human contact. I'm sure he found the thought of my touching him repellent.

Aside from my laconic datebook and sparse memories, there are a few letters from Aaron. Two dated May 25 make clear that, while keeping his rooms at the college, he was living mainly in London, both to do research at the Public Records Office and to escape the emotional tempests of Winchester Road. In one letter he disagreed with Blake and canceled that day's visit, but expressed sympathy for what I was going through and respect for my ability "unflinchingly to face so many tremendous issues of the past—and the future." He didn't think he could help with my "very private struggle," and was reluctant to be involved in what seemed a dangerous situation.

The other, longer letter was even firmer in his refusal to see me. I had evidently asked him to put off returning to London. He would not be "bullied" into changing his plans. My unfinished business was mine, not his. While "sincerely touched" by my feelings for him, he also felt "invaded" and "exploited." He asked me to please leave him alone, but still felt "warmly" toward us and hoped to remain our friend, but on his terms, which he assumed I would not find "acceptable, at least for the time being, but perhaps...later on." There is a P.S. about George's having just stopped in and Aaron being delighted at his safe return from Paris.

In the last letter from that period (June 17th), it's as if a dark cloud had lifted. Whatever I'd written on the 12th, he was touched and grateful and suspected that he had been most helpful by being honest about his feelings. Evidently I had persisted in my folly and become wise, had gotten over my infatuation and even discovered the reason for *its* persistence. I got him to give me a small photo of him. Because he reminded me of our Viennese friend, Norbert Neumann, Nunyu, and between my infatuation with Aaron and the psychiatric shenanigans, I began to solve the mystery of the age of thirty-six. Part of the puzzle was that I suspected a romance between Nunyu and Mother. According to a letter to Aaron, drafted but never sent, my aunts confirmed this, and Vickie told me that, when Isabella called to tell her that Nunyu had cancer, she said, "I can't say the word"—an extreme reaction if the cancer had attacked a mere friend.

George and I agreed that we would each confront our own parents with what we thought we'd learned that spring—or confront our mothers, as they were more available. When Mother visited us that autumn, I showed her the photo. Did it remind her of anyone? It didn't (it wasn't a good likeness), but I told her that its subject reminded me of Nunyu, and that I suspected that she had been in love with him. She gasped. "How did you know?" They had very nearly had an affair in the summer of 1937. It happened, or didn't happen, in Obersdorf. Paul and I were there too (and, judging by a photo, so was his wife Dora). As a five-year-old I sensed what was happening, as little children do, but the knowledge remained buried, unavailable to my conscious self until my attraction to Aaron began to unearth it from under layers of forgetting.

It wasn't until April 1972 that more pieces fell into place. At a friend's 39th birthday party, I chatted with a woman I hadn't seen since 1955.

> I told Thalia that when I was 30 I was so depressed to think in only 6 years I'd be 36, thought some adult I knew as a child must have been 36 & seemed old. [I also remarked that turning thirty was much worse than, shortly before this party, forty.] After I went to bed I thought about it & realized Mother was 36 when she nearly had an affair with Dr. Neumann.... And what was I doing at 36? That was when I was in love with Aaron!

Furthermore, I turned thirty-six in December 1967, just weeks after Aaron appeared in Oxford. Mother turned thirty-six on August 24th. So we were almost exactly the same age for our two non-affairs. What I'll never know is how Isabella and Nunyu felt about each other later, or even how he felt about her that summer. Did she have her hopes pinned on him when she suddenly, precipitously, decided to divorce Poldi in 1946? And if Nunyu, widowed in 1942, hadn't died of lung cancer in 1948, would they have married?

I never saw Aaron again but wrote him at Christmas, beginning in 1971. There are four roughly annual replies from him, and their tone now strikes me as just too too precious. "And God how I appreciate a minimum of quiet and good manners!" is one small example from the 1971 letter. In 1974 he finds "England steadily declining" and "civility" and "the standards of every service" eroding, which was perhaps true, but he didn't consider possible reasons for changing relations among social classes.

His last letter (January 1975) is from New York, to which he returned when his father had cancer. The father died and Aaron was the designated sole trustee of his mother, who suffered from dementia. He became a consultant, considered doing "something in the therapeutic consulting field," was enjoying New York's cultural attractions, playing violin in string quartets, and seeing "some but by no means all of my old friends."

I don't think I was hyper-sensitive to feel insulted by that last remark. I drafted an angry reply, pointing out that he'd been in New York for half a year but had written only after I wrote him. "Sure enough," I fumed, "you lump me (by implication only but clearly enough) with the old friends you don't see. And yet you write to me!" By then, thanks to actual therapy, I had the self-respect not to send this tirade. Nor did I write him at all, presumably, as there are no further letters.

From the little extant evidence, I suspect traits in Aaron that I didn't recognize in 1968, mainly a buttoned-up self-protectiveness, but also a passive-aggressive obsequiousness, a Mittel-Europa (Central European) specialty that makes it unbearable to be, or seem to be, in anyone's debt: you write me and I'll write you, but I'll never write on my own because I don't really want to write to you. (The jargon is shorthand for behavior that I believe justifies such weighty words.) I could be wrong. Perhaps with his fellow string players, with the friends he did see, he was loose and affectionate and jolly. Perhaps the call-and-response of our correspondence had to do with our history. Still, the style of his letters makes me wonder how I could have found him so irresistible. He reminds me

253

of someone accused of being pretentious who exclaims, in innocent amazement: "Pretentious? *Moi?*"

Did Aaron actually resemble Nunyu? In the 1970s I was attracted to Frank, another Jewish bachelor, who also regarded me at most as a friend. If the three could have been lined up, perhaps they wouldn't have struck anyone but me as similar—or not even me. Not only had Nunyu been married, but he was a good family friend, effectively another uncle—Paul recalled funny stories, I a snippet of one, in Yiddish, about the Hakoah soccer team—a role Aaron did not play with our children, but Frank did for the child of friends. Nunyu appears in my diary in June 1943, when we were moving from 6C to 6B: "Today Dr. Neumann came to help with the moving. Father was away, swimming most likely." So Nunyu, who didn't live there and wasn't athletic, was helping us move while Poldi, who *did* live there and *was* athletic, found something better to do with his Sunday and his muscles. An occasion for Nunyu and Mother to be together?

What was between them when Nunyu's wife Dora died, and four years later when she divorced Poldi, when Nunyu may already have had the lung cancer that killed him in 1948? In a 1968 letter, in response to mine about our unearthing early memories, she harked back to Nunyu without mentioning his name, in a sentence—in German except for the last word—that stood by itself, without explication: "Truth is good but is it also good when someone who cannot bear it hears that he has cancer." Might she have been happy with him, or was she mistaken in him as I was mistaken in Aaron? Not if he was as I remember him, affec-

Norbert Neuman, Nunyu, with his wife Dora, Paul Steiner, unknown girl, and Eva, 1930s.

tionate, interesting, unassuming. But who knows? Paul too knew him mostly as a child knows an adult, and now Paul has joined those who can no longer answer questions.

Mother assured me she did not say *"Um Gottes Willen"* as I "heard" her say at my relived "birth," but couldn't this be another case of a small child—an extremely small child!—sensing unexpressed feelings? Her husband had just left for several days of skiing. Why wouldn't she feel, even if not say, God help me? Whether it was a memory or a deduction from what I learned later, it came at me with the force of a repressed memory emerging, admittedly a slippery criterion. Can a thought or fantasy have a similar impact?

As we had agreed, George confronted Kay, late one evening at The Farm, about some not-so-pleasant childhood memories. Kay counter-attacked, denying there had ever been anything seriously wrong, and George backed down. "You were wonderful parents," he declared, and I felt betrayed. Kay was a formidable foe when fending off criticism. But he'd gone back on his promise, and I felt sure not only that they weren't wonderful parents, but that we were both suffering, in part, because of the parents they were.

Chapter 30
PLAINFIELD, 1968–70

*W*e spent our first two weeks in Plainfield in a cabin on Route 2. The French-Canadian Bertes owned cabins and an egg factory. In one henhouse, hundreds of birds ran around loose. In another, windowless house, pairs of hens were cooped up in small cages. With barely room to turn around, the birds literally henpecked each other. Lights were on day and night to speed up egg production. Mrs. Berte showed me around and I wondered whether the chickens didn't mind living in cages. "They're dumb brutes," she said, apparently one Catholic who believed animals have no souls. Inspired by Hinduism, I thought the Bertes' next incarnations should be as factory hens.

It was twenty years since Mother, Vickie, Paul, Claude, and I drove through Plainfield on US Route 2, past the sign for Goddard College, en route from Pinkham Notch in the White Mountains to the Adirondacks. Mother had arranged for us to meet Leo at Pinkham. He, Paul, Claude, and I hiked up Tuckerman Ravine and spent a night at Lakes of the Clouds Hut, below the summit of Mount Washington. Another guest, Alan Schoener, a physicist who at twenty-three seemed very mature to me, had been in the Navy during the war and learned Japanese. I was thrilled that he talked and listened to me, and played charades with us outside the hut after supper. Next morning we five climbed to the summit in wind and fog.

"Did you *walk* up?" More than one day-tripper, at the summit thanks to the road or the cog railway, was impressed; hikers were rarer then. When we descended there was a fluffy cloud around the summit, surrounded by blue sky. I'd learned that when you're *inside* such a cloud, it's not fluffy but cold and damp.

Vickie went home to New York, Leo home to Saranac Lake, and we four followed him there. This was the first of such baffling visits Mother arranged. It seemed odd for her to want to see his new family, odd for Ethel to put up with a visit by his ex-wife. I remember bright sunshine, two-month-old Toni in her mother's arms, and feeling awkward.

In 1968, the *Alexandr Pushkin* took us from Tilbury Docks below London to Montreal, the port closest to Plainfield. This Soviet ship had a pool, in which the water sloshed around wildly as the ship pitched and rolled, making swimming exciting for half the trip, when we also saw whales and icebergs. The other half was on the placid St. Lawrence.

Then, exactly twenty years after driving through Plainfield, I was there with husband and children to start a new life after four years abroad, beginning with a hunt for a house. As we couldn't afford a country place with land, we bought a small house in the village for $9,000, all we could manage after Kay lent or gave us $2,000 for the down payment. The house measured 16-by-24 feet, a third of that small footprint a screened back porch. It dated from the early nineteenth century; its low ceilings suited us short Moseleys. Its triangular lot fronts on Main Street and backs onto the bed of the defunct Montpelier and Wells River Railway. I made jelly from the chokecherries that grew at the peak of the triangle.

George prepared a plot for my vegetable garden, my first since I grew wilted radishes in a window box on 82nd Street. It was up a rise and through a small arbor on which nightshade, closely related to tomatoes and potatoes, climbed in summer. A subscription to *Organic Gardening* provided a stream of advice and ideas. Despite bugs and slugs, the garden was a moderate success; broccoli was especially delicious because cooked (barely) and eaten within minutes of being picked. Another triumph was growing cilantro in that northern climate; the berries, dried and ground, become coriander. The children showed little interest, so I was pleased when Tommy set up a vegetable stand; I bought some cucumbers. That evening he confirmed my suspicion: he'd sold me my own cucumbers. (This little entrepreneur became neither a crook nor a businessman.)

Volunteer tomato plants and cucumber vines growing out of the first year's compost reminded me of Mother's *Das ist nicht auf meinem Mist gewachsen*: "That didn't grow on my garbage (heap)." I'd known it meant "It wasn't my idea"; now I understood its origin—just as later, when laboriously removing old wallpaper, exposing cracks and holes, I surmised where the expression "to paper over" came from. And, poking seemingly fragile seeds into the cold, dark soil, I guessed the reason for fertility rites. If your life *depends* on your crops, as ours didn't, you will pray, dance, chant—whatever you believe will ensure that your seeds will sprout into plants that produce food, and more seeds.

Across the street, June Edson had a brick house backing onto the cemetery; she kept goats and students. A Goddard alumnus built sod houses and wore inflatable boots: the colder it got, the more air he pumped in. Down Main Street, Professor Rosenberg and his Chilean wife had twin daughters, whom Jessica often drafted for her dramatic performances. Near them lived a couple, also new to Goddard, with a small son. Told by his mother that he was special, he used this designation as a weapon against his contemporaries. It took a while for me to realize that he was special to his parents, as our children were to us: relatively special, not, as he thought, absolutely.

The Clouds, also newcomers, lived next door. Clifton worked for the state in Montpelier, Plainfield being a "bedroom town" for the capital and Barre. Natalie Cloud told me that, when they married, Clifton asked only for hot meals, clean clothes, and "a path through the house." This, and her Sunday supper of toast and applesauce, sounded unbelievably easygoing. She preferred stripping paint from the woodwork to the endless daily chores. Another wife to envy? Thirty years later, we learned that Natalie had decamped long before. Their easygoing marriage was evidently no magic formula for lasting happiness.

Clifton Junior and Tommy, early in 1969, "made 13 Snow-men in one day. Then we threw snow-balls at them and they fell down." So Tommy wrote Vickie and Rudi. Winters varied. In 1968–69 we had two heavy snowfalls; the walls of snow along the driveway towered over us. One sunny Sunday, Midge Eastman, who'd sold us the house, took me on my first snowshoe outing, across a field with only inches of fence-post visible, a peaceful way to spend a winter afternoon. In January 1970 the sun never shone, it snowed every day, and the temperature never rose above 15° F; the snow that fell remained powder. George put a large rock in the car's trunk for traction, and I learned that, while driving too fast in snow and ice can be risky, if you go too slowly, especially uphill, you may get stuck.

But before winter came we had to settle in. It was the first place in which we were meant to settle down, and the first house we *bought*. We had our doubts, I about Plainfield, George about settling down, though that wasn't apparent yet. We got the mortgage from Chittenden Trust Company, and our furniture from George's shed at The Farm. We couldn't afford a couch so he built one, and acquired an easy chair that I found uncomfortable. I showed it to Henrietta Gay, a student in the Adult Degree Program, and told her why George liked it and I didn't. "Do you call that an easy chair?" "No," said Henrietta, "I call it a difficult chair."

That wasn't the most difficult difficulty of the Plainfield years. Alex was right: it's hard to find friends at such a small college. Despite plenty of social life with faculty and students, I soon decided that, if I had to choose between town and gown, I would choose the town. George leaned the same way and became friendly with a campus cop, who came for coffee and acted out the stomping of stale, mostly-air doughnuts at the local police hangout.

This cop was later connected to the growing difficulties between George and me. In February 1969, I wrote Robert:

> We are indeed at Goddard & it has been—still is—probably the roughest year of our marriage. Options like divorce & suicide seemed real for the first time this year, but I suppose we will stick. We have ups as well as downs. At least no third party is involved, unless one considers Goddard a third party. It seems to be one of the more demanding colleges—not publication—hardly!—but just psychic energy, life-blood.

After a worried letter from Robert, I wrote again in May:

> Please don't worry about us—things are getting better. It seems once one opens up the Pandora's box of the psyche, one can't close it again & the little slimy, crawly things keep coming out. I'm sorry I wrote that asinine letter.... George is trying to write his thesis and add a couple of rooms on the house...& I'm giving German lessons, helping out with 4-H, baking bread, gardening, etc.

One of the "ups" was a day that first autumn when I fixed a picnic lunch and got George from the college. We went to a bit of woods, ate, and made love. Then he went back to work. A romantic tryst or a "comfort woman" bringing her man his comforts with the least possible inconvenience to him? Perhaps it's our subsequent history, plus women's lib, that makes me inclined to see it as the latter.

That outing was easy because Goddard is very near the village, which partly stretches along Route 2, partly is across a bridge over the Winooski River. It had only a few beautiful houses. Several, picturesquely down-at-heels, hung over the river, housing Goddard students, ex-students, and hippies attracted by Goddard's hippy atmosphere.

Three Plainfield stores sold groceries then. Bartlett's on Main Street was the sort of place you went when you needed a can of something at suppertime. Grandmotherly Mrs. Bartlett was Tommy's second-grade teacher, in a one-room schoolhouse up Middle Road. On Main Street near the bridge, Bea, tough and opinionated, presided over Kellogg's general store, selling groceries, woollen shirts, hunting caps, spades and other outdoor tools. She told me that when her father owned the store, the farmers did the shopping, driving their wagons into the village to sell their produce and buy staples they couldn't produce themselves. May's on Route 2 was attached to a gas station; May was from the Bronx. We did our serious shopping in Montpelier, Barre, or along the Barre-Montpelier Road. I disliked driving ten miles or more each way for groceries, and being in the car almost every day.

I first heard about the women's liberation movement from other faculty wives and disapproved of women who, in recouping their lives from sexist marriages, rejected—along with marriage and men—motherhood and children, half of them girls. Even accepting the premises of feminism, how could it be right to abandon women-to-be? It took more years and more experience for me to see the truly liberating aspects of the movement.

One faculty wife was particularly strident, often at the school, haranguing teachers and the principal. She may have been right about the school's shortcomings, and perhaps I was too passive in accepting the schooling my children were offered, but, unlike her, I wasn't sure that I always knew better than their teachers what was good for them.

I was sure, however, when the principal of Twinfield Elementary School wanted to put Jessica in third grade. She'd had four years of English schools. It's hard to compare English and American grades, but, sure she was ready for fourth, I said to Mr. Coffin, "Of course the schools in England are better." Not the thing to say to an American educator, as I realized even as the words popped out. But he tested Jessica—and put her in fourth grade.

The first year each child went off on a different school bus in a different direction. Jessica's school was in Marshfield, eight miles away. The recent merger of the two towns' schools was hard to accept, we heard, because they had been rivals at basketball. What seemed unfortunate was the long daily bus ride for the Plainfield kids, even if it was through the beautiful Winooski River valley, with the Groton Hills to the south.

I made that trip often, for I volunteered in the school library, cataloguing books and becoming friendly with Hazel Gokey, the librarian, a widow with grown children and numerous grandchildren. Working there made me feel a useful Twinfielder. In May 1969 I chaired a book fair; profits went to the PTA. I talked to Jessica's class about living on the coast of China, and helped chaperone a school outing. We had a view of Spruce Mountain, the highest of the Groton Hills, and I asked another mother, Joyce Fowler, if she had ever climbed Spruce. "No, but I'm not from here." "Where are you from?" "East Montpelier," she said. East Montpelier is three miles down Route 2 from Plainfield.

An annual potluck "international" supper at the school brought town and gown together. In 1968 I made Chinese "Lion's Head," ground pork meatballs steamed with cabbage. Everyone else brought pasta: spaghetti, lasagna, macaroni were Twinfield's (or perhaps America's) international cuisine. The next October I co-chaired a United Nations dinner for 225 mouths.

As further affirmation of my alliance with townies, I took on a 4-H cooking group and a Cub Scout den. Jessica was in the former, but Dorie Smith and I exchanged Cub sons. After completing prescribed activities: "Knights of Yore" in January and in February, Valentine cards made and delivered to "elderly people around the village," I substituted my own activity, having the boys build a compost pile, starting with

261

kitchen and yard waste, lime and soil, then fresh cow manure from the barn of Lou Irwin, Goddard's math professor. The boys gamely shoveled it into buckets and stirred it into the pile. Two days later I stuck a metal rod in. In a moment it was too hot to touch, a major triumph. I wonder if any of those boys remember their rendezvous with manure and the reason for it.

Our dens belonged to Pack 7 (Montpelier and Plainfield). Cubmaster Charles Corson wanted the eight- and nine-year-old Cubs to learn to march in formation with rifles. I wasn't the only parent who didn't want them turned into little soldiers, for the Montpelier *Times-Argus* published a bitter letter from Corson:

> We have tried to get parents to work as den mothers and committeemen and each one has an excuse for not being able to spend a couple of hours a month for the sake of their children. I have been accused of trying to run this pack in too military a fashion. I wanted these Cubs to know how to march, salute, and so forth. I feel this shows respect for their leaders and for our American Flag. Today we have hippies and drug addicts because their parents weren't around to care when they needed them.

And much more in this vein, with a few grains of truth, but he was evidently unaware that many of our soldiers—who knew how to march, salute, and shoot—relied on the drugs he decried to see them through their tours in Vietnam.

The Smiths with whom I traded sons had both been widowed. Each had three sons, and together they had a daughter. Dorie, with her six little boys, taught me the useful warning XYZ: eXamine Your Zipper.

Other Smiths, Sandy and Cary, were dairy farmers; their daughters belonged to my 4-H group, which did the usual "girlie" things, as Sandy called them. In a meeting with the Women's Society of Christian Service, the sewing girls, including Jessica, modeled or showed their projects; another girl showed how to make ribbon and checkerboard sandwiches. On a Saturday in April, the cooking class hosted a luncheon for the girls' mothers, serving tuna salad sandwiches, three kinds of pizza, an antipasto salad and ice cream with sauces prepared by the girls. I suspect that the antipasto and perhaps the pizzas were my innovations—and how alien did I feel with the Women's Society of Christian Service?

Cary, a Goddard alumnus, worked at the college. Soon after we met the Smiths at a party he had a motorcycle accident and was temporarily unable to milk. So we helped out, George having milked cows at Kent School. The Smiths still hauled milk from cow to bulk tank in buckets; milking machines and pipes to the tank came later. I fed the cows grain and washed the gear and felt virtuous and satisfied, till I realized that in twelve hours it would all be used again, and the same relentlessly twice daily all year.

Sandy was tall, strong, and energetic. She plowed, mowed, tedded, chopped corn, fixed the gutter cleaner and other machines; grew a large vegetable garden, pickling, canning, and freezing the results; in March collected maple sap; played competitive tennis and helped manage the Miss Vermont competition. She taught me how to can tomatoes, freeze vegetables, and make pickle relish—grinding ingredients outside, the juice seeping into the ground—and she hosted a Tupperware party: grown women singing and acting out "I've got that Tupperware feeling down in my toes (then ankles etc.)," reminiscent of Heather's Daily Vacation Bible School ditty.

Once Sandy and I rode her snowmobile to collect sap. The machine broke down and we had to tramp home through a foot of virgin snow. I despised snowmobiles but Sandy explained that they permit farmers, who do heavy physical labor, to recreate outdoors with little exertion. Getting outdoors can prevent cabin fever, or suicide. I saw her point, though most snowmobilers were not farmers. Plainfield was noisier in winter than in summer, the angry buzzing of the machines tearing at the quiet of Sunday afternoons. Snowmobiles are useful for rescue or forestry, but practical uses account for a fraction of the mileage, the gasoline, and the noise, and they can be dangerous. A convoy rode up a farmer's track one night, Sandy said. The farmer, unaware they were there, stretched a chain across the barway where they'd entered his land. Returning, the driver of the lead vehicle was decapitated.

Bathroom reading at the Smiths' consisted of breeders' catalogues. For the insemination of a heifer, Cary put on an extra-long rubber glove and wielded an enormous syringe loaded with semen ordered via one of those catalogues. My job was to keep the heifer from escaping one way. Sandy kept her from escaping the other way. It's amazing how puny a presence can intimidate such a large animal. Cary's procedure reminded me of the Bertes' chickens. Does a heifer feel something is wrong when she becomes pregnant without contact with a bull? Are cattle really "dumb brutes"? or are they, as the Buddhists say, "sentient beings"?

That animals have feelings, even romantic preferences, has been reported in news stories and books on animal behavior. Sandy told me about a non-romantic feeling in the dairy herd. The Smiths were changing from Jerseys to Holsteins. Jerseys' milk is creamy, Holsteins' less rich but more plentiful. As Americans began watching their cholesterol, it made sense to have cows that produced more, thinner milk. When they bought the first Holstein, Sandy said, the brown Jerseys shunned this black and white intruder. Perhaps prejudice based on color predates the emergence of Homo "sapiens."

With no degrees but curiosity and thoughtfulness about her own and others' lives, Sandy became my indispensable link to townie Plainfield, almost the only local acquaintance who didn't bore or exasperate me—due more to my out-of-placeness than to any deficiencies of the natives. She got me to join Home Dem, the US Department of Agriculture's extension program for rural women. The Hill 'n' Dale Homemakers' Extension group was also Plainfield's garden club; the women planted flowers outside the post office and cut the grass at a picnic area on Route 2. According to another *Times-Argus* story, in February 1970 I gave a talk about my "experiences in the Orient," playing some of the music recorded by the Macao "blinds." In a farewell speech that spring (we were moving again), I first described natural cycles of air and water versus our belief in "progress": Each year everyone is supposed to produce more and consume more, everything is supposed to keep getting bigger and faster. "We take fuels out of the earth and burn them; we take minerals out of the earth and make them into machines, buildings, gadgets; when we're through with them we dump them anywhere. Nothing is returned to the earth, there is no cycle." I suggested recycling, composting, eventually "reusing paper, tin cans and textile products," learning not to use "long-term pollutants like plastics and chemical sprays," and considering "the effects of what we buy and use on the Earth."

Waste products would be less of a problem if there were fewer people. [W]e need a new attitude toward motherhood… [W]e must stop thinking that six or seven children is better than one or two. Large families made sense when farmers needed lots of hands and when disease took a heavy toll of babies and small children. But now each child means bigger, more impersonal schools, each child will need resources [that] are not infinite. [W]e have to disapprove of parents who have five or more children or soon we may say that all parents are bad. And of course we ought to make sure that young people know how not to have children.

I showed them a diagram, which Mother had found, of how Native Americans see the world, with plants and animals, including humans, in a circle, while we see people alone in the center of the circle. "For the sake of the Earth and all its inhabitants," I concluded, "we should try to put ourselves back in the circle with the rest of nature's creatures."

Some women appreciated these ideas; one said she hadn't made the connection between farming and large families. For me it was uncharacteristic to speak out with controversial views, and indeed to speak in public. It was a small and not intimidating public.

Environmentalism had been emerging, slowly, for decades. Mother owned H. Fairfield Osborn's *Our Plundered Planet* (1948), focused on the importance of soil. From an environmental conference at Goddard I retained two interesting ideas, one an observation concerning our evolutionary cousins. Tree-dwelling monkeys simply drop the inedible parts of fruit out of their leafy world, the way children, and some adults, still drop things they're done with; it takes a deliberate mental effort to deal responsibly with our waste in a world with much more trash and fewer places, if any, to throw it out. (A later environmentalist said, "There is no 'out' anymore.") The second idea was a law to require any business that uses river water to build its intake pipe *down*stream from its effluent pipe.

We also got a taste of political shenanigans. For a town it *seemed* advantageous to assess farmland at market value, its price when sold for development, an issue especially in a bedroom town such as Plainfield. Market-value taxation would put family farms out of business, and perhaps large farms too. In the longer term this would almost surely not be financially advantageous. Cows were still said to outnumber Vermonters then, but if housing developments replaced barns, pastures, and corn-fields, who would want to vacation in Vermont?

At Plainfield's participatory town meeting, the issue came up after the dairy farmers left for the afternoon milking; luckily it wasn't decided behind their backs. Eventually state law decreed that farmland be taxed at a lower rate until it is sold for development. Preserving family farms may seem romantic, but small farms can produce better food; provide a hard but healthful livelihood; do more to maintain, even improve, soil quality than large mechanized farms; and preserve a varied and beautiful landscape. If we value things other than this year's or this quarter's bottom line, these virtues should outweigh quite a few dollars. (Since I first wrote this, interest in farming as a way of life has increased, as has criticism of industrial farming.)

On Plainfield's big day, the Fourth, the Cubs marched in the parade; 4-H had a float. There were booths, games, contests, a barbecue, and a band concert. Knowing I was sailing under false colors made it hard to enjoy it. It was the height of the Vietnam War, and the flag to me and many others meant not freedom and democracy but a stupid war waged by a misguided government on a small country that was no threat to us. On that major issue I was in tune with the college, not the town.

But a small incident could have been designed to muddle one's assumptions about who was politically left (and therefore right) and who was right (and therefore wrong). Goddard students spray-painted anti-war slogans on the brick wall of the library. Whose job was it to clean the wall? Vermonters who did the menial work at the college—very likely pro-war types. So the kids with the good politics about the war were in effect oppressing the local workers, whom they probably considered right-wing ignoramuses.

Goddard students could be maddening. Not entirely their fault, for the college coddled them in ways that were not helpful for kids floun-dering emotionally and intellectually, many using drugs, especially speed and marijuana. Goddard had never had exams or grades, but whatever expectations Tim Pitkin had of students evaporated when he retired and Jerry Witherspoon became president. During his first year the college showed *Arsenic and Old Lace*. When Edward Everett Horton comes to take "Teddy Roosevelt" to the asylum and introduces himself as Mr. Witherspoon, the students went wild, drowning out the rest of the scene. And their Mr. Witherspoon, we heard, soon left his family in the president's house and moved into a student dorm.

Several students thought learning those weird Chinese characters sounded "groovy." It was hard work, so most of the small class dropped the course. There were no consequences. Another instructor's student, reviewing a book, wrote that it was groovy to read it while in bed with a chick, smoking pot and listening to rock. A senior thesis recording a trip through India consisted mainly of the student's subjective reactions to what she saw and heard. Rebelliousness was rampant, based on no more serious a principle than aggravating adults, especially parents. I thought Goddard students should go to nearby Norwich University and vice versa, as each bunch needed what the other was getting. For some kids Goddard was a last resort, but the college's excessive laissez faire left many as aimless and confused as ever.

Some students did want to learn, not only those, like Henrietta, in the mostly off-campus Adult Degree Program. George took me along to an evening class on some aspect of East Asian history and politics. He was magnificent, glowing with enthusiasm, fully in charge of his topic. He never looked handsomer and I was never prouder of him.

We became friendly with a few students and alums, especially David and Liz, who introduced us to macrobiotics and invited us for a meal. We asked why the term "macrobiotic" and they explained that the founder chose that name because the diet promotes a "great life." (The Greek *makros* means "large," not "wonderful.") The meal was good, but when I saw Liz later she had given that diet up.

Another alumnus was one of George's helpers in rebuilding our house. I often gave the crew lunch. At one meal talk was about a female student who, hitchhiking from Barre back to Plainfield, was raped and left for dead in the woods. The alumnus in question said there is no such thing as rape. He simply ignored the fact that the man is nearly always bigger and stronger, and often armed. He couldn't imagine any woman not "wanting it"—even at gun- or knife-point. Unfortunately, he was not unique in believing this.

I had more formal connections with Goddard, once a course for adults in what I called "nature appreciation": pioneer plants, forest succession, quaking bogs, and so on. The instructor's vanity plate read WEEDS. Later I taught beginning German to adults, trying to speak only German. It was interesting, but I couldn't imagine starting new beginners off year after year.

Teaching at Goddard was sufficiently undemanding that George could moonlight in the history department at the University of Vermont, for the extra money and the extra line in his résumé. But the renovation consumed much of his time and energy. The house was cramped and the children would soon, by US standards, need their own rooms. We looked at larger houses but either didn't like or couldn't afford them—usually both. So we decided to replace the back porch—where the kids kept newts and other wildlife—with a two-story addition.

The snows of 1969 had brought down a nearby barn. George arranged with the owner to use its beams and boards for the addition, and got Allan Farnham to dig a hole with his backhoe to enlarge the cellar. Then weeks of particularly laborious work as George extended the dry-stone foundation to the new space. He framed the new rooms, and a small shed across half the back of the house, cutting those dense, heavy beams and sheathing the outside with barn boards. Fred Bonnie, a UVM student who owned a pickup truck, was another helper and became a friend.

George never slept much. Now he had two teaching jobs, worked on the house, and on the dissertation. After we left Plainfield, he told me that the day Farnham dug the hole "was the blackest day of my life." I was shocked that he had voluntarily taken on such an overwhelming task, and dismayed that he gave no hint of how he felt at the time. It seemed a betrayal to keep it to himself. But he wouldn't admit to any weakness, and probably I was supposed to know how he felt without his having to tell me. Something he said later indicated that he expected just that. He did not expect the reverse of himself. (Nor did I.)

The new shed is memorable because one afternoon George recruited Tommy to nail shingles on its roof. Tommy appeared to be in seventh heaven, skilfully wielding a hammer, for once doing real work for his father. But only once—and not one other Sunday afternoon, when

Tommy and friends were not seen or heard for an hour or more. Somehow we found out that they were lighting matches in the crawl space under the Plainfield Auditorium—a large wood-frame structure across the street. George got Tommy out and scolded and spanked him. But I don't think he again found useful work for him to do.

He was no longer the little boy who thrived in Mrs. Bartlett's schoolhouse, where, in an illustrated essay, he declared that he wanted to be a lawyer so he could be useful: if a pig were caught on a barbed-wire fence, he wrote, he would set it free. Where he got the idea that lawyers do anything so helpful is a mystery. Tom often hung out with older boys. I was impressed when a couple of them came to the door and asked, "Hey Tom, what are we gonna do today?" Was he always the idea man? What made him a leader? Intelligence or personality, or having been around the world and lived abroad? While many local kids had never been outside Vermont.

Our kids made friends among Vermonters and faculty children, and also branched out in the animal kingdom beyond cats. Early the first fall we acquired a puppy, eight weeks old, not quite ready to leave her mother. She whined all the way home, sounding as though she were saying "Ma ma ma." We named her Tuesday. George and the children had promised they would train and take care of her, but on Wednesday and nearly every day thereafter George went to work and the kids to school, and Tuesday and I were left at home. She whined, crawled between my feet as I washed dishes, chewed the furniture, and made puddles. Soon she was hit by a car and hurt badly enough that we had her "put down," the weasely term for euthanasia. Months later, George and the children went to see someone about a horse. Jessica had become quite the

Jessica and Tom on horseback in Montague, Mass., early 1970s. While we lived in Plainfield, Jessica brought home ribbons riding Western in local horseshows.

269

equestrian, riding Western in shows, bringing home ribbons. Tom rode too. They didn't get the horse but came home with *two* dogs, which tore the wash off the line and ran loose all over town and up to the college.

Two years of semi-rural life taught me that living in the country, with one's daily chores and obligations, is different from going there on vacation, and I gladly resumed living in cities. Country life suited George but Goddard didn't. When Tufts University, in Medford, Mass., offered him a position pioneering East Asian history and Chinese and he accepted, he had to wind up his work at Goddard and UVM and make the house rentable; the addition was closed in but not finished, nor was the dissertation. Shortly before our move I spent a week in San Francisco, where Mother was in the hospital after an operation for colon cancer. Despite this worry, George, as always when we were moving, was cheerful; for me Medford meant a kind of homecoming—not quite Cambridge but close enough; and the children were still young enough to adapt pretty easily to yet another change of address.

VII.

Coming Apart

Chapter 31
1970–71

$\mathcal{U}$nintentionally, George taught me that some men, maybe many, are susceptible to a feeling of redundancy, or were in the 1970s. Their role in reproduction is essential but momentary. (And with reproductive innovations, it may cease to be essential.) Their role in child-rearing may or may not be peripheral, depending on the culture and on individual inclination or dutifulness. If a man's *work* is problematic, and he, typically for Americans, has few or no close friends, he might find little reason to go on, at least to go on in the same direction with the same people.

"The children don't need me any more," George said that winter in Medford, apparently to explain his imminent departure. But I thought Jessica and Tommy wouldn't agree, that I needed him, that he probably needed them. Never mind the commitment he'd made, on February 28, 1958, to stick together through thick and thin.

He didn't claim that this was the reason he considered leaving; probably it wasn't, but an excuse to cover his confusion and wilfulness in withdrawing from the family. Unsure about what he wanted to do, often feeling he needed to be elsewhere, he enlisted the supposed needs of the children to make him look grown-up, altruistic, rather than confused or capricious. Although I disagreed, I'm unsure whether I did so out loud.

This was our thirteenth move in as many years. At first everything seemed to go well. Moving made George cheerful, and I was glad to be back in Greater Boston. We both rejected the first apartment Tufts offered us, too dreary even for George, but we snagged the shabby, pleasant second and third floors of what George called a faculty slum, a two-family house half a block from the campus and from an elementary school. An empty lot uphill from the house gave us extra light and air, trees and sky.

For George there was probably the appeal of the fresh start, like each September's new notebooks, another chance to achieve he-knew-not-what—something that would impress Kay, as I came to believe. This merged with his perpetual need to run away (from himself?). I doubt he learned the obvious, as poet Lucie Brock-Broido put it: "Wherever I went I came with me." A few weeks after our move he was tempted by a job announcement in *The New York Times*. "You can move to New York," I said. "The kids and I are staying here." Being firm wouldn't have felt so good had I known how prophetic my defiant statement was.

Not only had we moved enough, but he had a tenure-track job at a respectable university. Wasn't this what he'd worked so hard for, what we'd wanted, and been "poor" for? Yes, sort of, yet he reminded me more and more of Lord Ronald in Stephen Leacock's *Nonsense Novels*, who "flung himself upon his horse and rode madly off in all directions." He wanted to be in China, to raise sheep in Vermont, to import wood-burning stoves from Austria, to collect antique tools, build roads through the Vermont woods, research and write about China, make a lot of money. Some of these go together, some don't; some suited him, some didn't. For instance, he'd observed the ups and downs of the stock market and bought stock with inherited money. When the market dipped after Thanksgiving, as he'd expected, he lost his nerve and sold; the market went up, as he'd also expected, before Christmas, but he could no longer benefit.

Instead of reasonable pride in having arrived at a place where he could be useful and appreciated, he was restless. It was as if there was a destructive imp whispering in his ear, perhaps all his life. He told me early on, and once or twice more, that he expected to die young. Did he not feel entitled to live a good long life? He certainly was reluctant to settle down. At times he seemed tormented, but, instead of admitting and facing the torment, he pushed it out, mostly onto me, and at times onto the kids: he came into the kitchen one Saturday afternoon after a disagreement with Jessica, and said, "There are three bitches in my life: my mother, my wife, and my daughter." Jessica was eleven.

He was full of deep, unexplored contradictions that kept him biting his nails ("That's how I keep them short," another cover-up) and sometimes drove him to drink. The wildly contradictory views on Vietnam show that he wanted both to be free of his parents—defy them if necessary—and to please and impress them. I married him as a rebel against the conservative Moseleys. He seemed less and less a rebel as the years went on, so that, watching us both, it struck me that in middle age one becomes more and more like the parent of the same sex.

There were other contradictions. That first fall, George had a drink with Dan and Catherine Mulholland and came home flaunting a new word: sexism. When he explained it to me, I thought, "Well, you should know all about that." He didn't see that his actual view of women was sexism, not its opposite. Months later, Dr. L. tried to get him to talk about George and Eva rather than Men and Women, but George shared the views *not* of the women's liberation movement, but those that made that movement necessary.

And yet another contradiction. Dan Mulholland taught Russian history. Catherine, mostly at home with their three children, wasn't much of a housekeeper. Once I watched her peel green grapes, and eat the peels, then the flesh, explaining that the two tastes are different from that of the entire grape. I marveled at this pastime, and at Dan's apparent acceptance of her priorities as the grape peels accumulated and the house remained a shambles. In February we had dinner with them and, according to my diary, "Dan read to the kids, put them to bed, washed up [did the dishes]. Still Geo. thinks they're fine." (Much later I learned from Dan that the marriage was not a success and didn't last.)

When George complained, in Vermont, about "a dirty floor" and I didn't hand him the broom, we hadn't yet heard of sexism but were living it. It was the conventional division of labor: he brings home money, she manages house and children. George assumed that it applied to us, I had no choice about it, and he could decide that it needn't apply to other couples. Catherine could peel grapes; I still had to sweep the floor, while George derided sexism. (One example of what Dr. L. called a "whim of iron.")

Mostly I still agreed to the division of labor, but some expectations were ridiculous. He came home from Tufts, sat in the living room reading the newspaper as it got dark outside, and expected me to come from the kitchen, two rooms away, where I was cooking supper, and close the drapes. I said he should have married a Japanese woman. He took offense, but that kind of mindless subservience by the wife, and the husband's mindless bossiness, were a powerful tradition in Japan.

George had exhibited that same humorless, authoritarian male entitlement once when the children were at The Farm and he and I drove
from Plainfield to Grafton. We'd gone about half-way when I remembered that I hadn't packed his toilet kit. He hadn't packed it either, but
this was such a serious lapse that he drove back home, making sure I
understood it was my fault. We set out with the all-important toilet kit
the next morning.

Something as telling but also painful happened in Burlington, at a
UVM history department party, where I knew no one. I made my way
as best I could, spending a long time with the wife of the department
chair; she was not interesting but was willing to talk to me. When I'd
had enough of fending for myself I looked for George and found him
in a passionate embrace with a woman—not a friendly hug but a long,
intense kiss along with a more-than-friendly hug. I was angry, frightened,
humiliated. I got his attention and got him to leave. He was drunk, and
not contrite. After he had driven a few miles he got me to drive. That was
sensible, but after another few miles I pulled over and made him drive the
rest of the way, because of my fury risking making our children orphans.

Next day, the Saturday of the 4-H lunch, I was still angry and gloomy,
while he was quite pleased with himself. He thought the incident good
medicine: it would keep me from taking him for granted. Was it revenge
for the Aaron episode? Even if that was long over and I'd remained the
loyal wife, feelings and all? I didn't agree that I deserved this "good medicine," yet I swallowed the insult. How, why did I still love him? But I did.

While I expected that, having started a new life in Medford, we
would go on together, I also thought, "I have to be Eva as well as Mrs.
Moseley," without any idea yet how to go about it. George's view was
simple enough: "It's fine if you want to go to work—we could use more
money—but the house and the kids are your responsibility." Still good
at carpentry and other manual occupations, he wouldn't even look at a
drawer that stuck or a door that didn't shut. I had to call the Tufts housing
office, no matter how trivial the repair.

He was clearly disentangling himself from the family. Our house
became a home base, where he could get hot meals and clean clothes,
leave his stuff, and do things with the kids or me when he felt like it, and
not when he didn't. Already in Plainfield he wouldn't let me edit or even

see his dissertation. He didn't just want to split his infinitives at will; he was reading me out of his life.

At the same time he too seemed to be settling in. We bought a Yamaha studio upright piano, for me and maybe for the kids. We bought a washing machine. Even this feathering of the nest once created a little crisis. Whether it was a delivery or the removal of an ugly old couch, the movers had to maneuver a large, bulky object up or down a flight of stairs with a right angle halfway up and they bashed in the wall—Tufts University's wall!—just a little. George was angry and fearful. Angry at me for putting him in a situation he felt as dangerous. He became the martinet his father had been, excessively angry at me for "allowing" this damage and afraid that some large, powerful college official would punish him for the hole in the wall.

I wasn't good at putting all this together. The year before I'd talked at length with Edith, soon after the Milton family moved to a splendid Victorian house in Francestown, a village of splendid houses in southern New Hampshire. Aware that something was troubling me profoundly, I ranted on about Mother. After hours of this I realized that the trouble was between George and me.

For months, in Plainfield, my digestion had been more delicate than usual, tolerating only yogurt and cooked vegetables, and sending me for tests to Hitchcock Clinic at Dartmouth. The diagnosis was irritable bowel syndrome, and the gastroenterologist wanted me to take medicine to soothe it. I wrote him that I wanted to discover the cause, not just suppress symptoms. Psychiatry was what I was after and George, trying to be helpful—and assuming that I, not we, had a problem—brought a woman who worked at Goddard home for lunch; she had a therapist to recommend. Though unimpressed with her and what she told me, I took her advice and went to see Dr. Forest, retired head of the state mental hospital. This experience reminded me of Sartre's observation, in *Existentialism,* that, in choosing a person to get advice from, you choose your advice. By following the suggestion of someone I didn't respect, I got results that were at best inappropriate.

There were eleven sessions with Dr. Forest, enough to learn that our views were not in harmony, though I remember only a few specifics. He advised, when trying to get the children to pick their things up at the end of the day, to make "a play" of it. He was French Canadian; this was English for *un jeu*. Not bad advice; I already knew it was a good idea, but the pressure of daily chores and my own impatience and fatigue made it hard to follow, and he made no attempt to find out why I was tired and impatient or what could be done about it. It was up to me to make things right. No matter how I felt, or why I felt bad enough to seek him out, I should be jolly and patient with my children. As if I wouldn't have been that way every minute if I could.

The most interesting exchange though occurred when I told him that George complained of too little sex. "How old is he?" Dr. Forest asked. "Thirty-eight." He thought a moment and said, "That's still three times a week."

I knew that that exchange was all wrong, starting with the question of George's age. What about me? I was the same age. Is sex simply a service a wife provides for her husband's health, or any woman for any man's? And are his needs plotted out on a chart according to chronological age—like weight in relation to height? What about a wife's sexual needs? Is there a chart for those? How wrong-headed—and sexist!—this was became even clearer when I was in therapy with Dr. L., who stressed what ought to have been obvious: that there is a connection between what happens in the kitchen or living room before bedtime and what happens in the bedroom. George felt that he could be rude, nasty, demanding, insulting, depriving—drunk or not—but if he wanted it I should be sexually available moments later, and willingly. And Dr. Forest would have backed him up.

As if she knew all about this, for our anniversary Jessica gave us a risqué card. It showed a couple heading up the stairs at bedtime at three ages. As bouncy newlyweds, he carries her up and the caption reads: Tri-Weekly. Then they are middle-aged and he begins to look a bit doubtful. Caption: Try Weekly. Finally, he is bald, she grey. He carries a bottle of pep pills and prescription medicine (decades before Viagra appeared). Caption: Try Weakly. Dr. Forest could have designed this card.

After a few sessions he asked to meet George and we went together. The office was in the basement of the Forest house, a recent renovation. George began by rather pretentiously tapping the low ceiling—kicking the building's tires—and it was hard to get him to sit down. He held forth in the abrasive, unconvincingly self-assured mode he adopted when he felt on the defensive, his voice more metallic than usual. It was the last session, as he refused to pay for any more and I had no money of my own. Considering Dr. Forest's benighted view of men, women, and marriage, it was no great loss. Still, it took away a small ray of hope and I always wanted to ask him, "Now do you see what I'm talking about?" It was enormously helpful in my more serious and very long-term therapy with Dr. L. that he had gotten a good look at George. He was also infinitely more perceptive, and not hidebound by sexist notions. Perhaps Dr. Forest was better at managing the psychotic patients who used to be confined in state hospitals than he was at helping a normally "neurotic" woman in a rocky marriage. He provided neither support nor insight. I got more of both that afternoon with Edith.

But now, at Tufts, I thought we were going to make a new life, and I would find something grown-up to do beyond our four walls. Once my shoulder healed—for, as we played tennis on a Tufts court early in September, I dislocated it again, and had it put back at Lawrence Memorial Hospital. These episodes, of which there were two more before I had the shoulder repaired surgically, were painful and recovery was slow, my normally more useful right arm in a sling for weeks. George came home a few days after our tennis game feeling cheerful. "How's my girl?" he said brightly, putting his arm around me and squeezing *that* shoulder. That was probably only thoughtless, but soon after this he put his hand, palm up and heavy, on my throat as we lay in bed. "Are you caressing me or trying to choke me?" I asked, amazed at my daring. He admitted he wasn't sure which it was.

About then he told me that he had kept his service revolver in the bottom drawer of his bureau, among his sweaters, in our bedroom in Plainfield. It was a pistol with a short barrel, designed to kill at close range, I think .38 caliber. He kept it there even though a child could easily find it, yet that consideration didn't seem to be on his mind when, after he became friendly with that Goddard cop, he gave him the gun. In Medford he told me he did so because he was afraid he would use it on me.

Why? Was he like Tom Paley's jealous Knoxville murderer? What had I done? Nothing much, I thought, except fall in love with Aaron, and get over it, and expect George to be responsible for his family, to get his degree and either teach or pursue some other useful profession, which was what I thought, or hoped, he wanted to do. Partly he did want to do all this, and did do it for a time; partly he felt thwarted, confined, in a way that killing me would not have solved, aside from the likelihood of his being really confined as a result.

After the dinner at the Mulhollands', when Dan did all those domestic tasks, "we got home and [George] packed a suitcase & went to a room he [had] rented," on a trial basis. The kids needn't know yet; he appeared for breakfast and supper as usual. They were used to having him gone at all hours—presumably working at the office. But that they wouldn't know? A bit later, when it was clear that things were not going well and I was determined not to spring a fait accompli on them as had been done to me, I sat them down and said I had some bad news. "Are you getting a divorce?" Jessica piped up. It was twenty-five years and millions of divorces since the one that shocked me so much.

For a time indecision and ambivalence prevailed. The morning after the first night away he stayed on after the kids left for school. He'd thought better of it and wanted to come back. What I thought was: "One night and you're ready to come crawling back? How much could you have learned?" What I said was: "You've rented the room for a week. Stay the week and then come back, but we're going to get some counselling." And that was how I got him to go into therapy, just long enough to give Dr. L. a firsthand taste of George.

A while later he pointed out the house where he'd rented the room. It was two or three short blocks away! So his hurtful move was also rather touchingly pathetic. Later still I learned that it was a halfway house for male psychiatric patients. Was that what George thought of himself? Or the only room available?

But there was more. Betty, now Li-chiao, had been in Vienna and perhaps elsewhere. How long had they been in touch? He knew when she was in Hong Kong and she surely wasn't in Boston by chance. Smiling, he said I could see Hightower and he could see Betty, as if that were a fair deal, as if Robert weren't married and determined to stay that way while Betty was as always single, and as if I were still in love with Robert, which I wasn't. George was evidently shuttling between her and us. I guessed that he wouldn't have had the courage to leave if he hadn't had someone to go to. It was intriguing that both he and Van, in leaving their wives, took up not with younger women but with women from their early years. Another way to try to recapture one's youth.

Soon he said, again with a smile, that he wanted us to meet. I was not interested in meeting her (again!) but *was* interested in his proposal. He seemed to be saying, "Mother, I want you to meet my girl." He had in effect cast me as his mother, keeping the home fires burning while he did as he pleased, our apartment his home base rather than both his home and his responsibility. He'd turned all the responsibility over to me and to Tufts. And, like an adolescent, he didn't acknowledge the role Li-chiao was playing in my life, or the children's. An incident thirty years later evoked echoes of this moment: Mayor Rudolph Giuliani was told by a judge that no, he could not bring his girlfriend (later his ex-wife) to Gracie Mansion, New York's mayoral residence, while his wife and children were living there. Powerful politician and newly-minted critic of sexism: both devoid of common sense, common consideration, and self-knowledge.

A more distressing example of such obtuseness was Corliss Lamont, a brainy (and rich) Harvard alumnus and lifelong activist for labor rights, civil liberties, and other good causes. While married to the mother of his four children, he became enamored of widowed Helen Lamb and married her after "reluctantly" divorcing Margaret. "Much to my chagrin, considerable opposition developed among some of my relatives regarding my divorce and re-marriage [he wrote in *Yes to Life*].... Not one of my critics warned that the divorce would seriously upset my children and would hurt Margaret irredeemably. Those were arguments that could have stopped me." Which shows how dense a supposedly intelligent person can be.

In February I asked Henry if he would suggest a skiing weekend and try to talk George out of breaking up the marriage. This was not a smart move. Henry had been divorced twice (with two more divorces and three more wives still to come). Besides, it was dishonest, manipulative, the kind of thing Mother would do! But I was desperate, and I couldn't think of any other male authority figure, which was, I guessed, the only sort of person who could make an impression on George. It wouldn't have worked anyway, as George was determined to leave and Li-chiao to keep him, but Henry made sure it didn't by telling George that I had put him up to it. Fair enough that he wouldn't want in effect to be lying to his brother, but the honest course would have been not to agree to do it.

George came home from the halfway house on or about February 10th and endured several therapy sessions. He had let me find Dr. L., a neighbor and friend of the Hightowers, who recommended him highly. After a joint session, George went twice on his own; then it was my turn. Soon I was talking about my father. "How would you describe him?" Dr. L. asked. "Not too tall, well built, liked the outdoors." "Doesn't that describe George too?" he asked. Indeed it did. So in my prenuptial calculations of how they were *not* alike, I skirted their essential resemblance. Not that the three qualities I chose to mention got at the innermost essence of either one, but my choice of those qualities showed that the two men resembled one another, which I could have perceived in 1958 had I not been so determined not to. Those few sessions made clearer what sort of person George was, what oppressive ideas he had about marriage, how he resembled Poldi—and that I needed to understand why I married him.

Chapter 32
Lisl

$\mathcal{E}$lisabeth Kolberg was a good family friend, the daughter of a Privy Councillor who had been helpful to the Zetlins. She smoked incessantly and talked volubly, with a deep-throated laugh that often ended in a coughing fit, before the next drag on her cigarette.

As an adult she continued to live at home, a spacious apartment not far from Anna's in an elegant older building. She had had scarlet fever as a child, and her recovery was followed by six months in a sanatorium with some sort of mental illness, probably like my much milder and briefer post-flu depression in Hong Kong.

Through Lisl we got to know Elemer and Gisi Kardosh, a kindly Hungarian couple. Gisi had suffered from rickets as a child and was bow-legged all her life. I didn't learn, or at least don't remember, much about them, but Lisl had an impact on my life twice, once in a small and once in a not-so-small way involving the Kardoshes.

Lisl learned English and reviewed English-language movies for Viennese newspapers. When it became clear that we would all leave Austria if we could, she taught Anna some English, and Anna taught Paul and me what she'd learned. I liked the textbook, with its stories and songs, and remember singing "Bah bah bleck sheep/Hev you any vool?" There wasn't time to learn much before we left, but I was entranced by the *th* sound. I'd had a lisp, and spent some not-happy hours in speech therapy. Now, I told my family triumphantly, I would need that sound in English. Most of the adults never mastered it, alternating between *dot* and *zat*, never managing *that*.

In the US, Lisl lived in New Orleans, and then variously in Miami Beach and New York. In letters to Vickie from Florida, she often begged for photos of the children, which by then meant my children. My family,

Lisl Kolberg and Eva, probably 1935. Lisl was a good family friend, and the money she left me when she died of lung cancer was a great boon for me and my children.

both Steiners and Moseleys, included her in Christmas dinners and other occasions before she was immobilized by lung cancer.

Perhaps used to loneliness and frustration, perhaps tired of life, or just by habit a good sport in order to keep her friends, she seemed accepting and cheerful about her illness, or maybe only when she had visitors. I was busy with the children and not brave about hospital visits, so went to see her only twice. While we lived in the Bronx, she was at Columbia Presbyterian in Washington Heights. I brought her Dickens's *Pickwick Papers*, knowing she liked to read and figuring it would amuse and distract her. She told me she'd read it in Vienna but not since. She called me *the next day* and said, "That was wonderful." "How can you keep someone like that in books?" I thought. The edition I lent her has 817 pages of rather small print.

Later she was at Goldwater Hospital on Welfare Island, a city hospital for more or less indigent patients, where I remember Lisl sharing an enormous ward with what seemed like hundreds but was probably dozens. She died in the fall of 1971 and left me $1,000. Elemer Kardosh, her executor, made out the check but sent it via Vickie, so that I "should be spared of the obligation to acknowledge the receipt of it." But I wrote him a note and went to see him and Gisi in New York. Thanking them was more a pleasure than an obligation.

The timing of this bequest was providential. It was becoming clear that our divorce was going to be anything but speedy. It was already clear that it was anything but amicable. With a part-time job netting only fifty-some dollars a week and with George's support payments varying according to his whims, or needs, I couldn't afford Dr. L. Lisl's bequest was just the windfall that made resuming therapy possible. I could pay the cut-rate fee Dr. L. granted me; before Lisl's money ran out, I was working full time and could pay out of my salary.

I didn't deserve the money but was touched that Lisl wanted me to have it. It's gratifying to think that my family gave her enough pleasure that *she* wanted to thank *us* in the only way left to her. The money meant an emotional lifeline for me, and indirectly for the children, just when we needed it most.

Chapter 33
1971–72

*Y*ou'd think that T.S. Eliot had us in mind when, turning Chaucer's opening of the *Canterbury Tales* on its head, he began *The Wasteland* thus:"April is the cruellest month." Of my 90 Aprils so far, two have been cruel, the first in 1971, which saw our last session with Dr. L. Not only did George pontificate about Men and Women, but, as at Dr. Forest's, he wouldn't sit down—a pathetic way to disguise his discomfiture. In retrospect I have some sympathy for him, but why couldn't he admit he was confused? "Come off your high horse," I thought already in Plainfield, "and join the rest of us so we can muddle through together." If he could have done that (if I could have dared suggest it), he might have helped save the marriage, rather than wantonly damaging several lives, even if not "irredeemably." But he couldn't, or wouldn't—even if it was true, as Jessica says he told her later, that he was still in love with me.

Nor would he pay for any more therapy. I had no money to continue, and at first the point was to save the marriage; going by myself couldn't accomplish that. George admired Dr. L.'s ability to listen, understanding how hard it is to listen *usefully*. But this admiration didn't persuade him to continue. Perhaps just the opposite: he may have sensed that Dr. L. heard things George didn't realize he was conveying.

During a few uneasy, uncertain weeks, it once seemed he had come back, given Li-chiao up, and that day I was tentatively happy: he preferred me to her! Then he was out till 4 A.M. Unable to sleep, I listened to records—Haydn's trumpet concerto was one—that for years I couldn't hear without again feeling that night's rage and fear.

At about this time he said, echoing earlier complaints in a peevish tone and metallic voice, "I want sex." Presumably I had expressed reluctance because of what was going on, but in his view his edging away and his "other woman" were not supposed to have any effect on my "wifely duties." I felt both resentful and guilty, but Dr. L. cleared up my ambivalence, pointing out, as if to an ingenue, that George hadn't said, "I want you"—which would have made me readier to comply: after all, I wanted sex, with George, too, but he, in Dr. L.'s phrase, regarded me as "a source of supply." Whether it was sex or a clean floor, *his* wishes were what counted.

Also in that metallic voice, he said: "You think you're sexy but you're not." This interested me. *Did* I think I was sexy? I *hoped* I seemed so to him. For years he had thought so, as had some other men. He did have something of a point: those early encounters with Poldi had "trained" me to value sexual allure as a way to earn love, or attention. The nature of his attentions had led me to feel I had such allure, even as a toddler and even if those attentions didn't mean that he loved me as I needed to be loved. But George's remark, like his remark about us three bitches, said more about the accuser than the accused.

He began to go to Tufts social events without me, once coming home from a Friday happy hour too drunk to eat. I can still see him, his plate pushed aside, asleep on the table. At another supper he gave us a disturbing glimpse into his psyche. Tommy had been at the corner toy store and asked, for the second or third time, about something he had ordered. They promised it would be in soon, then it wasn't. "What do you conclude from that?" George asked. Tommy didn't know what to conclude, George did: the store owners were lying, stringing him along. I guessed that the supplier was unreliable, or the owners inefficient. George's view signaled both anger and paranoia, a sign of increasing irrationality.

Paranoia was perhaps one reason he quit therapy. Dr. L. was Jewish. That already made for a conspiracy. Maybe there was an unintentional one. I'd told Dr. L. about being expected to leave the kitchen to close the drapes while George sat within a few feet of them. In a joint session the doctor asked if I could do that. I said I'd try. Perhaps George sensed that only he took this seriously and felt we were laughing at him. In a way we were; the issue itself was ridiculous. But what lay behind it was not.

Soon what lay behind it came out in the open again, on Saturday, April 24th. I was cooking a pot roast when he announced that he was leaving, for good this time. The calendar says, in my writing, "George leaves." And one of the kids added: "HURRAY." I felt numb, resigned, both frightened to be left on my own, and determined not to be defeated, perhaps still hopeful that he would again change his mind. And glad I had the children, so as not to be alone but mainly as an anchor, something to give my life direction, limits, purpose. "Do your own thing" was in the air, people proclaiming the freedom to do what they wanted when they wanted. As I didn't always know what I wanted, it was good to have obligations.

So he left, taking *some* of his stuff. Although it was no longer a base to operate from, our apartment was still a convenient storage place. What surprised and appalled me more than this attitude toward the house was something that became apparent only gradually: that he had abandoned the children almost as much as me. His office was a five-minute walk away, so he could easily drop by to see if they were at home. That's what he mostly did: appear unannounced, stay as little as twenty minutes, not say when they would see him again. A note from that year enumerates these visits: "1 weekend + 7 times in 18 weeks (4 lunches, 2 dinners plus 1 afternoon (2 hrs.))." A further list includes "3 casual unannounced visits c. 20-30 min....12/12 took J. out for ½ hr." "The children don't need me anymore," he had said weeks before. But they did. They needed a father, although not the sort of father he'd become. And I needed a "him" that he no longer was. He had been a mostly willing, engaged husband and father earlier, but that was all gone. Was it a midlife crisis?—a new, trendy concept then.

It was appalling, if not surprising, how his departure hurt. I sat in a warm bath and cried and cried, an abandoned child, like the child sent into exile in 1935. I tore a dress he had bought in Oxford into shreds and flushed them down the toilet. There was little satisfaction in that gesture, or in tearing up his Yale diploma. The next summer I threw his car key into Casco Bay from the ferry between South Freeport and Bustins Island.

Soon he invited me for lunch at a Chinese restaurant. I expected he'd have something relevant or useful to say. But he chatted a little about nothing much, ate in near silence, batted his brown eyes with their long dark lashes at me, and at the end said, "We must do this again some time." The hell we must, I thought. I was still in love with him but not masochist enough to agree to casual dates with my husband while he lived with another woman and I raised our children virtually alone. Alas, he never asked again, denying me the pleasure of turning him down.

That day or another I told him I'd decided that couples should have psychotherapy before marrying. He had a different idea: having just seen a movie based on the Kama Sutra, the Hindu sex manual, he thought engaged couples should be required to see that. Was he serious? Did our views of marriage diverge so radically? Was he so much like Poldi, making a shallow joke of a family crisis?

Sometimes he was inappropriately jovial. Nine months after he moved out,

> Geo. walked in, without ringing or knocking, around 8. (No school today.) I told him not to do it. He said: What's for breakfast? I: Nothing for you. He played chess & poker with Tom, & asked for coffee; I refused. Asked him to go & warned him I'd get an injunction. Asked if he thought he had the right to come & sit around here, he said yes. Asked if Betty knew he was here—no answer. Told him he enjoys hurting 2 women. After he left I explained to Tom why I felt as I did—he looked so pale. Told J. also & called lawyer. [Unless otherwise noted, quotations are from my diaries; I resumed writing late in 1971.]

His opinions, actions, intentions were now inconsistent and unreliable, as was apparent to others too. "Winnie Chen said 2 friends had told her George had been nasty to them…. One used the word 'insane.'" At that early stage it bothered me when strangers saw him as unbalanced. I got no satisfaction from seeing him humiliated, even if he did it to himself, and even if he had sometimes humiliated me. But as he continued to be erratic, there was some consolation in hearing that his colleagues found him difficult, although when Dan Mulholland told me about George's shortcomings as a teacher, I "felt a little hurt to hear it." It hurt in a different way to learn that Li-chiao took "my official, public role as his woman" at a history department party. I'd lost my status as faculty wife and would have to make new roles, socially and professionally. Late in 1970 I saw that I needed to be Eva as well as Mrs. Moseley; a year later it looked as though I would be Eva and not Mrs. Moseley at all.

My calendar calls May 18, 1971, BLACK TUESDAY. It was the day a letter, addressed to Mrs. Eva Moseley, came from Charles R. Parrott of a prominent Boston law firm. In those days only a divorced woman would be addressed as "Mrs." and *her* given name. What hurt, more than George's going to a lawyer behind my back, was that whatever he said convinced Parrott that George had grounds for divorce. When I tried to learn what the grounds were from Parrott thirty years later, he didn't remember George and said that what he wrote was boilerplate, having nothing to do with this particular case. If only I'd known that then. But this was my first experience with lawyers.

Meantime, Mother, after her operations for colon cancer the year before, went to London in the hope that the Imperial Cancer Institute could cure her metastasized liver cancer. It could not, and in mid-June she came through Boston on her way home to San Francisco, where she died a few days later. This blow, just two months after George left for good, stirred up all the ambivalent feelings I had about her, as well as vertiginous loneliness—in still another sense an abandoned child—yet it almost paled beside the continual punishment of George's rejection.

If this makes me sound totally self-absorbed, so be it. I wouldn't compare my trials to the Holocaust or any other major disaster. We weren't hungry or homeless, no bombs were falling. But the future looked bleak. Financially and emotionally we were at the mercy of someone who had turned against us—against me mainly, but it spilled over onto the children. His behavior toward us was capricious, unpredictable, mirroring his own uncertainty—which he never acknowledged. In a dream I had about then, George had the children in an open jeep and was driving into deep mud; it began to sink, and Tommy was about to drown when I woke up in a sweat.

The kids started hanging out mainly with much older kids. I happened to be there when one was about to go for a joyride with Tommy and another boy in the trunk of a VW Beetle. They seemed defiantly pleased with themselves. It was stupid and self-destructive; I made Tommy get out. Another day a dozen kids were in our cellar sniffing glue in sandwich bags. I told them it could cause brain damage. "Oh yeah?" I guessed they had two contradictory thoughts: "Wow, that's exciting," and "It won't happen to me." Later some kids had guns at our house while I was at work. Sometimes one of the boys harassed Jessica. When I resumed therapy, the doctor helped me see that Tommy—and Jessica to a lesser extent—was trying to prove, mainly to himself, that he could do without a father, be his own father. They were almost having to do without one.

These would have been trying years anyway, with two kids entering their teens. Some of the contention and uproar might have happened even with George there, though probably not the guns or glue, or the run-ins with police. Jessica and I had frequent night-time altercations, I feeling that she was getting at me when I was feeblest, not being a night person; still, I would listen and explain as long as I could, though rarely long enough.

> Jessica & I had a fight last night, 11+ till after 12, because I wanted to go to bed before her. But in the course of it I told her I'm doing my best & don't feel guilty (she complained she had no parents—I don't act like one) & told her it's been rough, that Daddy "told" me he prefers another woman to me—and that he'd told her that too—that my Father did it to me so I know what it feels like. Really glad I said that, wish someone had said it to me. [December 4, 1972]

The kids had to work out their relations with their father; I tried to help by telling them facts while not raging against him out loud—no matter how his words and actions hurt—and by reassuring them that I would be there no matter what happened. Sometimes a remark by one of them gave me a jolt.

> Jessica's party—noisy—the boys (T., Tim, Michael) disrupted it. Tom still knows Geo. wouldn't chastise him. He said, "You think you're in charge of this house?" I said "Yes, who do you think is in charge?" He said, "Someone named Daddy." [December 4, 1971]

> Edith & Peter...had sent a beautiful cyclamen for my birthday. (Jessica said That must be from Daddy.) [December 22, 1971]

But sometimes one or the other would see what I considered, and consider, the reality of our situation. In February 1972 Jessica returned from a visit to Henry and his family.

> Jessica & I had a talk, about Henry's family & ours. She said she didn't know why we were getting divorced & I tried to tell her, when I talked about George telling her to protect Tom but not telling Tom to respect her, she cried (on my shoulder) & said, "I've never had a father." Said she wanted to stay in Annapolis because Henry was like a father.

Her conclusion about George seems right if hyperbolic; he had been a better father when they were little.

Sometimes they were the delightful children they had mostly been earlier.

> A nice supper, talk & good feeling—then the kids horsed around, mostly Jessica chasing Tom—& no disaster. Once Tom took refuge with me, threw his arms around me & hid his face in my shoulder. That's rare now, I'm glad it's still possible. [February 6, 1972, and the next day] Tom set the table behind my back.

One dinnertime in September, both "kids nice & helpful." Tom built a fence for my vegetable garden, one Sunday he straightened up the house while Jessica and I were at church (the UU church in Arlington, which she joined), and they both helped out at the Schlesinger Library. Jessica helped cook supper, cleaned the house on her own, and soon was cooking entire meals; in February 1974, I went to New York on library business for the day and Jessica vacuumed, washed the floor, and polished furniture. Sometimes they saw things my way: in November 1972 I told Tom about George's latest stingy offer for a settlement and "he said it's like a kid that does something stupid to make his parents angry!"

Although they were often with friends, and Tom especially would disappear for hours at a time, one Sunday in June we were all home all day, eating and talking and doing our chores, and on a Sunday in October I made green tomato jam, helped Jessica with her sewing, and taught

Tom the Greek alphabet. Just like a family. The constellation of a single mother with two teen-age children felt natural to me, because that was what I'd experienced as a teenager.

But such bright moments were interspersed in stretches of contention and misery, and I was often close to despair—lonely, angry, confused—while the children struggled with having only one parent at home, and the altered behavior of both parents. I might retire to my bedroom for several daytime hours, at the mercy of emotional pain and its physical manifestations brought on by George's rejection and abandonment and by the memories dug up in therapy. George continued his sporadic, perfunctory, unpredictable visits. In February 1972, "George...called twice today, from Tufts,...said he'd come to see them, then that he wouldn't," and in July, "Tom said, 'Daddy's coming'—he saw him coming down the street—but he kept on going."

One weapon George used against me, and us, was the car, a 1967 Toyota registered in his name. Before he left he kept finding things wrong with it, and had Precision Motors rebuild the engine. After it was fixed he took it back, claiming there was water in the oil, or something similar that sounded more Freudian than auto-mechanical.

He let me have it for most of 1971; then he took it so I had to ask to use it. This elicited suggestions from friends: "Anne Stevenson [poet, biographer of Sylvia Plath, formerly married to sinologist Mark Elvin] says—Let him have it, he'll have to pay the insurance. And Pierre Laurent [professor of French history at Tufts]: Wouldn't you rather be able to be mad at him about it than have the car?" I had enough other reasons to be mad at him and, with two children, friends in various places, and a psychiatrist in Auburndale (by public transportation more than two hours each way), it was hard to manage without a car.

One Friday in December 1971, I asked for the car to go to a party. "George said I could have it tonight instead of tomorrow" and added: "'I hope you'll restrict your use of the car.'!" The party was ending early, so I took the kids out for dinner and a movie instead. Was this whimsical self-indulgence as George's stricture implied? One day in January he promised to leave the car. Jessica called me at work to say it was there, "but when I got home, no car. Jessica & I toured the parking lot, no car, no George. [Next day he told me] he changed his mind & took it away! Partly because my lawyer called after I did—he was hurt by that! And said it was hard to share the car & he hadn't had a kind word since he could remember! He really is insane." Double standard: he could go to a lawyer but I mustn't; he could abandon and insult me but I should produce "kind words."

He again promised the car and again took it, for I got a ride to Dr. L.'s and went to work from there via that long trolley and subway trip. When I asked why he took the car, "he said there was no particular reason." Then he agreed that I could have it that Saturday to visit the Miltons in New Hampshire, and also leave the kids with him. Saturday morning he called: "'You won't believe this but I've lost the car keys.' He came & offered to go get the car (with my keys), I said I'd get it myself, didn't trust him."

If they were really lost, he soon found his keys, then lost them again and took Jessica to a father-daughter banquet by taxi. That time he behaved responsibly, but in June, having agreed to stay with Tommy while Jessica was away and I went to the Miltons' overnight, "George left [Tommy] here alone! Didn't eat with him either, though he spent the afternoon." At times the Hightowers lent me their car, and in August 1972 I bought an aged Opel station wagon, the first car I owned myself. By then, George and the Toyota were out of reach.

Aside from the car, my anger at him was often aroused by what he did to the children, the routine neglect plus some specific hurtful things.

> Jessica is 12 [I wrote on December 2, 1971]. George took her & Tom out for dinner. Later she told me he'd brought Betty along—I informed her that she was the woman he lives with. Luckily, J. doesn't like her—even so, it's hard to stomach imagining my children with her: it seems <u>dirty</u>—but I'll get over that.

I did get over it, but not over the conviction that bringing his mistress along to a dinner in honor of his daughter, without asking or even warning Jessica, was contemptible. The next Christmas Tommy made him a model of a boat, with a kit from that corner toy store. Soon a letter came; Tommy left it in the living room, which I took as license, even an invitation, to read it. George thanked him for the model and added, "You've got the right idea, but the workmanship is a little rough."

"How dare he criticize anything any of us does, when he takes no interest & hasn't for almost 2 years? What a cheap skunk!" I exclaimed to my diary. Only rarely had he taken the trouble to teach Tommy anything about carpentry or tools, and then he belittled what Tommy made for him. George had told me or Tommy or both that Tommy could have the tools he left behind, including a power saw, hardly the thing for an unsupervised ten-year-old to be using. Was he passing on his self-destructive tendencies too?

George did send money each month, the amounts determined by him. At first it was reasonable, about $345 plus our rent, which he paid directly to Tufts. Soon it was $300 plus the rent, and in January 1972, $200 sent late. I woke up to the fact that, whether or not we would end up divorced, the kids and I needed legal protection of our livelihood. It sounds antediluvian now, but I had suspended pursuing a career, helped him with his books, encouraged him to get a doctorate, willingly lived in a state of graduate-student poverty, and so at forty was not in a good position to earn an adequate living—while he was.

Realizing I needed a lawyer too, I'd seen Edward Barshak, recommended by Dr. L., in June 1971. "Since he is determined upon a divorce and now has a girlfriend," Barshak wrote in a file memo, "Mrs. Moseley is willing to go along with divorce. However, she is in absolutely no hurry. The two of them went to see a lawyer named Fitzpatrick in Medford who told them that neither one has grounds for divorce." He mentioned Parrott's letter contradicting Fitzpatrick. The implication is that, without my presence, George could cite grounds that wouldn't stick if I were there to contradict him. I never learned what those supposed grounds were. That I had been in love with Aaron? But I hadn't done anything except talk about my feelings, and eventually talk myself out of them. (While he had obviously been in touch with Li-chiao.) Perhaps it was the same offense(s) for which he'd wanted to shoot me.

Parrott was one of at least three attorneys with whom George was dissatisfied. One he hired and fired twice. One filed an (unsuccessful) motion to vacate the separate support order. He had dismissed one,

George told me, "for two contradictory reasons: that he wasn't moving fast enough, and also because George wasn't sure he wanted a divorce"; he wrote that he couldn't afford two households. Once or twice he talked about moving back, but when he brought the kids home after Jessica's birthday dinner and I asked if he really thought he might come back, he replied with a rueful smile that *I* didn't seem enthusiastic, avoiding the question of what *he* wanted.

Looking back from the fall of 1971, I noticed that, as soon as I stopped resisting the prospect of divorce and agreed that it would be best, he began to lose interest in it. While I felt that we should be making steady progress toward a settlement, often nothing was happening and it was uncertain that anything would happen. At times it seemed that he wanted to live separately without severing the legal ties between us. When I told him we could discuss his moving back, that didn't interest him. Just as well, I thought, for it was hard to see how he could live with us again unless we could agree about what was happening. "I don't want him to crawl," I wrote in a note to myself, "but if he simply lies, then there's no question of his coming back. Last week he said I threw him out—which is a lie; he wouldn't admit that Betty ever existed; he insisted that I'd been 'living high off the hog.' No hint of any pain he might have inflicted." I soon realized the idea of his moving back was just a distraction, a detour from the path to the inevitable.

When it became crystal clear that there would be no reconciliation, the legal wheels began to grind in earnest, if slowly and not always successfully. In the spring of 1972 there were efforts to forestall George's divesting himself of the Vermont land he had bought with his inheritance from General Moseley. (I'd begged him, in vain, not to buy land next to his mother's, for us to find land elsewhere in Vermont that appealed to us both.) I told Barshak about the land in December. We agreed to get a court order—which had to be tied to a divorce or separate support agreement—to keep George from selling it. But it was too late: in October George had signed some 190 acres in Grafton over to his mother, and sold roughly 80 acres in Chester to Ted and Eric of Potato Hill for a bargain price; the deed notes that "the transfer was made between friends." A memo to my lawyer cited Vermont statutes and case law indicating that

"Mrs. Moseley has an excellent chance of having Mr. Moseley's convey-
ances declared fraudulent to her rights as a creditor." But I was "leery of
starting anything we might lose. Want to get <u>free</u> of George."

Along with this contentious legal and financial struggle, I tried to be
the parent/s Jessica and Tommy needed; dig up my past, once I resumed
therapy thanks to Lisl, and figure out why I'd married George; earn extra
money with editorial projects; have some sort of social life; manage our
house in Plainfield, which was rented, and try to sell it; and later do a
fairly demanding new job, about which below. And everyday chores,
errands for the Tufts food coop, and a desultory hunt for a house to buy,
as I knew Tufts would eventually evict us.

We were in court at least five or six times, and I too had two more
attorneys, but they were more junior, and therefore cheaper, members of
the same firm, and it wasn't I who chose them. Ed Barshak had bigger
fish to fry but kept an eye on the case, as we got a separate support order
and found out about the land.

I sometimes tried to be charitable and see George's point of view,
but he didn't make it easy. He claimed I'd made life impossible for him
(without specifying how), and that I was "after him financially. Why
couldn't I trust him to feel responsible for the kids rather than get separate
support and besides the order said I had cause to live apart and I haven't."
He said this in court too—as if I could live with him after he moved out.
When I said, "What about adultery?" he said, "That's a technicality."

In a file memo my lawyer, Stanley Berkowitz, wrote that George's
attorney "indicated that Mr. Moseley is a most difficult client." George
defied the separate support order by not paying the full amount, so that
he soon owed $270, $90 for each of three months, equivalent to at least
twenty times that amount in early-21st-century dollars. After a constable
served the summons for a court hearing, "George said he doesn't want
a divorce: 'I have two children & they're the only children I'll ever have
& you're their mother so a divorce is ridiculous, meaningless.'" Which
would mean that he would be free but I wouldn't. But soon I began to
feel sorry for him—"poor crazy, lonely bastard."

I felt sorry for him because his vacillation made me think he was
alone. Perhaps these pendulum swings between impatience for divorce
and "divorce is meaningless" were a function of how he was or wasn't

getting along with Li-chiao. But very likely, as with my parents, the "other woman" was determined enough to get her man to overcome his occasional ambivalence. In September, Jeanne, the tenant in Plainfield, "said Geo. & Henry came up with 2 women, one of them Betty. I was surprised she's still around, regretted ever feeling sorry for him, but glad to hear Jeanne run her down." It was disturbing that Li-chiao was still with him, but balm for my wounds that one more person disliked my replacement.

Although my replacement was still in the picture, George continued to "talk vaguely of reconciliation" but wouldn't admit that it would take effort.

> [H]e thinks things will work themselves out. But why am I so soft? I feel so sorry for him, can't get angry. Why can't I remember, with <u>feelings</u>, that he sold the land, took the car, neglected the children, was unfaithful & deceitful. Is it because I feel I deserve such treatment? That must be it. God's in his heaven & all's right with the world when some sadistic, oedipal, vengeful martinet is dumping all over me. [July 6]

One day in January I "felt hurt that Geo., who was so dear to me, should be so crazy. He cannot admit that he has caused me any pain." The next day I "felt Geo. as an infant clinging to me & wanted to get him off." I was also crazed at times—though I tried to keep it between Dr. L. and me and my diary and me—because of what came at me from George, the children's troubles, and my own "issues": my having married a man who, despite admirable qualities, had rejected me and abandoned the family; and my tendency to fall for unsuitable men, men too young, married, gay, or just not interested. I called it my Man-of-the-Month Club and in November 1972 was relieved to look back on six months without an infatuation. Underlying these issues was a shortage of self-respect— a tendency (noted by Professor Ingalls) to try to please others even at my own expense, which usually means not pleasing anyone.

Dr. L. was enormously helpful. On June 5,

> he insisted on G being very responsible in being mean, nasty, angry, stingy toward me—& my worst crime is showing him the truth about

himself. He showed me again how I can't see the reality of George—blame Kay, Mullane [one of George's temporary attorneys]—& it's true, I'm still angry at Kay, was brainwashed early that women take the blame. Dr. L. said the only way to deal with Geo. is with the full weight of the law & hope he'd rather be out working than in jail.

Because of the $270 he owed, I was in court "nearly all day" on July 19th, partly with Berkowitz, partly with newcomer David Barry, who gradually took over the case.

Geo. lied about his salary but I let it pass & he made a speech about the order—that I don't need it, that I have no cause to live separately, that he hasn't harmed me (he said that twice)—when the judge said, "I take it you're not going to pay [the court-ordered amount]" he said "Correct."

I thought the judge owed him a warning: if you refuse to pay the full amount, I can send you to jail. Instead he simply sentenced him to the Middlesex House of Correction in Billerica for ten days, and then and there George was taken away. Much agonizing in my diary:

Rather a shock & I wonder what he'll do when he comes out…. Went home, slept an hour. Then Tom came in, he threw a rock (shot put) & broke Chris's windshield, I told her who did it…. Then Tom cried & I sat with him & then told him about Geo…. Then Kay called. Geo. had called Henry & said to tell Kay he doesn't want bail. Kathy says she'll pay what he owes. Tried to explain things to Kay & she half understood. Talked to Henry, very hostile though he wouldn't say so. The Moseleys' hostility hurts some, insofar as I feel guilty—but, I hope mainly, it makes me angry. As [a friend] says, he put himself in jail—& even Van said maybe he wants to hide there.

[July 20] David Barry confirmed the idea that he had put himself in jail—also, there is no question of bail as he's serving a sentence. He thought I or someone trusty could go to Billerica & explain things to Geo.—there isn't anyone he'll listen to—least of all me—but it might be worth a try. But what a nightmare it is: he's totally irrational, doesn't even restrain himself in court.

[July 21] David Barry told me George will be out after 10 days, if he doesn't pay we start the whole rigmarole (citation, hearing) all over again. [The] warden will talk to him but thinks it would help if I did too. I got the feeling he wouldn't want me to see him there, would think I was gloating & feel humiliated. David said he hadn't thought of that.

July 22 began with a 4 a.m. phone call that the Hightowers' car, which they lent me now and then, had been stolen from my driveway. Later Dr. L. and I struggled with the Geo. problem, he agreed I shouldn't go but thought my lawyer might ask permission to see him, & explain the realities to him. Talked to Barshak who said he'd never known anyone who didn't pay eventually (but this may be his 1st time!), said he'd write him a letter & send me a copy. He admitted the judge was a bit rigid.

[July 24] Barshak learned Kay came down Fri., paid the $90 (!, not $270) owing & Geo. got out [after two days]. I said, "Shit!" It's a relief to have him out but that story disgusts me. Tom asked, "Did she do it for you or for him?" I [said] if it had been even partly for me, she would have let me know.

The fact that he owed three times $90 had gotten lost. Are courts always so slapdash with the facts and figures? The sums sound trivial now, but I was earning $3.10 an hour; this was before the galloping inflation of the 1970s. I imagined Kay over drinks at Potato Hill, or at the Ballous' in Chester, indignant over the "fact" that Eva had George put in jail for a mere $90. The only satisfaction in all this came from Tom's astute question. Jessica was in Vermont; when I called and said I had bad news about George, "first thing she said—Why, is he dead?" Beyond that startling response, I didn't record her reaction.

While frustrating me and maybe making George more hostile (though he claimed to be chastened by his two days in jail), this episode changed nothing. He had resigned from Tufts when Ernest Cassara invited him to teach East Asian history at George Mason University, newly separated from the University of Virginia. Ernest, a colleague at Goddard, was the first chair of the new history department. Bob and Mary Jo Taylor had come for supper in June.

> We talked about Geo, who I guess was really a thorn in the history dept's side. Freeland Abbott, the department chair, wouldn't let Ernie Cassara into the history dept. when the divinity school closed, so Ernie & Geo. will have a gripe in common, or 2 gripes: Tufts & Goddard, not much basis for working together.

Whatever the dubious merit of such academic gossip, at George Mason George was not far from Dupont Circle, "where the action is," and many miles from me, which added the worry that it would be difficult and costly to serve him with court notices. He changed lawyers twice more, ending up with Joseph Klarfeld, whom my lawyers knew and found to be "disorganized."

George continued to send less than the court-ordered amount. Is it unfair to suggest that, like his failure to write or call, this miserliness indicates less than heartfelt devotion to the kids? He sent $350 instead of $450, and as he was no longer at Tufts he was no longer paying our rent.

Luckily by this time I had a higher and more reliable income. I had been constructing indexes freelance for Houghton Mifflin, typing for various people, and selling cleaning products for Amway, then for Shaklee. In September 1971 I got a job at the Arthur and Elizabeth Schlesinger Library on the History of Women in America, at Radcliffe. I'd gone to the Appointment Bureau as an alumna, looking for part-time work so I could be home afternoons. Offered a job at the library as the first-ever assistant to the curator of manuscripts (I heard later that the director, Jeannette Cheek, overrode the curator's doubts), I accepted, even though it meant working afternoons and so defeated one of my goals. Being in Cambridge made it handy; I had worked in libraries though not in archives; it was a definite offer and a somewhat familiar environment.

The curator, Diane Dorsey, taught me enough in one year that, when she went off to divinity school, she recommended that I take her place, and Jeannette agreed. I was about to go to Simmons College for a library degree; now that became difficult, and unnecessary. On my first day as curator, I was like a comrade of Trotsky, who "had many ideas…but…did not know what to do next." I decided to keep doing what I'd been doing as assistant and other things would follow of their own accord. They did. I'd stumbled on what turned out to be the perfect job for me, and the means to create the new status I needed. Being at a women's institution as the women's movement was beginning to have its greatest impact helped enormously, even if I didn't always agree with the more radical feminists.

Along with the job, I inherited a spot on the first-ever panel on women at the 1972 annual meeting of the Society of American Archivists (SAA). I expressed surprise that the same panel concerned women's archives and women archivists, two disparate matters, and was told, "You don't know what it took to get any session on women." When I delivered my paper in Columbus, Ohio, in November, I was so nervous my mouth was dry, but I was afraid to pick up a cup of water as my hands were shaking. The papers from the panel were published in *The American Archivist*, and I was invited to speak at the Phi Beta Kappa initiation at the University of Massachusetts the next May.

These were the first of dozens of talks at meetings of SAA, New England Archivists, and elsewhere. I learned to enjoy and not dread public speaking and became an archival "joiner": for SAA serving on the nominating committee and council, and an unsuccessful run for president; for NEA several times program chair and also president; helping found the Boston Archivists Group; for years editing the NEA newsletter (with the kids often folding, stapling, and sticking address labels) and later two issues of *The American Archivist*.

In 1994, when Jeannette's successor, Pat King, died of cancer, I was appointed acting director and in fifteen months learned more about budgets, personnel, and other administrative matters than I would ever need again, and about the inner workings of Radcliffe. I continued to serve as curator and also edited the proceedings of an international women's library conference we held as my term began. That concentrated effort made retirement look very appealing.

At an event to mark my retirement in 1999, Arthur Schlesinger jr. introduced me, Adrienne Rich read her poems, and the Massachusetts House of Representatives issued a proclamation in my honor (engineered by Representative Alice Wolf, granddaughter of Vickie's boss in Vienna). These and other honors gave me an inside view of people praising each other, best summed up by my reaction to being made a fellow of SAA. Who, me? Then I looked at the list of existing fellows: If x and y are on this list, there's no reason why I shouldn't be too.

Working for pay was a big boost to my morale and the promotion to curator much more so. The money was important but so was feeling competent and useful. At the same time various friends held me together during these months of melodrama. I babysat with the Chens' little girl and marveled at how distraught Winnie was when her parents, on Taiwan, divorced. They moved away at the end of 1971. History department colleagues were especially helpful. Pierre Laurent and Bob Taylor and their wives, Ginny and Alice Jo, the Mulhollands and Isabel Abbott provided various kinds of solace. I dropped in on the Taylors or Laurents for tea and talk; they might tell me news of George, invite me for supper, come to our house for a meal, give me advice, lend me garden tools.

According to my wall calendar, on five days in September 1971 Catherine and I canned together: plums, grape jelly, peach chutney, tomatoes, spiced peaches. Isabel told me that, after the full drill at Thanksgiving, at Christmas she made dinner simple: roast beef, rice, and frozen mixed vegetables; and that in her youth she started spelling her name Isobelle—until her brother took to calling her Eyesobelly. My diary records calls from all these Tufts friends to congratulate me when I was promoted to curator.

The Hightowers' oldest son Jamey and his wife Betsy lived around a couple of corners. Jamey played ping-pong with me or the kids, or chess with Tommy; they joined us, or me, for walks, bike rides or meals. We went to his parents' place on Bustins Island in Casco Bay with them, where for a few blessed days I forgot my troubles, where I watched, amazed, as Tommy split firewood: where had he learned to let the axe handle slide through his hands like that? Had George taught him more than I realized? Jessica helped with meals, as at home, and made friends with other summer people. With the younger or the elder Hightowers we went apple picking and hiking. On Mt. Wachusett one May day, Bunny pulled aside some dead leaves at the edge of the ski trail and revealed a clump of trailing arbutus—our elusive state flower.

Though further away, Robert and Bunny became to some degree my substitute parents. (In being further away—in another borough, so to speak—they resembled my actual parents.) On a particularly bad morning soon after George left, I asked Bunny if she could come over. She offered to come that afternoon. "Can you come now?" I begged. She did. I edited and typed one of her splendid novels for teenagers and gave her German lessons, tasks that added to my income; mainly though, like the manuscript job later, they made me feel useful and competent, while George undermined my tenuous self-respect.

The Hightowers invited me for meals, including a dinner party in September 1971, as Nixon and Kissinger were working to establish diplomatic relations with China, a prospect that interested the largely sinological company around the table. Holmes Welch referred to this "opening" as "a chink in the Great Wall," an unintended and unfortunate pun. Holmes gave me a ride home. George and I had been at a Welch dinner party, where his Polish wife Marek fed us sumptuous Polish dishes. She was not at this dinner; later I learned that the Welches too were divorcing. Though I told Holmes some of what I was going through, he didn't mention being in the same boat, the kind of reticence I resented—like Mother's silence about her abortion/s.

Jeannette Cheek produced the same feeling. Whenever I told her about the latest twist of the tortuous divorce proceedings, which dragged on even after she retired, she would understand if I stayed home to nurse the latest wounds. When I learned that her only son was getting divorced at the same time, it felt as if she'd said: "Yes, dear, I understand that you've made a mess of your life, unlike some of us." She would neither say nor mean this, but her silence about the mess in her own family implied as much. Partly it was a vestigial nineteenth-century reticence—or not wanting to impose her own troubles—but all I needed to hear was: Yes, we've experienced this too.

The Hightower house in Auburndale became almost a second home. But, although I liked and admired Robert and Bunny, from my diary it's clear that we had our disagreements—even that Robert sometimes annoyed me—due partly to disillusionment with the man I'd once wor-shipped, partly to instances of what still seems poor judgment. When (the next year) George asked me to reimburse him a per diem amount for the children's days at The Farm, Robert "was so shocked at its unreasonable-ness & how bad it looks he thought only dire need could drive [George] to it." To which I added the cryptic comment "Balls," reminiscent of his note on my term paper, that I didn't always express myself elegantly. Inelegant as the word is, it is accurate. And when I'd asked George why he saw so little of the children, in addition to assuring me it was (of course!) my fault, he said, "If you think it's so important for me to see the kids, how about letting them live with me next year?" Both Hightowers thought it would be "convenient." Yes, I could devote myself to work and pleasure and looking for a man without worrying about getting home for them, keeping them fed and clothed, safe and happy and educated. But I would miss them, miss seeing them develop as teenagers, and I would worry about them with their erratic, distracted father and his compan-ion—worry that they might be unhappy in Virginia or, conversely, that they might become estranged from me. The idea was simply out of the question, and it was disappointing to have such dear friends not see that. In case I had any doubts, Dr. L. said: "Do you love them? Do you want them to be with him? Would you miss them? Would you feel guilty? Do you care about what's good for them?"

That was in June 1972. A year later, with negotiations dragging on, Robert advised me to get a divorce before I needed one "because when I do [need one] I'll be at a disadvantage," and at the end of that conversation added, "Don't be vindictive." What Robert considered vindictive Dr. L. would urge as sticking up for my due, and the children's. So again, while appreciating his friendship, I had to defend myself, in my own head, against Robert's advice.

The one friend I could count on always to see things clearly, some-times before I did, was Edith. Especially during the months that I had no money for Dr. L., she became my sounding board and oracle. Not that she always had advice, but she understood and sympathized. Many years later, when I wrote to remind her how helpful she'd been, she replied that she remembered mainly feeling useless. Yes, she couldn't make George behave differently or prevent the divorce, but what a help to have her near enough for a day trip, sometimes in Boston for the day, or on the phone, listening, understanding, and occasionally straightening me out.

Even a busy social and professional life couldn't obscure an undercurrent of sadness and loneliness. Those years were just as hard for the children, as teenagers and because the divorce was trouble for them too. Ultimately they and I were better off without the person George had become, but it took time to accept that. It was disappointing that we hadn't done better than our parents, and that the epidemic of divorces was one historical trend we didn't skirt. There I was just like many others, not "different."

Chapter 34

MEN NAMED MAX

*W*hen friends named a new baby Max, Mother said, "*So jung und schon Max,*" and she quoted herself whenever the name came up: "So young and already Max." She hated the name; I don't think she ever explained why, but I may have discovered the reason.

But first there was one Max I liked particularly, and I think she did too: Max Kurz, the quintessential Nature Friend, a veteran of the Spanish Civil War and at Camp Midvale one of those World War II heroes, a communist with close ties to the GDR (East Germany), powerful on the volleyball and fistball fields, and a graceful and energetic folk dancer; he had a craggy face, and was outspoken and humorous. He once lent his bungalow to the wife and child of a jailed communist; the FBI watched him and in turn he helped guard the camp against local right-wingers.

This Max was an enticing but elusive presence during the coming-apart years. At Cardigan Lodge in 1973, Angie, who knew Max, was sure he would be glad to hear from me. I wrote in August and he replied:

> It didn't take me but a second to remember who Eva Steiner was. I was sorry to hear that your mother had died, I have very nice memories of her as well as of the little kid Eva. Last thing I remember of you was, that you married and left for the Far East. I hate to see people get hurt and I see from your letter that 1971 was a hurtful year. At least you have two consolations, two children you love. Whenever you come to New York please let me know, I would love to see you and my apartment is large enough to house you and your children (8 rooms). Then we can talk about old times and visit Camp Midvale, I still have a house there.

We exchanged Christmas notes, his 1974 one saying again, "I am looking forward to your call and I'm looking more forward to seeing you. Anxious to see how little Eva turned out." We planned a visit in February 1975. He again suggested a trip to camp and again offered to put me up, but I stayed with Ruth Loewenstein as usual, and we settled on Sunday the 23rd, which was chilly, gray, somewhat rainy. His friend Carl drove us to camp.

> I found [Max] very attractive [I told my diary]—though not handsome, he's aged a lot & balded some & his eyes are bad, he's 57—and just as nice & affectionate as I remember him. I…was happiest when alone with him…. Carl [is] very rigidly socialist…, Max is more human about it, though pretty blind too, but when we talked about education he said There'll always be problem children—while Carl thought under socialism there wouldn't— nor racism, etc…. I'd rather have gone on the bus and sat next to Max (he sat in back) as I did when he took me home. We did walk around camp by ourselves after lunch & up to Winfield Farm…, & after Carl left we had time together but I felt I shd. go home to Ruth's for supper—too bad.

His father was killed in World War I before Max was born, in 1918. He was very close to his mother but left Germany at seventeen; that, or soon after, must have been when he went to Spain. He was the first Jew who told me he had no use for Zionism or Israel; instead he was active in the US Committee for Friendship with the German Democratic Republic, helping produce its magazine and often visiting the GDR. He had been married, but for only a year, and worked in film or television.

We met up with another former Nature Friend with whom Max had some business to discuss. As they talked, he expressed annoyance with a vehemence that was a bit frightening. Did that short temper account for the brevity of his marriage? But I basked in warmth that was genuine: "…how nice to have him laugh at my funny remarks & put his arm around me, stroke my cheek, kiss me goodbye, & say I'm just as pretty as when I was a kid & you don't know how nice it is to see you—& so on. And he worried about my being alone, thinks I'm more alone than he is (probably so)."

His politics were his hedge against loneliness, I think. He was wedded to communism, to the GDR, which was after all his homeland, where he had been so close to his mother. He had apparently accepted his single state. My snotty "pretty blind" referred to his devotion to the GDR and communism. As Artie pointed out, admirers of communist countries generally compared their constitutions, rather than actualities, with unfortunate realities in capitalist countries. Max sent me some issues of the friendship committee's magazine and at least one article did just that.

But I still had a warm spot for Max, "pretty blind" or not. I did wonder whether I was attracted both by his endearing qualities and because he was potentially so hurtful. Nevertheless, when I got home

> I wanted so much to find a letter from him tonight & I didn't but one from Angie, largely about people she's met who know & like & admire Max. And Max asked me: who is this woman who told you about me? &, even when I described her, he cdn't remember her! It's so odd! She's so intent on him… & he doesn't know her.

Nothing from him until the usual Christmas note.

> For me 1975 was personally uneventful, but busy as all hell, organizationally. I hardly had time to make a living. Unfortunately I didn't have a chance to be even close to Boston. I really look forward seeing you again and you can be sure that if I am as close as 100 mile from Boston I'll make an "Abstecher" [detour]. When are you coming to New York again? Werde und bleibe gesund, Du schoene kleine Eva. [Become and remain well, beautiful little Eva.]

Although I went to New York two or three times a year and he was often on my mind, I didn't see him again for five years. Once I was at 130 East 16th Street—which housed his committee and also Women for Racial and Economic Equality—to talk to the women at WREE about its archives, but he was in Germany. Then in January 1980, we had dinner at Rolf's on Third Ave., pretty good German food. He told me about his wanderings in the 30's & his family. At 9:45 he said, Let's go to the movies—he thought it was 8. He pd. for dinner and took me home [to Ruth's] in a cab & a couple of times asked, What are you doing tomorrow? But I had no time so he asked me to Midvale this summer. He's a dear person & affectionate.

During dinner I hesitantly indicated that my politics weren't the same as his. He said we didn't have to agree about everything.

I couldn't have gone to Midvale with him if I'd tried: in New York after Thanksgiving, "Called Max & learned from a woman there that he'd been killed in a plane crash last March, she didn't want to tell me more. I kept thinking, 'Not Max,' but it hasn't really sunk in—I won't let it." I don't know who the woman was—something more than a housemate?—and I didn't quite believe what she told me—was she keeping him for herself?—until the WREE women, who were also fond of him, assured me it was true. Often since I've wished for his company. The name conjures up memories of someone warm and interesting who, during a sad period of my life, wanted to spend time with me—though admittedly he never did anything about it!

But for Isabella Max meant something different. Why did she hate the name? Max Kurz had nothing to do with it. Another Max I suspect did, though she never made the connection, not out loud to me anyway. In the twenties (hers and the century's), she was engaged to Max Friedmann. He emigrated to Palestine and she was to follow. She made her trousseau, but didn't go. I've been told that his mother broke it up, or that, not being an Austrian citizen, Isabella was afraid to leave and not be able to return if things with Max didn't work out. Perhaps it was both reasons, or something else. She did not go to Palestine, even though, according to his niece (Ruth Opper of San Francisco), Max wanted her to come and marry him even after Poldi got her pregnant. He married someone else.

In the '70s or '80s, Ruth O. told me that Max Friedmann and his wife were coming to Boston and I arranged to have dinner with them. This Max was intelligent, friendly, serious without being stuffy, courteous. I found myself wishing that she *had* married him, one of those impossible wishes, for then I wouldn't exist to wish it. He wasn't a wanderer and so couldn't stand in for her absent father. But it would have been better for her, even if his name was Max. And then most likely she wouldn't have hated the name.

Chapter 35
1972–74

*O*nce George moved away nothing much happened on the legal front. Barshak wrote him in July, when George was between lawyers, urging negotiations

> to work out financial arrangements…in a way that would be both consistent with her needs and with your needs and sense of responsibility. I understand that you have some feelings about the propriety of the existing court order and that you have not had any meaningful personal opportunity to participate in the shaping of the order. I would be very pleased to co-operate in such participation with you. In the meantime, the court order is outstanding and should be fulfilled by you.

No response. After a meeting between Klarfeld and my lawyers on September 1, 1972, only fruitless letters and empty promises, both George and Klarfeld proving elusive. I met with Barshak in late November and he promised to write again, "with threats but the choice of getting a lawyer we can talk to." Whether or not he wrote, it's clear that writing would be useless. After this meeting with Barshak, I felt "a touch of guilt & anguish for <u>him</u> [George]." Dr. L. dissected my feeling guilty when I was entitled to be angry.

> He used the candy-machine metaphor (for me): he puts his nickels in & expects candy-bars to come out—when they don't, he swears—what's the matter with this thing?—kicks it, eventually presses the Coin Return button. I had to laugh, it was so apt.

During the lull on the legal front, there was a brief flurry of communication about the Plainfield house, which we owned jointly. After a couple of offers, George wrote: "I don't believe there can be any solution for Plainfield house without a general settlement, and my lawyer indicates total frustration on that front." The pot calling the kettle black: the record shows that Klarfeld failed to contact Barry until Barry arranged a court hearing.

As before, George sent less than the court-ordered amount, in envelopes usually addressed to Eva, most checks payable to Eva Steiner. Did I no longer deserve the name Moseley, if I ever had? Was it nostalgia for the time when I *was* Eva Steiner? When it happened again, I thought: "When we had an agreement crummy enough to suit him, I was Eva Moseley!" If I was right, then Eva Steiner was the uppity bitch trying to milk him for all he was worth.

We had an agreement only briefly, until I realized it was inadequate; mostly we had a series of drafts, and disagreements. Early in 1973 Barry wrote me that he was "marking up your petition for separate support for a hearing on the merits," mainly "to stimulate Mr. Klarfeld" to persuade George "to negotiate seriously towards a settlement." With suggestions from me, Barry wrote Klarfeld in March to explain why we were going to court. He reminded Klarfeld that in September he had stated that George "was agreeable in principle to a final property settlement," and had since then "indicated repeatedly" that he would talk to George about the terms, but "there have been no terms forthcoming." He made him aware that George was $800 in arrears, that I was stymied in trying to sell the Plainfield house, and that, if there was no agreement, the court might *in*crease the monthly separate support payments. In his draft Barry wrote that I would accept a monthly child support payment less than what the court had ordered if there were "a reasonable division of property." I asked him to delete this sentence—"No point suggesting we might back down till we have to"—and he did. I'd taken Dr. L.'s lesson to heart enough so that—with time to think—I could be true to our interests.

The hearing was scheduled for April 10th. On the 9th, Barry told me it was to be continued to the 30th —Klarfeld had to be in federal court—but there was an offer from George: $350 a month and the house, which he [George] says I'll get 10G[rand] out of—I won't, of course, but less than 8G. Told Barry I want to be sure there's nothing to be done about the land & I want the stipend to change with his salary. Also told him I wished they'd let me know about the hearing. Later I thought I should ask for $400, make sure he has life insurance with the kids as beneficiaries &/or guarantees their education some way.

On the 9th I called Barry, not the other way around. I often had to prod my lawyers. While he went to court to get the matter continued, instead of getting dressed I went back to bed, "cried & slept." When I called to say I'd be in when I could, Jeannette said "not to be Spartan about it." I stayed home. Dr. L. gave me an extra appointment two days later.

> One thing he pointed out that hadn't struck me enough was that <u>we</u>'d set up a hearing & <u>they</u>'d knocked it down…& [Barry's] not letting me know meant, as he said, that no one was on my side, as when I was a child—Mother distracted by her own tsorres, Anna thinking everything was fine. With Geo.'s offer, I thought it over & came up with a self-respecting response—but my instantaneous reaction was, as he said, to shove not his chintzy offer but my self-respect. As I left he said, Perhaps we can narrow the gap—between my first & my second reaction. We have narrowed it already, but not enough & not in the most important situations.

Dr. L's analysis applied to Ron, whom I met contra-dancing—who, during our frustrating affair, would offer me one dance before dancing with other women, and I accepted it rather than, in the inelegant language of my diary, shoving it—and more consequentially to negotiations with George. Have lawyers become any more sophisticated in understanding their clients' psychology? Having the first hearing since the one that sent George to jail postponed was worse than a mere inconvenience, and not having Barry tell me till *I* called *him* made me feel neglected.

The affair with Ron lasted December to February, then one in April and May with a boring hiker. Although I had little luck in the romance department, now and then some man found me attractive, two in particular beyond Ron and the hiker. With a square dance caller I met at the Miltons' after a dance in Francestown there was clearly a spark, which was rekindled, if at lower voltage, at later dances, but there was a major obstacle: he was married and as we chatted in the Miltons' kitchen his wife was there too. Just as well; like other seemingly attractive men, he would not have been good news.

The other admirer, a younger cousin of Robert's, was clinically psychotic, certainly odd, if handsome and not stupid. We were both at the Hightowers' once, and later they told me that "Steven had been there & they learned that when he disappeared last year he was looking for me (in Vermont!), thinking: 'Eva, Eva—why can't I be Hitler & she Eva Braun?' Very flattering—yet in a way it is, & scary." Now I would not consider being attractive to someone so crazy a compliment, especially if it entails an analogy involving Hitler. Luckily Steven with his fantasies was safely far away.

Reading diaries and documents from that time thirty-some years later, I wondered whether the spring 1973 upsurge in juvenile delinquency centered on our house was partly caused by the appearance of first one man and then another. Jessica didn't like Ron and worried I might marry him; Tom was often sullen. The other kids, who, now that I was at work all day, made even freer with our house, were perhaps stimulated by signs of "romantic" goings-on. There was such an upsurge and it was discouraging.

But again there were bright moments with Jessica and Tom, and other kids were occasionally helpful or respectful. In May I "found a geranium with a note: 'Mom—Make the best out of the worst. Happy Mothers Day. Tom.'" The roses from the boring hiker were in the dining room, "but Tom's geranium is on the sewing-machine at the foot of my bed." Though often understandably angry or contrary, Jessica could be sweetly reasonable. When it came to a much older boy who was often around, "About Ralph I said, when someone attracts you, you notice all the nice things he does & ignore the others, & she agreed completely!"

After more delays, Barry wrote Klarfeld that a trial was set for June 4th and, "in fairness to my client, I cannot agree to any further continuances." We met at the courthouse and conferred for three hours. Klarfeld said: "You're the mother; you're the natural guardian of the children," and:

"I don't drink, I don't smoke, but I like women & you'd better believe it," evidently a traditional view of women, but no mention of (traditional) alimony. We reached an agreement of sorts: $350/mo., I get the house, G. to pay 3/4 of college tuition up to $2000/yr./child, and to be responsible for them for one month each summer during which he pays me nothing, and to have the life insurance he's got, at double his salary—now $28,000. Kay says she loves her grandchildren but is hanging on to the land. Then George raised the question of (my) remarriage, and said, about his monthly payments: "I ought to be able to see some bills," and then: "I visited the children recently and found them living in appalling conditions." I'd been fairly calm but that made me feel sick with anger. But we signed a divorce libel and got a court date: June 20th. When I told the kids about the agreement, they said they hadn't seen him, so evidently he was lying about "appalling conditions." Of course, if that meant the chaotic comings and goings of the kids' friends, I would have agreed with him, but where was I to get help to control them? Certainly not from him; even when he was nearby he never did anything to discipline that Winthrop Street crowd, perhaps was unaware of its existence. Most likely he just wanted to discredit me, but why? He didn't want custody. Just anger at me?

George had complained that he never heard from the kids. When I mentioned this to them, Tommy said he'd written George on his birthday and had no response. At Thanksgiving at Van and Mary's house, we learned that George had both written and called his father. He hadn't written *or* called his children. Jessica called him in early November about going to Vermont and he "said he won't come up & something about me 'putting him in jail' again. Jessica got upset talking to me about it."

On Sunday, June 10th ("The worst day of my life? How many of those have there been?"), after a morning of crying and remembering my early years, I called Dr. L. and got an afternoon appointment. It focused on how George had robbed his children with the land give-away and the whole chintzy settlement, which in turn reminded me of how I'd been robbed, meaning the deprivations of childhood. I regretted not insisting on better terms, but wrote that "he probably wouldn't have agreed to anything more & it isn't a matter of too much money. I thought I'd have Barry go after the money George owes me, but the hell with the stingy bastard, I spit on him. The earlier robbery is a bit harder to deal with." It took a while longer to see that if, instead of spitting on George and his money, I stuck up for the children and me, it would help reduce the effects of the childhood "robbery," which, along with my response to it, was the reason I was often so wimpy and compliant, not sticking up for me or the children. Thinking that the money didn't matter is one example.

But when the agreement came in the mail on the 16th and I saw it all in black and white, I called Barry and asked for changes to make the settlement less chintzy. "And I want the money he owes me," I wrote. "That's almost the hardest part, but why should I let it go? So I'm going to be unreasonable & change my mind & make a quick settlement impossible, but it was quick, with my cooperation."

On Wednesday (20th), after doing errands I made breakfast for Tom and Jessica's friend Debbie and me, ate and chatted with them, and went to court.

> The judge, Sullivan, got on his high horse & said Mr. Barry, you promised to come in here with an agreement—& he wouldn't hear anything. Klarfeld stood there glaring at David, the old faker. I didn't care, we're back to square one but I know better where to go next: get the money he owes me, or go after it anyway, and Barry says we'll try to undo the conveyance to his mother as fraudulent & get the land to cover his obligation…. Called the kids…& we went to Zum-Zum for lunch…& then to The Lodge, where I spent another $50 on clothes for them. Back to work, feeling good…—for good reason or bad?

For good reason: I had "insisted on my due." But halfway between the 16th and the 20th I'd begun to feel guilty about my new demands, realizing that "that's my biggest danger. And guilty is only part of it…. I'm afraid if I ask for this I'll lose everything…. [B]ut what have I to lose? He's already walked out and slammed the door!" (Echoing January 6, 1935.) All this raises another question about lawyers: why didn't Barshak or Barry or Berkowitz warn me that the children might have future needs that the proceeds of the house and steady-state support payments wouldn't meet?

I had repeatedly figured what it cost us to live; the amounts kept creep-ing up. Why did *I* have to think of a cost-of-living increase (in a time of increasing inflation), life insurance, and college tuition? Didn't such needs routinely come up in divorce settlements? Whatever the answers to these questions, having to take matters into my own hands made me feel abandoned by those I was paying to protect me. (Or, actually, going to pay when it was done.)

The day after the abortive hearing I had further thoughts about George's possible reasons for ending the marriage. I had speculated earlier that one reason, conscious or not, might have been my infatuation with Aaron. But I never wanted to end the marriage and wouldn't have left George, let alone the children, to go off with Aaron, even if he'd wanted me to. Whatever history lay behind the events of 1973, divorce was inev-itable and I tried to see it as a new beginning, even liberation. There was certainly plenty of time to get used to the idea.

While Barry tried to get a hearing, I'd added another complication. On July 23rd, having sent Tom off to camp and Jessica to a friend's house, I went to New York and the next day Will, a Midvale friend, drove Anna and me to visit Vickie and Rudi. On our youthful hikes, Will ran, puppy-like, ahead and back, covering a lot more ground than the rest of us; or he and Paul would play mental chess, without a board or chessmen. He came from an unhappy family and Isabella became a surrogate mother. After she died, he transferred some of his devotion to Anna. He had long been in love with me, at least on and off. So now, as I sunbathed and he played chess with Rudi, and Vickie and Anna chatted in the shade, I began to fantasize about Will, later speculating (erroneously) in my diary that what mattered was his connection with my family, Mother particularly.

I knew that I should be careful, so that when a letter was waiting for me when I got home three days later, saying he wanted to see me again soon, I fretted over what sort of answer to write, finally making it friendly but not unduly so. "Will is not one of those men that projects his weaknesses to hide his vulnerability. And, having been rejected by me once, he's taken a risk again & I do <u>not</u> want to hurt him, if it's avoidable. 'If it's at all possible, please include me in your life,' he writes. I don't dare trifle with someone as needy and vulnerable as I am." I wondered whether he was a "souvenir" of Mother, or a means to help me through a phase of therapy. There was as much doubt as hope.

> I mustn't encourage him any more till I'm sure I mean to. Never mind the geographical obstacles or the kids, could I seriously consider Will as <u>the</u> man in my life, forsaking all others? What kind of life would we make for each other? How would I feel introducing him to friends & colleagues as my husband? I don't know, but I have <u>serious</u> doubts. [A few days later:] I may be doing something bad in making him feel it's ok to love me & then perhaps ditching him.

He came by bus on a beautiful August Monday. I met him at the station and took him to Fresh Pond in Cambridge, we started to walk around it "& after a bit I took his arm. It was very lovely at first; we sat on a bench, talked & talked (etc.)." Later that day we took the kids and a friend to Crane Beach, where "the [three] kids acted up a lot," disturbed by this new role for an old friend.

Soon doubts reappeared. "What does one do with a person who says he is prepared to be anything I want him to be?" He followed me around, said "I want to be part of you," but I wanted another person out there, not another body part. When I suggested he bring with him a report he was having trouble writing, he said: "If you think it's important I'll try to work on it." (Reminding me of George's "If you think it's important for me to see the kids, ...") I refused to say it was important to me, but worried further: "Is it really oedipal clinging: it sounds & feels like it; or just an excuse for me to reject real love? More & more I think it's the former but it serves as the latter too."

By myself and with Dr. L. I was grappling with the Groucho Marx syndrome: Do I want to belong to a club that would have me as a member? Could I accept love from a man with such poor judgment as to love me? Along with passivity, cultural differences confused the issue: he had little education and you could hear it in his speech. I didn't want to take him to events at the library, or to meet most of my friends. Surely a bad omen.

[Aug. 8]: ...do I try very hard not to take advantage of him or do I... make him my creature until he rebels?... I always took advantage of him in a mild sort of way—he was company when nothing better offered but never my first choice.... [Does] this message of "We must do what Eva wants" mean "What will she do if I cross her?" & "If I don't please her I won't get what I need"?

I compared him to "a small child afraid to cross his mother" and potentially angry at her, "both for frustrating his wishes & for making him afraid." Often one of us was in tears over what was happening between us, sometimes both.

Despite the doubts, I hoped that he would be helpful with the children. He had started as a linotype operator at *The New York Times*, been promoted to supervisor, and worked nights on a schedule that allowed him to come to Medford twice a week. He could be at our house while I was at work. Nevertheless: "I felt more & more that he never could get on with the children, as a surrogate father. Have I just graduated from a naughty, hostile boy to a submissive, doting one?" August 30th, "I felt good being here with just my children. I can handle the friends too (up to a point) perhaps better than I can handle Will & kids."

Soon I was almost certain that his helping with the kids was "an idle dream." He was surprised that it was so hard for him to get along with them; he got on famously with one niece especially. It seems incredible now but I decided that he should stay at our house so he could help with kids and chores, then saw that "he was becoming part of my real life just when I didn't know if I wanted him to." Stupidly, I had him stay in my room with me, which was provocative for all the kids and painful for mine. The children would resent almost any man I chose to take their father's place; my ambivalence about Will fed their resentment.

They were variously wary, defiant, ready to wait and see. At first they still saw him as an old family friend. Jessica told me there was a letter from Will and said, sounding hopeful, maybe he's not coming, but another day "she said, Can Will stay all week & meet my best friend?" "Tom said, after he brings the record-player, why don't we throw him out?" In September Jessica "told me she likes him less each time she sees him," and when we had a long talk about him, "She was angry, said she doesn't need another father (she'd been trying to call Geo.) & then later it became clear she's worried about losing me, & I said if I had to choose I would stay with her & Tom till they were on their own."

The most devastating realization was that in this affair I assumed, though not deliberately or happily, the role of depriving parent, with Will the poor clinging child. He came from a family with a lot of kids, a lot of drink, and who knows what else. August 30th: "Tables really turned, I needing to get away & be alone (work more a refuge than ever), unable to read his letters or listen to him." As the dominant partner, I could push him around with little chance of losing him as a result. It was convenient but frustrating. He helped with chores, fixed things after his fashion, but when I asked what he wanted to do—he had, after all, gone to the trouble and expense of coming to Medford—he said, "What do you want to do?" I don't mind having my way—who does?—but I wanted another person with ideas, inclinations, not an echo.

Then again, an early letter showed him as "on the one hand super self effacing ('I will be what you want me to be at any time') & on the other each letter has ended with a demand: 'With the thought in mind that I am trying...,' & '...you must try to read my thoughts with under-standing.'" Sometimes his demands seemed unreasonable. When the kids' friends were causing even more trouble than usual, I called Will: "I tell him I'm nervous & worried & unsure how I'll get through the day & he says, How do you feel about me?"

Dr. L. explained to me that, "if Will loves me as he does there isn't just the guilt & sense that it's wrong, but disappointment, because—in being so loving—he's not Father!.... That means that whatever I have, I can't stand. If it's F. or G. or Ron, I remain anxious & starved; if it's Will, who feeds me so well, I yearn for the original cheap bastard." Despite this insight, the affair continued, my feelings swinging wildly between occasional joy and coldness, boredom, irritation, withdrawal. One good day, a November Sunday, Will came for breakfast, we did chores, and went to an apartment he'd rented in Cambridge. "I made lentil & left-over soup & we spent the day 'bed-ridden.' [His joke.] It was,...as I told him, heaven." More often it was limbo, or worse.

My contradictory feelings were driving us both crazy. Late August: "we had lunch by the [Charles] river...." I would rather have been alone and longing for him! Did he realize I was using him? Not deliberately, but I had surely started this affair because I happened to see him just a month after the distressing attempts at negotiation with George and Klarfeld. Only years later did I see that, unconsciously, I saw Will as a salve for my wounds, and he was ready to provide that, at least at first.

I took advantage of Will's willingness to do my bidding in other ways than emotionally. Beyond the occasional chores, which he did willingly but sometimes lazily—clearing the most minimal swath in the snowy driveway—he worked hard on the house I bought in July 1974, when Tufts finally evicted us. He helped us move, sanded and varnished floors, helped me strip wallpaper, paint walls, and buy used furniture for the three rooms I was renting out, and he offered to build a second bathroom.

We took space from the two rooms on the third floor, and a window from one. Helping carry sheetrock up two flights, I learned how easy it is to get hurt when doing construction. Will's asking whether I wanted a particular section of wall to come down, and, before I could answer, whacking it with a crowbar, I learned something about Will. As for the plumbing, he said he knew how to join old and new pipes of different gauges. One Sunday evening, after hours of cutting and soldering with the water turned off, with Jessica waiting impatiently to take a shower, he tried his new system. In no time a dozen waterfalls gushed all over the cellar.

Feeling cruel, I broke up with Will. He said I was making a big mistake. "You'll never find anyone who loves you the way I do," he declared, and he was right, but though it's nice to be loved devotedly, I wanted someone I admired, who wouldn't follow me around like a puppy, waiting to see what I wanted to do. It didn't need to be someone who could build a bathroom. I paid a carpenter to do that, and learned that the way Will planned to connect the drains to the stack would have been illegal. On a later visit to his house in New Jersey I saw that floors, walls, baseboards—nothing quite met.

Doing what I had foreseen I might do right from the start was trying for Will, but one needn't weep for him, for he married the mother of his favorite niece, ex-wife of a brother, in an almost Biblical pattern, only in the Bible she would have been a widow, not a divorcée. From all reports, they are devoted and happy.

George (who was a better carpenter but had ceased to be a reasonable husband) and I were still married and he was still sending his inadequate payments. In August 1973 he added a new wrinkle: he called about taking the kids to The Farm for four days and asked me "to contribute $100 for groceries, transportation, etc. I laughed & laughed (at George)." Needlessly, I wrote, asking what the expenses added up to, without saying I would pay. Today I wouldn't respond at all. After he figured the amount out, and I didn't pay as he asked, he deducted it from his next monthly payment. He'd claimed the money was for his mother. Did he really pass the money on? Had Kay always charged us for groceries?

After Barry tried to get a hearing on the money George owed me, the court set a date of November 29th for a hearing on the arrears and separate support. Klarfeld appeared but, claiming he didn't know what it was about, "got a postponement, to Jan. 7th. He told David he'd talked to G. & G. said, Get it over with; it's haunting me; I want a divorce." In the diary I added that George hadn't "made a single positive move toward getting one since I agreed to it. David reminded K. we'd had no response to our additional terms, & he said, Send me a revised agreement & I'll get back to you, won't delay a minute, I promise."

A small incident on the bus to court that morning showed that I was making progress. I "told a couple of toughies in the back to stop smoking. They argued a bit but they did it." Three years earlier, when still thoroughly Mrs. Moseley (as I thought), I wouldn't have tackled those guys, let alone prevailed. A combination of therapy and the job gave me the courage. Perhaps being cut loose from George, however much it hurt, helped too.

We revised the draft agreement and David sent copies to Klarfeld. As before, I was to get the Plainfield house. We omitted the summer month without child support and added stipulations that the monthly payments would always be 30 percent of his salary, that he pay part of my legal fees, and that we would exchange copies of our income tax returns as long as he was paying child support. Klarfeld got another continuance, to January 21st, and, according to an undated note in the file, George wanted to add that he would pay no support when he saw the children and to delete the paragraphs on the 30 percent, college tuition, life insurance, legal fees, and tax returns.

In January I wrote Barshak asking him to be present in court. No criticism of Barry, but "we are dealing with two devious and difficult people. It was you who was recommended to me, and I feel that at this crucial hearing I should have the benefit of your longer experience." Barshak did appear on Monday, January 21st.

> D-Day! I decided to go for a divorce. After another stab at an agreement, when George said that I had to return the money Kay gave us for the Plainfield down payment, Barshak said "The deal's off," and we had a two-hour trial. Despite some mistakes, we got most of the story across. Klarfeld asked what hours I work, how Tom gets home from school, am I home every evening with the children? I finally said, "Some evenings I'm home and they're not." Other questions about the children were also irrelevant: custody was not an issue.
>
> George said he paid a "friend" named Lin Li-chiao rent. Barry should have asked about the "friend" with the Chinese name, to expose adultery. Did George spend the $5000 (from land give-away) on the children? "No," and he started in about living in hotels. Barry cut him short. George raised his voice: I'm trying to answer your question. You've answered it, said Barry. We asked for $500/mo. child support, plus alimony, legal fees, and the house. Later Barry said he wished he could have made him flare up again—so did I!

The next day I "did a little work, told my story, lunch with Will—getting further away—& when I got back to the Library they gave me a surprise party: champagne & cake. It was lovely, I enjoyed the sisterliness. Told Will I was bad to him probably because he's a man & he said I'm also Will. Which is true. When I got home J. had cooked supper, that was lovely too."

With nothing to lose and no need to please George, we'd figured we might as well ask for the moon. We got moon rocks. On the 29th, "David called, he'd had the edict read to him: I got the house, $400/mo. (but he—judge—didn't say for how long) & health insurance. The house is to cover arrears [by then $1850]. I've got to get it soon so it doesn't

324

cover any more arrears!" Feeling cheated, I wondered how different the results might have been with a female judge; was ours perhaps a "male chauvinist pig" with a compliant, stay-at-home wife? The first female judge at that courthouse was sworn in later that afternoon! At our trial I was the only woman in the room.

Frustrating as the trial and the decree were, once I got used to the decision it was as if a weight had been lifted from my shoulders. The court had validated our claim to support, not as much as I believed we were entitled to but more than George would have granted. And it was *done*; no more fretting and scheming about what to ask for. George took five months to sign over his interest in the Plainfield house, so there was a stab at another contempt petition. After two more years of absentee landlady-ism I sold it to a woman who called it "a perfect house." That was good to hear; shedding the responsibility was even better.

George sent $400 regularly, except less one month, but otherwise his ways didn't change. There was little contact with the children and in January 1975 he charged me for the five days Tom stayed with him in December. An envelope bears his calculations: one-sixth a month for one child, or $33.33, deducted from his monthly payment; he did pay Tom's plane fare to Virginia.

Dr. L. had compared both Father and George to a teen-ager who considers his house a base of operations, and I'd criticized George for still considering 45 Winthrop Street his house. So I wasn't surprised when he wrote, in June 1974:

> I understand that you and the children will shortly be moving away from your present address, where I also lived prior to our separation. There are, I believe, a few things of mine which still need to be collected, and I would like to come there for this purpose at a mutually convenient time. I am thinking of the camphor chest and the tonsu (both of which my mother is anxious that I should have), the scrolls (four) of calligraphy, the picture of the God of War, my swivel desk chair, and at least one book.... I understand from my lawyer, Mr. Klarfeld, that the removal of personal effects such as the above is so routine that there was no necessity of bringing it up in court.

I saw no need to answer. The camphor chest and tansu were presents from Kay to both of us. I've written this book, and much else, sitting in the swivel chair, which we bought together at a Vermont yard sale; we bought the picture together in Macao and possibly one pair of scrolls. As he had left these things and they were mostly ours, not just his, there was no reason to hand them over. He thought he could store what he considered his stuff in a house no longer his and then take it whenever he wished. I didn't agree. Keeping these things was small recompense for the hurt he had caused, a bit of non-violent revenge.

Why had we fallen into this familiar pattern? Often it's a doctor whose wife raises the children and sees him through medical school, internship, and residency. Then he splits and marries someone else. George left us when he earned a doctorate and got a tenure-track position at a respectable university. What was behind this? For years the reason eluded me; then I found an answer in the interview with press agent Eddie Jaffe in Studs Terkel's *Working*:

> The truth is: it's psychologically important for stars to get rid of people who helped them get where they are. The client is the child and the press agent's the parent. The child has to grow up and leave the nest. It's part of living.

In 1998 I wrote Terkel to tell him what I'd learned from his interview with Jaffe:

> In 1958 I married a man uncertain of his aim in life but with a fascination with China.... After a couple of jobs, and with a couple of kids, he went back to school.... We lived on fellowships and my part-time work in genteel poverty, and I edited and indexed his books. In 1970 he landed a job at Tufts and got his doctorate. Half a year later...he abandoned the children and me.
>
> I knew this was an all-too-common sequence of events but never could figure out why people (usually men) behave this way. I found the answer in your interview with the press agent in <u>Working</u>. The helpful spouse becomes, like Jaffe in relation

to a successful client, a source of shame, a reminder of a time of dependence. Reading this made sense of an episode that had baffled me for years.

And then I had another revelation, thanks to a painting of Ariadne on Naxos. She lies asleep front and center; in the lower right corner one can just make out Theseus sneaking onto his ship. So the story isn't just common now; it's a classic/classical and perhaps universal tale. Ariadne actually saw him through graduate school: the sword and the thread she gave him represent her research and typing for his dissertation (the Minotaur); the outsmarted king might be his department chair. How one matches up the various elements could vary, but the story is the same: he could not have succeeded without her and, almost as soon as he has succeeded, he abandons her.

I'm truly grateful for the insight, which I haven't seen in print anywhere else. I should add that I see Jaffe's analysis as an explanation, not an excuse. My husband was just leading an unexamined life, acting out his impulses rather than observing and understanding them.

To my surprise and delight, Terkel sent a handwritten reply. He was impressed with "the Ariadne–Theseus analogy" and thought that "Eddie Jaffe, if he's still around, would be delighted to know that he let you in on something." (Jaffe was indeed still around then. He died in 2003, having represented, among others, Joe Namath, Jackie Gleason, and the Shah of Iran.)

Theseus succeeded his father as king of Athens, married a couple of times, fought a few wars, had a temple built in his honor. George and Li-chiao were married as soon as legally permissible, but it seems that life with her wasn't all he wished for. When, late in 1971, he talked of coming back, he said he'd expected "to do great things" once he left; I had somehow thwarted him. Instead of looking inside himself, he pinned the fault—if there was a fault—on me. "How much of a woman does he want?" Winnie Chen asked. Whether he got more or less "of a woman" is not for me to say, but leaving me didn't help him do those unspecified great things.

Jessica indicated that he and Li-chiao lived separate lives (was he her current meal ticket?)—and that he asked Jessica, aged fourteen then, whether a man could be in love with two women. Her (silent) response: how should I know? His attachment cum hostility seems to show that he saw me as having power I didn't have, as a child sees its parents. As mother/wife I was supposed to enable him to fulfill whatever dreams of glory he had and to know what those were without his telling me, even if he wasn't sure himself what they were.

Ariadne, waking up and finding herself abandoned, was grief-stricken, as I was for months. Venus took pity and gave her an immortal lover, Bacchus. His wedding present was a gold crown. When she died he threw it up into the sky, where it became a constellation. Just as George has no temple in his honor but did write four books in his field, so I had only a few short-lived liaisons, but my Schlesinger staff made me a crown of yellow plastic paper-clips, SAA made me a fellow, and NEA gave me a lifetime achievement award. For a mortal, not daughter of a king, those rewards, and many years of useful work—and children, grandchildren, and great-grandchildren—have more than compensated for the grief of 1971–74.

I do think people contemplating marriage should get very well acquainted first. George's idea about the Kama Sutra surely wasn't the whole truth about George, but it indicates differing expectations. Had we learned more of this in 1958, there might have been no marriage. Some would say that there would be many fewer marriages if couples became well acquainted, as many men and women look for different, often incompatible, benefits. Perhaps, but when, in my forties and fifties, friends of my parents asked me why I hadn't remarried, I said: "It's got to be worth it, and often the price is too high."

The price, of our rocky marriage and the divorce, was high for Jessica and Tom too. I tried to be more open and honest with them than Mother was with me, but not *too* honest: to keep them informed, as I was not about my parents' divorce, but not burdened with my anger, sadness, and fears. Divorce had become more ordinary, and more readily acknowledged, in the quarter century since 1946, yet Jessica tells me that, partly because only one Medford friend's parents were divorced, my children felt shame just as I had.

I've tried to make the story partial only in the sense of incomplete, but George would surely disagree with much of it, as might others who were there. As for making it "complete," had I not omitted most of the written record, this saga would make a fairly big book, as tedious to read as it was difficult to live through.

Chapter 36
ROBERT HIGHTOWER 2: THE LATER YEARS

*T*hose moments of annoyance at Robert recorded in my 1970s diaries surprised me when I read about them later, although I knew that my worshipful ardor had long ago cooled to a warm friendship. It resembled a pre-adolescent's disappointment in her father. He's not really so wise and all-knowing! He never claimed to be. It was I projecting my hopes and needs onto an attractive man with a wife—thus unattainable, almost a sine qua non for men I fell in love with. He was always honest and rueful about his shortcomings. "I must beg you not to endow me with too many improbable virtues; I'll be afraid ever to see you again," he wrote in 1957. Eventually I accepted him as a mere mortal.

In later years, describing relations with his father and others, he would say, "What a little shit I was." More than once, in the 1980s and '90s, as we sat by his study fire with the supper he'd cooked, he assured me that what he recalled best were incidents in which he was deficient: cowardly, inconsiderate, selfish, inadequate. I was taping an interview with Anna; her mostly self-congratulatory anecdotes contrasted with Robert's memories, together a refutation of the easy feminist assumption that men are more self-centered and smug and women more diffident and charitable. It *may* be true more often than not, but it's not always true. (Robert and I defied another gender stereotype: that only men remember and tell jokes. He enjoyed and forgot them, so I could tell him the same jokes more than once.)

In November 1976, during Robert's sabbatical year at the University of British Columbia, Bunny found a lump and in short order had a mastectomy—socialized Canadian medicine but no long wait. Home after six days, she was soon back to hiking, playing tennis, and "running the damn vacuum cleaner over the wall to wall carpets. I hate both," she wrote me, and urged me to visit. The next summer I spent ten days with them. Landing in Vancouver was spectacular, a vista of islands, bays, and mountains. The city was an odd blend of refined British and rugged western, literally English ivy climbing a giant redwood.

Gerda Hollenberg, a widowed Viennese refugee and friend of my parents, and her son's family took me on a day trip to Victoria, for the governor's garden party to mark the queen's birthday. At Government House we "shook hands with his honour and Mrs. Owen & had coffee & sandwiches & looked at the gardens." My diary doesn't mention my only vivid memory of the party: a guest entirely in pink: dress, hat, stockings, shoes, bag. Returning on the ferry, Gerda and I stood at the railing. "Now Eva, you're still young and you're still pretty," and she "asked why I don't find someone nice." What's the matter with you that you haven't remarried? I told her it's got to be worth it (without adding that I wouldn't have minded "someone nice") and that most men about my age were either married, gay, or dead. (About then, in a letter I read long after Vickie died, Hesse sent greetings via Vickie, which she didn't pass on, nor his message that at my age I shouldn't have to be "alone." He hoped I would find someone suitable, but not another "Goy"; he disapproved of mixed marriages, only Paul's an exception.) The Hightowers did not nag me about remarrying, but Robert did say, when I was becoming single again, "You'll have to get used to your friends fixing you up with dates." Yet neither they nor anyone else ever did; the sporadic male companionship of my later decades consisted of chaps I found on my own.

Back in Auburndale, Bunny's cancer returned. Shortly before she was to begin treatments, we took a trip north: I had to sort and pack papers for the Schlesinger Library in Brownfield, Maine. We got a room at the Tamworth Inn, near "the world's oldest professional summer theater," which had only one ticket left, so we had dinner at the inn and wandered over to the theater at intermission. Bunny knew people with summer places nearby, some of whom were in the lobby. The theater was founded by Francis Grover Cleveland, son of the president and named for both parents: Frances and Grover. Was he there? Yes, standing near the box office. This was 1979. His father, president 1885–89 and 1893–97, was born in 1837. The life spans of father and son covered nearly three-quarters of

At the Hightowers', ca. 1979. Bunny standing; Eva sitting with Betsy (first wife of oldest son Jamey), and Robert. Bunny was already suffering from the return of breast cancer.

the years since the US was founded. The "world's oldest democracy" was not very old.

The next day Bunny and I climbed West and East Rattlesnake, two hills overlooking Squam Lake. Soon she was too weak for hiking. Tom H. took a leave from Vassar and he and Robert took care of her at home, for which I did, and do, admire them beyond words. Not only that they did it, but that they did it unassumingly, without heroics, as if anyone would do the same, which most of us wouldn't.

Bunny died, at home, on March 6, 1981, Jamey's thirty-ninth birthday. She was only sixty-five. I still miss her, not as a mother substitute but as a friend. We were equals, each valuing the other's company, ideas, opinions.

For the next two decades, Robert and I had an ongoing regime: he cooked supper and I drove us to a play or movie or, more rarely, a concert. We generally agreed on the merits of what we saw. We both found Christopher Durang's *Sister Mary Ignatius Explains It All for You* sophomoric and not funny, though everyone else was in stitches. When I opined that "all these people went to parochial school," Robert thought that was self-evident.

At first he was often away for weeks at a time, traveling with his German friend Hedda Steiner, Josie's mother-in-law—to Florida, Prince

Edward Island, Malaysia, Kenya. Hedda, the more enthusiastic traveler, got more out of the trips. As he wrote a former student: "Each year Hedda writes up an account of our travels; when I read it, I am amazed at how much of it is strange to me." He was always glad to come home and seemed content tending his garden, cooking his meals, often with his own produce, and consuming breakfast and lunch in the kitchen, supper by the study fire. His pride in his cooking and baking—bread, cakes, desserts—struck me as a way both to bring back his mother and his wife, both of whom died too early, and to prove that he could manage without them, be his own mother/wife, at least in the kitchen.

He continued to let others, including me, arrange his social life. He almost never called me, sure that I would call him and suggest a movie or remind him of a play for which we had tickets. I learned to accept this but once the result was regrettable: Dan Ingalls's retirement dinner happened after Bunny died and Robert went alone, realizing only the next time he saw me that he should have invited me (as Dan's one-time student) to go with him. He apologized, which made being left out hurt a little less.

When Hedda died his travels ceased. It's ironic that, with both of us free of other entanglements, there was no urge to resume our 1950s romance. Whether so late in life he could imagine living intimately with *anyone* I don't know; while I could imagine it, the anyone would no longer be Robert, even if 1957's Eva would be incredulous that I didn't move myself and my belongings into the house that now had so many unused rooms.

Early in the new century macular degeneration kept him from enjoying plays and movies. At an eye check-up in his late eighties he was told that he was eligible for a white cane. "Can I carry it on my bicycle?" he asked. He was not given a cane. About then he wrote a friend: "For over two years I have been legally blind.... I still ride my bicycle, though I know I shouldn't. I don't go very far. [He'd had two serious bicycle accidents.] My other ailments are all chronic, untreatable, and painful. Otherwise I am in good health." Is this rueful or a joke? Perhaps a rueful joke, for when I compared him to Job, one affliction on top of another, he had thought of the resemblance himself. The white cane story showed his determination to remain independent. "Tom and Martine...came from Amsterdam to look after me," he wrote in that letter. "I was glad to have them here, though I didn't think that I needed looking after." While wanting to be as independent as possible, or more than was possible, he did learn to accept help, whether lighting the stove, taking things out of the oven, whipping cream for the inevitable homemade dessert, or the cleaning and heavier chores he used to take pride in doing himself.

Before he gave up his garden, he worked there lying down, the only way he could see what he was doing. For years it was a source of great satisfaction. Letters written in January tended to mention seed catalogues and one April he wrote a younger friend: "For a neurotic poet about to get religion [T.S. Eliot], April may well be the cruelest month, but for a gardener it is just the busiest." I was one of the beneficiaries of his bountiful garden, often going home with Swiss chard, tomatoes, and so on, and heard stories of his war on the little animals who often beat him to the harvest, such as the raccoon who took a single bite out of each tomato. Once I earned my supper by helping him transport a possum in a have-a-heart trap, a task he sometimes required of other visitors as well. We took the trap in my car across the Charles River and released the possum—an ugly little brute, not cute like Pogo—on someone else's property. I used to call Robert Mr. McGregor (the nemesis of Beatrix Potter's Peter Rabbit). He approved.

Cooking was as important as gardening and of course went on all year. At seventy-eight, he wrote a friend about two weeks of "a houseful of visitors":

> At one point...I couldn't make room for everyone at the dining table. They went through a ham and a 16-pound turkey in a couple of days. I like to cook and have cooked for as many as 100 people (when I was in internment camp [a World War II Japanese camp in China] during the war), but I find it something of an effort nowadays to produce a new dinner for eight or nine people every day. I wonder how my wife ever did it for the six of us. No wonder she always liked to be invited out to dinner. I didn't; because...we seldom got anything as good as what we had every day at home. I try to keep up her standards, not very successfully.

Several of those visitors were perfectly capable of producing those meals, but Robert liked to be in control of his kitchen—and of others' kitchens if they let him. He once scolded me for keeping the hot water at my kitchen sink hotter than necessary: that is, it shouldn't be so hot that you have to mix in cold water to use it comfortably. I agreed in principle and followed the rule: for me the hot water *was* the right temperature, but I was too intimidated (or polite) to say so, or to make suggestions in his kitchen, which would be implied criticisms. For instance, to wipe greasy pans with paper (I use partly used napkins, which would have appealed to his legendary frugality) before running water in them, or to pour hot liquids into glass jars rather than plastic containers; glass doesn't sag or leach out poisonous chemicals. Perhaps he would actually have appreciated such suggestions.

He had strong opinions about all sorts of things. News about professional athletes always reminds me of his contemptuous "Paid gladiators!" But he was willing to listen and learn. When I first had backaches he gave me a sheet of advice, one idea being to put a footstool "under your husband's desk." I pointed out that this was sexist, assuming that a husband has a desk and a wife doesn't. Robert said he would never have noticed that and was glad to be made aware but that didn't work with some literary sexism, in Schiller's *An die Freude*, the "Ode to Joy" of Beethoven's Ninth Symphony. The second stanza enumerates those who add their joyful voices: anyone lucky enough to have a close friend or to have won a lovely woman (*ein holdes Weib errungen*). I said that this was either sexist (the "anyone" assumed to be male) or it was promoting lesbianism. Perhaps I didn't explain it very well; Robert brushed it off.

Some things he said rankled. When he'd been listening to Bach keyboard music on the piano and I said I preferred it on the harpsichord, he called me a purist. Too hurt and baffled to respond, I let it pass but later decided that a true purist wouldn't just *prefer* the harpsichord but insist that this music *shouldn't* be played on the piano. If such remarks disturbed me, I can only imagine how his and Bunny's high standards and at times unbridled tongues weighed on their offspring. But that story, those stories, like those of my children, are for them to tell, or not.

It became ever harder for him to ignore his afflictions and in 2003 his children persuaded him to sell the Auburndale house. For eight months he lived with Jamey's family in Garrettsville, Ohio (where the barber calls his shop The Barber of G'ville). Then Jamey, who taught French at Hiram College, was taking students to France for a semester, so Tom helped Robert move to Josie's house in rural Elsen, in northwest Germany, idyllic except for the weather. After a few days there the next year I renamed the region, officially Sauerland, Sauwetterland—land of rotten weather.

At Jamey's he still fixed his own breakfast; at Josie's it had to be done for him. He was still using a particular spoon and other favorite items from Auburndale. When I arrived he was out walking, with two canes; these laborious walks soon ceased. One day I fixed Robert's breakfast, giving him the wrong tea, and he remarked that in his two weeks there Jamey would routinely forget the required tea. According to my diary,

> Josie and I discussed R. & she ran down his breakfast needs, making clear that it's nearly impossible to get it all right. But of course she cares for him in a devoted, loving way. A week after he lost his balance and fell Robert had his first shower since his fall, bit of an ordeal. Josie is a saint.
> On Saturday Bacon & pancakes for breakfast—the old Hightower tradition. Robert even ate some bacon. (Give me <u>half</u> a slice.— Now give me the other half.)

That he was at times grumpy or demanding is to be expected. He couldn't read but had to be read to, a favorite book being David Hawkes's *Letters from a Godless Grandfather*. (Hawkes was a sinological friend at Oxford and Robert was of course also a godless grandfather.) He could do less and less for himself. He had numerous pains and discomforts, as well as serious health problems. But his mind was clear, he still had his opinions and his sense of humor, he could still hold forth on all sorts of topics, still recalled the plots of plays and movies we had seen together that I had forgotten, and he was well aware of how good all four children were to him; he told me how lucky he was in them, and I think he told them too. When I remarked to them on their devotion, Tom said, "He must have done something right."

Robert died in January 2006. I realized, when leaving four months earlier, that it might be the last time I saw him. When Bunny died there was no event, no gathering; Robert and Tom didn't feel the need. Josie arranged an event for the interment of Robert's ashes in the local cemetery, and at my urging the East Asian Languages department at Harvard held a memorial gathering in October. One of his female students didn't attend because she wanted to keep believing that he was still alive. He had not cast that sort of spell over me for many years, but this marked the end of an era for me too — although the change that altered my week-to-week life had come three years before, with the sale of 321 Central Street, home to the Hightowers for half a century and for me so often a welcoming refuge.

Chapter 37
1975

*T*hat was the year of our second cruel April.

Again it happened late in the month, for George on Sunday the 27th, for us, Monday the 28th, when Pierre Laurent called me at work: on Sunday George had met a violent death. The *Washington Star* had called Tufts for information about George, which is why I got the news from Pierre. After I "absorbed a bit of the shock," I called David Barry and went home.

> I told the children & as I expected Jessica screamed & cried and Tom went off & was silent and (as he told me later) felt guilty that he wasn't crying. I asked if he'd ever felt angry & wished George dead & talked about regret & guilt—he said he was supposed to write him after his visit at Christmas and never did & that made us both cry, that awful feeling of infinite regret, as if doing something left undone could have made the difference. [Typical over-interpretation: it's not that a letter could have saved George's life but that it had become impossible to write one he could read.] I also talked about wanting to do things so George could see them, such as the table (which Tom had made in a school carpentry program), & he said he'd wanted to send him a picture of it.

Friends of the kids came and went; we talked to cousin Henry Moseley, Jr. and called my aunts. (The aunts didn't understand what happened or what it meant to us. In a letter to Hesse, Vickie wrote that George "had an accident and died"–which isn't what happened.) Henry Sr. called: the funeral would be that Friday at The Farm, and the children were the beneficiaries of the life insurance, "but if it's suicide they don't pay." My diary says we talked to Betty (Li-chiao), something I don't remember. George's Burmese friend Shwe called and asked for a ride to The Farm Friday.

> At 11:30 a man called & asked when we were divorced,(then told me Betty had said they were married 3 years) & asked if he'd ever done intelligence work. I told him I didn't know. He has other ways to find out. We'd watched some TV, had supper, and Tom went to bed. As I sat talking to Jessica I remembered with a jolt that he'd told me he always expected to die young. And he did.

Tuesday "I cried bitterly" recalling our first apartment, "it was spring & I was so hopeful, same old hope with the same blindness to reality, yet there was <u>some</u>thing good. Jessica went to school (she cried in art class & then slept) & I took Tom to school &, as he didn't wish it, didn't tell anyone there. Talked to John Fairbank, who already knew." I noted that "one of the first things I said to library colleagues was, I didn't want this to happen to him. And I thought I had little guilt to deal with." That is, why *say* I didn't want it to happen unless, half- or unconsciously, I did want something terrible to happen to him.

> Yet it is <u>so</u> painful today. I've asked him to come back, & when I went out midday & saw flowering shrubs I thought, He'll never see them again. I thought about Kay too & prayed: Don't let me survive either of my children. An article in the Washington <u>Post</u> said he had third degree burns, and was lying in a small back lane leading to a farm 40 feet from the car, which the police found in flames. A half-empty gasoline can was between him and the car. I was convinced he had done it. Both kids agreed he'd been unhappy, even Jessica, though she'd been saying the opposite—& I [said] that I'd gladly give him the tansu & camphor chest and the picture of the god to have him alive & I cried again, sobbing bitterly as she sat across the table & held my hands. Henry said the cap of the gas can was found in the front of the car, the trunk was locked, Betty knew nothing about the can & no gas station in the area had filled a can for him that night. [This was during the gasoline crisis.]

On Wednesday Tom went to school and Jessica came to work with me and read magazines. I wondered why I was there but stuck it out till afternoon. Betty Burch, who taught at Tufts, was at the library and when I told her the news she said that George "was a 'strange' man, didn't know much about China, & that he had to leave Tufts. She's even stupider than I thought, and nasty too." (Bob Taylor assured me that George did *not* have to leave, that Bob tried to talk him out of leaving.) Burch was certainly tactless. Dr. L. was both smarter and kinder that afternoon.

> "You feel you killed him," he said very simply & helped me see that suicide was practically impossible & that it was almost certainly homicide. After ½ an hour, at his suggestion, I invited Jessica to join us & she was wonderful, even acknowledging that it would have been worse if he had been living with us & agreeing when Dr. L. said, You really lost him a couple of years ago. It all took away much of my burden, but not all.

We did some shopping and I cooked supper, washed the dishes, and went to a meeting, with "some guilt at acting 'normal' so soon." Later I asked Tom whether he had told anyone. "No! Was he afraid he'd cry if he talked about it? Yes, if he <u>thought</u> about it." I still wasn't totally convinced that I wasn't guilty. The "burden" and the pain remained a while longer, but I learned how much easier such a loss is when it doesn't impinge on one's daily life. Not easy, but easier. For me there had been no contact since the trial except the monthly check; for the children it was the usual sporadic, unpredictable contacts. "Dr. L. asked if I still love him, & I said, I don't think so: I want him alive but I don't want him—I <u>think</u> that's true." And on Mothers' Day, as Jessica cooked dinner, "I cried a little again, thinking of the life we had together & my feelings of love, pride, hope. It wasn't death that took all that away! but George himself."

Like our wedding, the funeral was on a gray Friday. Shwe flew from Washington and we got to The Farm in a gentle, windless rain. The minister, Frank Moss, read from various psalms, the dedication poem from George's book of poems, and my excerpts from the Jewish prayer book (the piece we heard at Freeland Abbott's memorial service, with references to God omitted)—it seemed appropriate to include something

George and I had heard together. "The children laid down their carna-
tions & I my forsythia. Li-chiao grabbed the urn and took it back to the
house. There will be a burial when the ground is dry." At the gathering
at The Farm,

> I tried to smile at Li-chiao but she didn't want to be friendly. I
> kept thinking: He left me for <u>that</u>! She's not smart, she's not pretty
> (or not any more), she's not particularly nice— rather, I think,
> she's a sad spoiled brat. But she's Chinese & she was familiar &
> available. And he didn't <u>want</u> to live with a Mensch. Kay also was
> stand-offish (toward me) and Van was impossible: jovial & loud to
> the point of obscenity. Ted [Steele] & one or two other people
> said, It's nice to see <u>you</u> here. Kathy was friendly, and Henry
> helpful. I talked to him & Shwe about financial matters. Everyone
> is sure that George had the children's best interests at heart even
> though they know about the land—which is now in <u>his</u> name
> again! The only new fact was that his watch crystal melted and
> stopped the watch at 6:40. It seems as if he went straight there and
> quite possible that there was a rendezvous.

It's embarrassing to see how I took to the role of jilted first wife, and how
unforgiving I was toward Van, failing to see that his noisy good cheer was
a "manly" way to cover his grief. He and George were as close as Moseley
men got, I think. He surely felt the loss keenly, perhaps more than Kay.
Mary, his wife, wrote me on Sunday:

> It is hard to watch Van really suffer. He keeps wondering where he
> failed George. I regret that I could not be with you on Friday but
> asking Van to bring me would have been just too much. When
> he can I know he will write you, right now he cannot settle to
> anything for more than a few minutes. He is concerned about all
> of you and does not know what to do.

Poor Van felt even guiltier than I did, without the help of a "Dr. L.,"
believing that somehow he could have prevented George's death.
Someone told me Kay was annoyed at my Jewish text— "We don't know

George and Van Moseley (i.e., George Van Horn Moseley, 3ʳᵈ and Jr.)
at The Farm, 1950s, before I knew them or it.

any Jews"—and that she was still, or again, angry at me for "having put George in jail." (Years later she invited me to The Farm to talk about George, then had nothing to say or ask. And when Jessica and her daughters and I went with her to renew the flowers on George's grave, Kay rattled on about all sorts of things with no word about George.) Did she feel no twinge of guilt for conniving at keeping the land out of the divorce settlement? Or, conversely, did she regret signing it back to him? It would be sold and Jessica, Tom, and Li-chiao would each get one-third of the proceeds. If George had lived, the children might never have benefited by it. I used to sneer at talk about finances and inheritance at Moseley dinners—before I took part too, both because of the money and property and because of the feelings and relations behind them, often unacknowledged, hidden except for their manifestation in financial transactions.

When I called Kay on her birthday in late May, the burial was done, even though the family promised to tell the children in time for them to be there if they wished. It reminded me of the time, or times, when Kay called on Thanksgiving Friday: what a shame that Jessica and Tom couldn't be there the day before—only she hadn't invited them.

So what happened there in the woods? With articles on three consecutive days, the *Washington Star* tried to make a cause célèbre of this ugly incident; the *Post* printed one article. The Maryland State Police found George, with third-degree burns over half or all of his body (accounts vary), at 7:30 pm, some forty feet from his car, which was still burning. The gas can found between the body and the car was partly full. Li-chiao told the police that they had been in Washington earlier that day and George had filled the car's gas tank, said he should get rid of the gas can as it was leaking, and that he often went for rides on country roads to see the scenery and relax. It was so normal that she never asked where he was going. At first the police suspected foul play, but the autopsy turned up no evidence of wounds or strangulation, and the car had damage only from the fire, so by Wednesday the police were noncommittal: it could be homicide, suicide, or accident.

I saw the spot in 1976, when SAA held its annual meeting in Washington and, in pouring rain, Shwe took me to Point of Rocks. "It was shocking to see it, where the car was (the tree that stopped it still scorched) & where he lay. What was he doing there?" Back at the hotel, I cancelled an appointment, went to my room "& bawled."

Shwe had seen police photos and told me that George lay on his back partly curled up, probably due to the fire, with his arms relaxed in front of him. Even though the coroner found no bruises or wounds, Shwe—believing that it's possible to kill, or stun, a person with a blow to the temple that leaves no trace—thought he might already have been dead when set on fire. A later exhibition about Pompeii featured a replica of a woman overcome by lava. You could almost see her writhing in agony, *her arms, unlike George's, trying to protect her head.*

Was it suicide? The morning after the funeral, Tom helped me scrape ice off the windshield and we drove to Newton; Jessica stayed on at The Farm. I felt sad.

> But Dr. L. reminded me what a self-centered, angry, secretive bastard he was and very much reinforced the rendezvous theory (as a theory)—that he may have been involved in something & made the others so angry that they did what they did. He asked how often George had been apologetic, taken any blame on himself & I said that if there was any hint of it he would immediately include me in the blame. He said that (the mea culpa) would be

the suicidal type, not George, who evidently is more the sort to provoke murder.

This isn't scientific proof of course, and if it was murder, who did it? And why? Did he really drive around to "relax"? That doesn't sound like George. The "rendezvous theory" seemed, and seems, particularly apt, maybe also because that Wednesday, April 30ᵗʰ, was the day "Saigon fell," when all those Vietnamese and Americans scrambled to leave South Vietnam. Was George still somehow involved in US action in that tormented country? Did he promise to do something in that connection and screw up? The idea *that he got himself killed by others* (not killed himself) still makes the most sense—and fits well enough with his conviction that he would die young. It seems we'll never know whether that's what happened or only a reasonable guess.

From what I'd read about other murders, some quite old, I expected the police to follow up all likely leads, surely including an ex-wife. The Maryland police did not call me; I called them. On May 7ᵗʰ, "Talked to Officer Herring, he was nice but all I learned was that a 14-year- old girl who lives nearby said she'd seen him there a week before [which if true could support the 'rendezvous theory']. He asked about another woman etc. but I cdn't tell him anything." On August 7ᵗʰ, I wrote the Maryland State Police with questions Kathy Moseley raised in a letter:

> a) any developments <u>re</u> past or current government work
> *b) results of FBI test of various remnants to see if impregnated with gas or not
> c) any developments on the Bangladesh angle (after I told them of other letter found & of Indian types in car on road where accident occurred)
> d) The Print Shop - work - colleagues
> Jessica also mentioned George going off on some "secret mission" for the gov't, ca.1971. Is that anything? I would like to know if the police pursued <u>any</u> of these things.
> [The * is hers, to indicate importance.]

"I don't care nearly so much about the investigation," I added in the diary, "though it still seems dreadful that it can all subside so easily." "Trooper Herring" called on the 18th,

> with so-called answers: 1 George worked for the CIA 1956-7 & not later. 2 No petroleum traces [although according to the news accounts, the pathologist who did the autopsy thought "gasoline was involved"; she could smell it on his body and clothing]. 3 The Bangladeshi girl gave a talk to one of his classes—no suspicion there. 4 They don't know the name of the printing shop! & he [George] worked there such a short time it wdn't be any use to ask them!! I urged them to try anyway. Such rubbish—

The "printing shop" probably concerned historical maps of China that George had devised and printed. I told Herring what someone had told me: that the shop where he worked was in Springfield, Virginia. Herring said there were six in Springfield and they didn't know at which one George had worked. I hope I said, but may just have thought: why not check till you find the right one? Isn't that what police work entails?

This reminds me now, and did then, of earlier less-than-impressive police work. In the Bronx the "Ponyack" vanished and we reported it stolen. The police sent out a multi-state bulletin, but it was George, out walking with the kids, who found it. And in June 1974 Jessica called me at work: Ralph had been harassing her and she was afraid to leave her room. I told her to stay put and "went to get the Medford cops, who diddled around (needed a new switch for their blue light)." Luckily nothing dreadful happened to Jessica during this delay, but it might have. Now, in 1975, laziness? indifference? of the Maryland police made me wonder whether they had been told to leave the case alone, which was why I'd written Senator Ted Kennedy in May. On June 6th an aide, Ed Martin, called; he would pass the matter on to the office of Senator Charles Mathias of Maryland, and "they could put pressure on the Maryland attorney general." On June 25th I wrote Ed Martin that the Maryland police had told Kathy Moseley that "the case is 'suspended'"; he called on the 27th and said that "the police have the case open." Which was it? Who knows? I also wrote Senator Frank Church, who had been holding intensive hearings on the CIA. He replied: the committee's mandate did

not include pursuing individual cases. Should I go to Maryland and try
to force some answers? I concluded that it was up to the Moseleys, not
me. Kathy agreed that the investigation seemed "shoddy, at least, if not
peculiar. I have thought and thought about the details I know, and they
make no sense."

In 1979 I made one last attempt to throw some light on this mystery
by writing to Ed Lansdale, by then a general but a colonel when George
worked for him in Saigon in 1955–57. He answered almost immediately.
He knew only what he had read in the newspapers, invited me to come
for lunch when next in Washington, and regretted seeing little of George
while he lived nearby, although "I did have Chinese New Year dinner
with him … at a large party he hosted. He did tell me that he was going
to get married again, so I gathered that he was looking forward to the
years ahead."

It was more than a year before I made use of the map Lansdale sent
of his McLean neighborhood's winding suburban roads. One Sunday
in February 1981, Shwe drove us to Lansdale's and came in "for just a
minute but of course stayed all evening (as he intended)."

> I could see why George was so attached to Ed Lansdale—he's
> the way George wanted Van to be (and so did Van!)—smart,
> effective & humane. He fooled with a pipe as Van used to do,
> but he cooked supper (chao fan [fried rice]) and drove the maid
> home without complaining. I'd brought photos (of kids, and of
> Geo. with or without kids) and really wanted Ed to reminisce
> about George personally, but Shwe kept the talk political, also
> interesting but I wished I had the energy to change course. He
> gave us each a copy of his book, [*In the Midst of Wars*].

What I didn't record was that, while I admired Lansdale's personal qualities, I didn't agree with his Cold-War outlook. It was better than the
rabid anti-communism that led us to support anyone who opposed the
USSR and "Red China," but fighting communism figured prominently
in his choice of assignments and how he carried them out. He was the
model for Graham Greene's *Quiet American*, which was not flattering to
his type and their effect on Southeast Asia. And I again sold Van short,

having long heard the family ridicule him in his absence. Later I learned that when he jumped, as "the first man out of the first plane" on D-Day, and broke his ankle, he commanded his troops from a wheelbarrow all day, refusing to leave the battlefield before dark.

We (at least I) never found out who killed George and why, which made me wonder how many US murders remain unsolved every year. In 2009 an official of Law Enforcement Against Prohibition (LEAP), in speaking about the stupidity and destructiveness of the "war on drugs," reported that so much police time had been diverted to that hopeless endeavor that other work—such as solving murders—had increasingly been neglected. Could this explain the "shoddy" or "peculiar" (or non-existent) investigation of George's death? Perhaps a contributing factor?

Back in 1975, George's friends and colleagues jumped to their own conclusions. Shwe and Jay Wood, another old friend, suspected the CIA; when I saw him in May, Jay speculated that George might have left us "so we wouldn't be involved in whatever he was involved in. (Then why behave so badly?)" When I related this to Dr. L., "he said altruism was no part of George's nature." Jay told Shwe that in January he'd met with two men in Washington: "George's name came up and the State Dept. man said, He's with the CIA." This again didn't prove anything but per- haps there was still a CIA connection, despite Herring's assurances, and despite the CIA's assertion—when I wrote about survivors' benefits for the children—that George had worked for it only in 1956–57. Is it the CIA's modus operandi to tell civilians the truth?

Shwe suspected "Dragon Lady," as he routinely called Li-chiao. But probably all he had to back up this hunch was his dislike. Early in May he told me that the *Washington Post* reported that the police had ruled out homicide. "I was very disturbed by all this; it seemed such a tangle of deception & counter-deception," I told my diary; "it makes no sense to rule out homicide unless you know exactly what happened. I hate this part of it, the feeling that <u>no</u> one is to be trusted." Was there political pressure to deep-six the case? If so, from whom and why?

Allan Cole, an older fellow student at Yale, jumped to a different conclusion. He had seen George at his booth with his maps of China at the Association of Asian Studies (AAS) meeting in March, which "kept him from attending any of the sessions" and "exposed him to a sense of rejection." Cole had earlier tried to talk with him "more personally," and had "encountered his defences. So this (in some form) must have been gathering for some time." Any real change "would have required the will to be helped and to change, then the long work toward a lessening of the self-derogating patterns." Cole didn't say "suicide" but the assumption is clear enough.

Other acquaintances shared Cole's view of George's state of mind. Hod Briggs—who knew Cole and George at Yale—wrote that he had told his wife *at the time* of the AAS meeting that he found George "a very unhappy, lonely person, caught in a meaningless life." George told Hod that he still enjoyed reading and research but "was utterly bored and unhappy with teaching—a meaningless pursuit." At the 1973 meeting George had "tried to brush off the negative review of his book on modern China," while in 1975 "he was keenly—explosively—sensitive about criticism of his more recent work on minorities." Hod too wondered whether the "very simple maps of Chinese dynasties" merited renting a booth and missing conference sessions. He expressed shock and horror at the way George died. "You have our thoughts," he added, "in fact I can think of little else."

Mark Elvin, a sinologist we first knew in Belmont, wrote from Oxford that he had "lost several friends to violent ends but never anything like this." He could cite nothing from "desultory" correspondence with George that might throw light on "what certainly sounds like murder." Hal Kahn, our sinological friend from London transplanted to Stanford University, and Sandra were both active politically, therefore often had "shocking news about the treatment of friends and strangers. But the shocking never becomes commonplace. Nor does sadness." Ed Friedman had stayed with us in Hong Kong. "It was so good to see your name on the outside of the envelope," he wrote, "so awful to read the news in the letter inside." He had no illuminating information but, like others, asked to be kept informed of any news or explanations, ending: "I always had a great special affection for George + the greatest respect for you." He too wrote about George at the 1973 AAS meeting.

He was with his then–wife. [They weren't married yet; we weren't divorced yet.] I asked about his work, writing, his new job. I even asked about you. I don't remember much of his answers. George seemed subdued. I hardly looked at the woman. I remember thinking that I didn't believe George could believe he had made a life-affirming decision. I didn't like the new wife. I got no clue that he was active politically.

Henrietta Gay found the news "incredible, because my memory of George is as a young, vital teacher with a sparkling sense of humor. The semester I spent studying with him...meant more to me than either of the other semesters. George was an excellent teacher, and he loved China so that his enthusiasm was contagious. I'm still hoping to see China for myself, but I'm sad that I shall never be able to tell him that I'm going, and to ask his advice about things Chinese."

The only other former student I knew, Fred Bonnie, also expressed disbelief: "Foul play? I can't imagine who would want to kill George. Was he involved in governmental affairs? I just can't believe it. He told me that he wanted to move to the D.C. area, 'where the action is.' I just can't believe it resulted in this."

Fred had also been an employee, helping rebuild our house. Another former employee, Augusto, wrote from Macao: "I feel very sad learning that Mr. Moseley dead in such way. We were very close friend & helped me many times when I was in distress." He offered to repay money we had lent him; I thanked him but urged him not to.

Money was a problem for a while. Child support ceased and to get Social Security I had to be appointed guardian of my children, which took longer than expected. Meantime another complication with financial consequences descended on us in the person of a young Black man who came to rent a room the day before George's funeral. Two people from the local CETA (Comprehensive Employment & Training Act) agency brought him and seemed to be vouching for him. I was hesitant but let myself be persuaded that he was all right. He wasn't. He stopped paying rent; had lots of friends in his room, some overnight or tromping up and down stairs at all hours; took dishes upstairs and left them in his room gathering mold; ate our food; harassed Jessica; was often stoned; once left the third-floor shower running till it overflowed and destroyed the ceiling in Jessica's room. I called the police, who knew him but merely talked to him.

One July day, Tom called me at work: "there was white powder from a fire extinguisher all over the house and his stereo was gone." Also gone were a tenant's typewriter and other things. I imagined Donald and friends loading the loot in the small aluminum trunk George had had made in Macao for his books and papers and carrying it out in broad daylight, after setting off the fire extinguisher. The police were sure it was an inside job—no use to press charges though. The CETA people clucked in sympathy, and his parents, who lived nearby, were indifferent. Their upholstery was covered in plastic and I wondered whether Donald was still rebelling against this fastidiousness, only at my house instead of theirs.

"Jessica washed a lot of dishes & vacuumed some," I wrote that day, "& Tom had vacuumed and mopped." Looking back, recalling what they were going through as adolescents very recently made fatherless, I'm impressed and touched by their sense of responsibility—recognizing (in contrast to George) that the house was theirs to take care of too—and by their solidarity with me. Surely there were many things they would rather have been doing than mopping and vacuuming, yet they did their share without being asked.

Fallen ceiling, stolen food, burglary, and further misdemeanors notwithstanding, Donald was still there. I'm all for tenants' rights but Massachusetts law meant that it took weeks of lawyers' maneuvers and waiting periods until I was able to evict him legally. The evening I'd invited some Hightowers and others for dinner (including Kathy Kraft, a colleague at the library who had helped clean powder from walls, cupboards, and dishes), the sheriff permitted the eviction to happen. But I was responsible for Donald's possessions. Kathy's husband suggested putting the stuff in the garage and the sheriff agreed. So we had an "eviction party": packing up his clothes, taking down his posters, and figuring out how to keep him out. Next day the kids and I washed old food off the furniture and Tom moved furniture as I vacuumed.

A Medford acquaintance on the board of CETA said a friend had tried twice to rescue Donald and talk to his parents but decided he was a "con artist." Months later, as I was stopped at the level crossing in West

Medford Square, he ambled across the street in front of my car. "I could break his legs," I thought, seeing how necessary, and hard, it is to *feel what one feels without acting on it*. It became clear too how prejudice can ripen. The day he let the shower run, I wrote: "I despise him, I don't care what color he is." He happened to be Black. Wronged by one young Black man, I might begin to hate all young Black men, even all Black men or all Black people. The *feeling* may be unavoidable, but eventually benign or neutral contacts with other Black people—or whatever kind you've become prejudiced against—along with your own civilizing intelligence, will counteract and even wipe out the bad feelings. But it takes time, effort, and self-awareness.

Another lesson in self-awareness was to listen to my own doubts rather than others' empty promises, especially in a time of weakness. The shock of George's death weakened me, and in a way I replaced him, who in recent years had been so difficult, with another difficulty, even if not consciously. I let Donald into my house when I might so easily have refused. I trust CETA did other work that was useful rather than destructive.

Luckily I had other tenants, and of course my salary, and eventually we did get Social Security and some pension benefits of George's. Li-chiao asked the court to grant her a monthly allowance from the estate; it granted a smaller amount than she asked for. Presumably it came out of her share of George's estate. She also asked the estate to pay to move her and George's belongings to Vermont when she decided to live in Grafton. The bulk of the moving costs were for *her* piano, harpsichord, and furniture, which were not part of the estate, so again Louis Whitcomb, the Vermont lawyer who served as administrator (George left no will), granted her only a nominal amount. I resented it when she got one-third of a small royalty check for *The Party and the National Question in China*, which, as I wrote Albert Bolles, the Vermont lawyer representing the children, was "published five years before we were separated and dedicated to me."

Li-chiao evidently owed Kay $4,000 and she and George had other debts—including water and electric bills for $285—when George was making $17,000 a year (even with two children, we always paid our utility bills)—all of which she thought the estate should pay. As late as

September 1978 she was trying to get the estate to pay a debt she had incurred while a widow. Bolles, writing to my lawyer, Kathy McHugh, noted in September 1976 that Whitcomb "was having some trouble with the widow," and in December, that "the tone of [Whitcomb's] petition to the Court is such that he does not harbor too much sympathy for the widow." Even Li-chiao's own lawyer disagreed with her about the moving expenses and wrote Whitcomb about her "squawking about the payment of the Federal taxes." (If there were anything favorable to quote about her, I would include it, really I would, but there is nothing like that in the file.) All this confirmed my impression of her as the traditional gold digger. As keyboard performer and teacher she could probably have supported herself, but Gene had kept her in fine style in Tokyo, according to George, and when we saw her in Hong Kong it was in an elegant apartment on Victoria Peak. As a widow—after only eight months of marriage—she was entitled to one-third of his estate (except the insurance, which was only for the children); this wasn't much, but it was more than she would have collected if they hadn't married.

Once the land was sold, in 1976 for $50,000, she got one-third of that and of some cash and unspecified miscellaneous assets. Her allowance had stopped as she married again. I took this—maliciously?—to mean that she had discovered a good reason to marry. She married John Campbell, her agent, and moved to Toledo (Ohio, not Spain).

There was more dickering about the estate and much correspondence about who should pay the taxes, until Bolles urged "that the account be approved, and this case closed without spending more money and extra time that we cannot charge for." (It was news to me that lawyers ever spend time that they cannot charge for.) I wasn't sure that Jessica and Tom were well protected, but it was 1979 and they were no longer minors. I'd bought certificates of deposit with most of the insurance money and earned each several thousand additional dollars, so it was now up to them to spend or save their patrimony.

In an odd coda, by late 1982 Li-chiao too was dead. In some city a car drove up on the sidewalk and hit several pedestrians, killing her and perhaps others. Murder or accident? Another mystery? At any rate another death involving violence and a car.

In 1975, like George only forty-three, while coping with teenage kids, tenants, psychotherapy, a house in need of repairs and renovation, the job, and the legal and financial aftermath of George's death, I was still "looking." I had now and then seen Artie, Dolly's now ex-husband. He had called me in December 1974, a week after getting a Dominican divorce. He and Dolly and another couple had switched partners, but Dolly and her new partner, another physicist, were more certainly attached than Artie and the other ex-wife. One summer day,

> spent a long time at Halibut Point [on Cape Ann], which is so beautiful, then wandered around Rockport, which is a little too cute, and finally ate at the Blacksmith Shop.... Afterwards we walked some more and on a little, dark beach he took me in his arms, told me he had always tried to keep track of where I was. And he said, as if drawing a not-too-striking conclusion from a line of reasoning in physics, I love you. Only once—but I didn't respond. What could I say? I don't love you?

I might have said that I was flattered.

Artie was fun to do things with, but also exasperating and emotionally depriving. I saw him a few times in Medford or New York before and after George's death, and briefly entertained some hope that this "love" would amount to something. One day in August I drove us from New York to Lake Hopatcong in New Jersey, where Martha and Fred Gruenberg, my parents' friends who had visited us in Oxford, had a vacation house. We swam, ate, talked, and had a good time. And when I went upstairs to change Martha came with me and said "she hoped my life would get easier and how about getting married, and what about this 'boy'?"

It would have been gratifying to marry an old friend and brilliant physicist, but I soon saw that he wouldn't be what I wanted—even without the other ex-wife, whom he never mentioned. There were other things to ignore or get used to: for instance, as we left for New Jersey and I buckled my seat belt, his saying, "You're not planning to have an accident, are you?" It was stupid but his privilege (then, if not now) not to use a seatbelt, but it was stupid and mean to make fun of me for using one. With her talent for analyzing handwriting, Edith looked at his and "said he's confused, self-centered, very attached to his [birth] family, lies to himself & others." It doesn't really sum our friendship up, but I like a passage in my diary from February 1975, when I was in New York on library business: "went to Artie's, where I had supper & endless talk & it was too late to catch an express bus so I spent the night and sneaked out in the morning before he could start talking again."

In September I met Philip on a hike: about eight years younger, divorced after a brief marriage, recently moved to Massachusetts, high-strung, fairly trembling with fears and enthusiasms, attractive, and he was attracted to me. We had dinner that evening and he wanted more but I put him off. I dislocated my shoulder for the fourth time while in bed with him a while later, just from sitting propped up on my right arm, and he was helpful and solicitous during and after the repair at Cambridge City Hospital. But when hiking he looked for the perfect woman. His mother used to take him hiking, as my father used to take me. So when I went on hikes with him I had to watch as he "took off & cased all the women." He said it "hurt him to hurt me," but he went on hunting and I suffered while realizing that he too wasn't what I really wanted. I felt free to "ask about his mother & the perfect woman (neither of which he wants to talk about). What scares me is that he'll find Her & ditch me, but I know that it's just as likely that I'll find someone—i.e. not very likely." Once again grown-up, realistic Eva grappled with hopeful, deluded little Eva, sense vs. sensibility, and so it went on for more weeks before it petered out. (I had the shoulder repaired that fall and recovered at Harvard's infirmary, where Dr. L. came for a visit, a delightful surprise. Moments later Kay appeared. Correctly but unfortunately, Dr. L. deferred to her; I felt cheated.)

Decades later, reminded of those years of strife and Li-chiao's bizarre death, I thought: "I'm still here." It wasn't gloating, nor guilt, but simply true and comforting. Those who hurt me are dead. I may only rarely feel happy, but I'm alive and useful to some people, and I've got the tansu and the other things George tried to get from me, to use and to pass on to children and grandchildren, rather than have them go to Li-chiao's family or other strangers. Perhaps I was gloating!

George lives on too in a way. Ed Friedman told me that George's books were still cited as authorities on national minorities in China, and a younger scholar was impressed when I told him my connection to George: "You knew George Moseley? I have his book on my desk!" "Which book?" He didn't know there are several. I'm glad his work was still valued, and perhaps still is; he may have died in vain, but he didn't live in vain. Not attached to any prestigious "mentor," working largely on his own, he made his mark in sinology.

Henrietta was right that George's death was "a terrible shock. No matter what the final relationship becomes, I think that a person never stops having some kind of feeling for someone who has shared one's life so intimately." Photos of George, thoughts of places, music, food we shared, soften the memories. Love and admiration may come flooding back. Jessica added to this mellowing by reminding me, in 2008, that George used to sing to me: "Five foot two, eyes of blue" and "Hey, good-lookin', whatcha got cookin'?" "Do I have to rewrite all those later chapters?" I thought, for without Jessica's prodding I had no memory of George singing. But there is no natural law that says a person can't sing to a spouse one day, or one minute, and the same or the next want to kill her or him. George's traits that Dr. L. enumerated are real too. At seventy-five, I handed some chronic aches—exacerbated by injuries but at bottom nearly as old as I was—to a massage therapist. As over the weeks he dug ever deeper and found unexpected knots, out of the tortured, reluctant muscles came echoes of the feelings that had caused them to tighten up seventy or more years earlier. At one session a bottomless despair took me back to Vienna, to being worked over by another man, not for my benefit but for his sick pleasure. "You ruined my life," a voice in my head repeated. The "you" was my father, and also George, the "life" mine and also our children's.

George's conviction that he would die young was almost surely a result of early deprivation. I can sympathize with him as the child often overlooked by his parents (his mother especially?)—as I believe he was—while critical of his refusal to examine his own feelings, instead blaming me and depriving the children. Had he been willing to see the reality of "little George," his children's lives, and mine, could have been very different, and his own life better and longer. Instead, along with abandoning us, he succumbed to the attraction Dupont Circle exerted, as an emblem of public affairs centered in Washington—so that it was not far from Dupont Circle that he met the early death he expected. As Fred Bonnie all but asked, is that what he meant by "the action"?

Even with the violent death of someone so important to me, I partly skirted this all-too-common phenomenon. I didn't stumble on his body, nor see him dead. The children's lives were affected much more than mine. But for them too the major upheaval George caused in April 1971 was in its own way as devastating as that of April 1975.

VIII.
Family Portraits

Chapter 38

MUTTER, MOTHER, ISABELLA

Somehow one telling document survived when, at her death, I threw out Mother's papers, keeping only photographs. A *Wäge-Karte* (weight card) issued by the workers' health insurance agency in Vienna, it records my weight at various intervals from birth until May 1933, noting that I was *Abgestillt* (weaned) on March 27, 1932, at three months.

Discarding family papers seems an odd thing for an archivist to do, but June 1971, when Mother died, was three months before I began to become an archivist, and two months after George left. The papers were in San Francisco, the children and I living in Massachusetts. I regret the loss of the papers, but, considering our circumstances, have tried to forgive myself for this unfortunate decision. And I've tried to forgive Mother for her "crimes and misdemeanors," or at least to understand her better. Coming on that stray document in my early seventies started me on a belated attempt at a post-mortem reconciliation, based on skimpy knowledge of her early life, an almost total lack of archival evidence, and my own necessarily partial (in both senses) memory.

Thanks to Mother, I grew up with the conviction that of course you nurse your babies, which I did. But when, after three or four months, my milk became erratic, she did *not* tell me that she had stopped nursing me at that tender age. If she had—and had told me why—perhaps I might have overcome my own difficulties and continued for months more, as I longed to do. And it could have brought her and me closer together. So to me the *Wäge-Karte* documents a significant instance of Mother as dissembler. I think that isn't too strong a word, even though I don't believe she meant to deceive her children. Despite compassion because of her considerable tribulations, and admiration for her talent and her wisdom about human relations—though generally only those of other humans—I see much of her connection with me as a litany of deceptions.

The fact that she said nothing when she knew I was unhappy about trouble nursing is a sign of her wish to be seen as Earth Mother. She told me repeatedly that she was strong as a horse (*wie ein Ross*—actually a stallion) while I was delicate. Giving birth doesn't hurt, she said; it's just hard work. That's why it's called labor—although the German *Wehe* indicates pain rather than work, and it isn't true: childbirth hurts, and I doubt that it didn't hurt her. Mother told an anecdote about childbirth. A young woman in labor keeps moaning "*Oy Gott*," and the women who have come to help want to go in to her, but her mother says, "Not yet." Then the daughter cries, "*Oy Mamale!*" and the mother says: "Now!" This story undercuts the work-not-pain theory, but it portrays the kind of wise, perceptive mother Mother thought she was.

When she helped with my abortion, she couldn't bring herself to say: I did this too. Modern and prudish, she told me nothing about menstruation, even when my neighbor friend Pauline provided a way, telling me breathlessly that her mother had this terrible disease: when she went to the bathroom blood came out. When I told Mother, breathlessly, about this "terrible disease," she said nothing. Years later I asked her why she hadn't used this opening to explain menstruation. "Maybe I thought she *had* a disease" was her lame response. But why not say: Maybe yes, or maybe… and so tell me what I needed to know. (She *had* told me that a baby begins in the mother's belly when the father passes her a seed. She didn't say how he does that; I guessed that it was via a kiss.)

Mother was no braver than Pauline's mother. When I had my first period, at nearly thirteen, she crept into my room, sat on the bed, and said sheepishly, "I suppose you know all about this." Well, yes, I'd gotten information, perhaps some misinformation, at Kiddie Camp.

When I found menopause troublesome, I asked Vickie how it had affected her. She claimed simply to have stopped menstruating from one month to the next. "What about Isabella?" I asked. "Oh, we never talked about things like that!" she assured me.

It wasn't only Earth Mother matters. In the first years after her death, I often felt possessed by her, as if she were living in my body, making my facial expressions, directing feelings and gestures. Forceful in her views, she could be quite diffident in expressing them. In matters such as musical taste she said she didn't want to influence us. Yet somehow—in gestures or grimaces—she made her views plain enough. She didn't like opera, ballet, Tchaikovsky, or musical comedy. After her death, I gradually discovered that I like some operas and musical comedies, don't like ballet, and when I heard Tchaikovsky's marvelous piano trio I said he should have stuck to chamber works. Then a friend took me to Tanglewood. At intermission, with only a Tchaikovsky symphony to look forward to, he agreed to leave. We drove away with the radio on. "What is this gorgeous music?" I wondered. "The joke's on me if it's the concert." It was: the rarely performed second ("Little Russian") symphony, for me as marvelous as the trio.

More consequential than matters of taste were two instances in which knowing Mother's opinions could have changed the direction of my life. There's no telling whether it *would* have or, if it did, whether for better or worse, but withholding her thoughts about important choices I was making was not helpful. Both had to do with my education.

The perfunctory counselling for girls at Bronx Science steered us to colleges in the city, but I wanted to leave New York. Somehow I learned about Bard, and Annie Steinbach—still my piano teacher—told me about Mount Holyoke (MHC). Both offered me full-tuition scholarships. I visited Bard and liked it, but chose Mount Holyoke because it seemed better for physics and math (my likely majors) and because, if I wasn't satisfied, it was a better school to transfer from. That it was a women's college did *not* please me, yet I went there, being sensible but not true to my inclinations. After I graduated Mother told me she thought that Mrs. Steinbach recommended Mount Holyoke because Lucy was applying to Swarthmore and Radcliffe and her mother didn't want me competing with her. I was stunned, by the accusation and by Mother's silence. "Why didn't you tell me then?" I screamed in my head but not out loud. She couldn't tell me what was on her mind when it mattered, and I couldn't tell her what was on mine. Each afraid to make the other angry. But she was there first; it was partly from her that I learned to keep to myself anything that might make someone angry at me. Now, remembering that I heard about MHC only from that teacher at Lucy's school who was an alumna recruiter—but who evidently hadn't persuaded Lucy to apply there—I tend to think Mother was right, but she should have told me when it mattered.

She did it again with regard to my major. As I gave up physics and then math and opted for philosophy, she said nothing, kept sending me spending money—I remember it as a $60 check, always sent before I asked—with no hint of disapproval. Long after it could change anything, she said, "I always thought you would stay in physics." This was either after graduate school, when I was at sea about my future, or two years earlier, when I was heading to Harvard to study Sanskrit rather than quantum mechanics. Again I was stunned, even if less than at the Steinbach allegation: that she had harbored this disapproval in silence, and let it out when I could no longer act on it. Would I have decided differently if she had told me her doubts earlier? I don't know, but to consider my decisions and their likely consequences together might have clarified my own inclinations and choices, and it would have strengthened the bond between us.

There *was* such a bond. Although for years I was furious at her, simultaneously I felt close to her , closer than to her sisters. More than once, hurt by some man, I came home and found solace, and we usually saw eye to eye about politics and other matters; that was comforting too. But as she was so absent early in my life, she could seem to be one more aunt.

Her wilfulness often had her planning other people's days for them; her disability made refusing to comply seem boorish. Sometimes it was for her convenience, but not always—such as the one time I remember protesting. Living or staying at home, one morning I needed to get up early; she agreed to wake me but let me sleep. I let her know I was annoyed, preferring less sleep to having to rush. Why such misplaced solicitousness? Was she trying to make up for our childhood exile? If so, it was self-defeating; it only frustrated and irritated me. If my anger was out of proportion to any current offense, it was because of old, unspoken resentments.

Wilfulness was sometimes manifest in her opinions. One day she declared that Bach's compositions weren't really religious. I scoffed, silently, pretty sure that everything he wrote, liturgical or not, was for the greater glory of his God. But Isabella liked Bach's music and didn't like Christianity, so she rearranged reality to suit her inclinations. A more serious instance of wilfulness concerned our leaving Austria. She said later that she'd decided that we would leave together or not at all. Other parents were sending their children to England in the *Kindertransport*. Rather than save her children at any cost, was she really prepared to sacrifice us for family unity?—when, thanks to *her* arrangement, we had hardly been a united family. But it was never tested so remains an odd thing to say rather than a perverse thing to have done.

Some mannerisms drove me wild, again unreasonably so: the way she parked her glasses below her nose, the contorted face to show scepticism, which she did often. For instance when, in my teens, I reported something surprising I had learned and she said "If that were true, I would have heard of it before." "There has to be a first time," I thought but didn't say. If I had dared to disagree openly, my life might have been very different.

Two habits were particularly annoying. Mother liked to show off her frequent bruises, pulling up a sleeve, rolling down a stocking. It wasn't until 1967–68 that I dared to tell her that I didn't like looking at her black-and-blue spots. (I know when it was by where it was: in our second Oxford flat.) She was surprised, perhaps hurt, but it felt good to tell the truth. She was surprised too, when, about then, I thanked her for letting me have piano lessons. Bad as my playing is, it has given me some satisfaction, at times consolation.

Also annoying were the ways she asked for things. She might point imperiously, wordlessly at the salt shaker—as Frau Steiner, boss of her own business—or she would cock her head and with a little-girl smile say, "The salt, pleeeeeze," in a little-girl voice. "Why can't she just say 'Please pass the salt' like anyone else?" I fumed—to myself. Evidently she could be the superior boss or inferior little child, but never equal. Toward the end of her life by mistake she signed a letter to me "Isabella" rather than "*Mutter*." She added a P.S.: had she had the energy (she had cancer then), she would have retyped the letter rather than send it with that signature. I was in my late thirties, raising two children, but she didn't want me to see her as a woman just like me.

I found her penchant for making decisions for others, and cajoling others to make decisions for her irksome. It didn't seem friendly, mutual consultation but an unwelcome sort of entanglement. Even her talent as a couturière could be a way to impose her will. Vickie, whose position as the next youngest sibling was similar to mine vis-à-vis Isabella, complained that Isabella made her a purple jumper, which Vickie thought clashed with her red hair (dyed, to disguise her age, by Rudi as long as she was still going to work). Shortly after I married, I visited Mother one evening and we disagreed about a garment she wanted to make me; as I left she said, with her usual vehemence, "*Ich muss meine Begabung für meine Familie ausnützen*" (I have to use my talent for my family), or words to that effect. Granted that we did benefit from this talent, and that her wish to be useful is understandable, but it had to be on her terms, which weren't always the beneficiary's terms.

When I was a child she made me loose, A-line dresses with matching panties, both things that would become stylish—and I would come to appreciate—later, but *my* ideal dress, which I never had, had the conventional smocked bodice, gathered skirt, and attached sash tied in a big bow in back. The dress in my high-school yearbook picture was of red and blue wool, with two little wings in lieu of a collar (and that wide belt that annoyed Bob). I liked this dress *and* found it ungainly. Many admired

Isabella Zetlin, or Steiner, sewing.

a dress she sent me at college: blue Shantung silk—lovely color, lovely fabric—with pleated skirt, "self belt," short raglan sleeves with cuffs, and shawl collar ending in a little tie that made it resemble a Girl Scout uniform; it felt luxurious but alien. Evidently this isn't unusual: a friend told me that his sister never liked the clothes their mother made her.

It took some maturity to sort this out. When we lived in Oxford, she sent a suit of an expensive textured wool as a surprise, no doubt having purposely ordered too much fabric for a client. It fit perfectly but was not flattering: the skirt wrapped in front, making two layers of bulky fabric where I didn't need padding. I wore it on the last day of her next visit. On the way home I stopped at the greengrocer's in North Parade. Rebecca, the wonderful woman who staffed the shop, admired the suit, or "costume" as the British call it (in German, *Kostüm*). Would she like to have it? Well, yes, if I really meant it and it fit. I brought it to her, she took it home and tried it on. The next time I bought produce there were others in the shop. She said softly: "The costume"; a circle of thumb and forefinger indicated perfection. I was delighted.

I wrote Mother about it, explaining why the skirt was not flattering, beautiful as the suit was, adding that I wanted her to sew for me if we consulted about the fabric and the design, as we had often done successfully. My letter no longer exists, but her reply (in German) shows hurt, not acceptance: "It is absolutely not mean [*gemein*] if you say that I shouldn't sew for you. In this regard we never got along well, you and my mother were always my most difficult customers. And I hope too that from now on you won't find it necessary to accept anything from me." A sad and irritating reply: was she too hurt to notice what I actually wrote?

A memory quilt I made incorporates remnants of several of her creations, a brown wool dress from 1961 among them. "Oh good," I said trying it on, "it has pockets," as I put a handkerchief in one of them. "Don't *put* anything in them," she remonstrated; the pockets were fashion details, not utilitarian. Two years later she made a Jacqueline-Kennedy-style three-piece suit of a nubbly blue wool: straight skirt, jacket with three-quarter sleeves, and a top with short sleeves. I wore it to a ladies' luncheon and was uncomfortable: if it's cool enough for wool, you want longer sleeves; if it's warm enough for short sleeves, wool is too hot. But Mother could be practical as well as fashion-conscious: she took the lining out of each store-bought winter coat and added an interlining for extra warmth.

In her workshop she was deft, sure, energetic, quick, and often I was happy with what she made me. The quilt includes a remnant of a maroon velvet suit from 1957, the jacket of an interesting design with a single button. I wore it with a top of *changeant* silk, a remnant of one of Mrs. Harry Winston's Indian saris, maroon and green with a border of gold embroidery. I liked that suit, had some satin pumps dyed to match, and wore it at an IPR Christmas party. Alex collected me and we went to dinner and a play. I felt overdressed at the party, but Alex tried to convince me that the others were out of step, not I. Another velvet garment, a black skirt, was also a success but the pink blouse to wear with it, with my first high heels, to a Nature Friends banquet; felt lumpy. (It's only because of these garments that I recall that the Nature Friends had winter banquets in the city.)

As over the years I bragged about Mother's talent or accepted compliments on a dress or suit, it became apparent that people who hadn't known her assumed that she cut an elegant figure. In fact she had difficulty dressing herself with even remotely the flair she lavished on her clients. She made herself jumpers and wore them with plain or print blouses. Her blouse often rode up in back, creating an awkward little hump. Her scarf would come undone. Her hair, due to a childhood case of ringworm, was sparse and she never found a pleasing way to wear it. She put lipstick on without benefit of mirror, resulting in stripes of mouth with and without lipstick. I found a mirror that clipped onto a lipstick, but doubt she ever used it.

She wasn't true to expectations in other ways too. She wasn't a typical Jewish mother—not the "My son the doctor" kind, nor the "Eat, children, eat" kind. Although she became more dependent on Paul and me, she was concerned with public affairs and had interests beyond her family. Hearing about mothers of Jewish contemporaries, I came to realize how unusual she was, with her wider interests, her opinions on important matters, and her ability to take care of herself when necessary. But dressing herself so as to be both comfortable and elegant eluded her, probably due to her congenitally dislocated hip and to her plumpness. An inch or more under five feet, she weighed about 140 pounds. Perhaps she hated her body. Poldi's rejection would underline that. She remained not only single but, as far as Paul or I knew, had no regular, or irregular, male escort or companion. (We had no inkling about her and Nunyu.) When Claude's parents divorced, I suspect she had her eye on his father. But he married someone else, while Claude's mother took up with a genial Black man named Cliff. (Mother often got rides to Midvale or elsewhere with Charlotte and Cliff. Typically they were hours late. Cliff usually had to fix the car, and everyone except perhaps Charlotte suspected that in the course of fixing one thing he broke something else.)

At Camp Midvale a woman I barely knew said, "You're lucky to have such a wonderful mother." My (silent) response would be spelled "Grrrr." I was fifteen. At seventeen, I stood in the living room of Apartment 6B after an encounter during which Mother had infuriated me and thought, "Some day I'll have a daughter who feels about me the way I feel about Her." I'll leave it to Jessica to reveal, or not, whether I've had such a daughter. Now, from this safe temporal distance and from the land of the living to that of the grave, Mother appears to me as two women in one body, one the mother who arranged her life to exclude her two small children from her house and most of her daily routine, the other a gifted, creative, intelligent woman, living with a world and a body that thwarted and at times tormented her. I can sympathize with that woman without forgiving the *Rabenmutter*. That was a word she used for women she considered unloving mothers. Literally a raven mother. The dictionary says "cruel mother."

"Cruel" is too strong, but there was yet another way she made my life difficult. Throughout my childhood and youth she told me how graceful I was, how some acquaintance had admired the way I walked. She'd wanted to be a dancer. Of course! With a dislocated hip causing a limp that couldn't be corrected, in her youth she took dance and calisthenics classes and an instructor assured her that, yes, if only her hip could be repaired…. Instead it became increasingly troublesome.

Mother told us two facts that connect me to her hip, so to speak, though she never saw the connection—or never, as far as I recall, pointed it out. When she was twelve she had an unsuccessful operation to fix the hip, supposedly by one of the leading orthopaedic surgeons in Vienna.

And ever since she was twelve, she wanted a daughter named Eva. This wish was so definite that when Paul was born she was surprised to have produced a boy. She had no name ready for him.

All this suggests that after the failed operation she packed up that urge to dance and held onto it until she had a daughter to pass it on to. Abstractly, I was conceived then, in 1913, when she learned that she would never walk without a limp or dance as she longed to do.

Not to minimize her affliction, realizing how lucky I was to be born "whole," but trying to live out the impossible dream through a child is not a good idea. I duly took modern dance and hated it, but felt I had to live up to being graceful, because that's what she kept telling me I was. My release came in Oxford. Having to learn to ride a bicycle with hand brakes, I practiced at night, struggling not to brake with the pedals (as on American bikes) and falling over repeatedly. Soon I saw that I was neither inordinately clumsy nor inordinately graceful. It was liberating. I could enjoy folk- and square-dancing and the easier ballroom dances without guilt at not being a Dancer. And I wonder, again at this safe distance, whether my becoming a real dancer would have brought us closer together, or just the opposite. It would be all too understandable for it to make Mother proud but also resentful, envious.

Clearly I'm still angry at her, and why not? The harmful things she did or allowed, and the benign things she failed to do have overshadowed my whole life. The depth of my continuing anger has at times surprised and distressed me. But her abandonment, her neglect, her failure to defend me against an abusive father, despite years of therapy, continued to doom attempts at intimacy. Most men who interested me were examples of barking up the wrong tree, while Adam, whom I spurned, was almost surely a "right tree." Even I could argue that, as an adult I *should* have overcome these early setbacks, but perhaps one life isn't enough time, and even competent therapists not enough help.

Anger was never the whole story. Balancing it are the many things she taught me, and my attempts to see her as a fellow human being, not only as My Mother. How did her early experiences—the pogrom, the multiplying siblings, and the long separation from her father—shape her view of herself, her expectations of men, and her unfortunate choice of a husband? Her disability, which affected me somewhat, was a constant burden she could not evade. There are also the many ways I admired her. Sometimes it was just cutting through a bit of cant. During her last decade, Esalen Institute appeared, one of its specialties programs for troubled marriages. Couples would get together and, among other things, take their clothes off. Mother scoffed at this: "They've been taking their clothes off together for years and it hasn't solved their problems."

Aside from common sense, there is a repertoire of characteristic expressions, whether the Yiddish *Meschugge* (crazy) with her extra emphasis on the middle syllable, or habitual German ones: *"Da kannst lang warten"* (Don't hold your breath), *"Bild dir nix ein"* (Don't be conceited), *"Ausg'sucht ist teurer"* (Beggars can't be choosers). (Some are not literal translations but the equivalent English sayings.) Despite concern about her weight she would occasionally succumb to whipped cream, excusing this lapse with *"Wenn schon, denn schon,"* a cryptic and euphonious way of saying: *"If* I'm going to sin, *then* it has to be worthwhile." While I miss her emphatic tone and her grimace of doubt, disagreement, disapproval—and miss her as an older, wiser friend, not as a mother—I suspect that, were she alive, what annoyed me then would still annoy me.

With her interesting blend of prudish and emancipated, she sometimes ventured into the off-color—though Vickie said Poldi never told off-color jokes in Isabella's presence. A favorite expression that I understand very well denotes difficulty choosing among too many things to do: *"Ich will mit einem Hintern auf zwei Hochzeiten tanzen"* (With just one behind I want to dance at two weddings), an expression known in Germany as well as Austria. And Mother told an anecdote about a woman buying lingerie for her trousseau. "White or lavender?" asks the saleswoman. "What's the difference?" the bride asks. "White if it's your first marriage, lavender if it's not." The bride thinks a moment. "Do you have white with lavender trim?" As surprising as the fact that people still laugh at this story is that Mother told it. (She herself gave birth five months after her wedding, but that wasn't often mentioned.)

The little Yiddish I know I owe to her, including the definitions of the clumsy *Untam* and pathetic *Nebbich*: the *Untam* drops something, the *Nebbich* picks it up; and also of *goyim naches* (gentiles' idea of a good time): King George VI and Queen Elizabeth are to drive through New York.

It's cold and rainy but people stand waiting for hours. Finally the royal car passes. We see a nose, and a white glove waving. (Though not *goyim*, we waited too.)

Most of her jokes concerned Jews, including Jews who converted. One has Isaac inviting his priest for dinner on Friday and serving chicken. The priest remonstrates: "How can you serve chicken? You know we can eat only fish on Friday." Isaac explains: "You said, *'Jetzt bist a Yid, jetzt bist a Christ'* (Now you're a Jew, now you're a Christian), so I said to this animal: *'Jetzt bist a Huhn, jetzt bist a Fisch.'*" (A related joke I learned later has a Jew becoming a Protestant, and then a Catholic. A friend asks why. "If I tell someone I'm Catholic, and he says, 'But what were you before?' I can say: 'Protestant.'")

More seriously, Mother also enlightened us about Jewish traditions, even as we honored none of them in practice: some of the dietary laws, some holidays, and the meaning of the Sabbath. From Friday sundown to Saturday sundown no one is supposed to work, not one's slaves (their existence taken for granted in Scripture), not one's animals, nor gentile guests or travelers. The idea of a "Shabbes Goy," a gentile you pay to do work for you, is hypocritical enough. But this has evolved into the idea that turning lights on or off is forbidden. It used to be work, but flicking an electric switch is work only symbolically, and this debased idea has led to an odd practice of some Hasidim in Massachusetts, who, when leaving Friday night services, walk (driving being forbidden work) down the middle of the street so as not to turn on the neighbors' security lights. Mother would surely scoff at this perversion of the scriptural idea of a day of rest, that *unintentionally* turning lights on just by walking by is work.

Another tradition she told me about that I didn't follow, and I doubt she did, was not to prepare for a baby before it is safely born—not "counting your chickens" in a matter of life and death. When I mentioned this to a (gentile) dorm-mate at Mount Holyoke, Heather said, "Yes, if the baby doesn't survive you'd be stuck with all that stuff." This was not the point in Jewish lore! Whether Heather's obtuseness was a cultural or individual matter I don't know; perhaps there are Jews who believe that is the reason for the tradition.

She educated me in other ways as well. She took me to see Paul

Robeson as Othello, Marlon Brando in the original production of *A Streetcar Named Desire*, Ruth Draper in her astonishing one-woman shows, in which she portrayed an old Italian immigrant, a flighty Park Avenue socialite, and many other diverse characters. Not only was it amazing that one person could portray so convincingly misery and privileged nonchalance, intelligence and stupidity and every other human condition, but with her solo words and gestures she peopled the stage with those she was hearing, addressing, or talking about.

There were concerts, including Handel's *Messiah*. Everyone stood for the "Hallelujah Chorus" then. Now some do, some don't, and when I found myself standing almost alone I wanted to be back in Carnegie Hall with her, with everyone standing. She taught me two verses of the "Ode to Joy," so I can sing along with Beethoven's Ninth. She took us to Radio City Music Hall, for first-run movies and a stage show featuring the Rockettes, a huge organ that was played as it rose out of the floor, and other examples of talent in the service of vulgarity. There we saw the Don Cossack Choir, which sang in gorgeous harmony and, dressed in boots, fur hats, and belted tunics, danced vigorously, often with swords. It seem odd for us to enjoy Cossacks, known to use such swords to do unspeakable things to Jews of all ages, but I share her love of Russian and Ukrainian music and dance.

Decades after she died, I find myself quoting her, in my head or out loud. Neither a *Rabenmutter* nor the all-wise, strong, loving Earth Mother she imagined, she was a woman with a hard life, a great talent and, surely, inner struggles that she tried to ignore. Perhaps she regretted the weekly routine she and Anna devised for us, but she clung to an inadequate husband rather than the small children who needed her, and later, abandoned by the husband, tried to cling to the children, who no longer needed a protective mother but an affectionate companion, that "older, wiser friend," more and more an equal. I do wonder how lonely and unhappy she was, during her unsatisfactory marriage and her quarter century as a divorcée. That night in 1958, when we disagreed about what she was sewing for me, I went home to my new husband while she remained alone in the apartment that had housed a family. Determined to be *"Mutter"* and not "Isabella," she did not confide in me about such tribulations and I, young and full of my own concerns—and old resentments—did not, as far as I recall, ever consider how her lone state felt to her. Perhaps she did confide in others. Among the papers I threw out when she died were carbon copies of letters to friends I'd never heard of; in one she wrote more openly about her cancer than she ever wrote or spoke to me. Some may have known of her unfulfilled longings, her regrets, known things about her interior life that I can only guess at now.

I've long replaced her as grandma, as materfamilias, having followed in her footsteps in various ways, mostly not by conscious choice: having a girl and a boy (and an abortion); raising two teenagers alone; not remarrying; for many years working mainly with and for women; living in respectable but not elegant digs at the edge of a wealthy neighborhood; sewing some, usually with pleasure though never with her skill; being opinionated but not always courageous in making my views known; showing at least traces of Zetlin arrogance; even wearing lots of navy-blue garments and hardly any black ones.

Now I suspect that much of what she did (aside from sewing and wearing navy blue) she didn't do deliberately, and maybe much of it not happily. But to make sense (as far as that's possible) of my own life, I cannot forget that, especially in our early years, she was not the mother Paul and I needed.

Chapter 39

TWO ZETLINS: LYOVA AND ANNA

*E*ster Zetlin moved from Kursk, Russia, to Vienna with her children in 1905. Lyova, born in July 1904, was then the youngest. Anna appeared on Mozart's 150th birthday, January 27, 1906. As the only one born in Vienna, she likely felt more at home there than the others, as she had known no other place. Playing with the children of other Russian émigrés and speaking Russian at home were Anna's most explicit connections with her family's origins. Mama (Ester) learned some German, Anna told me, but spoke Russian so the children wouldn't imitate her not-so-good German.

In an early encounter with Anna, which I don't remember but often heard about, she was in the hospital after her skiing accident. Two years old, I sat on her night-table, one leg crossed over the other, babbling away, telling her I'd seen Lyova—or Loba as we children called him. "Paul knows Loba," I said. "Do you know Loba too?" Paul was my brother, Lyova hers. It was not the last time I told A about B when A knew B better than I did.

As the two youngest, when little Anna and Lyova were close. When all six family members shared two rooms, older ones stepped over them and their games, which they invented themselves, using whatever objects they could find, cutting paper dolls out of discarded scraps. They also exercised, then undressed and washed. When Isabella and Vickie declared that Lyova and Anna could no longer watch them wash, the youngsters, innocent of any knowledge of puberty, retaliated: You can't watch us wash.

But when he was about fourteen, Lyova lost interest in little sister, drawn to Hesse and other boys, and to pursuits he would follow all his life: botany, photography, appreciating architecture, tramping through the

My grandmother, Ester Zetlin, and four of her five children: Anna, Lyova, Victoria,
Isabella, before or during World War I. The oldest, Hesse, was probably at work.
As I saw him only when I was two or younger, he barely figures in this book.

city or the countryside. He took trick photos using double exposures; one showed him trapped in a bottle, in another he was a Lilliputian next to a giant cat. He read his poems to Hesse, no longer to Anna, and she was hurt.

It wasn't always totally peaceful among the Zetlin siblings. There were arguments, "but we didn't fight like your children," Anna told me more than once. (Tact was not among her virtues.) Her diary reports that, when someone sent postage stamps, "We fought again." Hesse gave the good stamps to Lyova, the damaged ones to her and Vickie. Once someone gave her a box; the others kept trying to take it from her. At twelve, she asked school friends whether she was cross-eyed. No. "Then why does Vickie keep pestering me?" she asked her diary. In old age she still recalled Vickie's scolding her on the trolley: "Don't do that. Don't sit like that."

More seriously, she told me that once Isabella, angry at Lyova, threw a pair of scissors across the room and just missed him. My children fought, but neither ever did anything so potentially lethal. Still, her diaries recount numerous outings with siblings to the Prater, known for its amusement park (colloquially *Wurstlprater*) but extending well beyond. It had been an imperial hunting ground; Kaiser Joseph II gave it to the city as a public park. The Zetlin apartment I knew, to which I think they moved in 1918, was two blocks from the Prater. Anna might go with a friend or with Lyova "only as far as the benches so that Vickie [or Isabella] could catch up with us." The diaries show solidarity among the four younger Zetlins, along with contention.

As Anna recalled her past late in life, others were often stupid or incompetent while she was clear-sighted and wise, at least common-sensical. Her motto might have been that of Peter Gay's Tante (Aunt) Hede, which he notes in *My German Question: Growing Up in Nazi Berlin*: "Unfortunately, I am always right." Anna had a version of what I've come to call the Zetlin arrogance. Lyova had it in spades. In my twenties, I once lent him a favorite record album: lutenist Suzanne Bloch playing and singing Renaissance songs. He returned it next day, his only comment: *"Die kann doch nicht singen."* ("That woman can't sing"), preceded by an expression of contempt, between *ach* and *ugh*. Anna produced a similar sound when I bought her placemats and she said, barely pulling them out of the wrapping, "I can't use that color." I share that arrogance to what I hope is only a small degree, acquired via "nature," "nurture," or both. There was plenty of exposure to Zetlins. Paul and I lived with Anna when we weren't living with Isabella, and Lyova was a major presence.

Was Anna as definite in her superiority when we lived with her as she was later? Probably not. As we grow older we become more ourselves. Earlier inhibitions, or disguises, due to aiming to please or proving one's worth, fall away and a truer nature becomes apparent. I noticed this already in my forties: I no longer had to prove anything so it became eas-ier to admit I'd forgotten someone's name or didn't know or understand something. As for Anna's later self-regard and tactlessness, when we lived with her she was happily married to a loving man; later she had much to be regretful, even bitter about, a possible impetus for self-aggrandizing stories.

Sometimes Anna was right, according to my lights as well as hers, about others' stupidity. In her first-grade religion class, the (male) teacher asked what the sky is and why it's blue. Anna volunteered that the sky is air. The teacher told her to sit down and approved another pupil's reply: *"Der Himmel ist eine blaue Decke."* ("The sky is a blue blanket," or ceiling; *Decke* has both meanings.) "How stupid!" Anna lost respect for this teacher.

The Zetlins were emerging from an orthodox past and there was little religious observance, but Mama taught them not to say anything disrespectful about God, and when she was nearly eleven Anna wrote that she and Lyova were going to make a temple for Hanuka, "with forecourt, sanctuary, and Holy of Holies, 4 priests and 1 High Priest all dressed in silk." There is no indication that they accomplished this; her devotion to the project almost surely signifies an interest in making things, rather than religious fervor.

It was a very different childhood from what most of us are used to in the States. Besides lacking space and privacy, during World War I they were hungry. The diaries tell of Vickie's going to market early in the morning and returning three hours later empty-handed; of the rationing of bread and other foodstuffs; of standing in line for coal. As Russians, the Zetlins were enemy aliens. The two boys attended *Gymnasium* in the autumn of 1914, Lyova for his first year, Hesse for his last, but after three weeks they were excluded and soon the girls were also barred from school. They were reinstated before the end of the war, presumably after revolutionary Russia withdrew from it.

Life wasn't all grim. After working as a censor of Russian mail, Hesse was an engineer in a cigarette factory. In April 1918 he was enrolled in the university but couldn't attend, perhaps because he had to work. Anna and Lyova were able to go to a vacation camp through the efforts of Privy Councillor Kolberg, father of our family friend Lisl. He also enabled Isabella to attend a commercial school, which she soon gave up for her true métier: haute couture. (A good many French words seeped into Austrian German while French itself apparently remained elusive. One anecdote had a Viennese writing home from Paris: "The people here are so smart. Even the children know French!")

In 1919 and 1920, Anna went to a Zionist family in Holland to be fattened up after the lean war years. Though she went to camps run by *Blau-Weiss* (blue-white, the Zionist colors), learned some Hebrew, and was intrigued—as I was thirty years later—by the applied socialism of the *kibbutzim*, she never seriously considered making aliyah. When, after the *Anschluss*, Lyova was afraid that everyone would get out and leave him there, Anna asked her Dutch foster parents to send an affidavit so he could emigrate. "They wrote me back, if you had gone to Palestine, you wouldn't have any problem," she told me. "So I got mad, and I wrote them, You didn't go to Palestine either and heaven knows what's going to happen in Holland." The Germans soon took Holland, the husband died and the wife went to Palestine, where she was unhappy. Here too Anna's contempt seems justified.

She was certified as a kindergarten teacher but it was hard to find work. Mama could have taken Austrian citizenship after World War I but didn't, so her children were not citizens. The school Anna trained in was attached to a municipal kindergarten, but only citizens could work in public kindergartens, the only kind there was, so she worked privately at odd jobs and for three years had a play group for the Schur children and their friends. Such well-to-do families left Vienna for three summer months. One summer she was offered a job in Grado, Italy, June to August. She couldn't afford to be unemployed all summer but as a non-citizen she might not be able to return to Austria. She had, however, found a solution to this dilemma.

Walking in Vienna's streets in her early twenties, Anna would eye young men and guess which ones she could like. Crossing the Praterstern, the circle with monument at the park's corner, and finding a tall, blond, bespectacled man walking near her interesting, she peered at him so intently that he said, "*Fräulein, kennen wir uns?*" (Miss, are we acquainted?) She replied, "I don't think so," but they walked on together, went to a movie, and made a date for the next week, Anna unsure whether he would appear. He did and they continued to go to movies, and on hikes in the Vienna Woods, becoming *well* acquainted. She loved to tell me about an incident in the Zetlins' tiny kitchen, where she handed him a hot kettle. She thought men couldn't deal with hot kettles, but he held it and said, "What should I do with it?" He had been a smith's assistant and so could handle hot metal. That impressed her, but it wasn't the main reason that Josef ("Beppo") Jarosik became Paul's uncle and in due course mine.

Nor was the main reason her need for citizenship so she could take the job in Grado. But she told him that they had to get married. He had his doubts because it was hard to get a place to live together. But they married, she went to Grado, and they got an apartment; it probably helped that he worked for the Social Democratic Party. The apartment was in one of "Red Vienna's" public housing blocks, one taking up not quite a city block in the Ninth Borough. Freud's house at Berggasse 19 is in the same borough. (Later, when the International Court decreed that citizenship came with place of birth, she said, "See, I didn't have to marry you." She laughed when she told me this; I suppose Beppo laughed too.)

Their apartment had a hall, small kitchen, toilet, and two bright rooms and a balcony overlooking the Danube Canal. Beppo slept on a day bed in the living room, Anna in the bedroom, with Paul and me when we were there. Years later, I asked her about this arrangement. She said that, after growing up in two-room apartments—Beppo with parents and at least two siblings—they valued privacy, and they could get together when they wished. For baths, Anna set up a tin tub in the kitchen and filled it with water heated on the stove. The communal top-floor *Waschküche* (laundry) had washtubs and scrubbing boards, and lines for drying on the roof. I remember the floor covered in slats, and a friendly female atmosphere, talk and laughter echoing in the steamy air. It was in this relatively cheerful place that Paul and I spent the better part of every week, except a few in the summers, for almost four years.

According to Vickie, in 1934 everyone they knew was unemployed. This was the year of a left-wing revolution in Vienna—quickly, ruthlessly put down by the government, its artillery killing people in municipal workers' housing—and the start of a homegrown fascist regime. Early the next year we moved to Anna's, and Lyova, as far as I know chronically unemployed, often—perhaps daily—took us on outings around the city.

Vickie, source of family secrets (whether true or not), told me that he had had an unrequited passion for a young woman, which may have contributed to his growing up to be an *Unicum*: original, unique, by implication odd. Many talents, much knowledge, and impatience with those who were more slow-witted or less informed, or whose opinions he considered rubbish. He refused to shave and to brush his teeth. He wore the same clothes whether hiking, in the Alps or the Sierras, walking around town, or later in the US working as an air-conditioning engineer: a shirt open at the collar and probably short-sleeved, a suit jacket, pants not matching the jacket, suspenders, and work boots. A belt was evidently as much an imposition as shaving.

Among spotty memories of outings with him in Vienna is Peterskirche (St. Peter's church) in the Inner City; in Vienna in 1982 I again looked up, as half a century earlier, at the painted ceiling in the high baroque dome. At least once it was a happy afternoon in the western suburbs, among allotment gardens. His laughter, his approval, were like sunshine, warm and reassuring. But May 11, 1937, when I was vaccinated against smallpox (the certificate has survived, hence the date), I cried because it hurt; Lyova, impatient, scolded me. I remember because it was so unusual—I usually "good," he proverbially fond of children.

Another incident that stands out: the bright, breezy spring afternoon when Lyova took Paul, me, and Walter, a neighbor child, to the Danube Canal. At the bottom of a steep grassy bank a concrete wall, just wide enough to walk on single file, rises a foot or two above the water. We were sailing Lyova's paper boats when Walter, in the lead, slipped and fell in, grabbing me, the next in line. Lyova, who couldn't swim, managed to pull me back but couldn't reach Walter. I recall men running down the grassy slope. They pulled Walter out, wet and frightened but not really hurt. Soon I was lying, minus my clothes, in a large bed under a scratchy gray wool blanket at a police station. Paul, wearing a cardboard party hat with an elastic band under his chin, stood by the bed looking down at me with interest. Having gotten only a little wet, and only a little frightened, I enjoyed being the center of some attention. Lyova became the center of another kind of attention: Walter's parents sued him. What the outcome was, I don't know. He was no "deep pocket," more an empty pocket.

A dozen years later I wrote "How I fell in the Danube Canal" for freshman English, asserting that I had written about this incident at every school I ever attended and wouldn't deprive Mount Holyoke.

The time I fell in my uncle, who seemed to have nothing better

379

to do, was providing us with paper boats to sail which enthralled us so much that Walter forgot himself and fell into the water, grabbing my coat for support. I wasn't much good for support, so I fell into the Danube Canal too. After this there was a lot of stuff about mobs of people and scratchy blankets in the police station and the silly hat my brother was wearing and my uncle's getting in trouble with Walter's parents. All this is irrelevant. All that matters is that you know that I fell into the Danube Canal.

Having not deigned to tell the story in detail, I added some actual irrelevancies:

> My father once went swimming in the Danube Canal; this is illegal and he was amply repaid by getting near a sewer outlet. Maybe it was my uncle (not the one with the boats; he can't swim) and not my father; we have a lot of athletes in the family.
> Everyone at Mount Holyoke College should also know that the Danube is green, except in winter, when it is grey.

Professor Brock didn't elaborate on her one-word comment: "Excellent," so I have to take her word for it, though now I find the tone unduly flip, and it's startling to see those verbs in the present tense: Lyova "can't" swim; we "have" athletes in the family. Swimmers and non-swimmers, they're all dead and gone.

While briefly in the US Army Corps of Engineers, Lyova had to shave and wear dress shoes, belt and tie, but I doubt he owned or wore those when not in the Army. In Vienna he lived with his parents and Vickie, the other siblings having married. In the States, after a brief stay with us in New York, he lived for several years in New Orleans, where he worked as draftsman/engineer.

In the mid to late 1950s he bought a small house in Montrose, near Los Angeles. One of the first things he did was kill the grass. Grass is boring. He replaced it with a jungle of flowering plants and shrubs. Inside were his enormous record collection and a darkroom. He cooked spicy food, claiming it was the only kind that agreed with him. He had a sizable following of young ones in Montrose and was usually patient with children, amused by their sayings and doings—and impatient, often unpleasant, with adults. I hadn't deliberately turned Jessica and Tommy against him, but they probably sensed that I was less than comfortable around him—due to past doses of impatience or disapproval.

A few days after that outing, I ran into Addie Tepper on Market Street in San Francisco. The Teppers and Lyova had become friends in New Orleans. She told me that at a Tepper dinner party, either because he found the conversation foolish or because he was being paid insufficient attention, Lyova said "I'm leaving," got up, and left. Learning that Addie, who liked him as a friend and wasn't stuck with him as an uncle, also had her troubles with him made me feel better.

Months later, he responded to a letter from me, criticizing my supposed child-rearing ideas, justifying hitting Tommy with a reference to the Danube Canal, and lecturing me about our family. "In our family the men have had no say. Our father not at all. And I not either.. All Jewish names with -lin or -kin are feminine names: Scheinkin, Tiomkin, Serkin, Zetlin, etc." [This and other letter excerpts translated from German originals.]

In my (to him unconvincing) reply I pointed out that if his father had no say it was because he was in Russia while the family was in Vienna, and that Lyova wouldn't have been responsible if Tommy fell in the water; I could have fished him out. The matronymics (Zetlin, etc.) may stem from the fact that a child's Jewishness is determined by the mother's. But matri*lineal* (if this even is truly matrilineal) is not the same as matri*archal*.

Lyova lived a life of constant and mostly competent activity, and left behind photo albums with clever captions; letters full of puns and word games in German and English, along with suggestions, complaints, accusations, and news; and evidently lots of friends and friendly neighbors, though perhaps others besides Addie had had their trials with him. That Lyova was vulnerable as well as gruff was evident when Hesse's first wife died. No Zetlin but Hesse liked Ina, but he adored and waited on her even though he worked and she didn't. According to Vickie, Hesse wrote Lyova that he, Hesse, was more to be pitied for being widowed than Lyova, who, not having had a wife, couldn't possibly understand how it felt to lose one. Lyova was appropriately hurt.

His letters are mostly in a blend of High German and Viennese dialect, with occasional English words spelled phonetically as if German. *Anyhow* becomes *ennihau*; a one-lane dirt road becomes a *won-lehn Dreckstrasse* (the latter a literal translation). He poked fun at my name and George's, addressing an envelope to "Mrs. Eva Van Horn Moseley III."

In the mid 1960s his health became increasingly problematic, and in many letters he fended off well-meant advice from his sisters. So to Vickie on December 6, 1967:

> I've just gotten a letter from Anna, in which she very naively asks me whether I EVER consulted a doctor. I long ago gave up asking doctors. After all it is they, along with chemists, who are responsible for my being constantly poisoned. Besides, it's clear that I'm not the only one whom they misdiagnose. Equally naive is her question whether I won't get a telephone. Some time ago I figured out that I've managed to save $1000 with my not-having-a-telephone.

The petulant tone, the blend of know-it-all and paranoia, which must have been very trying to his sisters, became more pronounced as his illness worsened; the fact that he kept writing shows that he valued their concern, even while rejecting it. It was probably in the fall of 1968 that he wrote Isabella:

> This time I'm making an exception to the habit of our family and especially my own, not to tell anything when something bad has happened. On Friday I had a stroke. Not paralytic—I was able to walk and speak, but it was bad and frightening. My entire left half was like a piece of wood, and is still partly stiff....I can imagine how you will react but for God's sake don't come here. It won't do you good, you won't help me, you'll be in my way and I'll only have to fuss over you too.

The sisters did not give up, despite his orders: "I hope you all will stop persecuting me, before I no longer know how to help myself except by becoming nasty. (really nasty.)"

In January 1969 his tone changes. He writes Isabella that he is feeling worse and worse.

> As I long ago became convinced that my troubles can be traced back to nerves—certainly the digestion, the heart, the breathing difficulties and probably everything else as well—and I observed that I feel better physically too when I have people to talk to, I guess I want to be visited. After the stroke I had masses of visitors, but since people saw that I wasn't lying helpless on the floor no one bothers about me any more.

He notes that Isabella had wanted to visit earlier, but now she has flu and can't travel. "I don't have any luck," he adds, ignoring that she, with flu, isn't having much luck either.

I don't know whether she visited him, but he died six months later, in July 1969, at just sixty-five. His siblings all lived longer. For me he was still the adored, admired, talented, and amusing uncle who had admired and been amused by me decades earlier, but the later reality was hard to avoid and hard to accept. Toni also found him diverting when she was little and offensive once she grew up—for instance, a remark that referred not-so-obliquely to her pubic hair. Sexual frustration must have formed part of his inner landscape. He was one of those who is harder on family than on friends, neighbors, or strangers, knowing that relatives will stick by him—not that this was a matter of cold calculation, but his sisters did remain loyal. He had the crotchety self-centeredness of someone used to arranging his life to please only himself, and I suspect the bitterness of one who feels cheated by life but who won't examine his own feelings. In me he inspired a mixture of anger, timidity bordering on fear, pride, and love. Making him laugh, saying something that interested him, felt like a great triumph. But when no longer a child I was never simply at ease in his presence.

Anna too aroused this combination of love, anger, and fear. Her contempt, disapproval, ridicule were not as biting as Lyova's and though she was short on tact she was not devoid of affection. Because she lived much longer, I had time to grow up more and so was better able to defend myself. Mainly I found her crotchety ways amusing, as I had to deal with them only rarely. Gloria and Fred Santillo, who dealt with them daily—having fixed up an apartment for her on their farm in Sharon Springs, where she spent her last decade—did so happily. Fred often imitated her accent and baleful glance when responding to his witticisms: "Fred, dot is not funny," and they recalled going out to eat with her and having to change tables four times. Gloria knew how to manage her. Not only her medications and hospital visits, but her contrariness. When Anna objected to round-the-clock caretakers, Gloria said, "It's that or the nursing home."

I wasn't so forceful, nor, as an occasional visitor, did I have to be. While at home, Anna preferred a wheelchair to the prosthesis. On one of my last visits, she rolled the chair to the kitchen sink and pulled herself up to wash a dish. The chair rolled away. "Why don't you use the brake?" I asked. "Because I don't feel like it," she said, in a tone generally reserved for assertions of fundamental principles. I rolled the chair back to her and shrugged off her peevish reply. Had I not been there, she might have fallen, as she did several times, bleeding enough, thanks to a blood thinner, to need medical attention. I shrugged too when, on a visit right after my annual physical, I told her that my blood pressure was still low and she said, "Mine was low till I was your age." Or shrugged and smiled when she told me she hadn't expected to live so much longer than her siblings, and invariably added: "You're no spring chicken either. How old are you now?" It had been mainly a relief when she didn't want to move near me, saying "I don't know anyone in Boston," while Gloria and Fred seemed to relish the extra responsibility. I had been afraid of her.

Her "Nuremberg divorce" enabled her, as a single woman, to go to England as a domestic. After some unsatisfactory jobs as live-in servant, when mothers went to work in munitions factories, Anna became director of a wartime nursery in Lincoln. In 1946 she secured a visa to come to the US and we went to LaGuardia Airport to meet her. I have an insistent memory of dreading her arrival, which feeling I can explain now only by assuming that it harked back to the time we lived with her and Beppo. She could make days interesting and fun for little kids. But there must have been something else—her version of Zetlin arrogance? or something worse?—that made her arrival unwelcome. Did I sense whatever it was again in the way she laughed, two decades later, at what two-year-old Tommy said or did as he played in her Brooklyn apartment? Or did I blame her for the Vienna exile, as if I thought she'd forced Mother to let her have us all week?

In about 1990, a stranger took us for mother and daughter because we looked so much alike. Looking in the mirror later I saw the resemblance for the first time; it didn't please me. And I didn't cry when she died. On my next visit to Sharon Springs I moved a box of gray stuff off a chair. "That's Anna," Gloria said. We designed a small stone, noting her dates and her profession, and Fred buried her ashes in their yard. At a memorial gathering there, her several caretakers and others expressed affection, exasperation, and amusement. If somewhere deep down I felt bereft, that feeling did not erupt in tears. Resentment just about cancelled out grief.

What buried feelings did she have that manifested themselves in rudeness, impatience, and those self-aggrandizing recollections? Because he was a Social Democrat, so not trustworthy, Beppo was assigned to burying fallen German soldiers on the Russian front. (A search of the military archives in Vienna turned up almost no information about him.) After the war he asked Anna to come back. She refused. Then she regretted refusing, but it was too late. Marriageable men were in short supply. He married someone else. Why did she refuse? Was it resentment that he abandoned her in 1938? even if it was a rational response to a terrible situation not of his making or choosing. Or even older resentment?

Anna and Beppo were among the "athletes in the family." One day in the winter of 1933–34 they took a trolley to the Vienna Woods to go skiing, agreeing that he would go from there to work and she would finish her last run and go home. It was dusk, she ran into a tree, and it was a while before the ski patrol found her. As a result, one leg was amputated below the knee. Did she resent this earlier abandonment? He behaved appropriately for the circumstances, but one can understand a bad situation intellectually and still rebel emotionally.

According to Anna, when she met Beppo he was in the army and belonged to one of the two soldiers' unions, the left-wing one. More reliable sources tell us that these were not labor unions for soldiers in a national army but militias of the two major political parties: the Social Democratic *Schutzbund* and the *Heimwehr*, roughly allied with the

Christian Socialists. Anna evidently preferred to deny this more sinister reality, as she denied the even more sinister realities of 1938, saying that Nazi atrocities "must have been in another part of the city." Other family members also didn't talk about such things (with me), but Anna's particular degree of denial may have derived from being the only native-born child in an immigrant family, and from having married a native Gentile. She never denied her Jewishness but she might have been reluctant to see Austrian Gentiles as her persecutors. The Jarosiks were not anti-Semites.

In a turbulent time of war, forced separation and migration, even those most prone to introspection would struggle to be honest and up-to-date with their feelings. As a Zetlin, even after attending lectures on psychology in the birthplace of psychoanalysis, Anna most likely suppressed any feelings that struck her as uncalled for—which wouldn't make the feelings go away. Not only complicated feelings toward Beppo but also survivor's guilt: about escaping while leaving Mama behind. If she ever wrestled with that, I never, as far as memory serves, heard about it; perhaps she confided in her sisters, or sympathetic friends. At any rate, the bright, outspoken, hopeful girl and young woman, the happy young wife, buffeted by the ugly public events of the twentieth century, which she couldn't entirely skirt, and by some private setbacks, became an old woman who could still be affectionate, and grateful to those who cared for her, but who was as likely to be rude, impatient, and crotchety.

Chapter 40

VICKIE AND RUDI

$\mathcal{V}$ictoria Zetlin, born April 7, 1903, became the middle child, bossed around by Hesse and Isabella, excluded from games and secrets by Lyova and Anna. In Anna's childhood diaries Vickie often appears with a headache; on outings to the Prater, while the others walked or played, often Vickie read a book. Once Selig, their father, became blind and came to Vienna, she took him to the library and read to him, which made her both proud and at times resentful.

She wanted to be a librarian but the family couldn't afford the schooling, so she became a bookkeeper, working for Jacob Engel's wholesale dry goods business in the Inner City, a shop crowded with piles of linens and bolts of fabric. Vickie was close especially to Renée Engel, the older daughter, later also to the younger, Jeanne (in Vienna pronounced *a la française*). In old age, Jeanne told me how, after the *Anschluss*, Vickie ordered her to do something about emigrating. The parents had died and Jeanne, not used to managing difficult affairs, kept procrastinating. "Have you gone to the embassy yet?" Vickie demanded each time they met. Jeanne did go to England, like Anna as a domestic servant, and then followed Renée, who with husband and daughter had emigrated to Boston.

Vickie was often with us on visits and outings, yet I have few memories of her from Vienna. In one incident—a secret she told me decades later—Poldi, with a few days free, wanted a companion for a hiking tour. Vickie had those days off too and Isabella encouraged her to go with him. They went, and Poldi, true to form, propositioned Vickie. This was not in the program as she—or Isabella—saw it.

Vickie lived with her parents until she emigrated. She was briefly married to Emil Russmann, one of those marriages that had to do with citizenship—his or hers. She was the first in the family to leave, in the fall of 1938. Once we were in New York she lived with us until 1943 and was again part of our outings, to Camp Midvale or Macy's or Saturday afternoon movies. She had lived on the meager wages from the job at Purepac in a rented room, with no luxuries beyond the occasional movie, which meant a newsreel, a cartoon, maybe a serial film episode, and a double feature. Those movies helped refugees learn English.

By 1944 she was a bookkeeper at an advertising agency, and later a "media (or space) buyer" in a series of agencies. Each had its array of friendships, annoyances, successes, and indignation-causing incidents. She often regaled us over supper with the day's news—the indignation-causing type especially—so we almost knew this ever-shifting cast of Madison Avenue characters. (Some firms really were on Madison Avenue.) Many years later I took Vickie and Anna to a Rockport seafood shack. Vickie ordered a lobster. I assumed that after all those Madison Avenue lunches she was savvy about lobsters, but when it arrived she looked at it in dismay and said, "Now what do I do?" I replied unhelpfully: "Don't ask me."

Vickie met Rudolf Pordes at Camp Midvale and married him on August 24, 1946, Isabella's 45th birthday. My parents had divorced in June. Now Isabella, used to being married, if not happily, was single, and her long-single sister was married to a man who told her that when she came into the room it was as if the sun came out. It's unlikely that my father ever said anything so romantic to my mother, or even had such a thought.

Rudi was born in Lemberg (its Austrian name), alias Lvov (Polish) and Lviv (Ukrainian), on September 29, 1906, one of two children of Jakob, a cantor, and Rosa. Jakob left and moved to Vienna. Rosa died while Rudi was a child; by late 1918 he had followed Jakob to Vienna and was living with him and his mistress, an uncomfortable arrangement for a child. He trained to be a furrier and attained the rank of master in 1931, having already established his own business. He was also drawn to photography and art.

Four months after the *Anschluss*, Rudi fled to Brussels, where he worked as a furrier and lived with a Belgian family. The Nazis invaded Belgium in May 1940 and in a hair-raising flight he escaped to France. Not a good move, but good moves were hard to come by. The French police arrested him as a stateless Jew and he was interned in a series of concentration camps—not as horrendous as what the Germans invented but bad enough. Transit camps for those expected to emigrate, they provided little protection from the weather and much more mud than food. His talents as a furrier were useless there, but at Camp des Milles, a former brickyard near Marseille, having managed to keep a camera, he became the camp photographer. Among his papers is an *Autorisation* allowing him to go to town to buy photographic supplies. On one such errand he simply didn't return. He once told us about his escape, but alas I didn't record it. Extant documents give only glimpses.

In Marseille the Vichy police picked him up. "We're looking for Rudolf Pordes from Lemberg," they said. "I'm Rudolf Pordes from Lvov," he replied, and the police, ignorant of eastern Europe's shifting borders, let him go. He had cousins and a fiancée, Golde Senzer, in New York. Some help came from there but they often didn't know where he was. With the help of the American consul, he sailed from Marseille in January 1942, at more or less the last possible minute, to New York but apparently via Spain and Portugal.

In New York he married Golde and worked as a furrier. Women wore fur coats, hats, jackets, capes, stoles, and muffs, or wool coats trimmed with fur. No one harassed them on behalf of the animals. The most bizarre confection was the fox stole: two foxes, the snout of each biting the tail of the other.

Rudi, divorced, lived at 108th Street and Manhattan Avenue; Vickie moved there and Rudi became a fixture in our lives just as Poldi almost disappeared from them. Rudi's checkered past had left him an at times charming and amusing, at times maddening psychological wreck. On top of early abandonment, the Nazis and the French, came the lesser shocks of a major slump in the market for fur garments, and a burglary that removed clothes, a fur coat he made, some silver, and several cameras, but the burglars left an overcoat with Golde's diamond ring in a pocket. He either still had a camera or managed to buy one, for we soon had that photo session with me in my junior high graduation dress.

Late in 1949 Vickie and Rudi returned to Vienna. He tried to re-establish himself as a furrier and they tried to start an export business, focusing mainly on ceramics. They also considered exporting enamelware.

A brochure among their papers startled me recently: the German for enamel is (the French word) *Email* but there was no email in 1949. (The English-language web site of a Viennese bank used to tell clients they could reach it by mail, telephone, fax, or enamels.)

Extant correspondence details troubles with landlords and friends, likely due to Rudi's difficult personality. They returned to New York and Rudi became an artist. Many of his paintings (some resembling Jackson Pollock's) and collages, in which he used coffee grounds, chicken bones, and other detritus, were inspired by the atom bomb and fears of the disintegration or destruction of the world. He had one-man shows in New York in 1958 and in their local library in 1971, and pieces in group shows on Cape Cod and Long Island. They built a tiny house in Mastic Beach near Long Island's south shore. We often spent weekends there, the best times when we crossed a nearby bridge to Fire Island with its miles of beach and dunes and the surf rolling in from the open Atlantic.

Vickie and Rudi moved to College Avenue in the Bronx, their apartment soon cluttered with the paints, tools, and objects he needed for his artwork. And with magazines and newspapers. When they moved again in 1967, to Port Jefferson Station on Long Island, he had two floor-to-ceiling stacks of *The New York Times*, which he planned to scour for items to use in collages. The flaw in this plan is that the *Times* is published every day, so he could never catch up. Vickie persuaded him to leave the papers behind. When he died thirteen years later, one room was again half full of newspapers and magazines, some from 1967.

Not all Rudi's work was deadly earnest. Some of his "found objects" sculpture was witty. He could be intentionally funny in other ways too. The Port Jefferson lot became his little estate where he gave enthusiastic tours of the vegetable garden, the fruit trees, the goldfish pond—all thriving in the wasteland the developers had left—plus his outdoor sculpture and waterworks. In a series of photos Rudi, wearing Vickie's plastic raincoat back to front, tests a homemade fountain, drenching the raincoat.

Along with his art and garden, we enjoyed his adventures with the English language. After early schooling in Polish, Rudi had to learn German; in the late 1930s, French; and finally English. The family joke was that he was inarticulate in four languages. With Paul as driver, Rudi warned fellow passengers, "No backside driving," and he might admonish a child: "Behave you." (It works in German.) As we waded in Mastic Bay, ostensibly clamming, Rudi stepped on an object half imbedded in the sandy bottom. "Something there is under the neath," he exclaimed. Alan Watts's book, *The Supreme Identity*, became "The Supreme Court Indentity." Cemetery became cementery. Sometimes the humor was in German, and maybe intentional: when I told him that a friend had had triplets, he asked "*Auf einmal?*" (All at once?)

Rudi learned to drive. He drove Vickie to and from the train, on errands, and outings to beaches and state parks. Beyond that, it was hard to get him to go anywhere. When we lived in Vermont, we repeatedly urged them to visit. Too far to drive. So why not take the bus? But no, he couldn't take a bus when he owned a car. This reasoning aroused George's "sparkling humor": "Rudi," he said, "is immobilized by his car."

Port Jefferson is a charming old village on the North Shore of Long Island, the terminus of the ferry to Bridgeport, Connecticut. Port Jefferson Station is inland, like their new house in a new development not what Vickie would have chosen. She wanted a place in some hilly, wooded region reminiscent of the Vienna Woods. Instead she got pine barrens, not even very near the salt water that Rudi evidently craved. Rudi's success in turning that semi-waste into gardens and orchard was admirable. His charm and humor and Vickie's affectionate nature endeared them to neighbors, especially to neighbor children, who were often at their house. My children were less enthusiastic, although they laughed when Rudi drove us by a particular house and asked, "Want to see my dental doctor?" and when he said something had to be done "right away or immediately."

But such flashes of intended or unintended humor were the bright spots in visits clouded by the demands and anger of this unpredictable man. He was jealous of Vickie's sisters, Isabella especially, and often made their visits unbearable. He needed endless attention from Vickie. She might be cooking or doing paperwork but he would repeat "*Vickie, hör zu*" (listen), tapping her upper arm with the back of his hand until that spot was black and blue. He could be charming, funny, irresistible company one moment and an angry, abusive scold the next, over the years driving away friends and neighbors, some permanently. We felt it too. In

1974, at the first Christmas in our Medford house, Rudi offered to put up some shelves. As I told my diary, he

> needed help with boards so I asked Tom to help him & pretty soon Rudi was yelling. At 1ˢᵗ I thought Tom could cope but then I saw he was leaving. Rudi carried on, I argued with him— saying Tom is a person (which he denied!)—& V. got into it & was soon in tears so I comforted her, but he went on & on—V. had to take a tranquilizer—& they decided to leave, or she did & he agreed, which they did at 7:30. Some birthday. But it was nice till Rudi got started.

Tom was thirteen. It seems likely that Rudi, deprived of his mother and launched into an alien world as a child, was jealous of a boy who had a mother. At other times too, whatever Tom did or didn't do, Rudi would erupt in self-righteous rage. Then he would lecture me about child-rearing, stressing *Disziplin,* pronounced dis-tsi-*pleen*, which sounds more disciplined than the English word. He had a point, but as Rudi was childless and not particularly disciplined himself, he was the embodiment of the proverb: "He who has no children brings them up well." Poor Vickie. She knew that, once he got started, there was no remedy but to get him away from the unwitting offender. My diary continues: "I'll never get him & the kids together again. V. talks of leaving him, as she has for years. Hope she does it."

(In a letter [in German] to Hesse, Vickie gives a different account of this incident. "It was very nice till the very end, when Rudi and she had a 'misunderstanding' and we left sooner than planned in night and fog, literally in snow flurries and arrived at 3 in the morning." What she called the very end became that only because of the "misunderstanding," with Tom more than with me. She also admired my "large and beautiful" house, thought it a shame that I had to rent rooms to pay expenses, "but she does what she wants and nobody can say anything." She thought a smaller house would have been cheaper, which was not the case, nor did I "want" to rent rooms. It's sad and irritating to be so misunderstood. I hope I'm not misunderstanding her; she can't, of course, correct me or defend herself.)

When she and Anna visited us in Oxford, she explained that she'd agreed to move to Long Island to please Rudi, who promised to behave but didn't, and she was often fed up, not least with the exhausting and chancy commute on the infamous Long Island Rail Road, and so thought of leaving him. But next morning she relented. "What will become of him?" she asked. Behind that question lurk others: What will become of me? Is loneliness better or worse than sporadic abuse? He still adores me; can I give that up? What if he finds another woman? She did not leave him, nor did I stick to my resolve not to visit with the kids.

She kept working into her late sixties or longer, but often slept at Anna's in Coney Island, the long subway ride less an ordeal than the LIRR. Rudi dyed her hair red, so she would fit in with the go-go Madison Avenue crowd; soon after she retired it was white. After that Christmas fiasco, she had another five-and-a-half years of adoration and exasperation, accompanied by failing health. After a probable stroke in her late fifties, her eyesight deteriorated, and she became increasingly deaf. (Was that to avoid listening to Rudi?) She wouldn't get a hearing aid. I nagged her, feebly, as it seemed dangerous to be a deaf pedestrian, especially in Manhattan. They both had heart trouble. Rudi's failed first, on July 10, 1980.

I came home to find a message from Jessica, who was there when Vickie called and promised to go to Long Island that Saturday. I called Vickie and "She was concerned mainly with funeral arrangements & what he would have wanted, seemed numb." Tom agreed to go too. Saturday was the first of three perfect summer days. The trip down was fine except for the kids' tail-gating (emulating their father). We found Vickie quite calm. Only at one point did she start to cry and say something about '*heu-len*' (wailing), some time. When Jessica and I stayed outside talking, she came out to look for us. I said we'd be right in but we talked longer and she got angry and said we'd talked nonsense all evening and couldn't we see she was hurting and only controlling herself. I said, You don't have to control yourself, but she said, Yes, I do, till after tomorrow. Anna, Vickie and I had coffee and talked "nonsense." I helped her decide about a dress and pocketbook for the funeral, and went to bed about 11 worrying about what to say.

Vickie had asked me to speak at the funeral, on Sunday the 13th. It should have taken place within two days, but couldn't be on a Saturday. To my surprise, she'd asked a rabbi to officiate. He hadn't of course known Rudi, so I was the only speaker who had known him. I didn't want to produce the usual don't-speak-ill-of-the-dead drivel, but also didn't want to offend or embarrass Vickie by saying, in effect, that Rudi was a pain in the ass who alienated nearly everyone they knew. After a bad night, I woke up early and wrote my speech. It all fell into place, a corroboration of the theory not to force words or ideas that won't come, but leave the task to one's un- or semi-conscious. Here is part of what came to me:

> Rudi came into my life in 1946, when he married my aunt Vickie. When we think of Rudi, we remember a funny, charming, affectionate, creative person. We also remember someone who was sometimes angry. Perhaps he showed anger that many of us feel and don't show. We know he had many things to be angry about, and perhaps the main one was death. He suffered a loss through death very early in his life, and in his adulthood, after rubbing elbows with fear and death for many months, he escaped from a continent where death seemed to prevail over life. Death makes us angry. It leaves a gap in our lives, and the bigger the gap in our lives day-to-day, the bigger our anger and our grief are likely to be. Today, one person here is afflicted much more than the rest of us. I hope that she especially will be able to "brood over her sorrow," as the text says, not to "embitter her grief" but enough to "lighten the heaviness of the heart."

The text I quoted was read at a memorial service for Freeland Abbott, the (gentile) chair of George's department at Tufts, and some of it at George's funeral. The little I said about Rudi was true, as far as I knew him and his history. To my relief, Vickie thanked me and seemed to mean it.

She was left in a cluttered house in a place he chose, unable to go to a doctor, grocery store, library, or train station without imposing on neighbors or hiring a taxi, unless Will or another friend or I came to help. I soon went back, drove her to the doctor, and we took newspapers, magazines, and other stuff meant to figure in Rudi's artworks to the dump. Will thought Vickie would make a good driver because she was good at reading maps, finding the way. This argument seemed as silly to Vickie as to me. She did take a few lessons (she was seventy-seven), until an elderly woman, backing out of her driveway, ran over a neighbor child she didn't see. "I don't need that," Vickie declared. She sold Will the car at a bargain price, which suited his Scottish soul, as did the low number on the odometer.

She looked at old folks' housing in Manhattan and settled on Isabella House in Washington Heights, a high-rise building of small apartments with a common dining room, a small garden, a few other amenities, and an attached nursing home. The floors were covered in linoleum tile and most furniture was institutional; residents were allowed at most two pieces of their own. I found it dreary, but Vickie didn't, nor Anna when she moved there later. They took care of plants and tutored local school-children. (Washington Heights, once full of refugees and other Jews, had become a mainly Latino neighborhood.) They took courses at the New School and visited Hesse in Israel, old friends in Vienna, and Anna's friends from her wartime years in England. Sometimes I went to Isabella House for a visit and a barely edible meal; or they met me in town, one day at the Museum of the City of New York.

As they approached, I thought: were they always so small? Of course not; it was part of growing old. When I pointed out to Vickie, who had sensibly taken to wearing running shoes, that she had them on the wrong feet, she said, "No wonder they weren't so comfortable today." Two omens for the future. By now, at ninety, I've lost more than four inches in height and am daily annoyed by increasing clumsiness and forgetfulness. When younger people tell me they are clumsy or forgetful, I assure them it will get worse; older people give me the same message. So if there are still doctors trying to lengthen life expectancy to 160, they should first make sure that we have teeth, eyesight, hearing, bones that hold us up, and well-functioning organs and brains for all or most of that time. As a society we can't take care of more blind, deaf, floppy, drooling, incontinent, lonely wrecks waiting to die—and we don't want to *be* those wrecks.

In 1982 I agreed to spend a month in Austria with Vickie. She would pay for everything; I would manage travel and luggage. We met in Geneva, where I had some archival business and where she and Anna landed after a tour. I took our suitcases to the train station to check them for the journey to Vienna; the baggage man claimed to speak neither English nor German (which seemed unlikely in that city of UN offices and tourism), so I had to make do with my hesitant French. And when we had lunch in a lakeside café in the *Jardin Anglais* on a warm summer day and I ordered iced tea, the waiter brought hot tea. "I ordered cold tea," I complained, again in meager French. "It'll get cold," he said.

We spent two weeks in Kärnten (Carinthia), at the *Kurhaus* (spa) in Weissbriach, a resort village. Friends of Vickie's stayed nearby and she was often with them, so I spent mornings hiking and afternoons with her. We became friendly with our assigned tablemates (there was no shifting about), Eva Fuchs and Annemarie Pordes, a teacher in Hong Kong who went to Weissbriach every summer and had arrived before us. Each place had a napkin case with a name tag. The management, not knowing my name, assumed that I was Herr Pordes. Annemarie, expecting meals with her ex–husband and his new wife, was relieved that "Herr Pordes" turned out to be Eva Moseley.

I needed hiking boots and Annemarie recommended the local shoe store. I chose a pair, the sky turned dark, and it rained hard for an hour. Everyone else had left, so the owner and I chatted about my history and other matters till the rain stopped. Next day, Annemarie picked up some shoes and told me that he said: "That American lady must be Jewish. But she's very nice." Such unconscious—and in this case relatively mild—anti-Semitism was endemic in Europe.

As was sexism. A local tour company ran day trips to Italy in a van driven by Walter, an outdoorsy chap originally from Vienna who had married a local woman, with whom he also ran a small hotel. I went to Venice with him, and Vickie and I to the Dolomites. At the border, among a fleet of bikers was a woman riding her own motorcycle. "See what women can do nowadays," said Walter. "Yes, what can't they do?" said a male passenger, and Walter muttered under his breath: "*Folgen* (obey)." He'd told me that his wife got up before dawn and worked into the night. But some women seemed just as sexist. On the train, an older woman couldn't open the door or manage her luggage. "When ladies travel there's always so much baggage," she chirped, deprecating herself and all other females; and when the conductor helped her, she said sweetly, "How nice to have a strong man's arm to help." I wondered: why not just a strong arm?

We spent our other two weeks in Vienna, except for a trip to Obersdorf in Steiermark (Styria), the last place we went for *Sommerfrische*, in 1937. (In 1938, no vacations or pleasure travel.) This trip, in a rented car, was more for my sake than Vickie's, but she was willing.

1982's Obersdorf aroused no memories but I was enchanted by its *Kalvarienberg,* a hill in the village with, along a winding path to the summit, wood carvings of the Stations of the Cross, expert folk art, proof of heartfelt Christian belief. I regretted leaving my camera in our room, while aware that the artist/s might have been glad that my ilk had been expelled from Austria.

Back in Vienna, Vickie asked a passerby for directions. As he raised his arm to point, she said, "Isn't it...?" and proceeded to tell him what she thought the answer was. His look said: "Lady, didn't you ask me a question?" I've caught myself similarly needing to show off what I know; this incident was a caution to stop doing that. (In *The Viennese*, Paul Hofmann writes: "Educated Viennese share with educated Germans the pedantic urge to parade their erudition." Not-so-educated Viennese also like to show off what they know.)

We spent time with her Viennese friends, ate and shopped; went to an organ recital in the Augustinerkirche, which Vickie slept through (she was seventy-nine and not in the best of health), and to the Israelitische Kultusgemeinde to learn the fate of her mother. We visited Beethoven's house and a cemetery where a friend who shot himself in 1925 had been buried, although the neglected grave had been given to another family. Evidently he had meant a lot to her.

We started an oral history interview. After a session about her early life, up to my parents' marriage, she said I'd gotten her to say things she thought she would never tell anyone. I transcribed it, a slow, tedious process, and sent her a copy of the transcript. Foolishly, I reused the tape, and later couldn't find the transcript among her or my papers. The tendency to divulge things that others preferred to keep hidden was one of the things I appreciated about her, so it's doubly a shame that this ninety-minute compilation of her memories, with bits of indiscretion, should have vanished, even if her memory was not as reliable as she thought it was. When I asked her about something or someone it seemed likely she would have known, she said, "If I had known it/her/him, I would remember." Though twenty-eight years her junior, I knew that there were many significant people and things I'd forgotten.

There was no chance to continue the interview. On June 4, 1986, I got the news from Anna: Vickie had died that morning, fairly quickly, of a heart attack. I felt almost nothing, partly that it was all so far away, but mainly I thought it was because of my annoyance at her egotism the last few years.

Next day I flew to New York and for two days Anna and I went through Vickie's things, Will and Carol coming to help and to take things they wanted. Vickie had a lot of stationery, blank checks, pencils, Rudi's wallets, and other such small items, "and about the 20th pocketbook we looked in was the one with cash: US, Austrian, British, etc."

Having talked to one of Vickie's Long Island neighbors, I realized some sort of ceremony was needed but neither Anna nor I felt up to organizing one. Nevertheless, Will and Carol drove Anna and me to Washington Memorial Park in Coram on Long Island. Two young employees buried a little casket of ashes. Harriet Christman said a few words. Anna, typically, interrupted her, saying that many people at Isabella House loved Vickie and would miss her but no one would miss her more than Anna. I wanted to say something but at that point my irritation with Anna and the whole family was at its height, so I just laid down the roses Will and Carol had brought. Other former neighbors arrived late, the wife crying, unlike Vickie's family. The heavens wept too, as it rained intermittently.

So Vickie joined Rudi in the cold ground. She told me that she never did cry for him, which surprised her, but I guessed that it was because of her mixed feelings. Thoughts of what one has lost bring forth grief but also, maybe more intensely, memories of unfulfilled promise, unreasonable demands, and one's own anger at dashed hopes. I hope this is not the whole story of Vickie's life but fear it is the story of much of it. Her "egotism"?! Maybe after thirty-four years with Rudi, she wanted to be a fully independent person. I'm not proud of my stingy feelings for her, or my unreasonable impatience with Anna, who had just lost her last sibling, or the annoyance recorded in my diary—but there they are, examples of how readily negative feelings may prevail even when a supposedly mature adult has to deal with older relatives.

Chapter 41
POLDI AND OTHER STEINERS

*W*e must have visited the Steiners in Vienna more than once, but I have only one memory of a cramped room with a sewing machine or two and grown men standing around. I don't remember the Steiner grandparents; Antonie died in 1933 and Isidor in 1938. He was a tailor, as were two or three of his sons. With his first wife, who died of tuberculosis, Isidor had two children: Frieda and Hans. Antonie bore five more: Margarete (Grete), Felix, Ignaz, Leopold, Rudolf—and, according to my cousin Eva, two younger daughters who died in childhood. Poldi and Rudi were the only ones to have "legitimate" children. In a 1982 letter (in German), Rudi claims that Hans had a son named Helmut who "was raised as a Nazi," and Isidor had a third marriage that resulted in one more son. So behind the seven siblings and Poldi's and Rudi's children there are these phantoms with supposed blood (or DNA) ties to the rest of us, but unknown and so mysterious.

Grete and her wealthy husband left before Jews had to leave Austria and eventually lived in Bel Air, a ritzy section of Los Angeles. I wasn't in touch with her but did send her an announcement when Jessica, the first Steiner descendant in the new generation, was born. She sent a check without a word, as if I'd sent a bill. I might decide otherwise now but I didn't announce Tommy's arrival, so it was a surprise when she left me a share of her considerable estate. There had been no contact in between and I assumed she'd forgotten about me, myself forgetting that Felix wrote that she had asked "a few times" about me.

In January 1985, Rudi, who had emigrated to Australia, phoned me from Grete's house: "Grete died and I'm in the will for 5%.... Will be there till end of Jan…, wants me to come out, to see if I want any stuff…& so we can meet." As he said, it would probably be our only chance to get acquainted. My life was complicated but I made plans to go on to L.A. after a meeting of SAA Council in Washington in late January.

Rudi's first words, as I got out of the taxi from the airport, were, "You're much prettier than I expected." Not necessarily a bad thing to say, but earlier remarks had made me wary. He'd expressed impatience with changes in my plans; when I figured how many days I'd be there, Rudi twice said, "And how many nights?" When I changed plans again, he complained, "One night fewer."

I stayed in the maid's quarters. He kept trying to get me to move upstairs. "Nothing will happen; I'm 78 years old," he said to reassure me. The idea that this uncle would even consider incest revolted me, especially as he wouldn't keep his hands to himself. He came up behind me as I washed my breakfast dishes, put his arms around me and pressed against me. When I protested, he asked, "How should I express my affection?" Like Poldi, he couldn't distinguish between affection and sex. "A big discussion about touching," I wrote. "I explained, using Katie as an innocuous analogy, that that involves <u>two</u> people & if one doesn't want, then the other should desist. I doubt anything registered."

At a restaurant he flirted with a young hostess. "He actually touched her blouse close to her breast, & she smiled & jabbered away & kissed him goodbye. He admitted that was silly, to prove his attractiveness—but he does it." As we watched a TV program that interested me, he talked incessantly, peppering his monologue with such remarks as "You have nice legs," and "Can an uncle marry his niece?" Toni, another niece, having had experiences similar to mine, disliked them just as much.

It wasn't just the inappropriate sex talk. "When I mentioned the importance of economic independence for women, he agreed—but he never let his wife work (she'd just finished nurses' training when they married)—'gegen meine Prinzipien' [against my principles]." On the second day:

> I managed to have breakfast when Rudi was not around. He still wasn't later, so I sat in the sun to read. He came out & said, "Na, Sehnsucht nach mir hast du nett." [Well, you don't have any longing for me.] I already hated him! Cindy, the housekeeper, took us to a camera shop, where Rudi bought a Canon (he had 2 other cameras with him). I thought it might be a present; it was: for

him. Another walk (with Rudi) to the mailbox & beyond. Of course I walk too fast.

His complaining was as irritating as the verbal and physical groping. "He is always right, judges everyone & *schimpft* [scolds] constantly at other people for things he does himself. Told me I'm rude, that he's disappointed in me, etc. I wore pants all 3 days. 'I don't like girls in pants,' he says (& I'm rude)."

I probably was rude, but it would have taken a very thick skin not to be. One exchange is a good example of how provoking he could be: "… he says he will give some of his inheritance to a Jewish charity. E: Which one? R.: One for Israel. E.: Were you ever there? R.: No, why should I go there? E.: It might be interesting to see. R. (defiant): Were you ever there? —& then a brief tirade about my hypocrisy." As if I'd said he *ought* to have gone to Israel. On the last day:

> …he asked how I'd slept. So-so, I said. *"Du sagst nie entweder ja oder nein."* [You never say either yes or no.] *"Du schimpfst mehr als 10 andere Leute!"* [You scold more than ten other people], I yelled somewhat illogically & slammed my door. I'd been scolded for saying something at the photo shop & elsewhere & had enough…. The voice, the bad jokes, the blaming, whining hostility—a real double for Poldi. (But I think nastier.) He didn't speak to me all day! I had to go upstairs to say goodbye, we just shook hands!

I must have written him soon after the trip, for he sent this reply:

> I am sorry that our recent meeting was far from being successfull and I take all the blame for that. However I am sorry to say I am too old to change and the only alternative is well we will not meet anymore and writing of any letters is futile and I suggest we give it a rest for 4–5 years and then if something is worth while to write about we can give it a go again. I found your letter a bit depressing and I cannot help feeling a bit more attention to your home affairs would or could help a lot. I know I should mind my own business so in a few years write if any changes are achievd. By the way your

way of answering a simple question by slamming doors is very childish and unpardonable but this will not happen to me again.

Now all the Best for your future, Rudi

P.S. Your visit to Australia is quite out of question!

I'll visit Australia if I feel like it, I thought, but certainly not you! Hilde had her own observations of Rudi and family:

I have broken off correspondence with Rudi, but am in touch with his daughters. His wife Elsie is really a heroine, because she endures all that. In June he was again in L.A. and then came also to Vienna. This year Eva [Rudi's daughter] was in Vienna at the same time as her father, but made no effort to see him. A peculiar family. You're right that the Steiners are not a "close-knit" family. [Translated from German.]

Perhaps Eva had similar reasons not to see her father as I had not to see mine. Rudi complained more than Poldi and was more of a self-centered tyrant, but both were blind and deaf about appropriate behavior vis-à-vis a daughter or niece.

Ignaz and Hans spent the war in Shanghai, in the Jewish ghetto that the Japanese tolerated, where life was ever harder as the war went badly for Japan. They returned to Vienna and Hans, who had often been in trouble with the law, was killed by a car while crossing the street. I wrote Ignaz ("Nazi" before the *Anschluss*) before our 1965 visit to Vienna, to establish some contact with Steiners; only Felix had been in touch with Paul and me. Ignaz let me have his ticket for *The Brothers Karamazov*. It seemed stupid to see a German play based on a Russian novel, but that's what was on offer (as the Brits say). We had a meal or a drink before the performance. I found him an alien being and, having much to learn about varieties of Jews, could hardly believe he was Jewish. He drank, smoked cigars, and seemed rather coarse, with nothing interesting to say. Hilde was kind and I saw her several more times, once spending those four days in Innsbruck with her. Ignaz and I corresponded and he chastised me for

403

not replying promptly. Damn it, I thought, if I hadn't taken the initiative we wouldn't be in touch at all.

Felix, another tailor, "was sweet & gentle," Paul and Norma told me. He and his wife Grete were in New York briefly in 1940 and stayed with us one night. In a 1974 letter, Grete recalled that "in the morning I braided your long hair." A store in Fargo needed a custom tailor, which is why Felix and Grete, a milliner (true to her maiden name, Margarethe Grünhut [Green-hat]), spent the rest of their lives there. Felix died, alas, before I thought of visiting Fargo. Once I almost visited its twin city, Moorhead, Minnesota, as the Schlesinger Library wanted the papers of Ada Comstock, daughter of a prominent Moorhead family and among other accomplishments president of Radcliffe, 1923–43. Her brother's widow was being difficult about the papers; Grete wrote that Felix had been George Comstock's tailor, and "Mrs. Comstock is a well to do woman, but rather odd and difficult."

Later, at a Schlesinger Library event at the Supreme Court (with Justices Sandra Day O'Connor and Ruth Bader Ginsburg), I met Ruth Landfield, a Radcliffe alumna from Fargo. "I have an aunt in Fargo," I told her. "Who's your aunt?" Ruth and Grete were old friends, via Fargo's synagogue, which Ruth's parents, the Goldbergs, had founded. Ruth took Grete to concerts and operas and kept an eye on her. I went to a concert with them in 1996: Fargo Symphony Orchestra, which sounds unpromising but was excellent. In 1994, Katie and I stopped there on a cross-country train trip. Ruth, driving us to her lakeside summer place in Minnesota, on the way passing various Goldberg/Landfield cattle spreads, told us about her father's operation at ninety-one. As she waited to wish him well, prep took an inordinately long time. She asked a nurse what was wrong. "We can't get his dentures out." The "problem" was that he had teeth, not dentures.

Not everyone ages so vigorously. Grete declined slowly. Still in her apartment in 1996, she died in a nursing home, at ninety-seven.

Frieda, who is a total blank to me, was the only one in that family to perish at the hands of the Nazis; she was sent to Theresienstadt in 1941 and died there or in Auschwitz. Like the Zetlins an amazingly lucky family, to have given the Nazi death machine only one victim. There is no explanation but luck—not foresight, importance, or virtue.

Rudi told Paul and Norma that "he admired Leo but that L. lorded it over him." To me he wrote:

> Poldi, your father introduced me when I was fourteen years of age to Socialismus, later on to Sport like swimming, ski and hiking. But we grew apart, as I did not like the circle of socalled Intellectuals which he belong to, who criticised the Soc. Dem. Party and never did any constructiv work to help to convert the easy going Viennese to understand the struggle for Socialismus.... I was always looked on as a political embryo by Isabella's friends, despite the fact that I held higher positions in the Youth Org. Swim- and Naturfriends. Poldi...liked Opera and I was happy with *Schrammelmusik* [Viennese popular music].

As far as I know, Poldi had political ideas but was not politically active, and his only job in Vienna was the one at Pick's store. In Oxford I had a dentist named Pick, the son of Viennese refugees. "Did your father own a sporting goods store in Vienna?" I asked him. "My father was a professor at the university," said he, in a tone implying that I had accused Herr Professor Pick of being something lower than a horse thief.

In New York, Poldi—to Americans Leo— first worked in the Racolins' apartment buildings. Briefly he helped Elemer Kardosh, Lisl's Hungarian friend, make mannequins for store windows. Next he was a machinist; after the divorce, a bookkeeper at a home for handicapped children; and then an X-ray technician, evidently inspired by his stay in a sanatorium with tuberculosis. He sent me an album made by a TB patient. In California he sold shoes and then Electrolux vacuum cleaners door-to-door, winning prizes, some of which he also sent me. His last job was as a machinist for Pullman railroad cars.

Ethel, his second wife, had been married but was childless and anxious to be a mother. Antonia was born in June 1948, while Leo worked at a sanatorium in the Adirondacks. After our brief visit there that August, Toni and I didn't meet again until the 1952 California trip, when she seemed a very self-possessed four-year-old, sprawled in our father's lap, legs wide apart, fingering her crotch, something I would never have dared do so publicly. She was a small bright spot in those painful visits to

Leo and Ethel. She told me later that she'd looked up to me and especially to Paul. He played with her then; later he wrote her off as hopelessly irresponsible.

Did Leo want to become a father again? Toni told me he would annoy Ethel by telling her stories or singing songs after Ethel had put her to bed, had her almost asleep, which sounds less like a good father than a mischievous older brother. She also told me about her parents' ugly divorce and about contention with her mother. Ethel arranged after-school lessons, French and piano among them, her idea, not Toni's. Toni soon gave up piano lessons, but later began playing on her own. She claimed that, right after she resumed playing, she came home from school and saw the piano going out the door, Ethel having sold it. It's possible that the sale predated Toni's new interest, but to her it seemed a deliberate thwarting of her wishes. Later Ethel sent her to Europe—according to a letter from Leo, "to get Toni away from her boyfriend." She came to us in Oxford twice, first, as I wrote Robert,

> in December 1967, on one of those European jaunts paid for
> by parents who would rather have her here than in the Haight-
> Ashbury. [S]he had tried that and said Nothing was happening
> there. She stayed in Marin County with an unemployed Negro
> musician twice her age. She smokes marijuana and takes LSD, she
> offered me some of the former, but as she also bought material
> for two mini-skirts and had one of those Indian bedspreads dyed
> purple to make a dress of, I had too much sewing to do to "turn
> on"—which might have expedited the sewing or stopped it alto-
> gether. Anyway, I don't find ordinary, linear, three-dimensional
> life boring. She also said that she didn't want to contribute to
> the economy (by working, for instance) and when I said you also
> contribute to it by spending money, even your mother's, she said
> she hadn't thought of that.

While Toni was in Europe, Ethel, without consulting or even informing her, enrolled her in a junior college.

I have some sympathy with Ethel's frustration, if not with her ways of dealing with it. She hoped for great achievements by her only offspring, who instead became a lifelong flower child, with no particular skill or occupation, although, according to her friends, with a great capacity for love and understanding. She had numerous men in her life and one daughter each by two of them; she was artistic and drawn to drugs and jazz (and jazz musicians) and to yoga and other strains of Asian philosophy seen through a California filter. She seemed to think it too worldly and unspiritual to own a car, but not to drive her mother's car. For me she was familiar and alien, loving and remote. When my marriage fell apart, she advised a macrobiotic diet. Great, I thought, that would make it impossible to eat with any of my friends. Another idea was to lie down and listen to music I love. Not a bad thing to do but it wouldn't feed my children, pay the lawyer, or make being abandoned hurt less. After Leo died, she told me how close they were toward the end, about seeing his spirit leaving his body. She was the only one of his three children to ask about a will. (There was none.) A sign both of her sense of entitlement—fair enough— and, under the patina of spirituality, a hard-nosed sense of reality, which however did not extend to trying to earn some money. I'm trying to be fair. She was a dear person, and probably more deeply wounded than she let on, at least to me. About Leo as a father she said, "He did the best he could," without admitting that his best was not good enough.

Toni is gone, having died suddenly and perhaps unnecessarily at the early age of fifty-four. At the gathering in her memory, at Ethel's house in Stinson Beach, there was chanting in various languages including Sanskrit, and talk of Toni's being in the room. Perhaps she was, but not according to my limited philosophy. When the ritual ended and the floor was open for others to speak, I, having known her longer than most, led off, saying that my remarks would be more down to earth. "Thank goodness," the woman next to me murmured. If only a fraction of what was said that day was true, Toni had touched and enhanced many lives. Even Leo, who had worked at unfulfilling jobs to support us and then her, could understand the life she chose: "I am not too sure myself what is right in regards of our young people. We are holding jobs which we hate just in order to have a comfortable life. Isn't it better to do what you want to do and enjoy yourself even at the expense of somebody else?"

Much has been written about alienation of industrial workers and other issues of our economy implicit in Leo's question. Ethel surely wouldn't agree with his reasoning. I liked stories of how awful she was to Toni, for I found her awful too. Not that I blamed her for my parents' divorce. But she seemed bossy and opinionated in a way that didn't take others'—not only Toni's—views or needs into account, a kind of interpersonal stupidity. When I was unhappy at TAF and unsure what to do, she suggested various possibilities, among them: "How about medicine? I love reading medical books." I thought: what does that have to do with me?

I have no idea why Leo and Ethel divorced. After they did, a therapist told him—so he told Isabella—that before marrying again he should learn to live alone, but after a short hiatus he married Elsie—a German Jew, cousin of the photographer Alfred Eisenstaedt (best known for the photo of a sailor kissing a "girl" in Times Square on VJ Day)—who was too old to have children. She had never married and, like Ethel, hiked with him. She baked and cooked for him, some of which food—I recall rich cakes—made him happy but may not have improved his health. And I'm as sure as I can be without real evidence that he was happy not having to compete with children for this wife's love and attention.

"Since I have been married with Elsie, we always talk problems over as they appear and I never felt more relaxed. This was not possible in my former marriages…. Elsie is just serving me some chicken soup with home-made matzo balls, which I like very much." So he wrote me in May 1969, five months after surgery for stomach cancer. Elsie was a nurse and had been living with her sister Lotte, who was jolly and fun until she developed Alzheimer's. Elsie and Leo bought a "six-plex" in Berkeley, a building with six small apartments, in one of which they lived. "Despite I am through with operations and cobalt treatments I am still weak and listless and barely can gain any weight," he wrote in the same letter. "We went on a hike with friends. Every trail seems to be much longer now. My doctor said that I get the proper medication, so I eventually will feel stronger again. I am permitted to go swimming, but I only went twice because I just don't feel like doing anything." He did not "eventually feel stronger" but died on July 2nd.

I think I understand why Isabella married Poldi, attracted by this handsome hunk, a wanderer like her father though for other reasons, and flattered that he would look twice at a woman more than two years older who, though pretty, walked with a limp. And she smoked. He detested smoking. So why, with differences guaranteed to cause friction, did Poldi marry Isabella?

Externally it was a shotgun wedding, on November 14, 1928, five months before Paul was born. For some now unknowable reason they, or she, decided to have this baby. (Vickie told me Isabella had one or two abortions later.) Perhaps she expected it to be her dancing "Eva." Vickie and a friend, Rudy Krauss, went with them to the equivalent of City Hall. It's striking how handsome Poldi is in the wedding photograph. More striking is that Vickie is standing between just-married Poldi and Isabella. Not your proverbial happy couple.

Why did Poldi marry Isabella? Seen through the prisms of adult-

My parents' unusual wedding photo:
Rudy Krauss (friend and witness),
Isabella Zetlin Steiner (bride), Victoria
Zetlin (sister and witness), Leopold (Poldi)
Steiner, groom, November 14, 1928.

hood, my own marriage and divorce, and years of psychotherapy, he was rather passive. Poldi facing divorce makes me think of a worm fought over by two robins. Which woman will it be? A shrug, a grin: which one is pulling harder? The main thing would be to have a woman to provide a home base to operate from, as Dr. L. helped me understand. Staying with Isabella would be alright. Leo wrote me that "I always respected your mother as a fine & decent person," yet when this fine person, exasperated and hurt by his philandering, wanted a divorce, he was ready to comply; he had Ethel to go to. When Isabella regretted her decision and wanted to take it, and him, back, he might have agreed to that too. Vickie is my less than totally reliable guide but this view seems to fit the facts. After all, why leave a fine woman who wants you even with all the faults she knows so well? The other robin was tugging harder and not letting go.

I knew little about this at the time and can't say whether I was hurt that his children didn't seem to figure in his decision to leave. I used to want to be hardy and tough to please and impress this outdoorsy father. But by 1946 I had largely given up on him as a father, so shame is what I remember as the only feeling I allowed myself to feel, or couldn't avoid feeling. Another kind of shame was involved too, one Vickie told me about much later.

One of the few permissible grounds for divorce in New York then was adultery, which one had to "prove." So Vickie and Nunyu had to come upon Leo and Ethel in a compromising situation. They arranged to find them half undressed, Leo sitting on the bed in which Ethel was lying. After they left the place, Vickie said, Nunyu spat in disgust. It may be my imagination or part of Vickie's description that Poldi sat there grinning— which could mean crassness, or embarrassment. I have a vague, general impression of him laughing off uncomfortable situations, especially ones he caused, a refusal to be a responsible participant in a situation in which he played a crucial part.

Except when he taught me the rudiments of skiing or the back crawl, his presence became mainly annoying or embarrassing, even before the divorce. He would break out in song, produce a pun or a joke; almost anything would set him off, a word, an idea, a news story. I don't want to be like him, yet in this way I am. Something will remind me of a song or joke and, if I'm not careful, like Leo I may bore, offend, or exasperate those around me. I don't recall his jokes, only the strained, metallic voice, the self-conscious grin—as if *expecting* his hearers to groan—and the way he would sit stiffly with arms folded and jiggle one or both legs, broadcasting awkwardness. He might say, "Did you know that there is a *Leopold-Steiner-See* [Lake] in Austria? But it wasn't named after me." (There is such a lake and perhaps he actually said this.) Yet about the time Isabella said, "Poldi, I'm going to get a divorce" after one of his jokes, I came upon them in the kitchen embracing. There was still mutual attraction, now and then anyway.

I know next to nothing about Poldi before 1928. We heard often that his mother made the sons who lived with her pay for cooking gas. If they were working adults, why shouldn't they pay? This was taken as a sign of an unloving mother's stinginess. Perhaps she *was* an unloving mother and perhaps Isidor really was a "tyrant," as "Fargo Grete" remembered him. (And perhaps a child molester, even of his young sons?) One other legendary symptom of Steiner stinginess were the separate lunch sacks of the Steiner boys, while other hikers pooled their food—the likely source of my youthful opposition to interdependence. I imagine them sitting apart, guarding their own lunches, while others ate together. Perhaps Poldi married partly to get away from a crowded Steiner household. And, as the second youngest boy, with two older sisters, it's likely he grew up expecting to be doted on and indulged by slightly older women.

As I talked about him during years of therapy, a picture emerged of an overgrown adolescent, not totally irresponsible but for whom his new home was a place to get hot meals, clean clothes, some companion-ship, some sex: not a joint project for him and Isabella but one for her, the mother/wife to maintain, while he kept a job and contributed his wages—as he had when living with parents—but otherwise moved about pretty much as he wished. I can hear angry voices on a sunny Sunday morning on *Hofstattgasse*. He is going hiking and fends off her objections in a whining droning voice, defending himself from her indignation at being left alone with the children—his children—while he hikes a dis-tance and at a pace that the rest of us can't match. He didn't always leave us behind; there are photos of him with us at a beach along the Danube or carrying me on his shoulders on the way home from an outing.

In New York he often took Paul and me hiking, Once Vickie was walking with friends when they came upon us in Van Cortland Park, which we reached by subway and through which we'd hike north into Westchester County. We'd had lunch, Poldi was lying with his head in the lap of a woman, Paul and I sitting nearby. I don't remember this. Either it is thoroughly repressed or it didn't happen as Vickie said—but it fits with what I think I know of him: the infidelity, the callousness vis-à-vis his children. Vickie's tale of their hiking tour fits too; any female was fair game, related or not, adult or not, which is why Rudi seemed so familiar.

My cousin Eva, Rudi's younger daughter, who was closer to the Steiners than I was, writes that Poldi had another daughter, "way before" my parents' marriage. It seems to have run in that family (not *only* that one!) to have half siblings as skeletons in the closet, sired by one's father, a discarded lover raising their child alone. Assuming these tales are true, did Poldi ever see this other daughter? Did Isabella know about her? Did she believe, as I might have in her place, that she had won him away from a rival and now he was safely hers?

Memories, facts, and hearsay about my parents make me wish to see them not as my parents only but as two people, at times lonely, confused, frustrated, frightened. Both had much to be frustrated and frightened about in those dangerous decades, even if they skirted the worst dangers.

As a parent Poldi did a lot of harm. Aside from what he did to me, I've heard—it isn't something I remember—that he belittled Paul, as if it were reasonable to regard him as a rival rather than a dependent little kid. According to a 1983 diary, "Paul said when Father came to Anna's to eat, he sometimes played chess with Beppo. In 1937 Paul had learned the moves & soon he could beat Father, who didn't like it a bit." I was glad to record this triumph of an eight-year-old, who found something he could do better than the father from whom he had gotten insults and competition more than pride and joy. In 2017 my first great-grandson, aged five-and-a-half, beat me at chess. I was delighted! But I'd had a satisfying career, not, like Leo, only jobs I hated.

What was Leo in himself, aside from being a problematic father? What would or could he have become in more benign times? Did he have some unfulfilled ambition: to climb the Eiger or Everest? Make a living with his outdoor avocations? Or something else entirely? Did he give himself away when suggesting that perhaps Toni was right to do what she wanted "even at the expense of somebody else"? It amazed me that he earned prizes selling vacuum cleaners. I tried to imagine him charming East Bay housewives into letting him in; to me he seemed stiff and anything but charming. Was he so different away from his family? Did he really like opera and consider himself an intellectual, superior to his resentful younger brother? He didn't seem intellectual to me, and I don't recall even talk about opera.

In 1983 I joined a Sierra Club group, hiking from lodge to lodge along the Rogue River in Oregon. Mornings and evenings were cool, days warm or hot, and I mentioned to a couple from Berkeley that I'd thought of making pants with legs that could be zipped off to make shorts. (Zip-off pants weren't readily available then.) A hiker they knew had made himself such pants. Later they asked what my maiden name was and said they'd hiked with a Leo Steiner—the hiker who had made the zip-off pants! If Leo actually made the pants, or even just added zippers to existing trousers, he must have had some of his family's tailoring skill. I'd never seen him sewing. Perhaps he had the zip-off pants made, but who knows what other hidden talents, what secret ambitions, he may have had?

Attempts to see him as a person on his own, aside from being My Father, are tentative guesses, questions rather than answers, as there is so little evidence. I can conjure up a modicum of sympathy, even grant Toni's "he did the best he could," as he appears to have been "damaged goods," offspring of an emotionally stingy family. For me he remains primarily the disastrous father because he did so much harm. His "best" wasn't nearly good enough for his children, nor for two of his three wives.

> That we all are influenced by our parents and even grandparents is probably true [he wrote me exactly a year before he died] but I would not search too much to find someone to blame for my shortcomings or whatever bothers one. You have a perfect right to be angry at me and at the same time I believe that you realize that you don't know enough what happened between your parents. I was obviously the bad man leaving the family on account of another woman. A few years ago your mother admitted that she also was to blame for my behavior. I promise you, that, whenever we meet again and you are interested, I'll give you my version about that happening.

We never did meet again, so I'll never know for what behavior Isabella took the blame. It isn't a matter of blame anyway, but of understanding: psychotherapy is research, archaeology. And it wasn't mainly the divorce that hurt; the abandonment and abuse of earlier years hurt much more.

In the 1940s, entranced by the movie *Pinocchio,* I borrowed the book from the library. Carlo Collodi's nineteenth-century diction and moralizing were off-putting and his Pinocchio wasn't cute like Walt Disney's, yet I read the book *six* times. Decades later I realized why: it is the story of a father who misses his wayward child enough to risk his own life to find him.

A great-grandmother entering my tenth decade, I'm still partly the little kid wanting to be cared for by a loving man who wants to spend time with me, for whom I'm neither a competitor nor a sex toy but a source of parental joy. I'm awed by women who speak or write about their fathers with true affection. The first impulse is not to believe them; the second, to envy them.

AFTERWORD: HOW LONG IS FOREVER?

A certain Zionist web site called me a "fake Holocaust Survivor," although I've always denied being a Survivor; we were refugees. Some who also left before Nazi ethnic cleansing became genocide call themselves Survivors, but true Survivors lived through the horror in Europe—in the camps, hidden by courageous Gentiles, resisting, or just surviving.[14] To claim the designation "survivor" when one escaped occupied, terrorized Europe is to dishonor those who lived through it all. Some may see suffering as glamorous and worth competing about, but I think that those who have not been oppressed ought to be humbly grateful and not solicit gratuitous sympathy.

My father was too young for military service in World War I and too old for World War II, for which my brother was too young. George was in Vietnam and Laos after the Vietnamese drove the French out and before the US was in a shooting war there. Tom was too young for Vietnam and avoided the draft. So it was just Beppo in the Wehrmacht, and Lyova in the Army Corps of Engineers, briefly and stateside.

I was in California or Europe when major hurricanes struck the northeast, felt only minor earthquakes in Vienna and California, and otherwise skirted natural disasters. We Moseleys skirted the Six-Day War in 1967 after skirting the spillover of the Cultural Revolution in Hong Kong. I drafted this chapter on a flight to Los Angeles while a bomb threat emptied the airport; when we landed all was back to normal.

Along with skirting disasters, I've sometimes been in the right place at the right time. During the Depression my family was just well enough off that I had no sense of deprivation; I grew up and older with an expanding economy, and though it didn't seem so wonderful, there was an underlying assumption of increasing possibilities that few now share.

I could stay home during our children's early years, George's income keeping us well above subsistence—never worried about our financial future.

More striking is the timing of my involvement with the Nature Friends (NFA) and the Schlesinger Library. When we first knew Camp Midvale, the NFA were solidly behind the US *and* the USSR in their common battle against fascist enemies. Not until I grew away from the NFA did the cracks appear, with the disillusionments of the Cold War and the un-American witch hunts, which threw a pall over American society generally, as the witch hunts tore the NFA apart. (I mean that the witch hunts were "un-American.") In the early 1950s a high-school friend and his much younger brother saw a movie about China during World War II. Little brother was baffled: "Are the Chinese the good guys or the bad guys?" They had been good guys during the war, but once the Communists won they became bad guys, just one sign that victory in World War II was not enough to secure the world of peace and "brother-hood" of our United Nations Hymn. Its birth, foretold in the song, is still in the future, if, given the way humans are, it is even possible; it should probably resemble the blend of *well-regulated* capitalism and socialism that the US used to have (without the racism, militarism, crypto-imperialism, and exceptionalism) and that much of Europe has had even longer. I once pointed out to brother-in-law Colonel Henry Moseley the irony that our military, supposedly defending the "free market," lives under socialism. He said brightly, "That's right!"

A quarter century after the Midvale bonfire celebrating Japan's surrender, I stumbled on the perfect job, at first not recognizing it as that. Thanks to the women's movement, the Schlesinger Library grew phenomenally—in holdings, staff, users, budget, publications, space, events, projects. During twenty-eight years there, I learned a lot of history and what our Chinese colleagues called archivology, and gained confidence about public speaking and managing a staff. No longer a non-joiner, I found work with professional associations mostly gratifying; archivists were lively and congenial, not the pale, dusty moles of the stereotype; my work made me a feminist; and it was gratifying to be part of the metamorphosis of an obscure little library into a prestigious institution, recognized in a *New York Times* editorial as a "national treasure." Through each I had a small part in controversial movements that protested, and to a degree changed, the status quo, in the case of Midvale labor rights, racial equality, and perhaps (though we didn't call it that) environmentalism; with the library, women's liberation and women's history. Unlike George, who seemed not to have found his true vocation—work that felt meaningful to him and provided a livelihood—I did find mine, by a happy accident. Mother and I had master's degrees of two different sorts, and were both lucky in finding, she early, I late, work that, more than a job, was a vocation, work that said to each of us: this needs to be done and you are just the person to do it.

My oldest friend, Alex Zwerdling—fellow Holocaust refugee, Kiddie Camper, Nature Friends Scout, and Bronx Science graduate—read early versions of some of the foregoing chapters and, as writer and English professor, gave me some good advice. Oddly, through most of our seventy-five-year friendship (he died in 2017), we didn't talk about how we got from Austria to the US. As he gave me memoir advice, he sent an essay about the Zwerdlings' coming to America: he and his parents were among the few passengers allowed to disembark in Havana from the ship *St. Louis*, which was turned away from the US and Canada and sailed back to Europe; many of its Jewish-refugee passengers were murdered by the Nazis. Alex suggested that the fears of 1938 Vienna and the dislocation of exile made me hesitant to assert myself, but I believe that what transpired in my family was more influential in those years than any public events: Anna seemed to have a rosy view of the Viennese, and Mother sheltered us from ugly realities.

It's impossible to assess definitively the effect of the Nazis on my life. I've speculated that I was triply deluded: that the *Anschluss* was good news for Paul and me, that I had somehow caused our return home, and that our parents were better parents than Anna and Beppo—deluded especially about Poldi vs. Beppo. I couldn't make Poldi loving as he wasn't, and I couldn't *make* Beppo loving as he already was! It's also possible that Beppo wasn't quite as wonderful as I remember him, and so much else about the Zetlins, Steiners, and Jarosiks is simply unknowable now.

As far as education, work, housing, and life's amenities go, I probably did better in the US than I would have in an independent, not-at-war

Austria—but there are so many conditions-contrary-to-fact involved that that's only a guess. (And I don't accept the very American idea that "you can be anything you want to be." It isn't only such drastic events as war or pogrom that impose limits and prove that we aren't totally free agents, subject only to our own will. I didn't aim to be an archivist, not being aware of that profession.) Nor am I sure how much exile and displacement to America disturbed me. In *Lost in Translation,* Eva Hoffman writes bitterly about her exile from Poland to Canada, and from Polish to English, but she was thirteen, an age when one hates to be torn from school and friends, one's embryonic own world separate from the parental one. I at seven and my children as pre-teens adapted to new places pretty readily. Once they're teens it's best to leave them in place if possible.

When I try to grasp what I perceived and felt in 1939, during the packing and moving, train and ship, it seems mainly an adventure—a *safe* adventure. My parents and Paul are there, and in New York Vickie too. I'm never mistreated or even yelled at by a German in uniform. My parents kept their anxieties to themselves, or maybe, relieved at our rescue from Dachau and Vienna, they felt sure that all would be well—as, relatively speaking, it was.

If those in my parents' generation suffered from survivor's guilt, they never spoke of it to me. Isabella, Vickie, Lyova, Anna—left their old, blind mother behind, but even when, in Vienna in 1982, Vickie and I learned her fate, Vickie was not visibly or audibly particularly moved or disturbed; she was more agitated about the friend who shot himself in 1925. How were relations between Ester and her children? I sense coolness, but there is no one to ask, and if there were, how truthful would the answer be?

Of course Paul and I neither could, nor had to, choose which exile we preferred. The Zetlins did not freely choose to move from Kursk to Vienna; the decision was thrust on them by military and political events, as was my family's decision—if it can be called a decision—to leave Vienna. Costs of exile pale next to what we escaped.

We were transplanted *from* a city that had, in my parents' youth, lost its empire and become the "hydrocephalic" capital of much-shrunken Austria, *to* the largest city of an already powerful country. A 2010 symposium—"Is America in Decline?"—helped me see that I had involuntarily become a citizen and taxpayer of "the world's only superpower," in total disagreement with its imperial aims and actions, appalled at its military command structure for the entire globe. Is the US in decline? I hope so. That is, I want it to give up its imperial ambitions, even as the supposed world's policeman (police are supposed to prevent and subdue violence, not instigate it, as the US so often does) and supposed promoter of democracy, to stop considering itself "exceptional" and become one country among all the 190+ others, a cooperative member of the world community rather than, often, a bully[15]. The *process* of decline may well be painful but the result should be a more humane existence at home and a friendlier presence abroad.

Aside from such political considerations, one price we paid was the "out-of-placeness" that Edward Said wrote about. Not that all those who have *not* known exile feel happily at home where they find themselves. Robert Hightower and I were probably drawn together, in part, by a common feeling of not fitting in at Harvard. He was born in Oklahoma; raised by grandparents in Indiana, then by his father in Colorado; later settled in Cambridge and Newton, Massachusetts, with stints in Germany, China, England, and Canada. Striking out on your own as a young adult is different from being forced to leave a place where you have roots; yet perhaps "mobility," which sounds active and upbeat, entails some of the same psychic cost as forced exile. And, again perhaps, had I been able to grow up in Vienna, I might have had less money, fewer possessions, a smaller dwelling, a less interesting career, but a feeling of being *rooted* in my native paradise, the feeling Berkley's lady had, and lost.

In 2009 evidence of the cost of being *up*rooted took me by surprise. Reading a passage in Carl Zuckmayer's memoir, where he reels off the names of mountains visible from a favorite spot near Salzburg—including Dachstein, and another peak near Wolfgangsee, about which lake there is a song I grew up with—I began to weep, with a long-buried sense of loss and longing. It's deeper in my psyche than I knew, as a child's feeling of being at home in a magically beautiful land full of sweet possibilities, the mountains huge, benign, protective; it exists side by side with a more realistic view of Austria, of what cruelty some Austrians were capable of, as well as how forbidding and dangerous mountains can be—like some large, handsome people. How different this loss is from anyone's lost childhood is probably anyone's guess.

Still, even if I'm never totally at home and still long for an Austria that never was, it is surely much easier to cope with changes of language, climate, money, food, surroundings, culture, at seven than as a teen or adult. For me, everything that followed arrival in New York was just my life as circumstances, people around me, and my own often tentative will made it, with only occasional reminders of being a stranger in a strange land—luckily in a city with many similar new strangers.

As for the adults, while I admire how well Zetlins and Steiners coped with our new world, not surprisingly they were the same people as before; relations among them and with us children didn't miraculously become ideal.

What was surprising to me, and impressive, was to see how Germany (contrary to the wishes of some Germans) has memorialized its own enormous crime. For years after our quick drive through it in 1965 I refused to go to Germany, but Katelin and I visited Dachau in 1997 and saw what sort of bunkroom Poldi slept in. Later I visited the Jewish Museum in Berlin, the mansion where the *Wannsee Konferenz* took place, and the former Gestapo headquarters in Cologne, the last two featuring copious text about Nazi atrocities. Has any other country done as much to make people aware of its own crimes? Ours hasn't, although it's being pushed to do so as I write.

And I suspect that many white people still believe that "They don't value human life as we do" and that "They only understand violence." "They" are non-white people, whether Japanese, Algerian, Vietnamese, Congolese, Palestinian—people suffering, as the political satirist Mark Russell put it, from "criminal swarthiness"—while the speaker is a "civilized" white person (American, European, Canadian, Israeli) in conflict with the "lesser breed" in question. Often the violence has been provoked by invasion, exploitation, oppression. And nearly always it is *we* white folks who do not value *their* lives. See the unequal attention paid to one or a few American or Israeli hostages or casualties, versus dozens, hundreds, even thousands of "others." Decapitating hostages is brutal; is bombing from 35,000 feet, or with drones controlled from the other side of the world, less brutal?

Almost the first thing I did when I retired in 1999 was to rejoin the (dormant) Cambridge Archives Committee (CAC), and start two other archives-related projects: an exhibition, *Growing Up Is Hard to Do: Harvard's Special Collections Document Some Trials of Our First 22 Years*; and an oral history project at The Cambridge Homes (TCH), the city's oldest retirement home. After some of us surveyed various repositories, the CAC—with the indispensable efforts of my co-chair, Charles Sullivan, director of the Cambridge Historical Commission—succeeded in getting a Cambridge history room included in the plans for the expanded main library, while I did a few interviews with TCH residents and organized the exhibition. (Charles kindly writes that he wasn't the indispensable one but only "provided the tables and chairs" for meetings.) Being more or less in charge of all three, even writing a (successful) grant proposal, resembled going to work, without the paycheck.

Soon I started working for other causes, using archival contacts to find repositories for the records of the organizations I worked with. One was the Funeral Consumers Alliance of Eastern Massachusetts (FCAEM), formerly called Memorial Society (MS). I'd been a member since reading Jessica Mitford's *The American Way of Death,* an enlightening, and at times amusing, exposé of funeral industries that gave MS a big boost in membership. We do educational programs, publish a newsletter, survey funeral homes' services and prices, and staff a phone line to provide advice on after-death care. Through FCAEM, I found others interested primarily in green or natural burial and joined the effort to find suitable, affordable land for a green burial ground, a search we continue as Green Burial Massachusetts, Inc. For me this is mainly a way to return what is left when we die to the soil, without which there would be no human life.

Along with these efforts looking toward the inevitable, I turned to political work. In Medford I'd been active in the nuclear-freeze movement and the Pledge of Resistance opposing US actions in Central America. When I moved to Cambridge I'd joined Massachusetts and Cambridge Peace Action, and helped them merge as MAPA, which has become a leader in peace and progressive campaigns; for some years I ran a fund-raising concert series, and helped plan and carry out other campaigns and events. When some leading members urged MAPA to take on Israel/Palestine as one of its concerns, I was at first opposed because other organizations that worked entirely on that were better informed. But then, recognizing how

The regulars at the weekly anti-war vigils in Copley Square,
Boston Public Library in the background, early 2000s. L to R: Eva, Michael Gilroy,
Cornelia Sullivan, Joe Kebartas, Elaine Antonia. Photo by a European tourist; some,
surprised at our dissent, asked us: "Are you Americans?"

central to US foreign policy the US-Israel tie is, I became a founding member of MAPA's Palestine-Israel Working Group (PIWG), which focuses almost entirely on changing US policy toward Israel.

When Israel was founded, I was entranced by the kibbutz idea, socialism not just for recreation, as with the Nature Friends, rather a total way of life. But for decades Israel was barely on my horizon, until 1982, when I considered buying Israel bonds, as Vickie and Anna did. Just then Israel invaded Lebanon. That gave me pause—and not only me—and gradually I became more aware of the situation of the Palestinians, partly thanks to a book by George's friend Gloria Emerson: *Gaza, A Year in the Intifada: A Personal Account from an Occupied Land.* In 2007 I joined a Cambridge group for ten days mainly in Bethlehem, with time in Jerusalem and Hebron. We learned about Palestinian life under occupation, saw Hebrew graffiti saying "Death to Arabs," and much else that made clear that Israel wants all the land between the Jordan River and the Mediterranean for a Jewish state, with as few non-Jews as possible.

Through PIWG's work: a conference in 2015 and lobbying for or against bills in Congress and the Massachusetts legislature, and thanks to the Bethlehem trip and to other books besides Gloria's, I've tried to sort out what I think and feel about Israel, as a Holocaust refugee and an American voter and taxpayer. Attitudes toward it among PIWG members vary but we all agree that Palestinians should have all the same rights as Jewish Israelis, which is not the case now, whether they live in the West Bank, Gaza, or Israel proper. Israel has dozens of discriminatory laws making non-Jews at best second-class citizens.

In the nineteenth century, Jewish "pioneers" mainly from Europe began to move to Palestine, a province of the Ottoman Empire. As in the Moses story in Exodus, there were already people in the Promised Land, with towns, agriculture, and a well-developed society. The Zionist assumption was that, after two millennia, Jews were returning to their homeland. There are questions about this assumption. Max Dimont, in *Jews, God and History*, wrote that in fifth-century Italy "perhaps a third of the Jews were not descendants of Abraham and Moses. Their ancestors were former pagans who converted to Judaism," and that in 740 the king of Khazar, a Tatar people, converted his whole kingdom to Judaism. Yet Zionists, only maybe descended from ancient Israelites, claim the Land *[Eretz]* of Israel because Israelites lived there 2000 years ago, while Palestinians who were expelled from their houses and towns only decades ago do not, according to every Israeli government, have the same "right of return."

Further complexities about our ethnicity: excavations by two Jewish archaeologists, Israel Finkelstein (an Israeli) and Neil Asher Silberman, of early Israelite villages show "that the people who lived in those villages were indigenous inhabitants of Canaan who only gradually developed an ethnic identity that could be termed Israelite." We were taught that Jews don't proselytize, but Shlomo Sand (emeritus professor at Tel Aviv University) writes that Jews have at times actively proselytized; that many married gentiles; that the Romans didn't expel whole peoples; that some Jews scattered during Roman times; and that many, even most, stayed put and, when Arabs conquered the area, most converted to Islam. So it's possible, even likely, that some Palestinians are descended from ancient Israelites while some modern Jews are not. The English translation of Sand's book is called *The Invention of the Jewish People*. The idea of a Jewish people is as questionable as the idea of a Christian people or a Buddhist people.

Does it matter? Theoretically, no—we're all one human family, so it could just be some interesting genealogy—but it does matter because the usual story has been, and is, used to justify not only the establishment of Israel but its push to settle and claim more and more of the land, even though that violates several UN resolutions, including the one that established a Jewish state (along with a mandated but never realized Palestinian state).

Among complicated feelings about Israel is a wish that that small region can develop true democracy and peaceful, satisfying lives for everyone there, Jewish and gentile, even if that seems a fantasy now. Three other things interest and worry me. Journalist and professor Peter Beinart wrote about one in *The Crisis of Zionism*: that many Jews still believe we are all victims, even though many of us are anything but. Jews in the US are represented in the arts, academe, sciences, and professions in disproportionately large numbers, as they were in my childhood Vienna. And here Jews have been Cabinet members and other prominent appointed and elected officials. Yet victimhood is hard to give up. It reminds me of my own and Vickie's penchant for indignation, the seductiveness of feeling wronged, whether or not one really is wronged. Israeli author A.B. Yehoshua suggests a reason for the temptation: "[O]ur having been victims does not accord us any special moral standing. The victim does not become virtuous for having been a victim. Although the Holocaust inflicted a horrible injustice on us, it did not grant us a certificate of everlasting righteousness. To be moral you must behave ethically. The test of that is daily and constant."

Second, Israel should not be immune to criticism. A concerted, largely successful effort, spearheaded by the International Holocaust Remembrance Alliance (IHRA), stipulates that criticism of Israel is anti-Semitism; all fifty US governors signed on, and the Pope, and many others. But as a sovereign country Israel is open to criticism of its policies and actions, along with praise and any other judgment, just like all the other countries in the world.

Third, on National Public Radio someone in Israel mentions Palestinians' human rights; an Israeli woman says, "They're not human." And a magazine article quotes a rabbi on the West Bank: "There is something infinitely more holy and unique about Jewish life than non-Jewish life." Without considering either of these extreme views typical, one needs to take them into account, as examples of all-too-common chauvinism and xenophobia, here even on the part of a spiritual leader of a group whose sacred book speaks of justice for everyone.

Although I worry about the future of that land with two peoples—each with a complicated history, each speaking a Semitic language, perhaps sharing common ancestors in Biblical Canaan—I worry more about three major evils, any of which could doom the Holy Land along with the rest of the biosphere.

When discussing their papers with actual or potential donors at the Schlesinger Library, I assured them that, once we accepted them and decided which portions were of lasting historical value, the intention was to keep them forever. At some point I started to say: **forever, however long that turns out to be**, although I wasn't yet as anxious about the future of humanity and the biosphere as I am now. I see three major dangers, all almost entirely caused by humans, so it should be in our power to avert them. But, because we have let them happen and many don't recognize them as dangers, or don't see or acknowledge them at all, I find little hope—unless there is a general awakening and enough people agree to cooperate to reverse the present trends.

The first danger is **nuclear weapons** and to a lesser extent **nuclear power**. Some say the power is carbon-free, but building power plants surely is not, nor has anyone found a solution for nuclear waste. As for weapons, the U.S. refuses to sign a no-first-use agreement and has many weapons on alert, ready to go off on too-short notice. It's an old story that few want to hear.

Almost as old, although we didn't hear about it until recently, is **global warming**. Now we know that some oil executives knew about this danger decades ago, but didn't want us to know so we could keep driving, flying, and heating our houses with oil without worrying, while they kept cashing in. Anyone paying any attention knows about the increase in wild fires—turning forests that could mitigate warming into infernos that increase it—the huge chunks of Greenland and Antarctica falling into the sea, and all the rest. But too many react by saying, Oh good, the Arctic is opening up, that will be a shorter trade route, and we can drill for oil there—of course leading to more warming.

Behind both these dangers, and especially behind global warming, is the third danger: **overpopulation—of humans**. The author of a 1948 book, *Our Plundered Planet,* was worried that the world's population, which had taken millennia to grow to one billion, was pushing two billion, which he thought would strain the Earth's resources. Now we are nearing eight billion. Most in "developing" countries will want comfortable, convenient lives like those many of us are enjoying, which will mean more consumption and more global warming. Partly because of fires, floods, and drought, as well as wars, there are ever more refugees, and signs of increasing competition for such basic resources as water. Population decline—even a *slowing* of population *growth*—is considered a worry, rather than a small step toward a more liveable world. The Earth hasn't gotten bigger, and it's not going to; somehow we must find the wisdom and the courage to convince and enable people everywhere to have fewer children, or adopt, or do without. Let's hope that the solution to overpopulation is not danger number one, above, or too much more of danger number two.

We need the cooperation of all imperfect humans, all "holy and unique," to overcome these dangers especially to younger and future generations.

When writing for the 40th reunion book of my Mount Holyoke class, I found it comforting to realize that everyone who read it would be my age. Now, closer to the 70th, I hope that people *not* my age will read this much longer outpouring of reminiscence and reflection, beginning with my own offspring, and hope they find—though I've long said that life isn't worth living if one can't complain—that even justified complaints have not dominated

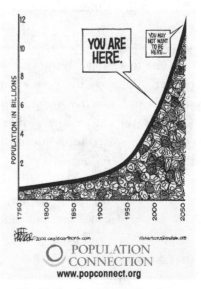

The *"J Curve"* in 2004. We're almost at 8 billion now. (Population Connection was formerly called Zero Population Growth, or ZPG)

these chapters. I don't want to seem like some Jews at a restaurant; after bringing their food, the waiter returns to ask: "Is *anything* all right?"[16] Nor do I want to sound like my mother-in-law. At one Thanksgiving, I suggested that we each tell one thing we were thankful for. When it was Kay's turn, she thought a moment and said, "I can't think of a damn thing."

I can think of many damn things to be thankful for, as well as many I wish could have been otherwise.

ENDNOTES

1   I don't use "herstory" because the "his" in "history" is not the genitive singular masculine pronoun but simply part of the Greek word "historia," meaning story or history. As my friend Edith said when "herstory" appeared, "Now we will all have herstorectomies."

2   Elizabeth Hawes, *Why Women Cry* (New York, 1943). Hawes made some of the same points Betty Friedan made twenty years later in *The Feminine Mystique*, about women's dependence and independence, work inside and outside the home, and so on. Perhaps it was too soon for these ideas, or they were unwelcome during wartime.

3   Some of the historical information comes from interviews with former Nature Friends conducted by Andrew Lanset, a radio producer and oral historian, in 1987 and 1988. From them he produced a radio documentary, "Camp Midvale: An Oral History," which was broadcast in 1988. NYU's Tamiment Library has summaries of the interviews and tapes of the interviews and the radio show.

4   In 2000 I asked Paul for information for this chapter, and he emailed back: "I remember your crush on Walter around 1944. As far as I know he is still available."

5   See Willy, see 'er go / Forty buses in a row. / No, Billy, them is trucks. / See what's in 'em: cows or ducks.

6   Later Buckingham, Browne & Nichols.

7   From a letter in his papers at Harvard University Archives. I rescued these papers from the curb in front of 321 Central Street the night before trash day; his children, overwhelmed by the task of cleaning out the house after 50 years of Hightower occupancy, had no time to deal with them, while as a retired archivist I knew where they should go.

8   In 2021 or earlier, Old Stage Road was, alas, renamed Stagecoach Road.

9 The name was dropped in 2021 because the founding Hastings had ordered mass killings of Native Americans.

10 This and most of the following notes refer to Swerdlow's *Women Strike for Peace: Traditional Motherhood and Radical Politics in the 1960s* (1993). Testing data quoted here are on p. 43.

11 In a latter-day whose-people-suffered-more competition, Jesse Jackson, while acknowledging the gay rights struggle, said that some slavemasters were gay and called the analogy with civil rights "a stretch...diminishing of slavery." At a conference session on Paul Robeson, Martin Duberman, the (gay) author of a Robeson biography, broached the same comparison; Robeson's son pointed out that one can hide gayness but not one's black skin.

12 In a 2005 study, European-Americans and Chinese were shown the same photographs; the former focused on the main object, the latter considered the background and the whole picture, indicating that there is merit in the clichés about greater independence, and isolation, of Americans vs. greater interdependence among Chinese.

13 The front steps of the church were the only place in the USSR where we saw beggars. The church must have served as a safety-valve, an oasis of traditional piety that the regime tolerated and that gave a few souls the solace they couldn't find in Soviet life.

14 At the 2003 Holocaust commemoration in Cambridge, I was billed as a survivor; I objected but was told that the term "officially" includes people like me. I still disagree, as did historian Peter Gay: "I had no right to claim the status of a survivor; I had never been hauled to a concentration camp, nor had my father or mother. I am among the lucky ones." (*My German Question*, p. 22). Although my father *was* hauled to a concentration camp, I'm also among the lucky ones.

15 See, e.g., Stephen Kinzer, *Overthrow: America's Century of Regime Change from Hawaii to Iraq*.

16 It doesn't have to be Jews; I heard it as Jewish women.